Singing Games in Early Modern Italy

MUSIC AND THE EARLY MODERN IMAGINATION
Massimo Ossi, editor

Singing Games

in Early Modern Italy

The Music Books of Orazio Vecchi

PAUL SCHLEUSE

INDIANA UNIVERSITY PRESS
Bloomington and Indianapolis

This book is a publication of

INDIANA UNIVERSITY PRESS
Office of Scholarly Publishing
Herman B Wells Library 350
1320 East 10th Street
Bloomington, Indiana 47405 USA

iupress.indiana.edu

♾The paper used in this publication meets the minimum requirements of the American National Standard for Information Sciences—Permanence of Paper for Printed Library Materials, ANSI Z39.48–1992.

Manufactured in the United States of America

Cataloging information is available from Library of Congress
ISBN 978-0-253-01501-3 (cloth)
ISBN 978-0-253-01504-4 (ebook)

1 2 3 4 5 20 19 18 17 16 15

FOR PRESCOTT
with love and gratitude

Contents

Acknowledgments

In a book about the pleasures of recreational singing it seems especially appropriate to thank not only some of those who made it possible but also those who made the process of writing it enjoyable.

Among many teachers I should first thank Rodney Haedge, my choir director at La Porte High School, who introduced me to the pleasure of singing madrigals with Orazio Vecchi's setting of "Il bianco e dolce cigno." Many years later in graduate school I arrived back at Vecchi through the guidance first of Barbara Russano Hanning and then of my dissertation advisor, Ruth DeFord. Both have been great sources of truly practical wisdom in my life as a researcher and teacher.

Work on this book has benefited enormously from the thoughtful comments of readers official and unofficial, including Massimo Ossi, Anthony Newcomb, Laurie Stras, and Seth Coluzzi; their recommendations have made the book you are now holding much better. Many other colleagues have been generously helpful in ways large and small; I would especially like to thank Allan Atlas, Bonnie Blackburn, Mauro Calcagno, Tim Carter, Lisa Colton, Anthony Cummings, Roger Freitas, Giuseppe Gerbino, Leofranc Holford-Strevens, Anne MacNeil, Melanie Marshall, John Milsom, Giulio Ongaro, Jessie Ann Owens, Massimo Privitera, Dennis Slavin, Jeremy Smith, Anne Stone, Andrew Weaver, and Anna Zayaruznaya.

Many of the ideas about recreational singing in this book came into focus through singing polyphony by Vecchi and his contemporaries in the company of good friends and talented musicians at workshops led by Peter Phillips, Andrew Carwood, Patrick Craig, Jan Coxwell, Deborah Roberts, Ghislaine Morgan, Don Grieg, and Jeffrey Skidmore. I am especially indebted to the members of the CUNY Graduate Center's informal Renaissance notation workshop, who have exemplified the fun of convivial singing from part books.

The publication of this book is supported by subventions from the Margarita Hanson Endowment and the AMS 75 PAYS Endowment of the American Musicological Society, funded in part by the National Endowment for the Humanities and the Andrew W. Mellon Foundation. At Binghamton University my work has been supported by a Dean's Research Semester and travel funding from the Dean's Office of Harpur College of Arts and Sciences and by a fellowship from the Institute for Advanced Studies in the Humanities. Also, the associates of the Center for Medieval and Renaissance Studies (CEMERS) have been a continuing source of collegial inspiration, especially Karen Barzman, Marilynn Desmond, Andrew Walkling, Olivia Holmes, Dana Stewart, Andrew Scholtz, and Tina Chronopoulos. Among other colleagues at Binghamton I must thank James Burns, Drew Massey, Tim Perry, Dan Davis, Christopher Bartlette, and Alice Mitchell of the Music Department; Sean Massey of the Department of Women, Gender, and Sexuality Studies; Bat-Ami Bar On of the Philosophy Department; Randy Friedman of the Department of Judaic Studies; Jennifer Stoever of the English Department; and in particular Harry Lincoln, professor of music emeritus, whose donated collection of microfilms and facsimiles in the library has been a wonderful—and wonderfully convenient—resource for my research.

For their assistance in research for this book I would like to thank the staffs of the Biblioteca Estense, the Archivio di Stato di Modena, the Archivio di Stato di Reggio Emilia, the Biblioteca Comunale di Correggio, the Museo Internazionale e Biblioteca della Musica di Bologna, the Staats- und Stadtbibliothek Augsburg, the Library and Muniment Room of Westminster Abbey, the British Library, the UC Berkeley Music Library, and the New York Public Library. I am also most grateful to the editorial staff at Indiana University Press for their clear and efficient help at every stage of the publication process.

Finally, I am grateful to my parents, Ginny Garrett and Bill Schleuse; my brothers, Martin and Stuart; my extended family of Garretts, McDermotts, Vanns, Fords, Hartlings, and Gehlings; and many other friends, but especially Joshua Ludzki, Alex Loughman, Amy Wielunski, Huntley Gill, Wick Taylor and Tom Lloyd, and Bill Kelley and Juan Escobar. They have all been a source of unflagging support and, when necessary, a welcome relief from work. Sarah Bridgman was a source of strength and clarity during the most difficult stages of producing the book. Most of all, my thanks and all my love to Prescott Vann, who has sustained me in every way.

Singing Games in Early Modern Italy

Introduction

The function of play in the higher forms which concern us here can largely be derived from the two basic aspects under which we mean it: as a contest *for* something or a representation *of* something. These two functions can unite in such a way that the game "represents" a contest, or else becomes a contest for the best representation of something.

The child [at play] is quite literally "beside himself" with delight, transported beyond himself to such an extent that he almost believes he actually is such and such a thing, without, however, wholly losing consciousness of "ordinary reality." His representation is not so much a sham-reality as a realization in appearance: "imagination" in the original sense of the word.

—Johan Huizinga, *Homo Ludens: A Study of the Play-Element in Culture*

[The] search for *suggestiveness* is a deliberate move to "open" the work to the free response of the addressee. An artistic work that suggests is also one that can be performed with the full emotional and imaginative resources of the interpreter. Whenever we read poetry there is a process by which we try to adapt our personal world to the emotional world proposed by the text. This is all the more true of poetic works that are deliberately based on suggestiveness, since the text sets out to stimulate the private world of the addressee so that he can draw from inside himself some deeper response that mirrors the subtler resonances underlying the text.

—Umberto Eco, *The Open Work*

This book is about singing as social play and music written and published to function this way in late sixteenth-century Italy. It is about the poetry that singers of such music encounter and how they relate to the fictive voices in this poetry, either being "transported beyond themselves" (in Huizinga's formulation) or "adapting [their] personal world to the emotional world proposed by the text" (as Eco describes). The particular historical moment I address was one when such relations were shifting radically, and the function of recreational singing—at least as represented in the music books issued by the Venetian printing industry—was shifting with them. In the middle third of the century, madrigals and other forms of part-song were most typically used for group singing without a separate audience, or at least for an audience of the singers' own peers. To be sure, instruments might double or replace voices in part-music, and more complex accompaniments might be improvised, but at midcentury these practices were ancillary to the kind of fully vocal realization implied by the texted part books in which madrigals were published. Larger-scale works written for performance at festive events were similarly the exception, not the rule. Solo performance by professional or quasi-professional singers was a practice still largely independent from the market for printed music.

Changes to this standard were under way by the 1570s, when, as Vincenzo Giustiniani reports, certain virtuoso solo singers inspired composers to create new styles of music both for solo voices and for group singing (my reading of Giustiniani's account opens chapter 1). By the 1580s Italy's wealthiest households were developing private, professionalized musical establishments whose display (and, often, concealment from display) marked their employers' status and *grandezza*. This professionalization of performance has been widely studied both as a late *cinquecento* phenomenon and as a precondition for the seventeenth-century preference for monody as the dominant texture in opera and other forms of literate music. My subject, however, is the tradition of recreational singing that continued in courts, academies, informal *ridotti* (salons), and intimate gatherings in bourgeois households; indeed, Giustiniani himself claims to have learned music in such houses. Although practices in these relatively modest settings are rarely documented in the kind of detail that survives for both public and private performances at courts, we can infer a great deal from the books of music that catered to recreational singers. The major Venetian music-printing firms provided a steady stream of reprint editions and anthologies of old pieces apparently known to have met with approval. Such books held less appeal for virtuoso singers or courts where more up-to-date music was the fashion and for which composers were issuing new books of increasingly—sometimes ostentatiously—complex madrigals.

The Modenese poet and composer Orazio Vecchi (1550–1605) makes an especially useful focus for this study for three interrelated reasons. First, as a composer employed for most of his career at churches in minor northern Italian cities he had little opportunity to compose for courtly settings. While this was evidently a source of personal and financial frustration, it freed him from the obligation to publish music befitting the elevated rank of a courtly patron (or to cloak such publications with apologies, as Orlando di Lasso did in his 1581 *Libro de villanelle, moresche, at altri canzoni*). Second, the relative compositional freedom Vecchi enjoyed, at least in his secular music, gave him free rein to innovate and experiment both with individual pieces and genres and on the larger conceptual scale of the music book. This innovative spirit informs his invention by the late 1570s of a new genre—the four-voice canzonetta—and his publications starting in 1590 of large-scale books of music in an unprecedented variety of genres organized around an aesthetic principle announced in each book's metaphorical title. Finally, Vecchi's unusual erudition equipped him both to write most of the poetry he set to music— sometimes in forms only coherent as *poesia per musica*—and to provide extensive commentary about his aesthetic motivations in the dedications and other prefatory texts to his books. All three of these aspects of Vecchi's life and work reveal a common theme: his music is almost always composed for the singers themselves as its primary audience, and their enjoyment derives from singing as a form of social recreation coexistent and imbricate with the conversation and game playing central to the social life of the courtly and subcourtly classes.

While this study focuses on Orazio Vecchi, it is not intended primarily as a comprehensive account of the composer's life and works. Many details of his professional biography are scattered through its pages, but it has not seemed relevant to discuss some interesting but incidental events of his life or his substantial (but generally conventional) body of sacred music.[1] My reading of Vecchi's secular music books aims to uncover how singers imagined themselves as embodying fictive characters, including Petrarchan lovers, pastoral shepherds, ethnolinguistic stereotypes, and rustic peasants. The poetry that gives voice to these characters plays with codes of decorum proper to polite society, especially within the sixteenth-century culture of *sprezzatura*. In performing such music, singers engage identities that define who they are, who they are not, and whom they aspire to be. This imitative play functions socially, I argue, in ways parallel to various kinds of games.

The conversational games described by Vincenzo Ringhieri in his *Cento giuochi liberali* (1551) and especially by Girolamo Bargagli in *Dialogo de' giuochi che nelle vegghie sanesi si usano di fare* (1572) provide a general model for early modern games, but their principles are applicable to a much wider variety of activities, including gambling and other games of chance. This process is explicit in musical works that depict social groups playing games, but it is implicit in the ways that recreational singing would proceed in the same kinds of social settings, with the choices of music in various genres analogous to turns in a game and subject to the same kinds of evaluation or discussion. Vecchi's music sometimes seems to demand just this kind of conversation, particularly in pieces that refer intertextually to other musical works or poetry.

Vecchi's Life

Orazio Tiberio Vecchi was baptized on December 6, 1550, in Modena, the third of six children born to Giovanni di Vecchi and Isabetta Garuti. According to the dedication of Orazio's *Sacrarum Cantionum* (1597), his earliest education was at the Benedictine monastery of San Pietro in Modena, but his musical instruction was with the Servite monk Salvatore Essegna, who included his student's madrigal "Volgi cor lasso" in his own book of four-voice madrigals in 1566. Essegna was appointed *maestro di cappella* at the cathedral in Siena in 1571, and Vecchi followed him there shortly thereafter. Vecchi is listed as a tenor in the cathedral's salary records through June 1574 and is represented by two madrigals in the heavily Sienese *Libro quinto delle Muse* of 1575.[2]

Vecchi had returned to Modena by the late 1570s and traveled with the Modenese nobleman Baldassare Rangoni to Brescia in 1577 and to Bergamo in 1578. A lighthearted *capitolo* penned by Rangoni first attests to Vecchi's abilities as a poet. Rangoni tells him:

La virtù Ermafrodita in voi risposta,	The hermaphrodite virtue resides in you,
Che inviduo (così) fa il canto a la scrittura	thus am I envious of the singing and writing
Fa che vi adora ognun a vostra posta.[3]	that makes everyone adore you in your place.

It was probably during these travels that Vecchi met Count Mario Bevilacqua of Verona, the dedicatee of Vecchi's first book of four-voice canzonettas, which he says were written over a period of some years prior to their publication in 1578 or 1579. In 1581 Vecchi was appointed *maestro di cappella* at Salò, and over the next dozen years he moved between various ecclesiastical positions in and around Modena. His book dedications to powerful figures in far-flung regions reflect a long-standing desire to find a courtly post.

Vecchi returned to Modena as *maestro* at the cathedral in 1583, and the following year he was awarded an annual stipend in return for a pledge to remain in Modena. Despite this, he departed again in January 1586, having negotiated a job in Reggio, where the Modenese Giulio Masetti had been appointed bishop. Vecchi is not actually recorded as having assumed this position, and in October of that year he was appointed canon at the cathedral in Correggio. In 1593 he resumed the position of *maestro di cappella* in Modena, which he held until shortly before his death.

Several violent events during this period led the eighteenth-century Modenese literary historian Girolamo Tiraboschi to characterize Vecchi as "uomo di umor alquanto bisbetico, e facile a risse" (a man of a peevish humor, and quick to fight), a description that other writers have echoed. Vecchi was attacked in the street on the night of February 5, 1595, and in a fight on June 18 of that year he himself wielded a knife against his sister-in-law's alleged lover. He also had a difficult relationship with the cathedral organist Fabio Richetti, who had been ousted as *maestro* when Vecchi was rehired in 1593; on April 21, 1596, Richetti apparently attempted to sabotage the music during Mass.[4] However, the chronicler Spaccini (Tiraboschi's source for these anecdotes) routinely recounted scandalous stories about prominent *modenesi*, and there is little justification for ascribing a particularly choleric nature to Vecchi on their account.

When Duke Alfonso II d'Este died without an heir in 1598 the territory of Ferrara reverted to papal control, and the much-reduced ducal court relocated to Modena, with Alfonso's cousin Cesare d'Este as duke of Modena. Vecchi was soon appointed Cesare's *maestro di corte,* also retaining his position at the cathedral. By this time Vecchi's ambition for a more prestigious post had apparently diminished, as in 1603 he turned down an offer to become *maestro di corte* at the imperial court of Rudolph II—though this move may have been linked to the town council's having awarded Vecchi a pension around the same time. In a final melodramatic turn of events (recounted more fully in chapter 6), Vecchi was fired from his position at the cathedral on October 7, 1604, on the grounds that he had been providing music for the cathedral convent, violating a prohibition from the bishop. Spaccini blames Vecchi's dismissal on the machinations of his pupil Geminiano Capilupi, who was appointed *maestro* in his place. Vecchi died on February 20, 1605, leaving his collection of music to another student, Paolo Bravusi, who was responsible for the posthumous publication of two more books of his teacher's music.

Vecchi's Music Books

After Vecchi contributed to a handful of madrigal anthologies in the 1570s, his first solo publication was the wildly successful *Canzonette . . . libro primo a quattro voci* (1578 or 1579), the first book to name this new genre on its title page. In chapter 1 I examine how these works' hybridization of the strophic *canzone villanesche* with the more complex madrigal created a genre particularly suited to recreational singing. This chapter also shows how Vecchi followed literary trends of the day in his second book (1580) by emphasizing the pastoral mode and how these two aspects—recreational singing and the depiction of an idealized arcadian setting—come together in "L'hore di recreatione," a seven-voice madrigal in three *partes* that concludes the *Madrigali a sei voci* (1583).

Chapter 2 reads selected pieces from Vecchi's remaining books of the 1580s with special attention to various kinds of intertextuality. At its simplest level, musical intertextuality connotes a quotation or variation of a preexisting work, as in the recomposition of Jacques Arcadelt's "Il bianco e dolce cigno" that opens Vecchi's *Madrigali a cinque voci* of 1589. A more complex network of associations is formed by multiple works in which Vecchi rewrites Giambattista Guarini's poem "Tirsi morir volea"; the scenario of pastoral lovers delaying their eroticized "death" recurs in madrigals from Vecchi's six- and five-voice books and also in both his third and fourth books of four-voice canzonettas (1585 and 1590, respectively). Finally, these later canzonetta books engage in a musical variant of the *proposta/risposta* tradition, setting poems of identical verse structure and closely related meaning to different music. Two such pairs of pieces appear in the third book, but Book IV engages in more extensive intertextual play, providing *risposte* to seven of the canzonettas from the first book, which had been reprinted several times in the 1580s. These poetic responses, written years after their notional *proposte*, recast the meanings of the original poems in ways that would come to light only if both pieces were sung in succession. The playful references of Book IV also include a sequence of canzonettas that may be read as a cycle relating to the episode of Alcina's enchantment of Ruggiero in Ariosto's *Orlando furioso*. This reading is far from explicit, but I argue that in the context of recreational singing and conversation witty and learned participants could tease out the clues that Vecchi planted in his music.

The year 1590 marks an important turning point in Vecchi's publishing career; it sees the last book of four-voice canzonettas and the first of an entirely new kind of music book. *Selva di varia ricreatione* is remarkable not only because of its unusual size and variety—it includes thirty-seven pieces ranging from three-voice arias to ten-voice polychoral dialogues—but also because the forest metaphor of its title reflects a particular poetic program for the book based on the association of variety and pleasure. Vecchi followed this innovative book with *Convito musicale* (1597), which presents the various dishes at a banquet as a metaphor for the book's contents. Chapter 3 shows how Vecchi's works represent a radical break with earlier books whose fanciful titles are simple metaphors for beauty. Vecchi defends and explains his titles at length in his dedications and prefaces, articulating his aesthetic priorities and displaying his erudition in a way matched in later years by Claudio Monteverdi in the prefatory texts in his madrigal books.

Chapter 4 approaches Vecchi's best-known and, historically, most misunderstood work, *L'Amfiparnaso* (1597) for five voices. Described on its title page as *comedia armonica,* this book combines elements of comic theater (long assumed to be the only theatrical style referenced in the piece) with scenes proper to the pastoral.[5] The representation of pastoral elements in *L'Amfiparnaso*—particularly of attempted suicides—is especially complex, since Vecchi's music depicts scenes that would not be enacted onstage in pastoral plays. The complex custom-made woodcut illustrations that adorn each scene in the *L'Amfiparnaso* part books thus play a particularly important role in conveying the work's meanings. This chapter concludes with a critical history of the so-called madrigal comedy, a genre label sometimes applied to *L'Amfiparnaso* and certain other books by Vecchi and others. This problematic term emerged in the early twentieth century as part of a half-successful attempt to disengage *L'Amfiparnaso* from the historiography of early opera, a confusion traceable to the earliest writings on Vecchi, including the inscription on his tombstone.

My framing of music making as a social activity analogous to game playing comes into sharper focus in chapter 5, which examines works by Alessandro Striggio, Giovanni Croce, and Vecchi that depict social game playing. Those by Striggio ("Il gioco di primiera") and Croce ("Il gioco dell'oca") involve gambling, and I read these games in the context of early modern warnings concerning the moral and social risks of gambling in etiquette books (Castiglione and Della Casa), genre paintings (Caravaggio and La Tour), and even writings in praise of gambling (Berni and Cardano). In musical depictions of games of chance, virtue is rewarded and lack of decorum is punished, reinscribing social values by instating order within notionally random outcomes. Vecchi's other depictions of games are more elevated and draw substantially on Bargagli's *Dialogo,* which was published in Siena in 1572 while Vecchi resided there. The *Dialogo* provides the model not only for Vecchi's *Le veglie di Siena,* his last published book, but also for two games depicted in "Il bando del Asino," a piece from *Convito musicale.* The *veglie* depict a complex series of games whose goal, I argue, is less to commemorate the Sienese Accademia degli Intronati (Bargagli's subject) than to engage the debates over modern music that had been initiated by Giovanni Maria Artusi in 1600.

Chapter 6 looks both backward and forward in reading works that imitate particular kinds of social interactions. Representations of social hierarchies articulate the outsider's suspicious view of the morals of other classes. This viewpoint is not unexpected in depictions of lower classes, but commentary on courtiers can be similarly deprecating, as I show in two pieces from *Selva* and *Convito* that depict courtiers as insincere flatterers but furthermore allude to sexual practices seen as unnatural. Drawing on Harry Berger's concept of "representation anxiety" in the sixteenth century, I argue that the discourses on class, behavior, and "naturalness" in these pieces reflect the pressure of constant (self)-policing on which the culture of *sprezzatura* depends. Vecchi's *vinate* take a more lighthearted approach, elevating popular drinking songs to the realm of polite sociability. One of these grafts a rustic song from the region of Marche onto a conversational game described by Bargagli; the other takes an archaic French chanson and gives it a comically rollicking final peroration. However, the moral danger of class mixing returns in an even more vivid form in another depiction of drinking, this time with a young city dweller sampling the wines urged on him by a rustic gardener. His growing intoxication expresses itself in musical and verbal terms normally reserved for erotic ecstasy, suggesting that the encounter between the young man and the gardener has taken on a sexual dimension. My goal with these analyses, and with this book, is to dislocate Vecchi from the margins of a teleological historiography of the later madrigal and early opera and to place him instead within a context of early modern print culture, music, and sociability that facilitates richer readings of his highly individual music.

1 The Four-Voice Canzonetta as (and in) Recreational Polyphony

> I will set down familiarly several thoughts that occur to me upon this subject, based upon the little experience I have acquired while I was conversing in houses where there was no game-playing [*esercizio del gioco*] but rather delightful occupations, particularly music, performed without assistance of paid performers by divers gentlemen who took pleasure and delight in it through natural inclination.
>
> —Vincenzo Giustiniani, *Discorso sopra la musica*

Vincenzo Giustiniani's *Discorso sopra la musica* is well known to musicologists as an important account of stylistic change in music of the last quarter of the *cinquecento,* in particular the rise of professionalized solo singing.[1] Written, as Angelo Solerti first demonstrated, in 1628, the *Discorso* not only remembers events at a half-century's remove but also places them in a context still meaningful in its own time. Far from describing the mere replacement of vocal polyphony with solo singing, however, Giustiniani recalls a musical culture in which enthusiastic amateurs enjoyed polyphony, and singing "per inclinazione naturale" was in fact considered superior to performances by "persone mercenarie."

In his account of Italian musical styles, Giustiniani describes—not always with great clarity—a shifting focus between solo and polyphonic practices, portraying the latter as drawing on recent developments in the former. This interaction can tell us much about Orazio Vecchi's canzonettas of the 1570s and 1580s, a period when the courts of Ferrara, Mantua, and elsewhere increasingly cultivated professionalized solo singing while amateur consumers like Giustiniani continued to support a market for recreational polyphony in up-to-date styles.

Giustiniani was born in 1564 to the Genoese governor of Chios, but his family moved to Rome two years later and became prosperous bankers. He recalls that in his childhood the best-regarded composers were the key mid-century madrigalists—Orlando di Lasso, Alessandro Striggio, Cipriano de Rore, Philippe de Monte, and the earlier but perennially popular Jacques Arcadelt—adding that accompanied solo singing was practiced more in the realm of the *villanella*. This opposition constitutes a background against which a more flexible performance practice emerged in the secular compositions of composers associated with Rome: "In a short space of time musical taste [*il gusto della musica*] changed and the compositions of Luca Marenzio and Ruggiero Giovannelli appeared with delightful new inventions, *either that of singing with several voices or with one voice alone accompanied by some instrument,* the excellence of which consisted in a melody new and grateful to the ear, with some easy fugues without extraordinary artifices."[2] This passage has been read as referring to Marenzio's and Giovannelli's madrigals published in the 1580s and also to Marenzio's three-voice *villanellas* from the same period.[3] In terms of these pieces' appeal to the changing tastes of amateur singers, their flexibility for use as polyphonic or accompanied solo works is crucial: the "new and grateful" *aria,* or melodic style, is especially suitable for the latter practice, while the "easy fugues" are appropriate for the former.

Although Giustiniani initially claims that his account is chronological, the changes he describes are not strictly ordered but relate also to different aspects of musical life. While the new canzonetta-related styles described above arose, Giustiniani tells us, in response to the changing tastes of listeners, concurrent developments reflected the innovations of virtuosic singers. Nevertheless, Giustiniani still emphasizes the constant influence of solo and polyphonic styles on each other, referring in particular to the music of Orazio Vecchi:

> In the Holy Year 1575, or shortly thereafter, a style of singing appeared which was very different from that preceding. It continued for some years, chiefly in the manner of one voice singing with accompaniment, and was exemplified by Giovanni Andrea *napoletano,* Signor Giulio Cesare Brancaccio, and Alessandro Merlo, *romano.* . . . They inspired composers to write similar works for several voices in the manner of a single one accompanied by some instrument, in imitation of the above-mentioned and of a certain woman called Femia. But they

[i.e., these composers] achieved greater invention and artifice, resulting in some Villanellas which were a mixture of Madrigals in florid style and Villanellas. Many books of these by the aforementioned authors and by Orazio Vecchi and others are seen today. But as the Villanellas acquired greater perfection through artful composition, so also every composer, in order that his compositions should satisfy the general taste, took care to advance in the style of composition for several voices, particularly Giaches Wert in Mantua and Luzzasco in Ferrara.[4]

Anthony Newcomb reads this passage as describing "the invasion of the polyphonic madrigal by the new style of vocal diminution, an evolution in which Ferrarese music played a crucial role."[5] Giustiniani makes a clear distinction, however, between virtuoso solo singing as practiced in Italian courts and polyphonic music intended to "satisfy the general taste" (riuscissero di gusto in generale) through its wider circulation in print.

The influence of the Ferrarese *concerto* (and its imitators) is less apparent in Vecchi's music from this period, which is neither highly ornamented in the luxuriant style nor particularly connected with Ferrara, his ties to the Este family having been firmly established only after the 1598 removal to Modena. Although Giustiniani identifies professionalized courtly singing as an important influence on composed polyphony, he also describes the new genres as hybridizing the *villanella* and the madrigal and as circulating widely in printed books, specifically those by Vecchi. This description can only refer to Vecchi's books of four-voice canzonettas, which first appeared around 1580 and were still being reprinted in Italy as late as the second decade of the seventeenth century.[6]

Vecchi's canzonettas were undoubtedly susceptible to adaptation for one or more voices with instrumental accompaniment—indeed, the three printed in *Selva di varia ricreatione* (1590) were provided with lute tablature— and such a performance could have accommodated the elaborate diminutions that were the specialty of professional singers. However, Giustiniani's account of his own experience as an amateur musician in Rome implies that recreational singing in polyphony was one important (and possibly the most important) use he saw for Vecchi's canzonettas and similar music.[7] In the mid-1580s Vecchi himself appears to have participated in a recreational musical *ridotto,* or salon, in Modena hosted by Mesin Forno, a canon at the cathedral.[8] In this chapter I show how selected four-voice canzonettas from Vecchi's first two books in the genre (ca. 1579 and 1580) particularly address themselves to recreational use in polyphonic singing. I then examine Vecchi's own depiction of this performance practice in the seven-voice work, "L'hore di recreatione," that concludes his book of six-voice madrigals (1583). This remarkable piece partakes of several of the strands we shall observe in the canzonettas: songs about singing, imitations of comic characters, and a depiction of courtly recreation in an (imperfectly) idealized pastoral setting.

The Origins of Vecchi's Canzonetta Style

As Giustiniani points out, the stylistic antecedents of Vecchi's canzonettas were the madrigal and the *villanella,* and the repetitive forms and strophic texts of the latter genre form the basic template for almost all of Vecchi's canzonettas. By the 1570s the most important formal markers of the *villanella* were a three- or four-stanza poem with a refrain (usually varied in the final stanza), a free mixture of *settenari* and *endecasillabi,* and a musical form of ||: A:|| B ||: C:||, in which the refrain may occupy either the B and C sections or only the C section of the music.[9] Vecchi uses some variation of this musical form in sixteen of the twenty-two pieces in Book I, either with or (in four cases) without a refrain. The remaining six canzonettas employ a simple binary form (||: A:||: B:||), three of them including refrains. Although binary forms were not entirely unknown in *villanellas* of the 1570s (including one whose text Vecchi set in Book I),[10] they may represent a slightly later range of compositional dates than Vecchi's pieces in the older form, since binary forms come to dominate the rest of his canzonetta books. Internal evidence from the binary-form canzonettas of Book I support this possibility. No. 1, "Canzonette d'amore," is in binary form and was likely written at a late date as an introductory piece for the book.

The origins of Vecchi's four-voice canzonetta style in the three-voice *villanella* are perhaps clearest in the vocal ranges and dispositions Vecchi employs. From its earliest printed examples in the 1540s, the *canzone villanesca alla napolitane* was characterized by a high-voice trio texture with a total range rarely exceeding two octaves. Donna G. Cardamone proposes that the origin of this style lies in the closely spaced harmonies of Neapolitan popular songs from an unnotated tradition.[11] Four-voice arrangements of *villanescas* began appearing in the 1540s by Adriano Willaert and in the 1550s by Lasso (some of which he printed only much later, in 1581).[12] The general method for these arrangements was to place the original canto line in the tenor an octave lower, often moving the tenor to the canto as well, while retaining the bass and adding a new alto. The ranges of these pieces conform to the conventional four-voice texture of roughly two and a half octaves, with each voice encompassing a distinct range of about an octave (bass ranges are often a bit wider), separated from the next-higher voice by a fourth or fifth. This alternation of ranges in relation to the final provided a framework for categorizing pieces by mode, with the canto and tenor range determining the authentic or plagal quality of the mode.

Vecchi's four-voice canzonettas stand apart from this practice. Instead, they usually retain the narrow two-octave total ambitus of the three-voice *villanesca,* with the top two voices (or, more rarely, the middle two) sharing essentially the same range, and the bass lying only an octave below the canto.[13] The narrow total range of each piece could facilitate singing in homosocial settings, either among women singing at something like modern pitch or by men transposing them downward by anywhere from a fifth to an octave. By the fourth book of 1590, however, mixed-gender groups of three women with one man had become emblematic of the genre: in the opening piece, "Udit', udite Amanti," the singers describe themselves as "tre leggiadre Ninfe / con un Pastore" (three graceful nymphs with a shepherd; see chapter 2), and the ambitus of most of the pieces is accordingly larger. In Book I, the few examples that encompass a wider total range do so not by distributing the voices according to the "usual" four-voice plan but by widening the individual range of the bass or another voice (nos. 7, 13, 18, 20, 21) or by separating adjacent voices by roughly an octave, leaving an apparent "gap" in the regular alternation of authentic and plagal octave ranges (nos. 9, 19, 22) (table 1.1).[14]

Vecchi's retention of the paired higher voices from the older *villanesca* forges a link with the more forward-looking style of the so-called *villanella alla romana,* introduced by Luca Marenzio in the 1580s. These three-voice pieces joined a similar high-voiced pair with a lower voice, but with an increasing sense of a harmonically determinative bass suitable for genres associated with accompanied solo singing. The contrapuntally distinct function of a harmonic bass appears sporadically in Vecchi's canzonettas but generally becomes more prevalent in the third and fourth books, suggesting that the influence of the accompanied styles described by Giustiniani was making itself felt in Vecchi's later contributions to the genre—though flexibility of performance options seems to have remained central to the canzonetta's identity and popularity.

Table 1.1. Vocal ranges in Vecchi's first book of four-voice canzonettas

	INCIPIT	CANTO	ALTO	TENORE	BASSO	TOTAL RANGE	SIGNATURE/ FINAL
1	Canzonette d'amore	g′–g″	f′–f″	f′–d″	g–g′	2 octaves	♭/G
2	Mentre io campai contento	f′–f″	f♯′–f″	b♭–d″	f–g′	2 octaves	♭/G
3	Occhi ridente	c″–g″	g′–f″	e′–d″	g–g′	2 octaves	♭/G
4	Son questi i crespi crini	g′–g″	f′–f″	c′–b♭	f–g′	2 octaves + M2	♭/G
5	Madonna, io v'ho da dir	g′–g″	f′–f″	c′–c″	f–g′	2 octaves + M2	♭/G
6	Chi mira gl'occhi tuoi	c′–c″	c′–g′	g–g′	c–c′	2 octaves	♮/C
7	Chi vuol veder un bosco	e′–e″	c′–b′	f–a′	c–d′	2 octaves + M3	♮/G
8	Cosa non vada più	e′–d″	b–d″	g–a′	c–f′	2 octaves + M2	♮/C
9	Cruda mia tiraniella	f′–d″	d′–d″	b–a′	B–d′	2 octaves + M3	♮/C
10	Raggi, dov'è 'l mio bene?	g′–a″	g′–g″	c′–c″	g–a′	2 octaves + M2	♮/A
11	Se'l vostro volto	d″–g″	g′–e″	c′–c″	g–g′	2 octaves	♮/A
12	Quando l'aurora	a′–a″	g′–a″	e′–d″	g–g′	2 octaves + M2	♮/A
13	Corse alla morte	f′–g″	c′–c″	b♮–c″	c–f′	2 octaves + P5	♭/F
14	Amor spiega l'insegna	e′–d″	e′–d″	f–c″	c–f′	2 octaves + M2	♭/F
15	Il cor che mi rubasti	e′–d″	c♯′–a′	c–a″	c–f′	2 octaves + M2	♮/D
16	Chiari lucenti rai	g′–e″	d′–c″	b–g′	d–f′	2 octaves + M2	♮/D
17	Io son fenice	e′–c″	c′–a′	g–a′	c–e′	2 octaves	♮/D
18	O tu che vai per via	d′–g″	f♯′–f″	d′–d″	d–g′	2 octaves + P4	♭/G
19	Quando mirai	b′–g″	f♯′–e″	c′–a′	c–d′	2 octaves +P5	♮/D
20	Nel vago lume	g′–g″	g–d″	g–d″	B♭–f′	2 octaves + M6	♭/G
21	Trà verdi campi	g′–e♭″	c′–b♭′	f–f′	G–b♭	2 octaves + M6	♭/G
22	Trà le chiome o de l'or	e′–d″	g–g′	g–e′	G–a	2 octaves + P5	♭/G

The First Book of Four-Voice Canzonettas: Inventing a Genre

The first book is dedicated to Mario Bevilacqua, a member and patron of the Accademia Filarmonica in Verona whom Vecchi must have met during his travels in the late 1570s. We do not know the extent of the composer's involvement with the Filarmonica or with the more informal *ridotti* he encountered, but these settings "in casa" (to use Giustiniani's term) must have been among the original contexts for singing Vecchi's canzonettas. Close readings of some of the pieces suggest the special appeal they had for amateur singers in private settings. The first edition of Book I does not survive, but it must have been published in 1578 or 1579 if we assume the dedication was written after Vecchi had the opportunity to visit Verona. The book's success was immediate, and demand for it was lasting: the Gardano firm issued reprints in 1580, 1581, 1585, 1591, and 1613 (this last by the successor firm of Magni). A Milanese edition was published in 1586, and Vecchi's canzonettas were ubiquitous in northern "omnibus" monographs and anthologies well into the 1620s.[15]

Although Vecchi is rightly credited with popularizing the four-voice canzonetta as a distinct genre—he was the first composer to use the term in a book title—his style appears to have evolved over the course of some years prior to his publishing his *Canzonette . . . libro primo a quattro voci* in 1578 or 1579. In the dedication Vecchi explains that most of the compositions had been in wide manuscript circulation throughout Italy in corrupt and misattributed forms: "Most of the present canzonettas of mine being dispersed around many parts of Italy under the names of various authors, it seemed to me appropriate to let the world know by means of the press that they are mine, as in fact they are. Therefore I have recalled them to their first origins, cleaned them up, and republished them as being the first."[16] This language must have had special resonance for Bevilacqua, who as patron of the Accademia Filarmonica would have been familiar with the sometimes haphazard transmission of music in manuscript.

More than merely claiming credit for corrected versions of the canzonettas, however, Vecchi describes the advantages of presenting them unified in print in a way that goes beyond mere authorial pride: "Now to make them seem happier and better in every part, all together: not torn apart and faulty, as they were up until now, but returned to their native appearance, and decorated with the most beautiful ornaments of the press."[17] This personification of the songs as "happier" when gathered together in a single book continues in the first piece, which addresses the canzonettas as subjects:

Canzonette d'amore	Canzonettas of love
Che m'uscite del core,	that issue from my heart,
Contate i miei dolori,	tell of my pains,
Le man baciando alla mia bella Clori.	kissing my lovely Cloris on the hands.[18]

The poet-composer addresses not the beloved Cloris but rather the songs contained in the new book themselves. Although such self-referential poems are part of the Petrarchan tradition (as in that poet's "Ite, rime dolenti"), the trope has special meaning in a printed musical setting. The songs are asked to kiss Cloris's hands, a conventional phrase in the context of a dedication but one with more significant meaning here, since songs—in their notated form—routinely touch and are touched by singers' hands, "kissing" them in a manner even more literal than that of an epistolary dedication. Cloris is cast not as one who merely listens to the song but as one who participates in singing it from the book.

The singers of such music are therefore in a position to imagine themselves both as the speaking voice of the poem and as the addressee, Cloris. This double subjectivity is defined in relation to the object held in the singers' hands, sent from the poet (Vecchi, but also one part of a singer's imagined persona) to its audience (recreational singers, both as real people and as the imagined Cloris). In the second stanza, the book's materiality is reemphasized through its location in Cloris's hands:

Ivi liete e vezzose,	*There,* happy and pretty,
Coronate di rose,	crowned with roses,
Contate i miei dolori,	tell of my pains,
Le man baciando alla mia bella Clori	kissing my lovely Cloris on the hands.

"Liete e vezzose" recalls Vecchi's description of the songs in the dedication as happy and decorated with printed ornaments. Now, however, the songs are also "crowned with roses," referring to Cloris's lips, as the printed notes are transformed into sounding music to speak of the poet's pain. The formal repetition of the last half of the stanza, with its return to the description of hand kissing, is dictated by the poetic form of the *villanella;* this form admits changes to the refrain text only in the final stanza, and Vecchi closes with an image that completes the penetration of Cloris's body with song:

Poi mirando il bel seno	Then, looking at her lovely breast
E'l suo viso sereno,	and her serene face,
Contate i miei dolori	tell of my pains,
In sen vivendo alla mia bella Clori.	living in my lovely Cloris's breast.

The gaze (fancifully ascribed to the songs on the page) that shifts from the breast to the face traces the flow of breath in the act of singing, but the song's final destination returns to Cloris's breast as the metaphorical location of the song's emotional effect. Cloris's hoped-for pity on the unhappy lover is felt in her heart but is expressed through her lungs and larynx; thus Vecchi uses not *core* but *seno* to describe the canzonetta's embodied home.

This poetic conceit from the book's opening is recalled in the final song, no. 22, "Tra le chiome d'oro," whose final stanza describes a "morte amando" (loving death) as coming to one imprisoned in the beloved's breast. Indeed, the body into which the canzonettas were previously asked to lodge themselves has now become a pleasant trap from which escape is both impossible and undesirable:

Trà le chiome de l'oro Amor ordisce	Among her golden hair Love weaves
Il laccio e la catena	the snare and the chain
Ch'à volontaria morte amando mena.	that lead willingly to a loving death.
Strali accesi son gl'occhi, e'l guardo	Her eyes are burning arrows, and her
è foco,	look is fire,
Che n'ancidono à torto;	which kills wrongly,
Cosi si resta alhor ferito e morto.	leaving one now wounded and dead.
E cosi dolce il laccio e la pregione,	The snare and the prison are so sweet
Che morir nel bel petto	that to die in that beautiful breast
Meglio è c'haver senza esso altro	is better than to have any other pleasure
diletto.	without it.

"Trà le chiome de l'oro" is one of only two poems in Book I (the other is no. 14) that entirely eschew first-person verbs. The happy victims of death within the beloved's breast can therefore be read not as the poetic speaker but as the canzonettas who were sent to live there in the opening song. The book having run its course, their "lives" must end.

However, in the 1580 edition "Trà le chiome" was only the penultimate piece, preceding "Trà verdi campi." This ordering was reversed in the third edition of 1581 and later reprints.[19] We do not know in what order they appeared in the lost first edition, but since the third edition agrees with the fourth, which Vecchi seems to have supervised (having signed the dedication himself), it seems that he approved the later ordering, whether it was a return to the original one or an improvement on it. In fact, both pieces have a claim to being an appropriate choice for the prestigious final position. The ordering of Book I reflects a certain degree of care. As table 1.1 shows, pieces with the same signature and final are generally grouped together, with the exception that those with a wider range and a lower-lying bass part (nos. 19–22) tend to appear toward the end of the book. "Trà verdi campi" and "Trà le chiome de l'oro" are the two lowest-range pieces in the book. While "Trà le chiome de l'oro" may be read, like the opening "Canzonette d'amore," as describing the book's songs themselves as residing in the beloved's breast, "Trà verdi campi" is perhaps an apt envoi for the collection in that it turns away from the mainly Petrarchan poetic vocabulary of the book toward the specifically pastoral vein that would become prominent in Vecchi's later books.

Vecchi's Poetic Style

The poetry of Book I—with distinct exceptions to be discussed presently—is founded on the metaphors, antitheses, and thinly veiled eroticism typical of Petrarch and his *cinquecento* imitators. Such poetry was of course ubiquitous in madrigals of the 1570s but had also become influential on strophic *villanella* texts of the same period. The uniformity of this poetic style is confirmed by the agreement between the anonymous poems (assumed to be by Vecchi himself) and the few that appeared in earlier (unrelated) musical settings or are known to be by others. These include Torquato Tasso's "Se 'l vostro volto è d'un aria gentile," set in no. 11; no. 13, "Corse alla morte," known from a setting by Giovanni Domenico da Nola from 1570;[20] and no. 6, "Chi mira gl'occhi tuoi," which had appeared in a three-voice setting by Gasparo Fiorino as recently as 1574.[21] Vecchi's poetic ability can usefully be studied in no. 7, "Chi vuol veder un bosco," which adapts a poem published in a setting by Cesare Tudino in 1566.[22] Vecchi maintained the poem's form but made many alterations in word choice (shown in boldface), creating a more rhetorically pointed text:

TUDINO (1566)	VECCHI (1578–1579?)
Chi vuol veder un bosco folto e spesso	Chi vuol veder un bosco folto e spesso
Venga a **veder** il mio misero core	Venga a **mirar** il mio misero core
Tante saette ci ha tirato Amore.	**Quante** saette ci ha tirato Amore.
Chi vuol vedere **due fontane vive**	Chi vuol veder **duo fonti d'acqua viva**

Venga a veder questi occhi **miei** dolenti	Venga a veder questi occhi **egri** e dolenti
Ch'Amor l'ha fatti due fiumi correnti.	Ch'Amor gli hà fatti duo fiumi correnti.
Chi vuol veder come arde una fornace	Chi vuol veder come arde una fornace
Venga a veder me sol ch'in ogni loco	Venga a veder me sol ch'in ogni loco
Amor m'ha fatto tutto fiamm'e foco.	Amor m'hà fatto tutto fiamma e foco.
Chi vuol saper **di cio chi n'è cagione**	Chi vuol saper **di questo la cagione**
Sappia ch'è di mia donna la beltade	**Miri costei, che sua rara beltade**
Chi non ha del mio mal nulla	**M'infiamma ogni hora e in lei non è**
pietade.	**pietade.**

Vecchi's version relieves some of the repetitions of "vedere" in the first two lines of each stanza with the more poetic "mirare," elevates Tudino's "living fountains" to "fountains of living water," and replaces Tudino's bluntly accusatory final stanza with a more poignant restatement of the third stanza's *fiamma* imagery.

In these early canzonettas, then, Vecchi mimics the literary poetic tone of the madrigal while retaining the strophic forms, repetitive structures, and musical texture of the *villanesca*. As recreational music this combination seems to have been extremely successful: although they partake of up-to-date literary topics, the pieces are easier to sing than the more complex five- and six-voice madrigals of the 1570s, and, thanks to their narrow range, they are more adaptable to different vocal groupings and instrumental participation. The persistence of the Book I canzonettas in reprints both in Italy and in northern Europe attests to the continuing popularity of this combination.

It is worth noting here that however popular his canzonettas were, they never won for Vecchi a place at court, nor, considering his choice of dedicatees, were they intended to. The audience for his canzonetta books seems mainly to have been typified by readers and singers like Vincenzo Giustiniani himself: the upwardly mobile merchant class and low-level courtiers whose interest in self-fashioning through music was based on participatory engagement rather than patronage of professionalized singers at court. The lyric poetic style of the canzonetta serves as a model for the elevated tone of courtly conversation and (re)inscribes for the singers the performative codes appropriate to a social milieu to which they may have had a peripheral or aspirational relationship. Yet social music making generally included a variety of different kinds of music, as Vecchi himself would soon demonstrate in "L'hore di recreatione" in 1583 as well as in later publications, including both positive models for courtly discourse and negative examples of comic foolishness.

Comedy in the Canzonetta

The didactic function of courtly poetry is especially relevant in settings sung recreationally in social settings, but the act of imaginatively personifying a poetic voice through song can take forms other than the emulation of a courtly ideal. Three pieces in Book I depart from the "mainstream" style by invoking the more varied playfulness of the older *villanesca*, though none of these texts are known from earlier sources. No. 5, "Madonna, io v'hò da dir," relates as gossip the story of a friar who was known by the phrase he habitually cried in the streets of Rome, "Fate ben per voi" ("Do good for your own sake"):

Madonna, io v'hò da dir una novella:	My lady, I have to tell you some news:
State a sentir, e riderete poi,	stay and listen, and you will laugh,
C'ha preso moglie il fate ben per voi	for the Fate ben per voi has taken a wife.
Vieni, Himeneo gentil', e i novi sposi	Come, gentle Hymen, and fill the new spouses
Empi di gaudio e riso, e vedrem poi	with joy and laughter, and then we will see
I pargoletti fate ben per voi.	miniature Fate ben per vois.
Nacque in Calabria, e poi frate divenne;	He was born in Calabria, and then became a friar;
Andò a la guerra, e tornò vincitore;	he went to war and returned victorious;
Al fin è fatto prigionier d'Amore.	in the end he became a prisoner of Love.

As Warren Kirkendale has shown, the Fate ben per voi was a real person described in contemporary documents, including an account of a popular song about the Fate ben per voi with a text similar to Vecchi's: "There was a hermit named after the words he was accustomed to repeat: 'fate ben per voi.' He was regarded as holy, and had such credit with the pope and princes that he was not denied anything which he requested, and he used the money to find husbands for perilous girls. He found one whom he liked, married her, and lost all the credit. . . . A song was made about him which said, 'Be careful what you will laugh about, when you will know that the Fate ben per voi has taken a wife.'"[23]

We cannot know the exact relationship between this song and Vecchi's canzonetta, but Vecchi probably knew of the hermit's accustomed cry. His voice is imitated in the musical setting where the Basso sings the words "fate ben per voi" on a slow, stuttering monotone (see example 1.1),[24] a figure Vecchi used again in the same form in "O messir," the bizarre nine-voice piece

Example 1.1. Vecchi, "Madonna, io v'hò da dir," mm. 11–18.

in *Selva* of 1590, in which the love-struck friar appears again.[25] The singers of "Madonna, io v'hò da dir" thus imitate not one but two comical characters: a gossip who tells the story (addressing a "madonna") and also, at least in the bass, an imitation of the ridiculous friar.

Singers get a chance to imitate a rustic character directly in no. 9, "Cruda mia tiraniella," which harks back to the older *canzone villanesca alla napoli-tana* style not only in its approximation of Neapolitan dialect and crudely erotic text but also in its use of parallel root-position triads. These are de-ployed in the three upper voices only, recalling the three-voice texture of the *napolitana,* and only on the second line of each stanza, precisely where the most eroticized images appear:

Example 1.2. Vecchi, "Cruda mia tiraniella," mm. 7–14.

Cruda mia tiraniella,
Quando succhio quei tuoi dolci coralli,

Triemo com'un gridasse, "Dalli, dalli!"

Dolce mia pazzariella,
Quando stringo quei tuoi bianchi
  cristalli,
Triemo com'un gridasse, "Dalli, dalli!"

O misero scontiento,
Che le labbra, le man, l'amico pietto

Legan quess'alma afflitta stretto stretto.

My cruel little tyrant,
when I suck those sweet corals of
  yours,
I tremble as though someone were
  shouting, "Get him! Get him!"

My sweet little crazy girl,
When I squeeze those white crystals
  of yours,
I tremble as though someone were
  shouting, "Get him

Oh miserable, discontented me,
for the lips, the hands, and the beloved
  breast
bind my afflicted soul so tightly.

The Four-Voice Canzonetta 23

The juxtaposition of crude and poetic vocabulary (e.g., "when I suck those sweet corals" for "when I kiss those sweet lips") is typical of the comical attempts of rustics in *villanesche* to mimic lyric poetry, but the joke depends on the singers' understanding an idiom that the character they imitate does not. This double subjectivity is emphasized by the contrast between the parallel triads of the second line and the more sophisticated point of imitation on "I tremble," using madrigalistic *fusae* (eighth notes) turns. The singers thus briefly engage in musical imitation of the rustic but quickly restore the distance between themselves and him by reasserting a normative style for the final refrain of each stanza (example 1.2).[26]

Vecchi depicts a more enigmatic character in no. 18, "O tu che vai per via." The poetic subject is a man in the street begging passersby to listen to his complaint. However, his dialect and vocabulary are those not of rustic imitations but of typical erotic courtly poetry, most obviously in his desire for death as code for sexual fulfillment. The incongruity of the scene is repeatedly emphasized by the speaker's references (in boldface below) to his own speech and to the listener's response:

O tu che vai per via,	**Oh you who pass along the street,**
Deh fermati, ti prego, in cortesia,	**stop now,** I pray you, out of courtesy,
Et l'aspra pena mia	and to my bitter pain
Odi, ch'io ti farò per meraviglia	**listen, for I shall make you, out of wonder,**
Stringer le labbia et inarcar le ciglia.[27]	**purse your lips and arch your brows.**
Il male è di tal sorte	My pain is of such a nature
Che sanar non lo pò se non la morte,	that it cannot be healed except by death,
Ne valmi il gridar forte,	**nor does it help me to cry aloud,**
"Ecco questa è l'acerba mia ferita	"Here is my bitter wound
Per la qual tosto io perderò la vita."	for which I shall lose my life."
Perche dal longo male	Because from long suffering
Hò quasi al viver mio volto le spale,	I have almost turned my back on my life,
Et contrastar non vale,	and fighting is useless,
Che chi gode di farmi ogn'hor languire	for she who enjoys making me languish all the time
Non mi vuol vivo e non mi fa morire.	does not want me alive and does not make me die.
Tal che meglio è finire	Thus it is better to end

Example 1.3a. Vecchi, "O tu che vai per via," mm. 1–6.

Questa aspra la vita, e di dolor uscire,	this bitter life, and to escape from pain,
E ti prego di dire	**and I beg you to say**
Che chi per donna ingrata perde il core,	that if one loses his heart to an ungrateful lady,
Morte è il remedio à cosi gran dolore.	death is the remedy to his great pain.

This self-referentiality makes singing "O tu che vai per via" an exercise in both performing and witnessing a lover's complaint: like the poetry, the musical setting puts the singers in the position of playing the listener as well as the speaker. The first and third lines of each stanza employ only three voices, leaving the fourth to listen as she waits to join in.[28] The opening line omits the Tenore, while the third line leaves the Alto silent first, and then in a written-out repeat the Canto (the Alto here sings the Canto's line; the repeat is other-

Example 1.3b. "O tu che vai per via," mm. 11–18.

wise identical). While it is not unusual in Book I to find a single line omitted in the Basso or, more rarely, the Tenore, the Alto and Canto only miss out lines in one other piece each (nos. 14 and 20, respectively), and "O tu che vai per via" is the only song to make such omissions in three different voices and to distribute these lacunae so purposefully through a varied repeat.

The emphasis in "O tu che vai per via" on the character's speech as a direct appeal to listeners within the singing ensemble is conveyed through other musical details as well. The octave leap that begins the opening point of imitation between the Canto and Basso throws each voice to the top of its range, encouraging a dynamic accent on the word "tu," and the shift to homophony at the Tenore's first entrance on "Deh, fermati" (m. 5) makes the supplication especially pointed (example 1.3a).[29] A similar moment, the entrance of the missing upper part on the fourth line (Alto in m. 16; Canto in m. 32) on "Odi" is even more strangely marked by the Tenore's irregular resolution of the suspension in the previous bar, leaping from the c#' leading tone up to the f', the third of the following D-minor sonority (example 1.3b). Though the following poetic strophes do not always take advantage of these moments in precisely the same way, they do highlight the self-quotation in the second stanza ("Ecco questa è l'acerba mia ferita") and the desired response in the fourth ("Et ti prego di dire / Che chi per donna ingrata perde il core"). By projecting onto the singers the roles of both speaker and listener and by highlighting the complaint as public speech rather than Petrarchan lyric reflection, Vecchi frames the desperate character as a figure of ridicule.

An altogether different take on the lover's complaint is no. 21, "Trà verdi campi a la stagion novella," which, we recall, was positioned as the final piece in Book I in the second edition of 1580. In both poetic style and imagery, it embraces the forward-looking pastoral mode more than any other canzonetta in Book I, adumbrating the ubiquity of pastoralism in Vecchi's later canzonettas and in Italian music of the 1580s in general. Though other Book I canzonettas would not be out of place in a pastoral context, only "Trà verdi campi" mentions the fields, rivers, nymphs, and shepherds that signify the pastoral and includes the lightweight pairs of *quinari* lines that would characterize much light Italian poetry later in the *cinquecento*.[30]

Trà verdi campi a la stagion novella	Among the green fields in springtime
Vince ogni fior una vermiglia rosa.	one red rose surpasses every flower.
Veggiola di lontano,	I see her from afar,
Ma stendo in vano	but in vain I extend
L'ardita mano.	my ardent hand.
Famosi fiumi, e tu, Colonia bella,	Famous rivers, and you, lovely Colonia,
Quanto de bene ha'l mondo in voi.	All that is good in the world resides
si posa	in you.
Veggiola ...	I see her ...
Cogliete i fiori in questa parte e	Gather the flowers here and there,
in quella,	
Ninfe, à honorar di voi la piu	nymphs, to honor the most famous
famosa.	among you.
Veggiola ...	I see her ...

Et voi, felici e cari umbrii Pastori,	And you, dear, happy, Umbrian shepherds,
Cantate in rime i suoi celeste honori;	sing her heavenly honors in verse;
E tu, rosa gradita,	And you, pleasing rose,
Beltà infinita	infinite beauty,
Dammi la vita.	give me life.

The text had already appeared in Serafino Candido's *Mascherate musicali . . . a tre quattro, e cinque voci* (Venice: Scotto, 1571). Only nine of Candido's thirty-four pieces are in fact *mascherate,* but almost all carry titles that euphemistically refer to sexual encounters.[31] "Trà verdi campi" is labeled "La ninfa Naria," the only title in the book that connotes a pastoral setting. However, if the context of Candido's *mascherate* renders the longed-for nymph as merely one of a long list of *cortegiane dishoneste,* then Vecchi's use of the same text almost a decade later in a book dominated by Petrarchan love poetry transforms her: by the end of the 1570s, pastoral literature had become a kind of roman à clef for courtly discourse about love. The poetic speaker in "Trà verdi campi" addresses the nymph just once in the poem and otherwise speaks to the community of nymphs and shepherds who populate the pastoral landscape.

This discourse is precisely that described by Giuseppe Gerbino in his account of pastoralism in the late *cinquecento* madrigal: "By relocating the inner life of the Petrarchist lover in the collective dimension of the pastoral community, Petrarch's introverted individualism was recontextualized as social fact. The 'Arcadianization' of the discourse on love adapted the solitary and introspective psychologism of the *Canzoniere* to the social structure of the court. The court, construed as a community of kindred spirits afflicted by a spiritual ailment called desire, shared and exchanged poetry and music in an attempt to comprehend and alleviate the malaise of human existence."[32] Strategically placed at or near the end of Book I, "Trà verdi campi" presages a transition in Vecchi's later canzonettas away from the comic elements held over from the rustic *villanella* toward eroticism couched in the pastoral style. The placement of this song at the end of the 1580 reprint of Book I, contemporary with the first edition of Book II, may have suggested a link between the old and new books (one which in later reprints was less pertinent than the programmatic placement, discussed above, of "Trà le chiome de l'oro" as the final piece). In any case, as a metaphor for a social gathering, the Arcadian setting of "Trà le verdi campi" stands at the leading edge of the pastoral trend that would transform Italian secular music from the 1580s onward.

"The New Sound of the Lyre": Pastoralism and Music Making in Book II

In contrast to the first book's canzonettas having been assembled at the end of the 1570s from pieces written over several years, Vecchi claims that those of the second book are of more recent composition. This assertion comes in the opening piece, "Vaghe Ninfe e Pastori," which (like "Canzonette d'amore" in Book I) serves an explicitly introductory function. The book's dedication to Camillo Pellegrini, the *podestà*, or chief magistrate, of Bologna, says almost nothing about the music except to imply that the pieces convey relatively little prestige either to the composer or to the dedicatee.[33] Such modesty, typical in dedications generally, is especially common in books of canzonettas, *villanellas*, and other genres perceived as "lighter" than the madrigal.

The increasing prominence of pastoral references in the poetry of Book II is paralleled by texts that refer, either incidentally or as their central conceit, to courtly music making and other recreational activities. As a book dedicated to a municipal magistrate in a noncourtly city and sold in its five Italian editions to a presumably wide range of music consumers, these representations of courtly leisure—in pastoral or more realistic terms—take on an aspirational quality. The erotic preoccupations of shepherds and nymphs are also encoded in Book II's discourses on music itself, and some of the polyphonic settings can be read as commenting on such subjects from the viewpoint of a peripheral observer. Vecchi's widely popular and technically accessible canzonettas may therefore reveal a more critical attitude toward courtliness than madrigals composed for the Ferrarese *concerto* and its imitators.

The pastoral mode is announced most explicitly in the opening pair of songs, no. 23, "Vaghe Ninfe e Pastori," and no. 24, "Hor ch'io son gionti quivi," which besides being saturated with pastoral imagery are unique among all Vecchi's canzonettas in their use of *sdruccioli*, strongly associated with the eclogic mode of Sannazaro's pastoral verse romance *Arcadia* (completed by 1489 and first published in 1504). *Sdruccioli*, poetic lines with a distinctive stress on the antepenultimate syllable (and, therefore, an extra weak syllable in what would otherwise be a stardard *settenario* or *endecasillabo*), would become increasingly emblematic of pastoralism in its late *cinquecento* revival. Moreover, the pairing of the two opening poems is evident in their shared stanzaic structure (a a b' B');[34] every other poem in the book has a unique form. As in many of Vecchi's books, the opening number serves a framing function for the entire volume, establishing an explicit emphasis on love that leads into the beginning of the second piece:

[no. 23]

Vaghe Ninfe e Pastori,	Pretty nymphs and shepherds,
Lasciate i primi ardori	leave your first flames
E quell'usanza vetera,	and old customs,
Meco cantando al nuovo suon di Cetera.	singing with me to the new sound of the lyre.
Vedrete à questi accenti	You will see the forests and groves
Le selve e i boschi intenti.	attentive to these accents.
Gli augelli desterannosi,	The birds rouse themselves,
E Canzonette mille indi udirannosi.	and a thousand canzonettas will be heard.
Poi vezzosetti balli	Then fearless flocks and herds
Guideran per le valli	will lead pretty dances
Greggi ed armenti impavidi,	through the valleys,
Del cantar nostro innamorati ed avidi.	inflamed with love by our singing.
Ma che? vedete intorno	But what? See all around
Farsi più bello il giorno,	the day becomes more beautiful,
E i campi che si smaltano	and the fields shine
Al cantar novo, e Greggi e Armenti saltano.	at the new song, and flocks and herds leap.

[no. 24]

Hor ch'io son gionto quivi	Now that I have arrived here
Frà questi boschi e rivi	among these woods and rivers
E queste herbette tenere	and these tender plants,
Io vo cantar del fier fanciul di Venere.	I want to sing of the proud son of Venus.

[three more stanzas follow]

The "first flames" in the opening stanza allude to the songs of Vecchi's own first book, implicitly recommending the newer ones of the second, but the broader reference seems to be to the new canzonetta style in general superseding older musical practices, in which the refined literary madrigal stood more clearly in contrast to the *villanesca* and its relatives. The invitation to "sing with me to the new sound of the lyre" suggests the possibility of instrumental accompaniment but also of multiple singing parts. As I have argued in connection with Book I, although the canzonetta accommodates a wide range of performance practices, Vecchi's musical settings reveal greater textual sensitivity and wit than genres (like the three-voice *villanelle* described by Giustinaini) in which polyphonically notated songs were more typically intended for accompanied solo performance. The pastoral image of singing to the archaic *cetra* therefore describes not (or not only) actual performance practices but rather the singing of imagined shepherds in the Arcadian landscape.

Elsewhere, Vecchi depicts courtly music making using the technical terminology of literate polyphonic composition, though with no loss of erotic subtext. No. 40, "Fa una Canzone senza note nere," is a song of seduction masked as a plea for musical simplicity in which the music reflects the text as literally as possible:

Fa una Canzone senza note nere	Make a song without black notes,
Se mai brumasti la mia gratia havere,	if you ever wish to have my favor,
Falla d'un tuono ch'invita al dormire,	Make it in a mode that invites one to sleep,
Dolcemente facendola finire.	sweetly bringing it to the end.
Per entro non vi spargere durezze,	Do not put dissonances into it,
Che le mie orrechia non vi sono avezze.	because my ears are not used to them.
Falla d'un tuono ch'invita al dormire,	Make it in a mode that invites one to sleep,
Dolcemente facendola finire.	sweetly bringing it to the end.
Ne vi far cifre ò segno contra segno;	Don't make proportions or signs against signs;
Sopra ogni cosa quest'è 'l mio disegno.	above all, this is my intention.
Falla d'un tuono ch'invita al dormire,	Make it in a mode that invites one to sleep,
Dolcemente facendola finire.	sweetly bringing it to the end.
Con questo stile il fortunato Orfeo	With this style the fortunate Orpheus
Proserpina la giù placar poteo.	was able to placate Proserpina there below.
Questo è lo stile che quetar già feo	This is the style that quieted
Con dolcezza à Saul lo spirto reo.	with sweetness the evil spirit in Saul.

The music lacks semiminims, mensural changes, and even the simple points of imitation that typically mark Vecchi's canzonettas; it is in fact almost completely homophonic and composed of root-position triads, with a "sweet" turn to E-flat harmonies in the refrain. The thinly veiled erotic content suggests the speaking voice of a woman who is willing to grant her favors to one who will not assail her bodily orifices (ears) with dissonant "durezze" (hardnesses) and will avoid difficult (and implicitly unnatural) combinations of mensurations. This style, the refrain promises, will earn the song's maker an invitation to bed, where he will find a sweet ending. The song's double entendre equates simple, pleasing music with normative sexual intercourse, as confirmed by the final stanza's mythological and biblical references, which promise that the simple style both pleases women "la giù" (there below) and calms men's "evil spirits."

Contrasting urges—both musical and erotic—are described in another of the Book II canzonettas, no. 26, "Fammi una Canzonetta capriciosa." Though placed near opposite ends of the book, the similarities of their titles invite singers to compare them, and the differences are striking:

Fammi una Canzonetta capriciosa,	Make me a fanciful canzonetta
Che nullo o pochi la sappian cantare,	that no one or few know how to sing,
E al tuon di quella si possi ballare.	And to its sound we can dance.
Non ti curar di tuono ò d'osservata,	Don't worry about mode or artfulness,
Che questo è meglio che tu possi fare,	because this is the best that you can do,
E al tuon di quello si possi ballare.	And to its sound we can dance.
Falla come ti dà la fantasia,	Make it as your fancy likes,
E affretta il corso col bel solfeggiare,	and speed up the step with beautiful sol-fas,
E al tuon di quella si possi ballare.	And to its sound we can dance.

It would be natural enough to assume that the song, like "Fa una Canzone," is intended to epitomize the kind of music it describes, but this seems not to be the case. Most obviously, the three-part *villanella* form is ill suited to traditional dancing. The first line is set to a simple point of imitation in duple (c) time, moving in minims and semiminims, while the second shifts to more syncopated lines mostly in *fusae* to represent a style that "none or few know how to sing." The third line shifts rhythmic style again, moving to triple-meter homophony that, while undeniably dance-like, undermines the plausibility that "Fammi una Canzonetta capricciosa" itself could serve for social dancing, which does not normally accommodate metric shifts within a single dance. The poem's ideal of the canzonetta as dance music is therefore metaphorical rather than literal, yet in comparison with "Fa una Canzona," the erotic subtext of "Fammi una Canzonetta" is distinctly more uninhibited. The desire for a fanciful dance song that "none or few" understand, that disregards proprieties of mode and rhythm, and that accelerates at the end with nonsensical *solfeggio* hints at a less constrained eroticism. However, to fully understand the metaphorical implications of both of these songs, we must parse their texts and subtexts in light of their social function.

The self-consciously tricky rhythms in the middle section of "Fammi una Canzonetta capricciosa" that "none or few" can understand are in fact only complex in comparison to the generally simpler style of Vecchi's canzonettas. They might well have confused some amateur singers upon a first reading, but they would by no means restrict performance of the piece to highly skilled musicians. In both this passage and the dance-like (but not dance-based) final section, then, "Fammi una Canzonetta capricciosa" points from the social context in which it is sung to a different and more inaccessible one: it expresses a desire for dancing and refined music that it does not fulfill. It gives singers who may not have the means or the ability to enjoy such courtly pleasures imaginative access to them. We have already seen this sense of play with social hierarchies in canzonettas that imitate comic urban or rustic characters, but imitation of the social elite—like the imitation of idealized (and erotically charged) shepherds and nymphs—is also a component of the canzonetta's appeal.[35]

The interplay of eroticism, imagination, and musical texture presents itself in canzonettas that do not refer to music as well. The speaker's erotic intent is unusually explicit in no. 38, "Lieva la man di qui": in his flirtation with Cloris, he describes his desire to kiss her, remove her veil, shower her with ambrosia, place her on his lap, and fill her with poison. Vecchi sets the poem in a thoroughly homophonic texture that subsumes each singer's subjectivity into a more distanced fictive one, but this reading is distinctive to the singers' experience rather than to that of a separate listener. To a listener a homophonic texture, in contrast to a contrapuntal one, may more clearly convey the text and therefore evoke a speaking character more sharply; for a singer, however, the experience of singing a first-person singular text in rhythmic unison with one's companions distances the poetic "I" from the social "we" that collectively sings the words.

No. 28, "O donna ch'a mio danno i ciel ti denno," achieves the opposite effect, its unusually persistent counterpoint giving each singer agency over her own words. The entire text comprises a series of *bisticci*, or tongue twisters, so that this contrapuntal technique captures the game-like nature of attempting to recite the text (example 1.4):

Example 1.4. (*above and facing*) Vecchi, "O donna ch'a mio danno," mm. 1–22.

O donna ch'a mio danno i ciel ti denno
Le belle treccie d'oro e 'l petto d'ira,
    D'Amore amaro ohime ch'io moro mira.

E se m'hà svelto il sonno e svolto il senno
Tua gratia, ch'in te spera, spara, e spira,
    D'Amor amaro ohime ch'io moro mira.

Le spirto esperto è sparto, e a ogni tuo cenno

Oh lady, to whom for my woe heaven gave
those beautiful golden tresses and a wrathful heart,
see that I die, alas, from bitter love.

And if your grace has taken my sleep and unraveled
my senses, which in you hope, struggle, and breath,
see that I die, alas, from bitter love.

My reason is set loose, and at every sign of you

Vola veloce ove tua voglia il tira.	flies fast to where your will draws it;
D'Amor amaro ohime ch'io moro mira.	see that I die, alas, from bitter love.
Se 'l tuo decoro hò caro e cura il core,	If I treasure your glory and my heart cares,
N'hà perche ardire, hor dir non deve ardore,	it has reason to burn, but must not speak of burning;
Mira ch'io moro ohime d'amaro Amore.	see that I die, alas, from bitter love.

The agonies of the Petrarchan lover are here depicted not only as a play of complex counterpoint but through the difficulty of enunciating the convoluted poetry, so that the *gravità* of the textual content is overwhelmed by the *piacevolezza* of the musical style. As with the middle section of "Fammi una Canzonetta capricciosa," the musical setting challenges each singer to get her part right—exactly the kind of challenge offered by the text alone. In his dialogue on conversational games of 1572, Girolamo Bargagli explains that *bisticci* belong to a lower category of games, since it depends on participants' errors for its competitive quality (see chapter 5)—an objection applicable also to singing recreational polyphony.[36]

"L'hore di recreatione"

The clearest illustration in Vecchi's early publications of both the recreational use of music and the imaginative conflation of courtly and pastoral life is "L'hore di recreatione" (transcribed in the present Appendix), the seven-voice, three-part work that concludes the *Madrigali a sei voci* (1583). I shall discuss that book in more detail in the next chapter, but the references in "L'hore di recreatione" to canzonettas and other "light" genres earn it a place here.[37] It depicts a group of ladies and gentlemen at leisure in an outdoor setting, passing their time singing, dancing, and playing a ball game. They would seem to be courtiers speaking and behaving in the idealized manner of the pastoral, but their choice of songs and sometimes disruptive behavior undercut such a straightforward reading, repeatedly exposing the cracks in their self-mythologizing façade. The opening describes a pastoral landscape complete with birds that sing in the style of a *concerto delle donne,* but the humans choose instead to sing a simpler song in which all can participate:

Hor che le piaggie ridon d'ogn'intorno,	Now that the slopes laugh all around,	
E spuntan fuor viole e gigl'e rose,	and violets, lilies, and roses sprout forth,	
E gl'augelletti per le vall'ombrose,	and the birds through the shady valley	
Cantan'in stile adorno	sing in an ornamented style	
Leggiadre Canzonette e amorose	gracious and amorous canzonettas,	
Donne e donzelle leggiadrette e belle,	lovely and beautiful ladies and damsels,	
Ch'in gioia a tutte l'ore	since joyfully in you at all hours	
Con gran piacer in voi s'annid'Amore,	lurks Love, with great pleasure,	
Deh, tutti uniti insieme:	now everyone join together:	
Cantiam qualche ballata o Canzonetta!	let's sing some *ballata* or canzonetta!	

A discussion of the disposition of parts follows, in which individual voices claim the Canto, Alto, and Basso parts, while two voices share the Tenore part. The canzonetta that follows, though sung by all seven voices, is thus represented as a piece in the four-part style of Vecchi's previous books and is in fact an expanded version of the first stanza of "Chi mira gl'occhi tuoi," from the first book. The bass line is transposed down a fifth, moving the final from C to F, and the remaining parts are adjusted to accommodate the fuller texture. While the texture and the use of a single stanza are typical of the larger-scale *canzone* or canzonetta (including Vecchi's six-voice canzonettas of 1587), the text suggests that the fictive song heard by the characters is nevertheless in the four-part style:[38]

TB^2B^1	Chi farà il Basso?	Who will be the Basso?
B^1	Io!	I will!
CA6	Chi fara il Canto?	Who will be the Canto?
5	Eccomi qua!	Here I am!
CTB^1B^2	Chi fara l'Alto?	Who will be the Alto?
A	Io!	I will!
tutti	Del Tenor' ve n'è coppia, or commenciamo!	For the Tenor there is a pair, now begin!
	Chi mira gl'occhi tuoi	Whoever looks at your eyes
	E non sospira poi,	and does not then sigh,
	Credo che non sia vivo,	I believe is not alive,
	O di giudizio privo.	or is without judgment.

The *seconda parte* begins with a disagreement. Four voices call for an immediate repetition of "Chi mira gl'occhi tuoi," while the remaining three repeatedly respond "non più!" and then call for a dance, to which the other voices immediately assent. The call for the repetition, "Un'altra volta, senza intervallo," is itself modeled on the opening of Cipriano de Rore's "Un'altra volta la Germania strida."[39] The other singers' rejection of this request therefore also humorously rejects the elevated style of the serious political madrigal. The dance that follows, "Ballarestu fantina," appears to be of a nonliterate popular origin, since it reappears in two different prints in 1608 with a slightly different text.[40] Its rustic dialect leads to laughter, which breaks off the song:

5A6B[1]	Un'altra volta, senz'altr'intervallo!	Again, without a break!
CTB[2]	Non più, facciam'un ballo!	No more; let's have a dance!
tutti	Non più, facciam'un ballo!	No more; let's have a dance!
5ATB[1]	Ballarestu fantina, Da la farza turchina?	Will you dance, my girl, like in a Turkish comedy?
CA6B[2]	Ballareve ben mi, sa savesse con chi!	I dance well, knowing whom to dance with!
tutti	Ballareve ben mi, sa savesse con chi!	I dance well, knowing whom to dance with!
C5A	Non più, non più frenate il riso!	No more! Hold back your laughing!

After this somewhat lowbrow interlude the group seems to attempt a return to the more decorous tone appropriate to their pastoral surroundings, noting again the birds' affinity for more refined singing. The general call for a song in honor of a beloved lady is sung *tutti,* blurring the group's identity momentarily into the first-person singular subjective voice of the love lyric (as thoroughly conventionalized in the madrigal). However, the comic element intrudes again with the observation that "we" have nearly a hundred lovers. The lyrical mode breaks down as some in the group—the upper four voices, to be precise—return to the group subjectivity of the first-person plural. This dialogic alternation of voice groups here enacts the comic interruption, and the lower four voices sheepishly respond that they do not remember the lady's name:

T6B[2]B[1]	E, poiché dolcemente	And, since the birds
tutti	Cantano gl'augelletti ai nostr'accenti,	sing sweetly to our accents,
CATB[1]	Piacciavi di cantare	be pleased to sing
tutti	Quella che sì diletta a mio compare.	of she who appears so delightful to me.

C5AT	Come si chiama, che n'abbiam ben cento?	What is her name? We have nearly a hundred!
T6B²B¹	Non mi soviene.	I cannot recall.
C5A	Or stia ciascun'attento:	Then let each one listen:
tutti	Or va Canzona mia, non dubitare...	Here goes my *canzona*, without a doubt...

The full group now begins a seven-voice arrangement of "Or va canzona mia," a *villanella* first published in 1560 in an anonymous three-voice version and later in a five-voice arrangement by Giovanni Ferretti in 1567.[41] As with "Chi mira gl'occhi tuoi," Vecchi expands the texture of his model in a way that allows all the singers to participate, minimizing any sense of an audience-directed performance.

The song is next interrupted even more abruptly when a single voice cries "Fermatevi!" and calls for a comic *giustiniana,* a genre that enjoyed a brief popularity in the 1570s in music mostly by Vincenzo Bellavere and Andrea Gabrieli. Vecchi himself revived the genre starting in 1590, including them in all of his four large-scale collections. *Giustiniane* typically depict a foolishly lovesick old Venetian, a stereotype that also gave rise to the Pantalone figure in the *commedia dell'arte* tradition. Though typically scored for a low-voiced trio (and sometimes in fact depicting a trio of men), the *giustiniana* on which the company of "L'hore di recreatione" embark is again scored for all seven voices and takes its text and melody from one of Bellavere's songs in the genre, "Tutto il di ti te spampoli" (example 1.5).[42]

B²	Fermatevi!	Stop!
CA6	[Perché?]	Why?
B¹	Perché[43]	Because
A6B²B¹	quella ch'io voglio	what I want
A6B²B¹	È una Iustiniana!	is a Giustiniana!
C5ATB²B¹	Sì, sì, gliè ver, or dite allegramente:	Yes, yes, he's right. Now cheerfully say:
tutti	Tutto il dì ti te spampoli Che mi son un petagolo E che par'un coruogolo Con la coa tutta toccoli...	
CA6B¹	Or io mi sento raddolcito il core,	Now my heart feels refreshed,
5ATB¹	Doh, viva l'amore!	O, long live love!
C5B²	Doh, viva l'amore!	O, long live love!
tutti	Doh, viva l'amore!	O, long live love!

Example 1.5. Bellavere, "Tutto 'l di ti te spampoli" (first stanza only shown; middle part book does not survive).

In the *terza parte,* the party plays a ball game, beginning with a somewhat obscure discussion of prize money and a process of determining who will take the first turn—stages that map onto the conventions of more learned games of the period, a topic to which I will return in chapter 5. Once play begins the game quickly dissolves into an argument, though since the exact nature of the game is unclear, this passage is difficult to parse. The mood is quickly soothed by a return to singing with the line "Ben venga maggio," the opening line of a poem by Angelo Poliziano that reaffirms the springtime setting of the entire scene.[44] In terms of the recreational function of the *terza parte,* it is particularly noteworthy that Vecchi sometimes employs consistent vocal groupings to set dialogue, but during the heated argument the groupings shift in ways that blur the distinctions between characters and eventually include the full ensemble on the climactic line "Fuor di qui ci parleremo," suggesting that the entire company has gotten caught up in the fracas, including the voices that, a moment later, seek to restore order:

5A6B¹	Or tocca a voi:	Now it's your turn:
CT	diamo principio al gioco!	start the game!
5AB¹B²	Chi ha la palla di voi?	Who has your ball?
CT6	Eccola qua!	Here it is!
5AB¹B²	Eccola qua!	Here it is!
T6B¹B²	Facciam'a duoi a duoi.	We'll go two by two.
C5AB¹	Battete!	Strike!
C6B²	A voi!	To you!
5ATB¹	Glìe fal la prima volta!	The first turn is false!
CAB²	Non già, ch'io non l'ho colto!	Not yet, I wasn't prepared!
5A6B¹	Voi v'ingannate, che glìe fallo marzo!	You're wrong, for you paid the ante!
CTB²	Non dite il vero!	You don't tell the truth!
5A6B¹	Fuor di qui ci parleremo!	We'll talk outside!
tutti	Fuor di qui ci parleremo!	We'll talk outside!
5A6B¹	Signori non gridate,	Gentlemen do not shout,
CAB²	Ma piuttosto a cantar voi ritornate	but rather come back to sing
tutti	A l'ombra di quel faggio:	in the shadow of the beech:
	Ben venga Maggio!	Welcome, May!

Though some general principles can be observed in the dialogue's voice combinations (e.g., the alternation of Canto and Quinto voices as the top line), these are not entirely consistent and do not clarify the structure of the dialogue (as, for example, divided choirs do in sung theatrical dialogues).[45] Indeed, there are at least three distinct characters represented in this passage. As he would do most consistently in *L'Amfiparnaso*, Vecchi varies the vocal combinations to enhance the sense of play for the singers themselves: looking at an individual part book, one cannot discern the full sense of the text and therefore must engage the piece imaginatively by both singing and listening.

"L'hore di recreatione" lays bare some of the tensions and contradictions inherent in courtly codes of behavior. Although the company enjoy their leisure in an idealized pastoral setting where refined music and nature are seemingly in harmony with one another (particularly as embodied in birdsong), their musical choices descend in decorum from a simple canzonetta to rustic dialect songs. The only reference to a refined madrigal—the paraphrase of Rore's "Un'altra volta"—comes in lines that, within the fictive setting, are not sung but spoken and are in any case quickly rejected. The group's behavior follows a similar path, from the cooperative distribution of part books in the *prima parte,* to the interruptions and accusations of amorous promiscuity in the *seconda parte,* and finally to the outright argument over the ball game in the *terza parte.* In a move that we will see repeatedly in music that imitates sociability (see especially chapters 5 and 6), social concord is restored at such moments through the imposition of musical harmony.

2 Intertextuality in Vecchi's Canzonettas and Madrigals, 1583–1590

As we have seen in chapter 1, by 1580 Vecchi had effectively invented a new genre: the four-voice canzonetta, a kind of music that found immense popularity in print and that was particularly suited to recreational singing. In his first two books of canzonettas, he established the genre's kinship with the older *villanella* and with the pastoral poetic vein then coming to prominence in the contemporary madrigal. In the next decade Vecchi produced two more books of four-voice canzonettas (published in 1585 and 1590) and one of six-voice canzonettas (1587), but he also turned his hand to the more high-status madrigal in books for six voices (1583) and for five voices (1589).[1] While Vecchi had contributed to two significant madrigal anthologies in the 1570s, his single-author books of the following decade demonstrate his maturation in the genre.

In this chapter, we will see how Vecchi's madrigals and canzonettas reflect their different poetic priorities and cultural registers, particularly in the ways they frequently point to other poems or musical works either through explicit responses (*risposte*) to other works of his own or through poems modeled in various ways on some of the most popular texts of the period. These intertextual references do more than simply situate Vecchi's music in relation to these other works, however: they create a virtual dialogue between pieces that was realizable as actual conversational dialogue among recreational singers. Both by singing related songs sequentially and by discussing the similarities and contrasts between such songs, their formalized discourse about music, poetry, and love (the ubiquitous subject of so much *poesia per musica*), participants follow a pattern comparable to another recreational activity: game playing. As described in treatises on games by Innocentio Ringhieri and Girolamo Bargagli, courtly games are nothing other than structured conversations about a given subject.[2] Game-like conversations are also depicted in Baldessare Castiglione's *Il cortegiano* and Antonfrancesco Doni's *Dialogo della musica,* the latter illustrating how songs alternate with conversation in a social setting.[3] Musico-poetic *risposte* thus interact both with the works from which they are derived and with the conversations in which they are embedded; the point is not that such references are so obscure that only the most musically knowledgeable will find them but rather that holding multiple works up next to each other prompts the kind of game-like conversation that early modern sociability prized.

The *risposta* tradition is especially prevalent in the four-voice canzonetta books of this period, and I believe Vecchi's fourth book takes the idea a step further by creating an implicit cycle of songs referring satirically to the episode of Ruggiero and Alcina in Ariosto's *Orlando furioso*—a kind of narrative linkage that Vecchi pursued in various ways in his later books of the 1590s. My examination of intertextual connections in Vecchi's music of the 1580s concludes with a reading of three works in different genres that all imitate Battista Guarini's "Tirsi morir volea," one of the most popular madrigal poems of the century, though one that Vecchi never set in its original form.

Vecchi's Dedications: Context and Careerism

Although by 1583 Vecchi's four-voice canzonettas had proven their popularity, the first book having been reprinted twice and the second book once in a matter of two or three years, the composer seems to have wanted to prove himself in the more serious genre of the six-voice madrigal, not coincidentally, at a moment when his career may have been somewhat unstable. Vecchi had been *maestro di cappella* in Salò since 1581 and was granted a salary of fifty scudi there for a three-year term in 1582.[4] However, he was appointed *maestro di cappella* at the cathedral in Modena on February 16, 1583, and was subsequently dismissed from his post in Salò on June 24, 1584.[5] By March 1584 Vecchi was well-enough established in Modena to declare to the town council his intent to remain there permanently in order to care for his aged father, for which he was awarded a stipend of ten lire per month.[6] This confirmation of his new position may well have prompted his formal dismissal from Salò a few weeks later.[7]

Although the appointment in Modena was no doubt attractive to Vecchi for both personal and professional reasons, the *Madrigali a sei voci* suggest that between his initial appointment and his official commitment to remain he still sought another position further afield. The dedication, signed in Venice on September 1, 1583, is to Alberto (Albrycht) Radziwiłł (1558–1592), marshal (*marszałek*) to the king of Poland, whom Vecchi had apparently never met: in the dedication he notes that Claudio (Merulo) da Correggio had brought his music to Radziwiłł's attention and that the latter had enjoyed it. The title page names him only as Orazio Vecchi, without the "da Modena" he normally appended to his name, a strategy he adopted again for books that seem to have been tied to bids for employment elsewhere.

In contrast, Vecchi's third book of four-voice canzonettas was dedicated on November 30, 1585, to the gentlemen Camillo and Thomaso Rubini. Vecchi here retained the "da Modena" styling of his name, and he was apparently not seeking employment through this dedication. The dedication to the Rubini brothers expresses the composer's hope to secure "some friendship or service that could be fruitful, good and true friends being so few," but Vecchi is clear that the dedicatees' names are intended to add allure to the book for others: "To you I therefore give and consecrate these my verses, and these songs, which gain strength and quality through going out adorned with your name. To your name they will perhaps also serve as glorious incense and myrrh in perpetuity, and consecrating them with the same affection I commend myself to you, and kiss your hands."[8] This passage is most notable, of course, as Vecchi's most explicit claim of authorship for the poems he set to music, and indeed the third book of canzonettas contains no poems that can be securely attributed to others.[9]

Despite his earlier pledge to remain in Modena, in January 1586 Vecchi was found to have been secretly negotiating an appointment as *maestro di cappella* at the cathedral in Reggio and was dismissed from his position at the cathedral in Modena; he was subsequently released from his obligation to the town council.[10] Vecchi remained in Reggio only a few months, however, and in December 1586 was appointed a canon at Correggio, where he would remain until 1593, having been named archcanon in 1591. His years in Correggio were unusually productive: he published no fewer than six books between 1587 and 1590.

Vecchi's dedications during this period serve contrasting purposes. Dedications to relatively minor figures seem to represent gratitude for patronage already bestowed: the modest *Lamentationes cum quattuor paribus vocibus* (1587) and the fourth book of four-voice canzonettas (1590) are dedicated to local patrons (Bishop Sisto Visdomini of Modena and Count Camillo d'Austria of Correggio, respectively) and identify Vecchi as "da Modena." The other four books are dedicated to figures Vecchi had never met, and these dedications suggest greater ambition. The *Canzonette a sei* were dedicated to Marco Antonio Gonzaga, *primicerio* in Mantua, the head—independent from the bishop—of the church of Sant'Andrea.[11] The more courtly *Madrigali a cinque* of two years later were dedicated to Duke Vincenzo Gonzaga, a powerful potential patron but no more than that: the dedication commences with an elaborate apology for Vecchi's having been away when the duke visited Correggio: "I was profoundly pained, my most serene Lord, not to find myself in Correggio when it pleased Your Highness to honor this city with your presence, because on that occasion I could for once have achieved what I had already for a long time ardently desired, that is, to discover for myself, as a devoted Servant, that which I have heard about from those who have some understanding of your greatness of spirit and of the Heroic virtue with which it is so richly adorned."[12] The dedication goes on to report that Vincenzo had nonetheless heard some of Vecchi's music while in Correggio and had praised it (a detail obviously reported for the benefit of the reader rather than the duke). We can surmise, therefore, that these two dedications did not reflect past Mantuan patronage but were rather meant to solicit it in the future; Vecchi pursued this campaign through a dedication not only to the duke himself but also to another influential member of his family. The other two books published in 1590 were dedicated to Wilhelm V, duke of Bavaria (the *Motecta*), and to the brothers Johannes and Jakob Fugger of the wealthy Augsburg banking family (*Selva di varia ricreatione*), suggesting a new ambition to seek employment in Germany.[13] As with the 1583 dedication of the *Madrigali a sei,* none of these aspirational dedications succeeded, and Vecchi's relationship with the highest levels of courtly culture remained that of an outsider looking in.

Poetic Adaptation in Vecchi's Madrigals

As the dedicatory patterns outlined above suggest, Vecchi aimed his madrigal books at higher levels of the aristocracy—and thus at different potential performance contexts—than his popular canzonettas. By the 1580s in such courtly circles generally and in the Gonzaga court at Mantua in particular, madrigals were increasingly performed primarily for the benefit of listening audiences. Although in printed form they certainly found use in the hands of amateur singers, we can read their engagement with literary and musical traditions from the overlapping perspectives of listeners, singers, and readers. This overlap would also include performances, such as those documented for the Ferrarese *Concerto delle donne,* at which listeners were given copies of the music being sung.[14]

Like Vecchi's first book of canzonettas, the *Madrigali a sei voci* seem to be drawn from a range of works composed over a considerable time prior to their appearance in print. They also rely heavily on compositional techniques associated with Vecchi's canzonettas, favoring four- or five-part homorhythmic textures decorated with Giustiniani's "easy fugues," reserving the *tutti* texture for important cadences, and emphasizing the large-scale sectional repetitions of the canzonetta (especially in final sections). Moreover, six of the fourteen pieces set texts by, or modeled on those by, other authors:

1. O che vezzosa Aurora
2. Ardo sì, ma non t'amo (Guarini)
3. Ardi e gela a tua voglia (Tasso)
4. Occhi soavi che m'avete il core
   Seconda parte: Altre parole e leggiadrett'accenti
5. Scioglier la voce umile
6. Non veggio ove scampar mi poss'omai (Petrarch)
7. Che fia lasso di me?
8. L'onde lascia e gli scogli (after Strozzi)
9. Amor di propria man congiunti avea (after Guarini)
   Seconda parte: La Ninfa allor con voc'ebra d'Amore
   Terza parte: Così con lieto gioco
10. Tu dolce anima mia
11. Se più t'ammassi, ingrato (Guarini)
12. S'odon le Gierarchie nel ciel cantare
    Seconda parte: S'ammirano i Pastor
13. Dolce cantava a l'apparir del sole
14. Or che le piagge ridon d'ogn'intorno ("L'hore di recreatione")
    Seconda parte: Un'altra volta senz'altr'intervallo
    Terza parte: Ormai poniamo fine al nostro canto

Two other anonymous poems in Vecchi's book are found in previous settings and therefore may not be his own. No. 7, "Che fia lasso di me?" was set by

Andrea Feliciani in 1579 in his *Primo libro di madrigali a cinque voci*. However, since Vecchi and Feliciani would have known each other from the Sienese *cappella* in the early 1570s, the poem is likely to date from that period and may be by Vecchi. No. 10, "Tu dolce anima mia," was set by Giovanni di Macque also in 1579, but this Roman composer is less likely to have known Vecchi, so the poem's authorship is more uncertain. As for the securely attributable poems, by drawing on high-status literature Vecchi may have sought to elevate his madrigals above the canzonettas for which he claimed authorship of words and music.

Even when setting poems by others, Vecchi may have adapted them to suit his purposes. Guarini's published version (from 1598) of no. 11, "Se più t'amassi, ingrato," reverses the gender of the addressee, beginning "Se più t'amassi, ingrata."[15] Vecchi's setting of only the first quatrain from Petrarch's sonnet "Non veggio ove scampar mi possa omai" is more straightforward but proves poetically unsatisfying, since the second couplet lacks the *acutezza* necessary to justify its extended canzonetta-like repetition. A more creative adaptation of another poet's work is Vecchi's setting of "L'onda lascia e gli scogli," which substantially rewrites a poem by the elder Giovanni Battista Strozzi:

STROZZI	VECCHI
L'onda lascia, e gli scogli	**L'onde lascia e gli scogli,**
Delle sempre atre nebulose rive	Le selv'e le fontane,
E qui Meco **t' accogli**	**De le sempre atre, nubilose rive,**
O Filli in questi poggi, e'n queste **olive**	Arno, deh, **tu l'accogli!**
Dove l'alma si vive	Ninfe vaghe'e sovrane
Sì riposta, e lieta;	Ghirland'al vago crin di verd'**olive**
Che tal non si consola, e non s'acqueta	E di lauro e di mirto ognor tessete
Afflitto pellegrino	E Virginia, splendor di quest'etate,
La ver la sera al fin di suo cammino.[16]	Cantando, al Ciel'alzate!

Vecchi's version of the poem may have been intended for ceremonial use. The references to the Arno and to Virginia suggest a possible connection to Virginia Vagnoli (since 1571 the wife of Alessandro Striggio) or to Virginia de' Medici, perhaps as a wedding piece. The latter's engagement to Francesco Sforza was called off in 1581 when he accepted a cardinalate, but she went on to marry Cesare d'Este in 1586, subsequently becoming duchess of Modena (and Vecchi's direct patron) twelve years later. The event for which "L'onda lascia e gli scogli" was originally composed cannot be identified, but Vecchi's Florentine connection is clear: he had already collaborated in the celebrations for the marriage of the Grand Duke Francesco de' Medici to Bianca Capello in 1579.[17] Those who recognized the poem's opening line as that of a Florentine poet might have been surprised to find the poem altered, but they would have been satisfied that its Florentine identity had been maintained.[18]

The most obvious form of intertextual reference in *cinquecento* secular polyphony generally is the *proposta/risposta* pair. The answering poem may take its poetic structure, end rhymes, and significant words from the first poem, and it usually constitutes either a response to the subjective voice of the first or an antithetical poetic position.[19] These paired poems were sometimes written more or less together, but more characteristically the *risposta* is (or poses as) a later response by a different poetic voice and, often, a different poet, defining the earlier poem as a "proposal" only retrospectively. Vecchi's paired settings of Giambattista Guarini's "Ardo sì, ma non t'amo" and Torquato Tasso's *risposta* to it, "Ardi e gela a tua voglia," were the first in what was to become a prominent tradition, particularly in the 1585 collection *Sdegnosi ardori,* which is completely devoted to settings of these poems.[20] For the purposes of the present study they represent a continuation of the broader tradition of setting *proposta/risposta* poems as paired madrigals and Vecchi's first unambiguous linkage of pieces within a single music book. While *proposta/risposta* pairs appear in prints as early as the 1550s, they were to become a dominant feature of Vecchi's subsequent books of canzonettas and constitute an early form of the large-scale integration of his more varied collections from 1590 onward.[21]

After the proliferation of resettings of "Ardo sì" and "Ardi e gela" emerged in the later 1580s, of course, so did the playful sense in which each new setting of either poem functioned as a *contrarisposta* to the previous tradition. But in 1583 Vecchi's settings could be read only in relation to each other, since neither poem had as yet appeared in print. They mirror the poems' similarities while remaining sensitive to their syntactical differences:

GUARINI	TASSO
Ardo sì, ma non t'amo,	Ardi e gela à tua voglia,
Perfida e dispietata,	Perfido et impudico,
Indegnament'amata	Or Amante, or nemico.
Da un sì leale Amante.	Che d'incostant'igngeno
Né sarà più che del mio duol ti vante,	Poco l'amor io stimo, e men lo sdegno.

Perch'ho già sano il core	E se l'amor fu vano,
E s'ardo, ardo di sdegn'e non d'amore.	Van fio lo sdegno del tu cor insano.

I burn, yes, but I do not love you,	Burn and freeze as you will,
treacherous and pitiless one,	treacherous and shameless one,
unworthy to have been loved	now lover, now enemy.
by so faithful a lover.	For, from a fickle mind
No more will you take pride in my pain,	I esteem love little, and scorn less.
for my heart has already healed,	And if your love was in vain,
and if I burn, I burn with scorn and	vain too shall be the scorn of your
not with love.	demented heart.

Though the poems share a poetic scheme (abbcCdD), they divide syntactically at different points: after line 4 in "Ardo sì" and after lines 3 and 5 in "Ardi e gela." While accommodating these differences, Vecchi's settings use similar harmonic trajectories, both establishing a tonal space defined by clear G cadences at the end of line 1 and D cadences in line 2 before moving farther afield, eventually returning to G at the major divisions after lines 4 and 5, respectively. The final peroration is in each case marked by E♭–D motions before the final cadences to G.

Despite some obvious similarities, notably the withholding of *tutti* textures until key lines, Vecchi's use of textural shifts in "Ardo sì" is perhaps more effective in projecting a sense of the subjective character than that of "Ardi e gela" (table 2.1). For example, the Guarini setting places the first-person complaints of line 1 in the upper voices and introduces the Quinto and Basso only for the second-person-directed lines 2 and 3 ("perfida e dispietata, indegnamente amata"), which are then quickly repeated with thinner textures. The *tutti* texture is reserved for line 4, "Da un si leale Amante," where the focus shifts back to the first-person speaker of the poem. This entire passage, moreover, is dispatched in only eighteen semibreves; the remainder of the poem takes thirty-one semibreves and is then given a complete repetition with only the usual voice exchange between the Canto/Sesto and Tenore/Quinto voice pairs. The final three lines thus account for just over three-quarters of the madrigal's length, far exceeding even the typical repetitions of final sections in canzonettas and canzonetta-influenced madrigals. A more conventional setting might have repeated only the final line or perhaps the final couplet, but Vecchi seems to have taken pains to return to the powerfully deictic line "Né sarà più che del **mio** duol **ti** vante" before the final peroration on the entirely self-directed final line "E s'ardo, ardo di sdegn'e non d'amore."

Table 2.1. Comparison of voicing in Vecchi's "Ardo sì" and "Ardi e gela"

C	6	5	A	T	5	B	"Ardo sì"	C	6	A	T	5	B	"Ardi e gela"
C	6		A	T			Ardo sì, ma non t'amo,	C	6	A	T			Ardi e gela à tua voglia,
C	6		A	T			*Ardo sì, ma non t'amo,*	C	6	A	T			*Ardi e gela à tua voglia,*
	6	5	A	T		B	Perfida e dispietata,		6				B	Perfido et impudico,
	6	5	A	T			*Perfida e dispietata,*							
C	6		A	T		B	*Perfida e dispietata,*							
C	6		A	T		B	Indegnament'amata	C	6	A	T		B	Or Amante,
	6	5	A	T	5				6		T	5	B	…or nemico.
C	6	5	A	T	5	B	Da un sì leale Amante.	C	6	A	T	5	B	Che d'incostant'ignegno
C	6	5	A	T	5	B	Né sarà più che del mio duol ti vante,	C	6	A		5	B	Poco l'amor io stimo,…
C	6		A	T			Perch'ho già sano il core	C	6	A	T	5	B	…e men lo sdegno.
C	6	5	A	T			E s'ardo,	C	6	A	T	5		E se l'amor fu vano,
C	6	5	A				…ardo di sdegn'…	C	6	A	T	5	B	*E se l'amor fu vano,*
C		5		T			…e non d'amore.	C	6		T	5		…*fu vano,*
C	6	5	A	T	5	B	E s'ardo, ardo di sdegn'e non d'amore.	C	6	A		5	B	…*fu vano,*
C	6		A	T		B	Né sarà più che del mio duol ti vante,	C	6	A	T	5	B	…*fu vano,*
C	6		A	T	5		Perch'ho già sano il core	C	6	A	T	5	B	…*fu vano,*
C	6		A	T			E s'ardo,	C	6	A	T	5	B	…*fu vano,*
C			T	5		B	…ardo di sdegn'…							
C	6	5	A	T	5	B	…e non d'amore.							
							E s'ardo, ardo di sdegn'e non d'amore.	C	6	A	T	5	B	Van fio lo sdegno del tu cor insano.

Note: C = Canto, 5 = Quinto, A = Alto, T = Tenore, 6 = Sesto, B = Basso. Text that is repeated with a different voicing is shown in italics.

In "Ardi e gela," on the other hand, the shift from upper to lower voices is preempted by the *tutti* repetition of the opening line. The emphasis on the Quinto and Basso in line 2 instead sets up the alternation of high and low voice groups to underline the purely symbolic opposition of line 3, "Or amante, or nemico." The similar alternations between voice groups for the repetitions of "fu vano" in line 6 have a more rhetorical character: in replying to each other, even with the same phrase, each half of the ensemble is reminded of this poem's status as a *risposta*. Moreover, Vecchi's relatively extended treatment of this section is possible because no large-scale repeat is necessary to drive home the dialogic function of the poem, since the second-person address is vividly contained in the final line, "Van fia lo sdegno del tuo cor insano." As the termination of a poetic *risposta*, this phrase, with its eloquent inversion of the *proposta*'s line "ho già sano il core," effectively closes off the pair by throwing the first speaker's words back in his face.

As the foregoing analysis reflects, in his six-voice madrigals, Vecchi uses textural variation and textual repetition—both devices that evoke his canzonetta style—as a primary means of projecting subjective poetic voices. The lines of generic distinction can be seen most clearly by comparing the six-voice madrigals to the book of six-voice canzonettas printed four years later. Like the five- and six-voice *canzone* that appeared in the early 1570s by composers such as Alessandro Merlo and Giovani Ferretti, Vecchi's six-voice canzonettas set short poems of a length and style resembling the initial stanza of a longer strophic text, reflecting these genres' origins as expansions of strophic *villanelle* or, for Vecchi, four-voice canzonettas.[22] That these texts were (or were readable as) the initial strophes of longer poems is confirmed by the later appearance of five of them with additional strophes that may or may not have been by the same poet.[23] The canzonettas use more extensive sectional repetition than the six-voice madrigals, resembling in this sense their four-voice counterparts, but their counterpoint and harmony are only slightly less complex than that of the madrigals.

Consistent with this hybrid quality, the *Canzonette a sei* sometimes partake of the playful quality of the four-voice canzonettas we saw in chapter 1. The initial poem, "Gitene, Canzonett'al mio Signore," addresses the songs themselves, commanding them to go and be heard by a dedicatee, similar to the opening piece of the first book for four voices, "Canzonette d'Amore":

Gitene, Canzonett'al mio Signore	Go forth, canzonettas, to my lord
E 'l cor mio gli porgete;	and carry my heart to him;

E se v'accorgerete	and if he recognizes
Che grato il don gli sia,	the gratitude of the gift,
Scioglliet'il suon' a la Sampogna mia.	let loose the sound of my bagpipe.

However, whereas "Canzonette d'Amore" describes a fictive female character singing the music herself, holding a part book in her hands and allowing the songs to alight in her mouth and penetrate her breast, here the songs' destination is a male superior—most obviously the book's dedicatee, Marc Antonio Gonzaga, but also a fictive listener separate from the singers in any given performance. The reference to a bagpipe (*sampogna*) casts the poetic voice as pastoral, and the onomatopoeic imitation of that instrument's drone at the end of the piece evokes an imagined instrumental accompaniment (example 2.1). The rest of the book ranges widely in affect from the pastoral mode of the opening through bitter renunciations of love, consistent with Vecchi's emerging interest in encapsulating a wide affective range in a single collection. It concludes with an amorous serenade, "Vaga Nigella, hor sù non più dormire," that marks the inevitable return to love.

The seventeen pieces in the *Madrigali a cinque,* addressed in the dedication to the Mantuan court, represent Vecchi at his most sophisticated, both as a composer and as an increasingly self-reliant poet.[24] He relies far less on the expansion of canzonetta techniques seen in the six-voice book from six years earlier and sets only four poems known to be by others. These are all among the best-known poets of the age. Besides Giovanni Guidiccioni's "Il bianco e dolce cigno" and an excerpt from Jacopo Sannazaro's *Arcadia,* both discussed below, they include the octave from Petrarch's sonnet "Ite rime dolent'al duro sasso" and Guarini's "Dice la mia bellissima Licori."[25] Settings of a fifth poem, the anonymous "Cara mia Dafne, a dio," were published in 1584 by Alessandro Milleville and 1585 by Lelio Bertani, so Vecchi is probably not the author, though his own setting of it had appeared in the Ferrarese anthology *I lieti amanti* in 1586.[26]

The book opens with Vecchi's best-known adaptation, that of Arcadelt's "Il bianco e dolce cigno," perhaps the most famous madrigal of the century and one that appeared first in almost all of the many reprints of Arcadelt's first book.[27] Vecchi begins by quoting Arcadelt's madrigal an octave lower and in longer note values. In answer to this lugubrious opening, the Canto and Quinto enter with roulades on the word "cantando" (singing), which are soon taken up by the lower voices as well before an affective chain of suspensions on "more" (dies) leads to a dissolved cadence (example 2.2). The

Example 2.1. (*above and facing*) Vecchi, "Gitene canzonette," mm. 32–46.

40
a,
Scio-glie-t'il suo-n'a la Sam-
a,
Scio-glie-t'il suo-n'a
Scio - glie - t'il suo - n'a
Scio-glie-t'il suo-n'a la Sam-po - gna, Scio-glie-t'il
a, Scio-glie-t'il suo-n'a la Sam-po - gna, la
a la Sam - po -
44
po - gna mi - - - - a,
la Sam - po - gna mi - a,
la Sam - po - gna mi - a,
suo - n'a la Sam - po - gna mi - a,
Sam - po - gna mi - a,
gna mi - a,

Example 2.2. (*above and facing*) Vecchi, "Il bianco e dolce cigno," mm. 1–19.

moment bespeaks a powerful sense of intertextuality and historicity; Arcadelt's style had been described as "troppo vecchio" (too old-fashioned) as early as 1544 in the *Dialogo della musica* by Antonfrancesco Doni, for whom it already exemplified the madrigal's past.[28] In Vecchi's opening, the lower voices present Arcadelt's music in a register and speed that, even allowing for variability in pitch and tempo, must have sounded stodgy and dull compared to more familiar presentations of "Il bianco e dolce cigno." The disruptive entrance of the upper voices in a faster and notably up-to-date style bridges the historical gap between the 1520s and 1580s in a way that a more thorough resetting of the text could never do.

James Haar has discussed some of the relationships between the two settings, including the similar dotted rhythms in the final peroration on "di mille mort' il di sarei contento" (I would be happy for a thousand deaths a day) and the use of a poignant harmonic shift on the word "piangendo" (weeping): for Arcadelt, a move from F to E♭; for Vecchi, a more pungent shift from F to A major, with direct chromatic motion in the Alto.[29] Vecchi's most obvious departure from his model comes in the move to triple meter for the repeated words "ed io moro beato" (and I die happily). Arcadelt's setting handled this line discreetly, downplaying the obvious double entendre on "moro" in favor of an extended melismatic passage on "beato," cadencing to D, the most harmonically distant strong cadence in the piece. This move leads elegantly into the completion of the sentence "Morte che nel morire / M'empie di gioia tutto e di desire" (a death that, in dying, / fills me completely with joy and desire), which cadences to F, the modal final (example 2.3a).

In Vecchi's setting, the perky triple meter of "moro beato," besides enlivening the rhythm, accentuates the thrice-repeated "moro beato" as a more determined future-tense "morò beato" (I *will* die happy), and this insistence is rewarded when the phrase arrives at F just after the return to duple meter (example 2.3b, mm. 41–45). This closure creates a strong sectional division in midsentence, making the "happy death" explicit in a way that Arcadelt had avoided. Having achieved the harmonic (and symbolic) climax of the triple-meter passage, Vecchi continues the sentence with music that harks back to the beginning of the piece, with a low-voiced trio in long note values answered again by a faster-moving Canto and Quinto (example 2.3b, mm. 48–58). Vecchi sets "se nel morir" (if in dying) to exactly the same shift (using the same chromatic voice leading) from F major to A major that he used for "piangendo" in the opening phrase, ratcheting up the harmonic tension even further with a move to E♭ before the humorous peroration on "Di mille mort'il dì sarei contento" and its repeated cadences to F. This recapitulation can be read as the ubiquitous erotic "return to life" and further arousal. Of course, Vecchi's point in transforming "Il bianco e dolce cigno" and placing it at the head of his madrigal book in the first place was surely to demonstrate the contemporary madrigal's increased potential to respond promiscuously to poetic meanings. It prompts a conversation amongst the singers or listeners comparing the two "competing" versions.

If "Il bianco e dolce cigno" begins Vecchi's book by engaging a "classic" madrigal and the tradition that it anchors, the book ends with a setting drawn from a similarly foundational literary source, Jacopo Sannazaro's *Arcadia*.

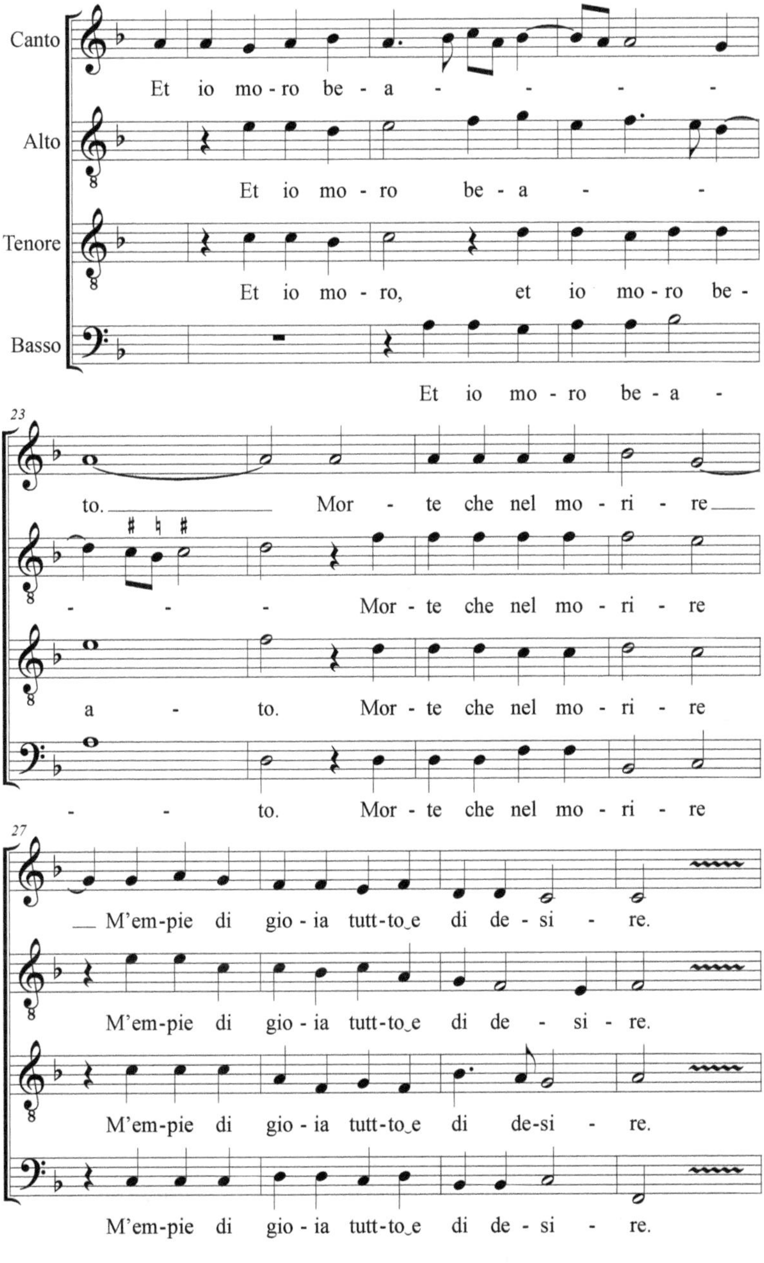

Example 2.3a. Arcadelt, "Il bianco e dolce cigno," mm. 20–30.

Example 2.3b. (*above and facing*) Vecchi, "Il bianco e dolce cigno," mm. 39–58.

Here the sense of contest is present within the text itself, "Quella ch'in mille selv'e 'n mille fratte," an excerpt from the ninth eclogue of *Arcadia*, depicting an unusual dialogue between the shepherd Ofelia and the goatherd Elenco, with two interruptions and a final conclusion spoken by another shepherd, Montano. The poem is comprised of *terze rime* that alternate consistently between the speakers, a rapid changing of voice suited to their energetic argumentation. In the opening fifty-one lines of the eclogue, written in *ende-casillabi sdruccioli,* Ofelia and Elenco trade insults and challenge each other to a singing contest. Montano agrees to act as judge, and the meter changes to *endecasillabi piani* for the contest proper: a sequence of alternating tercets on the theme of love that nevertheless lapses repeatedly into barbs exchanged between the two singers. Eventually, Montano declares that the contest's only winner has been Apollo, for granting the competitors such wit.

Out of this dialogue Vecchi sets a passage of six tercets (lines 79–96), arguably those that best exemplify the spirit of the singing contest, without the insults with which it is elsewhere contaminated. Though the *Madrigali a cinque* print does not identify the speakers (shown below on the left), Vecchi's shifts of texture between three-voice subsets of the five-voice ensemble (shown on the right) clarify the dialogic structure of the poetry. Each tercet is sung primarily by a three-voice group, meaning that each change of character voice requires one singing voice to continue singing "as" the new character. To compensate for this, Vecchi leaves this voice out just after the shift, so that each trio is initially answered by two before the continuing voice reenters to complete the new three-voice texture.

ELENCO: She whom Love makes me follow in a thousand forests	ATB
and a thousand coverts, I know she makes complaint,	
although she flees me still, although she hides her.	
OFELIA: And my Amaranth constrains me, it is her will	C5
that still I sing at her chamber door, and she	CA5
makes answer with her sweet angelic words.	
ELENCO: Phyllis is constantly calling me [Ofelia] and then hiding,	TB–T5B [C]
and she throws an apple, and then laughs, and indeed desires	
that I see her gleaming whitely amid green leaves.	
OFELIA: Yea but my Phillis waits for me by the river,	CA
and then so gently doth she make me welcome	CAT
that I let my flock, and myself, sink in forgetfulness.	
ELENCO: The woods are shady: and were not my soul	5B
now present you would see in novel fashion	T5B
the flowers withered and the springs exhausted.	
OFELIA: The mountain is bare, and there is no climbing further;	CA
but if my sun appear there, I shall see it yet	CAT
clothing itself with grass in a pleasant shower.[30]	*tutti*

Vecchi's choice of this passage, and his subtle textural response to it, is itself a kind of *risposta* to Luca Marenzio's setting of the previous passage (lines 37–75) as "Vienne, Montan," the final piece in his *Madrigali a quatro voci* from 1585.[31] Marenzio uses various textures for the introductory tercets but sets the contest itself in alternating duets, with the Canto and Alto representing Elenco and the Tenore and Basso Ofelia. Vecchi's setting, which

Example 2.4. Vecchi, "Quella ch'in mille selve," mm. 39–45.

prefigures the shifting textures he uses for dialogues in *L'Amfiparnaso,* is more subtle than Marenzio's alternation of unvarying voice pairs.

Vecchi also, curiously, interferes with Sannazaro's poetry in the third tercet by answering Elenco's phrase "Phyllis is always calling me" with the Canto's "Ofelia, Ofelia" (example 2.4). Read as part of the poem, of course, the added word "Ofelia" disrupts both the meter and the meaning: the Canto seems to be singing the wrong name—if she is calling the "me" of this line, she should be singing "Elenco," not "Ofelia." Is this a simple mistake on Vecchi's part, or is he playing with the dialogue in a more complex way? Sannazaro's interlocutors are never named in this excerpt, so only those closely familiar with *Arcadia* could notice the Canto's use of the "wrong" name in the interruption. Readers and listeners ignorant of the eclogue might naturally assume that the main speaker here is named Ofelia and that the little solo in the Canto represents Phyllis calling his name, thus introducing a marginal third character into the dialogue. But literary *cognoscenti* will know that the speaker here is in fact Elenco and that in the next tercet Ofelia will also claim a lover named Phyllis who is decidedly less shy. The added utterance in the Canto is therefore Ofelia himself, mockingly interrupting Elenco with the subtext, "Phyllis is really calling me, and though she hides herself teasingly from you, she gives herself to me completely." The viciousness of this insinuation seems out of place within the madrigal's text, but again, those who know the theme of the eclogue from which it is taken will recognize it as consistent with the rest of the poem's more brazenly argumentative style.

Tirsi Dies Again

One of the most illuminating examples of Vecchi's adapting and rewriting well-known poetry in the 1580s is his ongoing engagement—even fascination—with the scenario depicted in Guarini's "Tirsi morir volea," one of the most frequently set poems of the decade.

Tirsi morir volea,	Tirsi wanted to die,
Gli occhi mirando di colei ch'adora;	gazing into the eyes of she whom he adored,
Quand'ella, che di lui non meno ardea,	when she, who burned no less than he did,
Gli disse: Oimè, ben mio,	said to him, "Alas, my love,
Deh non morire ancora,	oh, do not die yet,
Chè teco bramo di morir anch'io.	for I want to die with you."
Frenò Tirsi 'l desio,	Tirsi restrained his desire,
Ch'ebbe di pur sua vita allor finire;	which had already almost ended his life;
Ma sentia morte in non poter morire.	but he felt death in being unable to die.
E mentre il guardo suo fisso tenea	And while he held his gaze fixed
Ne' begli occhi divini,	in the beautiful, divine eyes,
E il nettare amoroso indi bevea,	and drank the nectar of love,
La bella Ninfa sua, che già vicini	his lovely nymph, who already nearby
Sentia i messi d'Amore,	felt the messengers of love,

Disse con occhi languidi e tremanti:	said, with languid and trembling eyes:
Mori, cor mio, ch'io moro;	"Die, my heart, for I die,"
Cui rispose il Pastore:	to which the shepherd replied:
Ed io, mia vita, moro.	"And I, my life, die."
Così moriro i fortunati amanti	Thus the lucky lovers died
Di morte sì soave e sì gradita,	a death so sweet and so pleasant
Che, per ancor morir, tornaro in vita.	that, to die again, they returned to life.

As with "Il bianco e dolce cigno," much of the poem's appeal for Vecchi seems to have been its playful equation of death with sexual climax. However, the scenario of "Tirsi morir volea" is specific enough that Vecchi's adaptations of it (even when he does not use the name Tirsi) can be read as responding specifically to Guarini's poem rather than to general themes of sex and death. While the association of death with erotic love is ubiquitous in *cinquecento* poetry, the more suggestive image of lovers dying and returning to life to die again brings the eroticism out into the open, transforming a Petrarchan trope of suffering in love into a scene of pastoral sensuality. "Tirsi morir volea" pushes the metaphor a step further by depicting the male lover intentionally delaying death at the behest of his partner so that the pair can die together. As Laura Macy has shown, some early modern medical writings (in the tradition of Galen) prescribed the necessity of simultaneous orgasm for procreation, and Guarini, though not addressing the question of procreation, reinscribes this necessity as idealized sexual behavior; his nymph signals her readiness for orgasm by telling Tirsi to climax in a verse whose lexical and phonic symmetry emphasizes mutuality: "Mori, cor mio, ch'io moro" (Die, my heart, for I die).[32] Vecchi adopted this scenario—and played with the expectations it raised with readers and listeners—in at least four different pieces, including one each from the second book of canzonettas ("Lucilla, io vo morire," in which a rustic girl begs her doubtful lover to wait before dying), the *Madrigali a sei,* the third book of canzonettas, and the *Madrigali a cinque.*

When Vecchi's *Madrigali a sei* were published in 1583, "Tirsi morir volea" had already appeared in printed madrigal settings by Luca Marenzio, Benedetto Pallavicino, and Giaches Wert. For his madrigal "Amor di propria man," Vecchi did not use Guarini's poem as a formal model (as he had done with Strozzi's "L'onda lascia, e gli scogli"), but the specific situation depicted is exactly the same: Tirsi and his lover (here named as Galatea) work to reach simultaneous orgasm, expressed in the usual terms of death:

Amor di propria man congiunti avea	With his own hand Love had joined
In loco chiuso duo fedeli Amanti,	in a secluded place two faithful lovers
Per dar fine a lor pianti;	to bring an end to their laments.
L'uno era Tirsi e l'altro Galatea,	One was Tirsi, the other Galatea,
E perch'ognun di lor avea desire	and so each of them desired
Di provare il morire.	to taste death.
Fu'l primo Tirsi a dire,	Tirsi was the first to speak,
La sua Ninfa gentil stringendo forte:	strongly embracing his nymph:
"Vita mia cara, io son vicino a morte!"	"My dear life, I am close to death!"
La ninfe allor con voc'ebrea d'Amore,	The nymph then, in a voice intoxicated with love,
Stringendoselo al petto,	embracing him to her breast,
Piena d'alto diletto,	full of great delight,
Disse: "Non far, speranza del mio core,	said, "Don't do it, hope of my heart,
Non mi far consumar a poco a poco,	don't make me expend [myself] little by little;
sia'l colpo egualem poich'egual' é'l foco."	let the blows be alike, since the fire is alike."
Così con lieto gioco	Thus with a happy game
L'uno e l'altro morio, con viva speme	one and the other died, with the lively hope
Di gioir mille volte ancor' insieme.	of enjoying it together a thousand times more.

Despite the unmistakable similarity to "Tirsi morir volea," Vecchi's poem is more plainly sexual than Guarini's. Gone are the extended references to the lovers gazing into each other's eyes—along with the significant erotic power of that gesture—and the emphasis on Tirsi holding himself back from orgasm ("Frenò Tirsi il desio") that marks the second part of most settings of the Guarini.[33]

Vecchi's Galatea has a different desire: her concern is that if Tirsi climaxes too soon, she will be deprived of an orgasm altogether, and her arousal will merely dissipate "poco a poco." While a simultaneous orgasm may be the result, the line describing their climaxes is not precise about the question either: "L'uno e l'altro morio" can be read as referring to a single event or to two successive ones. The final three lines parallel Guarini's, but they expose the talk of death as the double entendre that it is: Tirsi and Galatea are only playing a "lieto gioco," and they live on in the hopes of enjoying the game a thousand times more. The peroration on the final line (just over half of which is shown in example 2.5) paraphrases the end of Arcadelt's "Il bianco e dolce cigno" both textually and musically, with dotted rhythms, falling melodic lines, and an extravagant degree of repetition leading to the final cadence.

While Vecchi marks the transitions between narrative and character speech with textural shifts that encourage and require singers to act as audience as well as performers, the real "dialogue" of the poem is with Guarini's better-known treatment of the same subject. Listeners familiar with Guarini's poem or any of its settings will, in all likelihood, find humor both in Vecchi's blunter, earthier treatment of the scenario and in recognizing his reference to "Il bianco e dolce cigno." The successful recognition of these intertextual references constitutes one of the game-like aspects of recreational singing that pervade Vecchi's music.

Vecchi adapted the scenario of "Tirsi morir volea" to the scale and formal constraints of the canzonetta in "Con voci da i sospiri" from his third four-voice book of 1585. The concise text depends on readers recognizing the familiar scene from fairly vague clues:

Con voci da i sospiri	In a voice by sighs
Interrotta, dicea un Pastor dolente,	interrupted, a sad shepherd said,
"L'alma vicin'a mort'homai si sente"	"I feel my soul near death."
Disse la Ninfa al'hor con gran desio,	The Nymph then said with great passion,
"Non posso piu tardar, i moro	"I cannot wait any longer; I am dying
anch'io."	too."
Il Pastor sospirando	The sighing shepherd
Si la strinse, che piu forte non stringe	squeezed her as tightly as
Olmo novella vite cho lo cinge,	a young vine squeezes an elm,
Et ella disse, "ò che felice sorte,	and she said, "O what a happy fate,
Se non sopravenisse à noi la morte."	if death should not overcome us."

The poem is sung entirely by the lower three voices until the nymph's comment in the final line of each stanza, at which point the Canto sings a scale descending from d″ to d′ (inflecting the penultimate note to e♭ for the word "moro"). Although the correspondence of text to music is less exact in the second stanza, Vecchi here plays on the literary elaboration of Guarini's poem: to avoid being "overcome" by erotic death evokes both the conven-

Example 2.5. (*above and facing*) Vecchi, "Amor di propria man,"
terza parte, mm. 33–46.

39
me, an - cor in - sie - me,
me, an - cor in - sie - me, Di gio - ir
me, an - cor in - sie - - - me,
me, an - cor in - sie - me,
me, an - cor in - sie - me.
an - cor in - sie - me, Di
43
Di gio - ir mil - le vol - te an - cor in - sie - me.
mil - le vol - te an - cor in - sie - - - me.
mil - le vol - te an - cor in - sie - me.
mil - le vol - te an - cor in - sie - me.
gio - ir mil - le vol - te an - cor in - sie - me.

tional image of the return to life and a desire to avoid climax and prolong the sexual act.

Vecchi reimagines this scenario yet again in the *Madrigali a cinque* of 1589 in another three-part cycle, "Tremolavan le frondi e la marina." The poem begins with a long scene-setting passage that comprises the entire *prima parte* and gives no hint of the erotic conceit, which is revealed only in the second and third parts. Mariarosa Pollastri has aptly described how this poetic gambit makes the latter two parts "give the impression of having been added by another poet who wanted at all costs to insert an erotic human action into a charming scene of Nature."[34] Even more striking in comparison with "Tirsi morir volea" is the explicit conflation of the narrator with the male character. Though this identification of the narrator with Tirsi is implicit in Guarini's poem—and is central to the structure of settings such as Wert's—in Vecchi's poem his subjective voice is emphasized at the beginning of the second part with the strongly deictic "quando," "ecco," and "mio," locating him as the voice of the more descriptive first part.

Tremolavan le frondi e la marina,	The leaves and the sea were trembling,
Aure dolci spiranti,	sweet breezes blew,
Increspava la sua fald'azzurrina.	rippling the pale blue water.
E gl'augelletti gai,	And the happy little birds
Co'i garriti e co' canti,	with their chattering and with their songs
Givan sfogando amorosetti lai.	cast forth amorous lyrics.
Quando ecco il mio bel sole	When here my beautiful sun
Con tacite parole	with unspoken words
Piene d'affetto, di ferventi ardori,	full of emotion, of burning desires,
Disse: "Ben mio, deh mori,	said, "My love, oh, die,
Ch'io moro, ohimè, i' moro!"	for I am dying, alas, I die!"
Ond'allor io languendo,	So then I, languishing,
Con luci tremolanti	with trembling eyes,
Anelando e morendo,	yearning and dying,
Nova vita immortal dolce riprendo.	sweetly returned to immortal life.

The preliminary description of the desire for death and the partner's entreaty for its delay are taken completely for granted, replaced instead in the first part by a strikingly dispassionate and highly pictorial scene that acts as a foil to the rest. The images of trembling leaves, waves, and singing birds lend themselves to the contrapuntal madrigalisms to which Vecchi sets them (example 2.6).

Example 2.6. Vecchi, "Tremolavan le fronde," mm. 1–7.

The subjective viewpoint in the second part is established through a more consistent homophony in which the three lowest voices—representing Tirsi—take special prominence at moments that frame the action, singing alone the first word, "quando" (when), and the introduction of the quoted speech, "disse" ([she] said). The depiction of climax in the female partner's quoted speech is especially clear: the repeated settings of "ohimè, ohimè,"

Example 2.7. (*above and facing*) Vecchi, "Tremolavan le fronde,"
seconda parte, mm. 35–52.

sung to expressive falling minor thirds, lead to a vivid interrupted cadence
followed by a rest at the end of the *parte* (example 2.7). This incomplete cadence and the notated silence that follows it represent her inability to speak
at the moment of orgasm rather than the more objective "completion" that a
regular cadence would suggest.

44

ohi - mè,   ohi -

ro, mo - - - ro, ohi - mè,

mo - ro i' mo - ro,

mo - ro i' mo - ro, ohi -

mo - ro i' mo - ro, ohi -

48

mè, ch'io mo - ro i' mo - ro!

ohi - mè, ch'io mo - ro i' mo - ro!

ohi - mè,_____ ch'io mo - ro i' mo - ro!

mè, ch'io mo - ro i' mo - ro!

mè,_____ ch'io mo - ro i' mo - ro!

After this musical depiction of sexual ecstasy, the third part, "Ond'allor io languendo," returns to the speech of the male lover just at the moment when he must describe his own climax. The text here recalls Guarini's description of the female lover's "occhi languid' e tremanti," but in Vecchi's poem Tirsi is now describing his own languishing and his own eyes. The climax occurs in the setting of "anelando" (yearning; example 2.8), which replicates in its last

Example 2.8. Vecchi, "Tremolavan le fronde," *terza parte,* mm. 24–30.

repetition (mm. 29–30) the exact setting of the female's cry "mori, mori" from the second part (mm. 37–38 of example 2.7), varied only by word-interrupting rests commonly associated with sighing, depicting Tirsi, like his lover, as unable to speak coherently at the moment of orgasm.

The up-to-date expressivity of "Tremolavan le fronde" befits its status as a five-voice madrigal and Vecchi's ambition for that genre, trading in the expressive style of *seconda prattica* composers like Marenzio, whose setting of "Tirsi morir volea" Vecchi surpasses in his realistic imitation of sexual climax. If one of Vecchi's goals with the *Madrigali a cinque* was to offer his services to the Gonzaga court as both poet and composer, then "Tremolavan le fronde" was an apt demonstration of his skills but perhaps betrayed an uncourtly lack of musical decorum.

Risposte, Dialogue, and Intertextuality in the Third Book of Canzonettas

Vecchi's third book of canzonettas (1585), like his first two, declares itself implicitly as a musical book in its opening piece, no. 44, "Hor che'l garrir," with references to pastoral birdsong and to a nymph, Isabella, whose rose-scented breath attracts Cupid to settle in her mouth.[35] As in "Canzonette d'Amore," the opening song of Book I, the singers of "Hor che'l garrir" identify both with the poetic speaker and with Isabella, whose sweet exhalations vividly suggest that she is not merely breathing but singing. Love lodges itself in the mouths of singers through Vecchi's amorous words, underscoring Vecchi's claim of authorship for the poems as well as the music in Book III.

Book III includes two pairs of songs that partake of the *proposta/risposta* tradition. In the first of these, no. 51, "Sia maledetto Amore," and no. 52, "Sia benedetto amore," both poems present the same speaker, first cursing and then blessing love.[36] The love imagery in each stanza of "Sia maledetto Amore" (arrows, torches, and chains) is reinterpreted in a positive light in "Sia benedetto Amore." Vecchi's musical settings depict the idea of reversal as well: each canzonetta opens with the same rhythm but an opposite melodic contour. In "Sia maledetto Amore" it appears first in the Bass, descending from c' to g before being taken up by the Alto and Canto. In "Sia benedetto Amore" the corresponding motive begins in the Canto, moving up from g' to c", and is then imitated in the lower voices. "Sia benedetto Amore," however, has an additional fourth stanza that turns the blessing on the beloved herself and states the Petrarchan paradox of love explicitly:

Sia benedetto insieme	May she also be blessed
Colei che mi fa sempre	who always makes me
Provar contrarie tempre,	feel contrary states,
E fa ch'a tutte l'hore	and who always makes
Io benedichi e maladichi Amore.	me bless and curse love.

Besides confirming that the *risposta* represents the same voice as the *proposta,* this stanza changes the relationship between the two, since it forms a necessary link between them: "Sia benedetto Amore" makes no sense as an independent piece. The "dialogue" implied by the *risposta* is thematic rather than dramatic: read as songs to be sung in sequence in a social setting, the contrasting characterizations of love recall the kinds of games described, for example, in Ringhieri's "Giuoco d'Amore," which revolves around questions about the experience of love.[37] These include "What are the greatest harms and the greatest benefits one receives from love?," "Would it be better or worse if love did not exist in the world?," and "Which is the stronger passion, love or hate?" In social conversation or in more formalized game playing, Vecchi's paired canzonettas might be used as prompts or as answers to such questions.

The second *proposta/risposta* pair in Book III, no. 59, "Caro dolce mio bene," and no. 60, "Amante se ti piace," presents a contrast between a graphic male plea for love and a haughtily dismissive response:

NO. 59, "CARO DOLCE MIO BENE"	NO. 60, "AMANTE SE TI PIACE"
My dear, sweet love,	Lover, if you please,
comfort of my pains,	do not disturb my peace;
your eyes, which are sapphires,	if my eyes are sapphires,
be content that I may always gaze	they were made for me, and not to be
on them.	gazed on.
My dear, beloved soul,	You will not kiss me,
refuge of my life,	no matter what you say;
those rosy lips,	My rosy lips
let me kiss them in unaccustomed ways.	are reserved for a more faithful lover.
You, my dear contentment,	Too rude and wicked
remedy for my torments,	is your evil desire.
those unripe apples, also,	These apples that I have in my breast
let me taste them before I die.	are not bait for you, false Bireno.[38]
And your ivory breast,	My ivory breast
let me hold it tightly	is not a haven for you.
until love's messengers	Listen to love's messengers,
we both feel in amorous burning.	for you don't deserve to pluck so
	beautiful a flower.

"Caro dolce mio bene" is musically consistent with the comic/rustic musical style Vecchi employed in his earlier comic canzonettas: it highlights the text through an almost entirely homophonic texture and rhythmically concise text setting, particularly in the crudely erotic second half of each stanza. As I have argued, such textures downplay the identification of individual singers with the subjective voice of the poem. In contrast, "Amante, se ti piace" employs contrapuntal writing and shifting textures, encouraging each singer to imagine herself as an individual embodiment of the more virtuous and eloquent female poetic voice, participating in her disdain for the crude advances of the previous song.

Since each stanza of the *risposta* is a specific response to the corresponding stanza of the *proposta,* readers are implicitly encouraged to read the poems simultaneously, alternating stanzas. Indeed, this would be an effective way to sing the two pieces together rather than sequentially: the increasingly graphic imagery of the man's advances would more naturalistically prompt the woman's increasing disdain. The possibility of such a practice is hinted at by a *proposta/risposta* pair set as a madrigal by Giuseppe Caimo in 1564 that sets the lines of each poem in alternation.[39] Vecchi's books do not explicitly call for an interleaved performance, but the strophic form of the canzonetta and the musical similarities between the paired settings conspire to make this practice highly evocative of the conversational habits of the social settings in which they were sung.

The Fourth Book of Canzonettas: Amorous Dialogues

In 1590, five years after the publication of Book III, Vecchi produced his fourth and last book of four-voice canzonettas. The year 1590 also saw two books that, like the *Madrigali a sei,* suggest that Vecchi was seeking employment abroad: the *Motecta* and *Selva di varia ricreatione* (discussed in chapter 3). These were dedicated, respectively, to William V, duke of Bavaria, and to the brothers Jacob and Johann Fugger of Augsburg, and in both dedications Vecchi explicitly proclaims his interest in employment. The fourth book of canzonettas stands apart from this campaign, being dedicated to Count Camillo da Correggio d'Austria, whose local, small-scale patronage Vecchi had, according to the dedication, already enjoyed.[40]

Like its predecessors, Book IV reflects a keen interest in the music book as a resource for social singing. This is nowhere clearer than in the opening piece in the book, "Udit', udite, Amanti," which places the book, by name, in a fictive pastoral context of polyphonic singing.[41] The first stanza establishes the pattern:

Udit', udite, Amanti,	Listen, lovers,
E voi, Pastori eranti,	and you, wandering shepherds,
Tre leggiadre Ninfe	to three pretty nymphs
Con un Pastor lungo le chiare linfe	with a shepherd by the clear streams
Cantar con voci elette	singing with sweet voices
Il Quarto libro de le Canzonette	The fourth book of canzonettas.
Udite Donne belle,	Listen, beautiful ladies,
Udite, voi Pulcelle,	listen, maidens,
Tre vezzose Dive	to three pretty goddesses
Con un Pastor lunga l'herbose rive	and a shepherd by the verdant banks
Cantar con gran diletti	singing with great pleasure
Il Quarto libro de miei puri affetti.	The fourth book of my pure affections.
Udite, Abete e Faggi,	Listen, firs and beeches,
Udite, ò Dei Selvaggi,	listen, O sylvan gods,
Tre gentil Regine	to three gentle queens
Con un Pastor con voci pellegrine	and a shepherd, with rare voices
Cantar'i dolci amori	singing the sweet loves
Del Quarto libro de miei vani ardori.	of the fourth book of my vain ardors.

Once again, the singers imagine themselves as embodying two subjective identities at once: as a group they obviously represent the four-voice ensemble described in the poem, a fictive group that transforms from nymphs into goddesses and queens, though humorously anchored in their pastoral context by an unchanging shepherd. Yet the first-person singular "miei" sung at the end of the second and third stanzas in connection with the fourth book itself constructs the poem as Vecchi's own utterance. The songs that follow, especially the *risposte* to previously published pieces, reinforce the powerful sense that singing Vecchi's canzonettas involves interacting with a printed book, performing multiple identities, and giving voice to the poet-composer himself.

As with most settings of the "Ardo"/"Ardi" poems, poetic and musical *risposte* were ordinarily printed together so that they might more easily be compared and read in relation to one another. Vecchi himself had followed this pattern not only with his settings of the Tasso and Guarini poems in the *Madrigali a sei* but also in the two *proposta/risposta* pairs in Book III. The seven *risposte* in Book IV, however, are labeled as responses to poems not present in the book, and only the titles of the retroactively designated "*proposte*" are given, with no clue that they are to be found in Vecchi's oft-reprinted first book. They thus present singers with a riddle, though not an especially challenging one for those familiar with Vecchi's ubiquitous first book. Jennifer King's description of the Book IV *risposte* as a "marketing tactic" is therefore somewhat reductive: they also serve a poetic and social function by drawing the two books into a virtual dialogue with each other and prompting reader-singers into conversation about these intertextual relationships.[42] Indeed, while encompassing a range of rhetorical positions with respect to their models, the *risposte* consistently cast them in new lights and suggest new meanings for them.

CANZONETTAS FROM BOOK I	RISPOSTE IN BOOK IV
2. "Mentre io campai contento"	67. "Mentre io vissi in dolore"
4. "Son questi i crespi crini"	68. "Se da le treccie mie"
17. "Io son fenice"	73. "Non ha, finto amator"
6. "Chi mira gli occhi tuoi"	74. "Se son' quest'occhi tuoi"
15. "Il cor che mi rubasti"	75. "Il cor ch'io ti rubai"
10. "Raggi, dov'è'l mio bene"	80. "Raggi, dov'è'l mio male"
19. "Quando mirai"	83. "Tuo cor non hò per furto"

Two of these pairs, "Mentre io campai contento" / "Mentre io vissi in dolore" and "Raggi, dov'è'l mio bene" / "Raggi, dov'è'l mio male," present a reversal of imagery in complaints about love that seem to come from the same speaker, the same configuration we have seen in "Sia maledetto Amore" / "Sia benedetto Amore." However, in the Book I / Book IV pairs the reversals of imagery are purely rhetorical: they do not reflect a change from unhappiness to happiness in love but rather a stronger sense of loss. "Mentre io vissi in dolore" achieves this through a variation of the final refrain. Each stanza describes the agony of past sorrows and concludes with the refrain "Now, free of cares, / time flies and the years flee away," but the final stanza brings this thought to the conclusion that fleeting happiness leaves one always in misery: "Alas, joy is brief / and melts away like snow in the sun, / but my heavy pains / last forever and never end."

"Raggi, dov'è'l mio bene" and "Raggi, dov'è'l mio male" present a simpler contrast between losses in requited and unrequited love. However, Vecchi's *risposta* is also a reply to Monteverdi's setting of "Raggi, dov'è'l mio bene" in his *Canzonette* of 1584, which Vecchi paraphrases in the opening of "Raggi, dov'è il mio male."[43] As the Canto sings the melody of Vecchi's "Raggi, dov'è il mio bene," the Alto and Tenor sing runs of *fusae* similar to Monteverdi's main subject.

The remaining five *risposte* in Book IV take the more usual form of a female speaker responding to a Petrarchan male voice either positively, by allaying his doubts and returning his praises, or negatively, by rejecting his claims of amorous suffering and subverting his poetic language. These responses are conventional enough, but Vecchi also draws our attention to relationships between the *risposte* themselves if we read them in relation to their *proposte.* The clearest example of this is between the adjacent pieces no. 73, "Non ha, finto amator," and no. 74, "Se son' quest'occhi tuoi," which present negative and positive reactions, and both play (once again) on the imagery of "Tirsi morir volea." These are the only ones of Vecchi's *risposte* to disagree with the modes of their respective *proposte,* yet the texts still encourage reading and singing stanzas of the two pieces in alternation. More remarkably, Vecchi reuses not only the metrical form and rhyme scheme of the original poem but the specific end rhymes and usually the rhyme words themselves. The layout below alternates stanzas of the two poems, with those of the *risposta* indented:

IO SON FENICE

(*risposta:* Non ha, finto amator)

Io son fenice, e voi sete la fiamma	I am a phoenix, and you are the flame
Che m'arde a dramm'a dramma,	that burns me little by little,
Ma la morte m'è dolce e si gradita	but death is so sweet and pleasing to me
Che pur anco morir ritorno in vita.	that even as I die I return to life.
Non ha, finto amator, la vostra fiamma	Your flame, false lover, does not have
Di fe pur una dramma,	even an ounce of faith,
E voi volete che mi sia gradita?	and you expect it to please me?
La fede sola è de gl'Amanti vita.	Faith alone is the life of lovers.
Voi sete il Sol, ed io liquida cera,	You are the sun, and I am liquid wax,
onde convien ch'io pera,	so that I should perish,
Ma la morte m'è dolce e si gradita	but death is so sweet and pleasing to me
Che pur anco morir ritorno in vita.	that even as I die I return to life.
La vostra fede è come mole Cera	Your faith is like soft wax
Ch'al sol si strugga e pera,	that softens and dies in the sun,
E voi volete che mi sia gradita?	and you expect it to please me?
La fede sola è de gl'Amanti vita.	Faith alone is the life of lovers.
Voi sete bella, e si ve ne n'avvedete	You are beautiful, and if you notice
Ch'ogni hor più m'accendete,	that you burn me more all the time,

Dunque, ben mio, non è miracol s'io	then, my love, it is no miracle if I
Sempre rinovo e struggo il piacer mio.	constantly renew and destroy my pleasure.
E pur senza la fe non v'accorgete	Don't you see that without faith
Ch'inarno v'accendete?	you burn in vain?
Dunque ò fuggite ò non fingete, ch'io	Therefore either flee or do not pretend,
A perfido amator non do il cor mio.	for I will not give my heart to a traitorous lover.

The female speaker of "Non ha, finto amator" responds eloquently to her suitor, not only reshaping his verses but also reinterpreting his metaphors for sexual climax and renewal as images of inconstancy in love. The initial image of the burning phoenix, made vivid by the repetitions of F's and D's ("fenice . . . fiamma" / "arde a dramm'a dramma"), is answered by the accusation of falseness ("finto") and the extension of the alliteration on F to the second line, where "fenice" is, in effect, truncated to "fe" (faith). This emphasis on fidelity undermines the erotic conceit in "Io son fenice" of dying and returning to life by redefining it in nonerotic terms.

The reversal of meaning in "Non ha, finto amator" is, however, reversed again by the next canzonetta in Book IV, "Se son quest'occhi tuoi," a response to "Chi mira gl'occhi tuoi," a canzonetta from Book I that Vecchi had already quoted in "L'hore di recreatione" (see chapter 1). Once again, the poetic imitation extends not just to form but to most of the rhyme words as well. Here the relatively tame death/life imagery of the original poem is elevated in the *risposta* to the specifically erotic desire for simultaneous death:

CHI MIRA GLI OCCHI TUOI

(*risposta:* Se son quest'occhi tuoi)

Chi mira gli occhi tuoi	Whoever looks at your eyes
Et non sospira puoi,	and does not then sigh,
Credo che non sia vivo,	I believe is not alive,
Ò di giudicio privo	or else is without judgment.
Se son quest'occhi tuoi,	If my eyes are yours,
Perche sospiri poi?	why do you sigh?
Non sai ch'io di te vivo	Don't you know that I live for you
E ogn'altro amant'ho a schivo?	and scorn every other lover?
Perche n'escano rai	For from them come forth the rays
Non visti altrove mai,	never seen anywhere else,

Che fanno l'huom morire	which make a man die
Senza dolor sentire.	without feeling any pain.
Mercè de tuoi bei rai	Thanks to your beautiful rays,
Per cui legata m'hai	with which you have bound me,
Et mi vedrai morire	will you see me, too, die
Senza dolor sentire?	without feeling any pain?
Et s'avien ch'egli mora	And if it happens that he dies
Ne la medesma hora,	at that same moment,
Con la belta infinita	with your infinite beauty
Voi lo tornate in vita.	you return him to life.
Ma se pur vuoi ch'io mora,	But if you really want me to die,
Moriam nell'istess'hora,	let us die at the same time,
C'havrò gioia infinita	for I shall have boundless joy
Morendo gustar vita.	tasting life in dying.
Miracoli d'Amore,	Love's miracles,
Che fa che tutte l'hore	that at all times
Con disusata sorte	through unaccustomed fate
Gustiamo vita e morte.	make us taste life and death.
Tu fammi gratia Amore,	Do me a favor, love,
E abbreviami poi l'hore	and shorten the hours
Che pari sia la sorte	until fate will be the same
Frà noi e in vita e in morte.	for us in life and death.

Again, Vecchi substantially reinterprets the original poem, of which he was probably not the author (see chapter 1). While "Chi mira gl'occhi tuoi" presents a one-sided Petrarchan view of love, the introduction of the female character voice in the *risposta* creates an intertextual dialogue that accommodates a more poetically up-to-date longing for simultaneous climax. The stylistic tension between the two poetic voices culminates in the final stanzas: he reflects abstractly on the paradoxical miracles of love, while she longs for the physical union with her lover.

The complex of interrelated texts represented by "Non hà finto amator" and "Se son quest'occhi tuoi" is well suited to the social contexts in which they would often have been sung, prompting conversation about love, disdain, gender, and (in some circles, at least) sex and theories of procreation. That complex would also have sparked consideration of the way in which well-known songs from a previous decade could be answered by a contemporary voice and a monologue transformed into a dialogue. A close reading of one final *risposta* from Book IV opens a window onto the possibility of another, even more complex (and interpretively promiscuous) series of poems related to an episode in Ariosto's *Orlando furioso*.

The "Sorceress of Love" and a Canzonetta Cycle

As we have seen, Book IV opens, as is typical in Vecchi's canzonetta books, with an invitatory piece, followed by "Mentre io vissi in dolore," the *risposta* to the second piece in Book I. The third piece, "Se da le treccie mie"—another *risposta* to a canzonetta in Book I—begins a sequence of five songs that can be read as a narrative. Once again the strategy of reading (and perhaps singing) the stanzas of the model and its *risposta* in alternation highlights the transformation of monologue into dialogue:

SON QUESTI I CRESPI CRINI
    (*risposta:* Se da le treccie mie)

Son questi i crespi crini, è questo il viso	Are these the curly locks, is this the face
Ond'io rimango ucciso?	that leaves me dead?
Deh dimilo, ben mio,	Oh, tell me, my love,
Che questo sol desio.	for this alone I desire.
Se da le treccie mie, se dal mio viso,	If by my tresses and by my face,
Cor mio, restai ucciso,	my heart, you were killed,
Io che d'amor son Maga	I, a sorceress of love,
Ti sanerò piaga.	will cure your wound.
Questi son gli occhi che mirand'io fiso	Are these the eyes that, when I gazed intently on them,
Tutto restai conquiso?	left me completely conquered?
Deh dimilo, ben mio,	Oh, tell me, my love,
Che questo sol desio.	for this alone I desire.
Se gl'occhi miei t'han superato e vinto,	If my eyes conquered and defeated you,
Credei l'amor tuo finto,	I believed your love false,
Ma hor sei vincitore,	but now you are the victor,
Che sei di me signore.	for you are my lord.
Questa è la bocca, è questo il dolce riso	Is this the mouth, is this the sweet laughter
Ch'allegra il paradiso?	that cheers heaven?
Deh dimilo, ben mio,	Oh, tell me, my love,

Che questo sol desio.	for this alone I desire.

E s'allegrar pò la mia bocca e 'l viso	And if my mouth and face can cheer
La terr'e 'l Paradiso,	the earth and heaven,
Rallegrati, ben mio,	rejoice, my love,
Che sol'in te viv'io	for I live only in you.

Ma se questo è, che non mi par bugia,	But if this is true, which does not seem false to me,
Godianci, anima mia,	Let us enjoy ourselves, my beloved,
Et l'alma al duolo avezza	and my soul, accustomed to pain,
Mora la dolcezza.	will die of pleasure.

Non star in forse, e prendi, Anima mia	Do not hesitate, my beloved, but take
Di me la monarchia,	from me my sovereignty,
Che per soverchia voglia	for if I am arrogant toward you,
Io morirò di doglia.	I shall die of pain.

The female respondent's description of herself as a "sorceress of love" is unusual in Vecchi's poetry, as is the general discourse introduced in the *risposta* regarding lordship, sovereignty, and submission. The implied scenario is more resonant with that of the epic and romantic styles of Tasso and Ariosto.[44] Vecchi was perhaps motivated to pursue this imagery by certain similarities between "Son questi i crespi crini" and a description of the sorceress Alcina in canto 7 of Ariosto's *Orlando furioso,* as she is seen by Ruggiero:

Di persona era tanto ben formata,	She was so beautifully formed
quanto me' finger san pittori industri;	no industrious painter could feign the like;
con bionda chioma lunga ed annodata:	with blonde hair, long and in a knot:
oro non è che più risplenda e lustri.	gold is not so shining and lustrous.
Spargeasi per la guancia delicata	On her delicate cheeks were scattered
misto color di rose e di ligustri;	the mixed colors of roses and privet;
di terso avorio era la fronte lieta,	of polished ivory was her cheerful brow,
che lo spazio finia con giusta meta.	and shaped in perfect proportion.

Sotto duo negri e sottilissimi archi	Beneath two black and most thin arches,
son duo negri occhi, anzi duo chiari soli,	two black eyes, or rather two bright suns,
pietosi a riguardare, a mover parchi;	pitying their looks, gentle their movement;

intorno cui par ch'Amor scherzi e voli,	around them Love seemed to play and fly,
e ch'indi tutta la faretra scarchi	and then shoot his whole quiver,
e che visibilmente i cori involi:	and visibly steal all hearts.
quindi il naso per mezzo il viso scende,	Down the middle of the face, the nose,
che non truova l'invidia ove l'emende.	where envy could find nothing to change.
Sotto quel sta, quasi fra due vallette,	Under this, as if between two little valleys,
la bocca sparsa di natio cinabro;	the mouth, strewn with native cinnabar;
quivi due filze son di perle elette,	here two rows of choice pearls
che chiude ed apre un bello e dolce labro:	where beautiful, soft lips close and open:
quindi escon le cortesi parolette	from here emerge those courteous words
da render molle ogni cor rozzo e scabro;	that soften every coarse and rough heart;
quivi si forma quel soave riso,	here is formed that pleasant laughter
ch'apre a sua posta in terra il paradiso.[45]	that makes a paradise on earth.

Although the correspondences are not exact, both descriptions describe a beautiful face, following the viewer's gaze from the hair down to the mouth, whose laughter is said to create heaven on earth. "Son questi i crespi crini" describes this laughter as "cheering heaven," but in "Se da le treccie mie," Vecchi refers to both earth and heaven in a way more similar to Ariosto. Little of this description is compelling enough in itself to read Vecchi's pair of canzonettas as a direct reference to Ruggiero and Alcina—indeed, Ariosto's characters do not perform a dialogue analogous to Vecchi's. Nevertheless, the resonances of the bewitched knight and the enamored sorceress continue through the following four canzonettas of Book IV in a way that I believe would not have escaped the attention of readers or singers already acclimated to the spirit of dialogue engendered by the *proposta/risposta* genre.

"Se da le treccie mie" is followed by no. 69, "Dove s'intese mai," a declaration of love for a woman named Barbara, playing on the pun (*barbaro*) of that name—a conceit also used by Guarini in his madrigal "Dunque può star con barbara fierezza."[46] Each stanza contrasts the name's negative connotations with the woman's favorable character and her beauty, in this later aspect touching on precisely the same physical attributes as "Son questi i crespi crini" and "Se da le treccie mie": the hair, the eyes, the face, and a voice that "cheers the world." The final stanza concludes: "The qualities of Barbara do not correspond to her name. . . . Love, who sits within her heart, proves it." The poem's conceit can stand alone as a commentary on the paradoxes of love, but, if we read the lines as the words of a Ruggiero-like lover under the thrall of an infidel (i.e., barbarous) enchantress, we recognize that he has mistaken the otherwise obvious reality of the situation.

The sequence continues more clearly in no. 70, "Partirò si," which with its expressive tone and explicit references to the "sorceress of love" can be read as a monologue spoken by Ruggiero after Alcina's spell over him is broken by the "good" sorceress Melissa in *Orlando furioso* (canto 7, stanzas 64–65) before he makes his escape from Alcina's island:

Partirò si, si ch'io mi partirò,	I shall leave, yes, yes, I shall leave,
Vera Maga d'Amore,	true sorceress of love,
Che piu non soffrirò,	for I shall no longer bear,
Che piu non seguirò,	I shall no longer follow,
Che piu non mirerò, no no no no,	I shall no longer look at,
Gl'occhi, cibo à la vist'e tosco al core.	those eyes: a feast for the sight but poison for the heart.

[two more stanzas follow]

The poem and music are both unusually emphatic. "Partirò si" is one of only two of Vecchi's canzonettas to employ *rime tronche*, the shortened and end-accented poetic lines that often signal assertive speech.[47] In Vecchi's setting of "Partirò si," the tenor voice is strongly set off in the opening with a rising fifth, sung twice, against which the other voices sing in subdued homophony; this individuation of a single singing voice creates an atypically strong sense of character. The defiant rejection of the sorceress refers readers back to her speech in "Se da le treccie mie" and resolves the paradox observed by the hero of the seemingly misnamed "Barbara" in "Dove s'intese mai."

Vecchi's recasting of a plot from epic romance in the genre of witty canzonetta poetry injects a dose of humor into the proceedings by providing quasi-pastoral speeches for the knight both before and after the spell is broken. No. 71, "Non sarò piu ritrosa," likewise depicts a departure from chivalric expectations: a female character who vows to indulge the desires of her future lovers:

Non sarò piu ritrosa à chi mi segue,	I shall no more be hesitant toward those who follow me
Se la sorte risponde al mio desire,	if fate answers my desires;
Anzi vorrò servire	rather, I will serve
Quei che sofrir per me pena e martire.	those who suffer pains and torments for me.
Non sarò disdegnosa à chi mi brama,	I shall no longer be disdainful to those who desire me,
Ne vorrò sopportar ch'altri si mora,	nor will I want to let them die;
Anzi che ad hora ad hora	rather, from time to time
Trarrò gli Amanti miei di pena fuora.	I shall rescue my lovers from pain.
Io sarò piu pietosa ai gran tormenti	I shall be more merciful toward the great torments
Che soffersero già i leali Amanti,	that my loyal lovers have suffered;
Anzi darò altretanti	then I shall make them more
Contenti, quanto all'hor versaro pianti.	content, the more tears they have shed.

The obvious implication is that the speaker was recently heartbroken by an affair in which she had been unyielding. The sorceresses in romances like *Orlando furioso* and *Gerusalemme liberata* have histories of ensnaring men and withholding their love from them, and both are eventually abandoned by the men they love. However, their response is not to look forward to future loves but rather to lament their losses in the conventional alternation of grief and rage and to attempt to recapture their escaped lovers.[48] Within a narrative reading of this canzonetta cycle, the sorceress of love is here responding in kind to the extreme rhetoric of "Partirò si," but with a vow that moves her from the realm of romance to that of Pietro Aretino's comically lascivious tales.

This comic vein continues more strongly in no. 72, "Trista novella"—the last in the sequence—with a comic description of an old woman that inverts all the physical attributes described favorably in "Son questi i crespi crini" and uses pairs of *quinari* (five-syllable) verses that would mark the lightest poetry of the coming decade:

Trista novella	Sad news
Di Donna bella:	of a beautiful lady:
Mira le bionde chiome	see her blonde hair
Farsi d'argent'e quell'amato nome	turned to silver, and her beloved name
Languir in basso stato.	languishing in low repute.

O innamorato	O lover,
Mal consigliato!	ill-advised!
La Primavera	Springtime
Piu non si spera.	is no longer a hope.
Mira, deh mira i fiori	See, oh see the flowers
Del tutto inariditi e i bei colori	all dried up, and the beautiful colors
Nel bel viso cangiato.	of her lovely face changed.
O innamorato	O lover,
Mal consigliato!	ill-advised!
Le perle elette	Her choice pearls
Hor son neglette,	are now neglected,
E i rubini vermigli	and her red rubies
Cadon come col sole e rose e gigli.	fall like roses and lilies in the sun.
Di Basilisco ha 'l fiato.	She has the breath of a basilisk.
O innamorato	O lover,
Mal consigliato!	ill-advised!
Le luci belle	The beautiful eyes
Che già fur stelle	that once were stars,
Mira con meraviglia	see with amazement:
Horride in vista, e le stellanti ciglia	horrible to see, and the shining eyebrows
Ch'altrui rendon turbato.	that left men disturbed.
O innamorato	O lover,
Mal consigliato!	ill-advised!
Dunque per tempo	Therefore, while there is time,
Prendi il buon tempo.	have a good time.
Godi se puoi d'Amore	Enjoy while you can
Il dolce fruto e de l'etad'il fiore,	the sweet fruits of love and the flower of youth,
Che non sarai chiamato	so that you will not be called
Innamorato	lover,
Mal consigliato.	ill-advised.

Although by itself the poem is merely a portrait of a grotesquely faded beauty, it once again echoes the fate of Ariosto's Alcina, as seen by Ruggiero once the spell is broken:

> [H]e was astonished to find that in place of the beauty he had just parted from, he was confronted with a woman so hideous that her equal for sheer ugliness and decrepitude could be found nowhere on earth. / She was whey-faced, wrinkled, and hollow-cheeked; her hair was white and sparse; she was not four

feet high; the last tooth had dropped out of her jaw; she had lived longer than anyone on earth, longer than Hecuba or the Cumaean Sibyl. But she made such use of arts unknown in our day that she could pass for young and fair.[49]

The cycle has thus come full circle: the beautiful "sorceress of love" embodied through the vivid dialogue of "Son questi i crespi crini" and "Se da le treccie mie" is now an object of laughter and scorn described in the third person, with an exhortation in the last stanza to a new "you"—the reader or listener—to seize the day and enjoy love before time takes its toll. This trope was to become—almost literally—something of a personal signature for Vecchi, who invoked it again in a dance-song, "Gioite tutti," labeled "Saltarello detto il Vecchi" in *Selva di varia ricreatione.*

The main themes I have emphasized in Vecchi's fourth book—the commentary on older pieces through newly composed *risposte* and the construction of a canzonetta cycle that alludes to epic literature but eventually devolves into low comedy—resonate strongly with the recreational contexts in which canzonetta books were used, prompting conversations about the relationships between poetic registers and views of love. They also adumbrate another concern that was to take central importance in Vecchi's subsequent books: the large-scale organization of a music print in ways that combine strongly contrasting moods, registers, and genres. This new interest emerged contemporaneously with the fourth book of canzonettas, in *Selva di varia ricreatione* of the same year. Although in 1597 Vecchi would write, in the dedication to his single book of three-voice canzonettas (coauthored with Gemignano Capilupi), that he had previously thought to "close the vein of canzonettas and sing with the maturity of my age," the sense of play and witty juxtaposition he developed in the canzonettas and madrigals of the 1580s were to form the foundation of his subsequent books, taking on the poetic role of representing nothing less than the full range and variety of human experience.

3   Forest and Feast
The Music Book as Metaphor

Beginning with *Selva di varia ricreatione* (1590), Vecchi began publishing his music in large collections of pieces in a variety of genres, an approach not taken up by other composers until the rise of the *concertato* style in print after 1600. In the prefatory texts to *Selva* and to *Convito musicale* (1597), Vecchi explains the books' metaphorical titles in learned and witty terms, and although these collections include a few large-scale works clearly written for performance at courtly festivities, most of the music serves the same recreational function as Vecchi's publications in the 1580s. Both books offer a variety of genres, Vecchi explains, because variety is a source of pleasure. This argument resonates with contemporary literary debates about generic hybridity, particularly regarding the status of the pastoral tragicomedy, though Vecchi's books crossed different sets of genre boundaries. Furthermore, both books are organized internally to reflect the principles set out in the prefaces: *Selva* includes groups of pieces that exemplify the categories of *grave, faceto,* and *danzevole,* which he describes in the dedication, while *Convito musicale*'s more complex alternation of *grave* and *piacevole* genres seeks to balance a range of affects—a goal reflected in the titular metaphor of a banquet and in the anti-Epicurean philosophy to which Vecchi alludes in the preface. Although these large and somewhat unwieldy books did not enjoy the multiple reprints of Vecchi's successful canzonetta books, they reveal his continuing desire to cater for the contexts of recreational singing, articulating a poetic of imitation, variety, and pleasure by presenting a music book as a coherent aesthetic statement.

1590–1597: From Correggio to Modena

By 1590, as we have seen, Vecchi was well established as a popular composer of madrigals and, especially, canzonettas. The wide availability of his music in reprint editions does not, however, imply financial gain for the composer himself, since reprints and editions published abroad were normally financed by the printer and did not profit the composer. Although Vecchi's position at Correggio was secure (he was promoted to archdeacon in 1591), he apparently aspired to a more prestigious courtly appointment.[1] Of the three music books he published in 1590, only the most modest, the fourth canzonetta volume, was dedicated to a local patron, Count Camillo d'Austria of Correggio. The other two bore aspirational dedications of the kind Vecchi had written in the 1580s to members of the Gonzaga family, but by now he was setting his sights farther afield, dedicating *Selva di varia ricreatione* and the *Motecta* to potential patrons in southern Germany, where Vecchi's popularity is attested by his inclusion in anthologies beginning in 1588.[2]

Selva was dedicated to the brothers Jacob and Johann Fugger of the powerful Augsburg banking family. The *Motecta,* for four to eight voices, was dedicated to Duke Wilhelm V of Bavaria, and in that dedication the composer explicitly expresses his desire for employment:

> By such vigilance on my part I can indeed trust that you, in your kindness, will support me as one of those who enjoy your patronage; then I could easily show you how much my soul is bound to you, as one especially worthy of reverence and respect. And further that I might come to know by sight those learned men of the sort with which your house is filled (I do not mean to cite their fame; their virtues are already apparent to all); if I attain all this, I will soundly judge the fruits of this little gift of mine to be not so meager.[3]

Obviously, winning favor with the Fuggers could have been helpful to Vecchi in attaining a position at the ducal court, and the dedication to *Selva* identifies Vecchi's connection to Wilhelm as well as to the Fugger brothers. Vecchi explains that he has never met the Fuggers personally (indeed, there is no evidence that he ever traveled outside of Italy) but that he knew of them by reputation:

> [I devoted myself to you] . . . when long ago I heard Signor Pietro Antonio Pietra, among many others, spread an ocean of praise in speaking with me of your greatness and magnanimity, which, although they are well-known in the theater of the world, I was nevertheless glad to hear spoken of by such a great virtuoso. I now dedicate the present work as a sign of my devotion and small token of my service. Nor should it seem a wonder to you that I could be such a devoted servant to you only through reputation, without ever having seen you, because it is not for Princes and Lords to know, but to be known and admired, as it behooves me now to do.[4]

Pietro Pietra was a tenor in the Munich *Hofkapelle* from 1586 until 1625, working under Orlando di Lasso until Lasso's death in 1594.[5] How Vecchi met Pietra is not known; Pietra may well have been Italian, but just as Vecchi never traveled outside Italy, Pietra is not documented as having gone there after his appointment in Munich in 1586; *Hofkapelle* records indicate that he made several trips with members of the court, but not to Italy.[6] Nevertheless, the reference to Pietra links Vecchi to the Bavarian court in a way that underscores Vecchi's career ambitions in 1590. Alfred Einstein surmised that Vecchi must have been aware of Lasso's failing health and was angling to take his place as *Kapellmeister.*[7] The possibility that *Selva* was intended partly as a demonstration of the range of Vecchi's talents is supported by pieces in it that resemble music of Lasso, particularly in their use of figures from the *commedia dell'arte* and the comic German mercenary known from Lasso's "Matona mia cara."[8] However, Vecchi's main purpose in *Selva* is to reimagine the music book both as an expression of a poetic theory and, in a more practical sense, as an *omnium gatherum* containing the full range of genres that might be desired in social music making.

In any case, no Bavarian position was forthcoming, and Vecchi published no new music books until 1597. Besides reprints, his music only appeared during this period in Venetian anthologies issued by Gardano, his regular publisher. Of particular interest among these is Gardano's mammoth *Dialoghi musicali di diversi eccelentissimi autori, A Sette, Otto, Nove, Dieci, Undeci, & Dodeci voci* of 1590, which among its wide array of fifty-nine large-scale pieces includes six works by Vecchi, a number matched only by Wert and surpassed only by Lasso, who has eight. Vecchi's works include three of the five dialogues for twelve voices, the others being one each by Giovanni and Andrea Gabrieli. These pieces, like the eight- and ten-voice works in *Selva,* suggest that during his time in Correggio Vecchi had opportunities to write for staged spectacles: his texts, which are all pastoral, favor first-person-plural character voices well suited to theatrical choral scenes. He must have composed such large-scale works with some regularity but without choosing to have them printed: a book of similar dialogues by Vecchi was published posthumously in 1608.[9] The 1590 *Dialoghi* surely exceeded the usual resources of the individuals or institutions that enjoyed typical books of canzonettas and madrigals, but there was sufficient demand to justify Gardano's financing the edition without the support of a dedicatee. This risk paid off to the extent that a second edition was issued in 1592 and possibly a third in 1594.[10]

Despite the continuing popularity of Vecchi's small- and large-scale works, however, he did not find the kind of courtly appointment he had been seeking, and in 1593 he returned to Modena as *maestro di cappella*, the same position he had left seven years earlier, for which the town council restored his former subsidy of ten lire per month.[11] Whatever the reason for his seven-year hiatus in publishing after 1590, the floodgates opened in 1597. That year saw *L'Amfiparnaso*, *Convito musicale*, the *Sacrarum Cantionum Liber Secundus* (a sequel to the *Motecta*), and the three-voice canzonettas with lute accompaniment, a collaboration with his pupil Geminiano Capilupi. With the exception of *Convito musicale*, these books are all dedicated to local figures or institutions, suggesting that Vecchi was no longer actively pursuing employment abroad and enjoyed at least modest private patronage at home.

The *Canzonette a tre voci* are strongly marked as works for a local Modenese context. Besides Vecchi's having collaborated with his Modenese student Capilupi, the book is dedicated to Signor Paolo Calori, the head of one of the city's oldest families, and the dedication implies that Vecchi's music had been performed in Calori's house. The first two pieces make reference to the Calori family and to Laura Cortese, who may have been Paolo's wife or daughter, while another mentions Leonara Pio, presumably a member of the ruling family of nearby Sassuolo.[12] The first canzonetta, "Deh, cant' Aminta un'aria a la romana," also functions as a proem in Vecchi's usual self-referential manner, inviting the reader (reimagined in pastoral terms as Aminta) to sing these new Roman-style canzonettas and recommending in the closing lines that for maximum effect they should be accompanied by lute (for which tablature is provided):

Ma se desii contentarmi pieno,	But if you want to satisfy me fully,
prendi il liuto,	take the lute,
Ch'è grande aiuto	which is a great help,
e senza quest'ogn'aria è manco grata,	without which every song lacks grace,
ma il suon e 'l canto è gemma in or	but playing and singing are joined
legato.[13]	together as a jewel in gold.

Similarly, the *Sacrae Cantiones* are dedicated to the abbots of the Cassinense Congregation of San Pietro in Modena, and in the dedication Vecchi describes himself as one of the congregation (on an honorary basis, apparently) and his music as having been "born" within the congregation's house.[14] *L'Amfiparnaso* is dedicated to Alessandro d'Este, whose brother Cesare became duke of Modena and Vecchi's patron in 1598. In the dedication, Vecchi refers to Alessandro's having heard *L'Amfiparnaso,* but he does not say when or where.[15]

The only aspirational dedication among Vecchi's four 1597 books is that of *Convito musicale,* dedicated to Ferdinand of Austria, who was to become Emperor Ferdinand II in 1619. In a familiar pattern, Vecchi recommends himself to the would-be patron through a mutual acquaintance, here Pietro Antonio Bianchi (ca. 1540–1611), who was Ferdinand's *Kapellmeister* at his court in Graz from 1595 until his death.[16] As with *Selva,* the variety on display in *Convito musicale* may likewise be read partly as a demonstration to the dedicatee of Vecchi's compositional range, though Vecchi's title and prefatory texts argue for a purpose both more poetically motivated and more pragmatic for a book of recreational music.

Forest Imagery and *Selva* as a Book Title

Single-composer music books conventionally bore generic titles that simply announced the kind of music on offer and the ordinal number identifying its place in the composer's publications (i.e., *Canzonette di Orazio Vecchi da Modena libro seconda a quattro voci*). Anthologies collecting music by multiple composers were often given names evoking fruit, flowers, or other imagery to create a kind of brand identity, a strategy only very rarely employed for monographs. In some special cases, a music book's title might reflect a unifying poetic theme, as with the Petrarchan Ferrarese anthologies *Il lauro secco* (1582) and *Il lauro verde* (1583), but as a rule a metaphorical title cannot be read as a description of the book's contents or organization.[17]

The function of Vecchi's title for *Selva di varia ricreatione* was entirely novel. It was unusual enough for a composer to assign a metaphorical title himself, but the real innovation was the meaning of the title Vecchi chose. In his dedication, he takes pains to explain that *Selva* was not an arbitrary title like those seen before: "If I had wanted to be silent, O Most Illustrious Gentlemen, about the reasons that prompted me to title these musical notes of mine 'FOREST,' either it would have implied that I chose the term by chance, or this title might have been interpreted in a way far from my intentions."[18] He goes on to explain the metaphor's meaning, attaching to the forest image the other key words in his title, variety and recreation:

> I say "FOREST," then, because it does not follow a continuous thread, just as we see the trees in forests placed without the order that we see in artificial gardens.

... To this title "FOREST" I then add "of RECREATION," because just as in a forest one sees that the variety of grasses and plants offers so much delight to the observers, so must the variety of diverse harmonies in these songs of mine resemble a "FOREST." And I have likewise joined in one the serious style and the familiar, the heavy with the humorous, and with the dance-like, to give rise to the variety that the world so enjoys.

The comparison with "artificial gardens" can easily be seen as a reference to the long tradition of flower- and fruit-based titles used for collections that, like most music prints, contained only a single musical genre. For Vecchi, then, the forest metaphor refers not just to the fact that the book is a collection but to the principle of variety and, ultimately, the pleasure that variety affords. Vecchi pursues the idea of recreation and pleasure further in the opening piece, labeled "proemio," which like the first pieces in his canzonetta books introduces the book as a whole:

Se desio di fuggir vi spron'e move	If you are moved by the desire to escape
I rai del sol estivi,	the rays of the summer sun,
Saggi amici pastori,	wise, friendly shepherds,
Tutti lieti e festivi,	all happy and festive,
De prati usciti fuori,	come out from the meadows,
E lasciando gl'armenti	and, leaving your herds
A pascere l'herbett'e i fiori intenti,	to graze on the grasses and flowers,
E da lupi sicuri e d'ogni belva,	safe from wolves and all wild beasts,
Venite à ricrearvi in questa	come to entertain yourselves in this
SELVA.	FOREST.

The addressees of this poem, imagined as shepherds who are called to relax in a shady wood, might conventionally be read as stand-ins for the Fugger brothers, but they are also construed as the readers or singers, who are invited to enjoy themselves by singing the music in the book. As in Vecchi's canzonetta books, the opening poem constructs a complex subjectivity in which the singers, by reading Vecchi's words on the page and singing them aloud, become both the "you" and the "I" as they begin to sing, read, or browse through the book.

Though *Selva di varia ricreatione* was a uniquely meaningful title for a music print, it had a long history as a title for other kinds of books. The Latin *silva* was used as a book title by Statius in the first century CE for five books of occasional verse in various meters, which he describes in the preface to Book I as having been written with great speed.[19] However, the classical literary sense of the word encompasses not an idea of variety but a kind of raw material. This meaning is described pejoratively by Quintilian: "There is a fault . . . into which those fall who insist on first making a rapid draft of their subject with the utmost speed of which their pen is capable, and write in the heat and impulse of the moment. They call this their *rough copy* [*silvam*]."[20] But another classical meaning for *silva* can be surmised from Aulus Gellius (ca. 123–169 CE) in the preface to his anthological collection *Noctes Atticae:*

> But in the arrangement of my material I have adopted the same haphazard order that I had previously followed in collecting it. . . . It therefore follows that in these notes there is the same variety of subject that there was in those former brief jottings. . . . I have given them the name *Attic Nights,* making no attempt to imitate the witty captions which many other writers . . . have devised for works of this kind. For since they had laboriously gathered varied, manifold, and as it were indiscriminate learning, they therefore invented ingenious titles also, to correspond with that idea. Thus some called their books "The Muses," others "Woods" [*Silvarum*]. . . . [Gellius goes on to name many other books with metaphorical titles.][21]

Statius's monographic *Silvae* are not the "Woods" to which Gellius refers, since *Noctes Atticae* is a collection of pieces by multiple authors. Vecchi's conception of his *Selva* draws on both Statius's collection of his own light verse and Gellius's description of a highly varied anthology. A small but coherent group of book titles beginning *Selva di varia* . . . appeared in the mid-sixteenth century in imitation of the classical tradition, starting in Spain and spreading quickly across Europe. The most prominent of these is Pedro Mexia's *Selva di varia lettione,* whose first part was printed in Seville in 1540 and to which Mexia added three more parts in later editions. This work, a combination of world history and general encyclopedia, was widely translated and reprinted throughout Europe but most notably in Venice, which produced no fewer than twenty-three editions of all or part of it between 1544 and 1682; Francesco Sansovino even added a fifth part to the work in a Venetian edition of 1563.[22] In phrasing notably similar to Vecchi's, Mexia described this book as "an orderless forest in which, according to the author, all the accumulated knowledge of his time was collected in his readings, like the trees and leaves in the forest."[23]

Other works from the period with similar titles attest to the continuity of the tradition associating the forest with all-encompassing variety. They include Juan de Mendaño's *Sylva de varios Romances, en el qual se contienen muchos y diversos Romances de hystorias nuevas* (1588),[24] Carlo Passi's *La selva di varia istoria* (1572),[25] and one musical work, the *Libro de musica de vihuela intitulado Silva de sirenas, en el qual se hallara toda diversidad de musica,* assembled by Enríquez de Valderrábano in 1547.[26] This massive and meticulously organized book—it lists nine different genres in its table of contents—includes both original works and transcriptions for solo vihuela, vihuela and voice, and the only known works for two vihuelas.

However, the tradition of *Selva* titles for music books moved in a new direction after 1590. In the seventeenth century, at least four musical works appear with *selva* in the title, all notable for their unusual size and variety. The range of Giovanni Francesco Anerio's *Selva armonica, dove si contengono motetti, madrigali, canzonette, dialoghi, [e] arie a una, doi, tre, et quattro voci* of 1617 is remarkable in comparison to Anerio's *Diporti musicali* of the same year, which contains only madrigals for one to four voices.[27] Three years later Francesco Rongoni published *Selva di varii passaggi*, a two-part pedagogical work with a prefatory "Avertimenti à Cantanti" that emphasizes the book's recreational function: "Whoever does not find, in this first forest, fruit meeting all his desires, should go on to the second, which, with greater breadth and depth, will abound in tastier and more delicious fruit."[28] Claudio Monteverdi's *Selva morale e spirituale* of 1640 is in the same mold as Vecchi's *Selva*, containing a wide range of Latin sacred music and Italian *madrigali morali* and *canzonette morali* in various *a cappella* and *concertato* textures.[29] Finally, in 1664 Bernardo Storace published *Selva di varie composizioni d'intavolatura per cimbalo ed organo*, a book of keyboard music consisting mostly of variations on various ostinato bass patterns.[30]

Whether these later books took their titles directly from Vecchi's *Selva* or not, new trends in Italian music and music publishing made a title like *Selva* increasingly apt for seventeenth-century collections. Variety is a prominent feature both in Monteverdi's last three madrigal books and in the earliest Florentine operas, which consisted of a mixture of dramatic recitative, canzonetta-based arias, instrumental ritornellos, and choral refrains. Although the error of drawing connections between Vecchi's late books and early opera has been much rehearsed (usually in reference only to *L'Amfiparnaso;* see chapter 4), the similarities between Vecchi's late publications and the Florentine musical humanists should not be overlooked.

Selva and Vecchi's Aesthetics of Variety

Vecchi's humanist orientation is explicit in the dedications to both *Selva* and *Convito musicale*. In *Selva* Vecchi defends the inclusion of "lighter" genres in the book with a reference to Horace:

> I know well that perhaps some people at the first hearing may judge these Caprices of mine lowly and light, but they should know that it requires as much grace, art, and nature to play a humorous character in a Comedy as to portray a prudent and wise old man. And they do not know that the Musician should sometimes mingle the serious song with the familiar, taking the example of the Poets. For while Tragedy should stay within its limits, not using the domestic speech of Comedy, and vice-versa, Horace says in the *Ars poetica:*
>> Often the Comedian elevates his style,
>> And sometimes the Tragedian has reason to use
>> A style that is humble and low.

The lines attributed to Horace are an Italian verse paraphrase of *Ars poetica*, lines 93–95. Although Vecchi's music in *Selva* and elsewhere sometimes draws on the *commedia dell'arte* tradition, the theatrical reference here is only an analogy. It can be read as an answer to the theorist Gioseffo Zarlino, who quotes an almost adjacent passage in the *Ars poetica* in his *Institutioni harmoniche* of 1558:

> We ought indeed to listen to what Horace says in his epistle on the *Art of Poetry:*
>
> "A theme for Comedy refuses to be set forth in verses of Tragedy . . ."
>
> . . . For if the poet is not permitted to write a comedy in tragic verse, the musician will also not be permitted to combine unsuitably these two things, namely, harmony and words.[31]

In the original passage Horace affirms the categories of classical poetry but also notes that these conventions may be broken in order to move the affections:

> These are the characteristic ways and tones of different kinds of work: if I cannot keep to them as described, or am ignorant of them, why do people call me poet? Why, in false shame, do I prefer not to know than to learn? Comic matter refuses to be expressed in tragic meters; similarly, the feast of Thyestes cannot be suitably related in strains that are careless or perhaps even suitable for comedy. Let each individual subject be allotted its proper place and keep to it. Yet sometimes even comedy raises its tone and Chremes in anger protests his case with outpuffed lips; and frequently a tragic character laments in ordinary

language, a Telephus, or a Peleus, when, poor and in exile, each casts aside bombast and words a yard long, if he is concerned to touch the spectator's heart with his complaint.[32]

Ultimately, Zarlino and Vecchi both invoke theatrical proprieties only metaphorically to justify exceptions to convention. Though Vecchi's argument seems to predict Monteverdi's justification for breaking Zarlino's contrapuntal rules, the two are not writing about music in the same terms. While Zarlino and Monteverdi wrote about counterpoint, Vecchi's unorthodox generic juxtapositions in *Selva* instead address the poetics of assembling a music book and the practicalities of using such a book in social music making. When Vecchi says that he has "giunto in uno" (joined together) the serious, the humorous, and the dance-like, he does not mean that he set serious poems to light music, or vice-versa, but rather that he mixed works of different genres and styles in a single book, recognizing that recreational singers would enjoy this variety.

The defense of variety in the *Selva* dedication is more clearly relatable to contemporary theories of poetic genre, particularly as they evolved in the ongoing polemics over the works of Ariosto, Tasso, and especially Guarini. Throughout the second half of the sixteenth century, poets and literary theorists issued lengthy critiques and counter-critiques of the emergent genres of romance, tragicomedy, and pastoral, comparing their aesthetic ends and means to the epic and dramatic poetry of classical literature, especially as codified in Aristotle's *Poetics*. The relative merits of unity and variety were among the most hotly debated aspects of contemporary poetry. Defenders of unity cited classical authority and the dramatic coherence of the single plot, while advocates of variety rallied around concepts of verisimilitude and pleasure in arguing for plots described (with various shades of meaning) as double, mixed, or complex. The most important of these treatises is Guarini's *Compendio della poesia tragicomica*, a defense of the tragicomedy and the pastoral first published in 1601 but that circulated in a preliminary form as early as 1588 in *Il Verrato*, a response to Giasone Denores's critique of *Il pastor fido*. Like Vecchi, Guarini explicitly links imitation and pleasure in terms drawn from Aristotle's *Poetics*: "[The end of tragicomedy] is to imitate . . . an action invented and combining all those tragic and comic parts which can stand together in a verisimilar way and with decorum, corrected under a single dramatic form, with the end of purging through delight the sadness of the listeners."[33] For Guarini and Vecchi alike, imitation, variety, and pleasure form an interconnected aesthetic matrix. Vecchi engages this debate with his reference in *Selva* to the "variety which all the world enjoys," with his comment regarding *L'Amfiparnaso* (1597) that "through its diverse personages [it] represents all the actions of the private individual," and in *Le veglie di Siena* of 1604, stating "I have no other purpose in representing people with dramatic poetry than to imitate better the things of life." On the other hand, Vecchi preemptively defends *Selva* against literary critics' charges of incoherence when he writes, somewhat cryptically, in the dedication: "Because where there is no order there cannot be anything good, it may be said that this is a confusion, which if not as a whole, then at least in its parts, is ordered and distinct." This response to hypothetical criticism may simply refer to the tension between the book's diversity of genres and the orderly way in which it is organized. In any case, we should not make too much of Vecchi's polemical tone here, because, as with the reference to Horace, the terms of the literary debates only apply indirectly to collections of music. As Jonathan Morgan has observed, Guarini's response to his critics was to argue that he had not mixed, and thereby confused, established genres but that he had created a *new* genre hybridized from elements of older ones; Vecchi makes no such claim and in fact insists on the coexistent variety of the genres contained in his collections.[34] But these distinctions refer more to each artist's rhetorical strategies than to his poetics; the aesthetic interest in combining elements that were conventionally segregated is clearly a shared one.

Exemplifying Variety: The Five-Voice Pieces

Despite Vecchi's defensive talk of confusion and discontinuity in the dedication, *Selva*'s contents are in fact organized quite simply: pieces are grouped together first by number of voices and then by genre within these groups. The number of voices increases regularly, except that the five-voice pieces are placed first, followed by those for three, four, and then six voices (table 3.1). Placing the five-voice works first gives pride of place to the madrigals, the most respected secular genre, confirming the book's intellectual rigor and engagement with contemporary poetics. More precisely, the five-voice group as a whole demonstrates the variety that Vecchi promises in the dedication when he writes: "And I have likewise joined in one [book] the serious style with the familiar, the heavy with the humorous, and with the dance-like, to give rise to that variety which all the world so enjoys."[35]

Table 3.1. Contents of *Selva di varia ricreatione*

	GENRE	INCIPIT	CLEFS	SIGNATURE/FINAL
1	Madrigali a 5	Se desio di fuggir	g2/c1/c3/c3/c4	♮/G
2		Se tra verdi arbuscelli	g2/g2/c2/c3/c4	♮/G
3		Al bel de tuoi capelli	g2/g2/c2/c3/f3	♭/F
4		De la mia cruda sorte	c1/c3/c4/c4/f4	♮/E
5	Capricci a 5	Margarita dai corai	g2/c2/c3/c3/f3	♮/C
6		Tich toch. Ch'è quel?	g2/g2/c2/c3/c4	♮/C
7		Cicirlanda. Che comanda?	g2/c2/c3/c3/c4	♮/C
8		Ie veu le cerf du bois salir	c1/c3/c4/c4/f4	♭/F
9	Balli a 5	Gitene, ninfe	c1/c2/c4/c4/f4	♮/A
10		Gioite tutti	c1/c2/c4/c4/f4	♮/A
11		Saltarello detto Trivella	g2/c1/c3/c3/f3	♮/A
12		Mostrava in ciel	c1/c2/c4/c4/f3	♮/D
13	Arie a 3	Se gli è ver, Himeneo	g2/g2/f3	♮/A
14		Amor, opra che puoi	c1/c1/c4	♭/G
15		Io spero e temo	c1/c1/f3	♭/G
16		Non vo pregare	c1/c1/f4	♮/A
17	Justiniane a 3	Sanità e allegrezza	c4/c4/f4	♭/F
18		Deh vita allabastrina	c4/c4/f4	♭/F
19		Mo magari, colonna	c2/c3/c4	♮/C
20	Canzonette a 4	Damone e Filli	g2/g2/c2/c3	♭/G
21		Che fai, Dori, che pensi?	c1/c1/c2/c4	♭/G
22		Deh preg'amor	c1/c1/c2/c4	♭/G
23	Aria a 4	So ben mi ch'ha bon tempo	c1/c3/c4/f3	♮/D
24	Fantasia a 4	(untexted)	g2/c2/c3/f3	♮/D
25	Madrigale a 6	Sovra le lucid'acque	g2/g2/c2/c3/c3/f3	♭/G
26	Serenata a 6	Tiridola non dormire	g2/g2/c2/c3/c3/f3	♮/C
27	Canzonetta a 6	Affrettiamoci tutti di fruire	g2/g2/c2/c3/c3/f3	♮/A
28	Villotta a 6	O bella, o bianca	c1/c3/c3/c4/c4/f4	♭/F
29	Dialogo a 7	Dolcissima mia vita	1st choir: c3/c4/c4/f4	♮/A
			2nd choir: c1/c2/c4	
30	Lotto amoroso a 7	Chi mett'al lotto olà?	1st choir: c1/c3/c4/f4	
			2nd choir: c1/c3/c4	♭/F
31	Dialogi a 8	Ecco, nuncio di gioia	1st choir: c1/c3/c4/f4	
			2nd choir: c1/c1/c3/c4	♮/D
32		Vieni o morte.	1st choir: c1/c3/c4/f4	
			2nd choir: c1/c2/c3/c4	♭/G
33		Echo rispondi	1st choir: c1/c3/c4/f4	
			2nd choir: c1/c3/c4/f4	♮/A
34	Diversi linguaggi a 9	O messir	"Marenzio": g2/g2/c2/c3/f4	♮/C
			"Vecchi": g2/c3/c3/c3	
35	Dialogi a 10	O felici e cortesi habitatori	1st choir: c1/c3/c4/c4/f4	
			2nd choir: c1/c3/c4/c4/f4	♭/G
36		Ecco sul Tauro	1st choir: g2/c2/c3/c3/f3	
			2nd choir: g2/c2/c3/c3/f3	G/♮
37	Battaglia a 10	Accingetevi, amanti	1st choir: g2/c2/c3/c4	
			2nd choir: g2/g2/c2/c3/c3/f3	G/♮

The twelve five-voice pieces divide neatly into four serious madrigals, four humorous *capricii*, and four dances, an alternative ordering to Pietro Bembo's familiar binary of *gravità* and *piacevolezza*.[36] Vecchi's tripartite division does not map onto this continuum; though he describes the style represented by the madrigals as *grave* and *serio*, the *capriccio* style (characterized as *famigliare* and *faceto*) sits uneasily with our understanding of *piacevolezza*. As Martha Feldman has shown, Bembo's theory of *variazione* in his *Prose della volgar lingua* in fact incorporates not only the *grave/piacevole* opposition, but also a theoretically distinct division of styles into high, middle and low.[37] Yet his general association of *grave* expression with the high style and *piacevole* with middle and low, as well as other logical slippages, prevents his theory from being reducible to a schematic system. Likewise, Vecchi's inclusion of the category of *danzevole* in his description opens up a broader field of expression in which he moves between multiple poles of affect (*grave* and *piacevole*), language (Tuscan Italian vs. dialects), musical forms (through-composed vs. strophic), literary mode and setting (pastoral vs. urban comedy), and register (elevated eroticism vs. blunt obscenity).

The five-voice group, then, explicitly fulfills the book's stated aesthetic principles—unlike the rest of *Selva*, where groups of a given ensemble-size generally emphasize binary contrasts between genres. By virtue of this arrangement Vecchi also invites us to read each piece as in some way exemplary of its genre. This principle plays out clearly enough in the madrigals, but less so in the *capricci*—a genre-label whose meaning was quite flexible in 1590—or in the dances for vocal ensemble, a formal genre unique in the music of the time.

Within the five-voice section of *Selva* each genre-group is further ordered based on thematic links, narrative progression, and musical styles. Careful ordering of pieces in motet and madrigal books is not uncommon; modal ordering is the most familiar strategy, and had appeared as early as Rore's *Madrigali a cinque voci* of 1542.[38] As Mauro Calcagno has shown, thematic organization reminiscent of the ordering of Petrarch's *canzoniere* can be detected in madrigal books by Wert and Marenzio.[39] Books with more obvious narratives were soon to appear, notably Marenzio's seventh madrigal book for five voices (1595) and Monteverdi's fifth book (1605), both of which draw their texts and narrative structures primarily from Guarini's *Il pastor fido*.[40] Of course, Vecchi would later organize *L'Amfiparnaso* according to the structure of a *commedia dell'arte* play, but that is not his strategy here.

Instead, the genre-groups present contrasting narratives to highlight the differences between them. The madrigals relate a story of unrequited love in the pastoral manner, different only in its small scale from the *canzoniere*-like ordering of madrigal books described by Calcagno. This opening group is symmetrically balanced by the dances, also in the pastoral mode, in which a love story ends more happily with physical consummation. The middle group of *capricci* has no continuous narrative, but rather presents a chaotic (that is, anti-pastoral) series of scenes in city streets and taverns. These narratives and their contrasts would be readily apparent to readers browsing through the book and to singers who might choose to sing pieces in order, providing the pleasure that Vecchi refers to in the dedication, as well as fodder for social conversations about poetry, love, and decorum.

The Madrigals

While elsewhere in *Selva* Vecchi experiments and stretches convention, the five-voice madrigals that open the book remain squarely within the tradition of the genre in the 1580s. Musically and textually they are in the style of the more conservative pieces in Vecchi's *Madrigali a cinque voci*. None of the poems juxtapose narrative and character voices, though as monologues they variously address the reader, a beloved, the speaker himself, and the allegorical figure of Fate. While linked by certain kinds of imagery, Vecchi's poems thus employ most of the rhetorical positions found in contemporary madrigals, encapsulating the genre in only four pieces.

As we have seen, the dedication's theoretical depiction of the forest as a place of pleasure is restated in the introductory "Se desio di fuggir" in terms of pastoral recreation by inviting the addressee (potentially the dedicatees, readers, or listeners) into "this Forest"—that is, both the imagined pastoral landscape and the book itself. The second madrigal, "Se tra verdi arbuscelli," continues the idyllic forest imagery of "Se desio di fuggir," but the edenic setting soon prompts the speaker to remember his lover. The poem does not construct a clear addressee; unlike the multivalent subjectivities of "Se desio di fuggir," the speaker in "Se tra verdi arbuscelli" essentially talks to himself:

Se tra verdi arbuscelli	When, among green saplings
O lungo à fresca riva	or beside refreshing banks
Di limpidi ruscelli	of clear streams,

Vien mi à ferir nel viso	the breeze of Paradise
L'aura di Paradiso,	strikes my face,
Amor sovien mi il giorno	love reminds me of the day
Che spirò la dolcissima mia Diva	when my sweetest goddess blew
L'aura al mio cor intorno,	the breeze around my heart,
Per cui se tutt' avampo	for which, if I am all inflamed,
E l'aura e il foco	both the air and the fire
Mi fia gradito in ogni tempo e loco.	will be pleasing to me forever and everywhere.

Vecchi continues the contemplation of the beloved in "Al bel de tuoi capelli," but now in the form of direct address, even as he returns to the image of the sun's rays from "Se desio di fuggir." On its own the poem can be read as a pastoral monologue, but by recalling the bright sunlight that the imagined shepherds escaped earlier the speech is resituated in the "here" of the forest and its function recast as a recreational performance.

Al bel de tuoi capelli	The beauty of your hair
L'oro ogni pregio tiene	is as precious as gold,
Ch'al paragon piu impallidir si vede.	which in comparison appears to grow paler.
Son cosi forse i velli	Thus, perhaps, are the locks
De l'Auriga celeste	of the celestial charioteer
Quando di raggi il mondo infiamma e veste.	when with rays he clothes and inflames the world.
Febo vinto si rende	Apollo gives himself up defeated,
Mentre piu chiaro luce	while purer light,
Dunque di che risplende	therefore, shines
D'un vivo raggio de l'eterna luce.	from a living ray of eternal light.

These three opening madrigals thus effect a subtle shift from an invitatory proem through a Petrarchan soliloquy to a pastoral speech, the implied addressee shifting in each case. The final madrigal of the set returns to the Petrarchan mode in a darker vein. The speaker laments his beloved's disdain, a disruptive turn of events similar to the *accidente* expected in the *canzionere* narratives of Petrarch and his sixteenth-century imitators:

De la mia cruda sorte	Of my cruel fate
Ben à ragion mi doglio	I have good reason to complain,
Non di colei chi hà del mio cor la chiave	not of her who holds the key to my heart.
Ch'ella piu che la morte	For she hates, more than death,

Piena d'ira e d'orgoglio	full of anger and pride,
Odia colui sotto il cui peso grave	him who, under this great burden,
Vive e vita non have.	lives and does not have life.

Ahi sorte priva di sapere e d'arte	Alas, fate, without wisdom or skill,
Vieti dunque à due Amanti	thus you prevent two lovers
Stringersi in nodi santi	from clinging together in holy bonds.
La sentenza non cade in giusta parte	The sentence does not fall justly,
Che un resti afflitto è solo	that one remains afflicted and alone,
Congiunto l'altro con eterno duolo.	bound to the other in eternal pain.

"De la mia cruda sorte" employs not only a pathetic text but also several musical references to the musical style then current for such texts. While many pieces in *Selva* are written with a ¢ signature (the distinction between c and ¢ had largely dissolved by the 1590s), this is the only one in which it actually signifies that the music moves in a *tactus* of semibreves rather than minims.[41] This self-consciously archaic mensuration typically signaled a particularly serious tone, as it did in Marenzio's *Madrigali a quattro, cinque, e sei voci, libro primo* of 1588.[42] The opening, moreover, is directly modeled on the *exordium* of Marenzio's "Dolorosi martir," another madrigal in ¢.[43] The pathetic style is also expressed in more audible features, particularly the setting of the final line, "Congiunto l'altro con eterno duolo," marked by cross-relations in mm. 51–54 and then by a dramatic descent through a tenth in the Canto in mm. 58–62 (example 3.1).

The language echoes Petrarch in the final paradox of the first part, "Vive e vita non have" and in the parallelism of the second part's conclusion, "Ch'un resti afflitto è solo / Congiunto l'altro con eterno duolo." Despite the madrigalistic mixture of seven- and eleven-syllable lines (*versi sciolti*), the two-part formal and rhetorical structure mirrors that of the sonnet (table 3.2; I have indicated a relevant text repetition in Vecchi's fourth line). Vecchi's versification, while not precisely that of a sonnet, does echo the structural features of one, as does its two-part setting. The *prima parte,* with the binary scheme abCc-abCc, corresponds to the sonnet's *ottava,* establishing the poem's theme and culminating in the statement of a paradox. The six-line *seconda parte* (Dee-DfF) corresponds to the *sestina,* in which a general point is drawn and a final state of affairs is named. In a narrative reading of the madrigals, "De la mia cruda sorte" is a wrenching plot twist transforming a pastoral erotic tale into a Petrarchan tragedy, concluding with the narrator's bitter resignation and acceptance of his fate.

Example 3.1. (*above and facing*) Vecchi, "De la mia cruda sorte," mm. 46–64.

Imitating Obscenity: The *Capricci*

Vecchi's *capricci*, read in sequence after the madrigals, could hardly be more of a disruption. They are characterized not by any common form or style but by idiosyncratic musical features and texts that depict low-status characters, often trading in sexual innuendo of a far coarser kind than that found in erotic madrigalian texts. The term *capriccio* appears as a genre-label only for "Margarita dai corai"; the next piece, "Tich-toch," is labeled *dialogo* and is followed by the two *vinate*. I categorize all four pieces as *capricci* for three reasons. First, the rubric "capriccio primo" over "Margarita dai corai" implies

53
duo - lo, con e - ter - no duo - lo, con - giun-
lo, con - giun - to l'al - tro,
con e - ter - no duo - lo, con - giun-to l'al -
tro con e - ter - no duo - lo, con e - ter - no
tro con e - ter - no duo - lo,
57
- to l'al-tro, Con - giun - to l'al - tro con
con-giun - to l'al - tro, Con - giun-to l'al -
tro, Con - giun-to l'al-tro con e - ter - no
duo - lo, Con - giun-to l'al - tro con e -
Con-giun-to l'al - tro con
61
e - ter - no duo - - - lo.
- tro con e - ter - no duo - lo.
duo - lo, e - ter - no duo - lo.
ter - no duo - lo.
e - ter - no duo - - - lo.

Table 3.2. Sonnet-like form of "De la mia cruda sorte"

PETRARCHAN SONNET		VECCHI'S "DE LA MIA CRUDA SORTE"	
VERSE FORM	RHETORICAL FORM	VERSE FORM	
A	Establishment	a	De la mia cruda sorte
B	of theme	b	Ben à ragion mi doglio
B		C	Non di colei c'hà del mio cor la chiave
		c	(c'hà del mio cor la chiave).
A	Expansion of theme,	a	Ch'ella piu che la morte
B	with paradox	b	Piena d'ira e d'orgoglio
B		C	Odia colui sotto'l cui peso grave
A		c	Vive e vita non have.
C	General statement	D	Ahi sorte priva di saper' e d'arte
D	derived from *ottava*	e	Vieti dunqu'à due Amanti
E		e	Stringersi in nodi santi.
C	Conclusion, with	D	La sentenza non cade in giusta parte
D	rhetorical *acutezza*	f	Ch'un resti afflitto è solo
E		F	Congiunto l'altro con eterno duolo.

that it is followed by more *capricci*. Second, the groups of four madrigals and four dances that precede and follow these pieces imply that they should likewise be read as a group of four. Finally, they share a tone that can be described, then and now, as "capricious," and they are all in mode 12, which Vecchi uses exclusively for the most comical pieces in *Selva*, including the *giustiniane*, the six-voice *villotta* and *serenata*, and the nine-voice *Diversi linguaggi*. This modal consistency probably reflects the use in several of these pieces of popular tunes from nonliterate traditions, or at least tunes that were intended to evoke a popular style.

The first *capriccio*, "Margarita dai corai," combines a poem in the form of a *villanesca* (rhymed couplets with a repeating refrain), a northern (Lombard) dialect, a refrain of nonsense syllables, and a through-composed musical form based on a popular melody that is varied from verse to verse (example 3.2).[44] The melody of "Margarita" appeared again in a duo by Giuseppe Giamberti published in 1657, and Marcello Conati has shown that the song remained current in northern Italian folk traditions at least into the 1970s, citing several examples transcribed in the Po valley.[45]

"Margarita's" popular roots account for its dialect text, which draws on a series of sexual metaphors not readily apparent to the modern reader and belongs to a tradition of equivocal allusion that Vecchi drew on throughout his career:

Example 3.2. Reconstruction of "Margarita dai corai" melody with Vecchi's text underlaid.

Margarita of corals,
get up, the cocks are crowing,
and I don't think of it,
   La la diridon.

My husband is a fool;
he knows it himself,
and I don't think of it,
   La la diridon.

My husband has gone to Pavia
to buy a Malvasia
to make soup for the donkey,
   La la diridon.

My husband is a gentleman,
a good but poor man,
and I don't think of it,
   La la diridon.

The crowing cock of the opening stanza, of course, suggests sexual arousal, and this text is associated with other settings of the tune. The subsequent stanzas are unique to Vecchi's setting and may be his own invention: they switch to the voice of Margarita herself, mocking her foolish husband in terms that allude to his irregular sexual proclivities and hint at her availability to other lovers. If singers recognize the tune and imagine a rustic social context in which it might be sung, then the imagined Margarita is more or less making herself available to a group of men.

She describes her absent husband as a fool who has gone to Pavia to buy Malvasia (the wine also known as Malmsey). Both the city and the wine carry equivocal associations. Pavia was referred to as a city of corrupting influence as early as the twelfth century by the Archpoet in the *Carmina Burana*:

Quis in igne positus igne non uratur?	What, placed in fire, does not burn with fire?
quis Papiae demorans castus habeatur,	Who, in Pavia, is to remain chaste,
ubi Venus digito iuvenes venatur,	where Venus's finger beckons youths,
oculis illaqueat, facie praedatur?	with ensnaring eyes, and preying faces?
Si ponas Hippolytum hodie Papiae,	If you put Hippolytus in Pavia today,
non erit Hippolytus in sequenti die:	he won't be Hippolytus the next day:
Veneris in thalamos ducunt omnes viae,	all roads lead to Venus's bedrooms,
non est in tot turribus turris Alethiae.[46]	and among those towers is no tower for Truth.

More specifically, Malvasia is invoked in connection with sodomy in Pietro Aretino's *Sonetti lussuriosi,* poems penned to accompany the pornographic engravings by Giulio Romano known as *I modi.* In the eighth sonnet, a dialogue concerned with the relative merits of vaginal and (heterosexual) anal sex, the male partner declares:

Finisca in me la mia genealogia,	May my genealogy end with me,
Ch'io vo fottervi dietro spesso spesso,	since I want to do you very often in your rear;
Per gli è differente il tondo, e'l fesso	for the circle and the slit are as different
Come l'acquato dal la malvagia.	as rainwater is from wine.[47]

Two lines of parallel images are developed here: the "slit" (the vagina) and water (symbolic of female humidity in Galenic thought) are contrasted with the "circle" (the anus) and Malvasia.[48] References to cooking carried sexual connotations in equivocal poetry as well, and the mention of poverty, or "need," in the final stanza refers to the husband's sexual appetite.[49] This stanza shifts to triple meter, which, as in some of Vecchi's other pieces, carries in its dance-like rhythms a sensation of embodiment and, where the text supports it, eroticism.

The nonsense phrase "La la diridon" also appears in two of Vecchi's later faux-rustic *villotte,* and although in all these cases it may be heard as an imitation of an instrument (as it is in Lasso's similarly obscene "Matona mia cara"), it can also function as a stand-in for obscene lyrics. I discuss these *villote* in chapter 6; they are distinct from this *capriccio* in their nonstrophic texts and simple homophonic style. "Margarita's" contrapuntal, through-composed setting of variations on the tune, on the other hand, foregrounds compositional virtuosity in a way that distances the tune—and its racy text—from its low-class origin. "Margarita" uses imitation between voices in every verse, with only occasional homophonic passages. The basic melody is presented on several pitch levels and in triple meter for the final verse. This structure and degree of refinement have some relatives in the five-voice *canzonas* of Ferretti and others, which use strophic texts in through-composed settings and in some cases parody the three-voice *villanellas* on which they are modeled.[50] Vecchi may likewise have derived "Margarita" from a polyphonic *villanella* that is now lost, but any such piece would itself have been based on the popular (i.e., nonliterate) tune that survives in Vecchi's setting and elsewhere.

Vecchi's second capriccio, "Tich-toch," begins as an imitation of a theatrical dialogue between the clownish *zanni* and a higher-ranking—but no less foolish—*vecchio*, a scene-type central not only to *commedia dell'arte* performances but also to the disreputable mountebank shows out of which they evolved.[51] The conversation eventually departs from convention, however, descending first to the *zanni's* suggestive description of a sexually charged act he intends to perform publicly with his wife, in which he shows off his "baboon" and she her "monkey," both euphemisms for genitalia. The text then shifts from dialogue to a third-person description of the act itself, allowing the singers to imagine an obscene display without implicating themselves as participants in it. The climax of the piece, in which the "monkey" dances and the "baboon" leaps, moves—as does "Margarita"—to an eroticized triple meter and the first full homophonic texture of the piece, vividly evoking the sexual imagery while distancing the singers from the imagined "performers."[52]

Vecchi's last two *capricci* carry the label *vinata*, and their depictions of real drinking games and songs are discussed more fully in chapter 6. While popular songs associated with drinking must always have existed in oral traditions, their appearance in notated music before *Selva* is rare (though references to wine in more courtly song are not), and Vecchi was the first to label such pieces *vinate*. However, two northern treatises published subsequent to *Selva* mention the *vinata* as a secular genre, shedding light on the social status of the *vinata* and on the theorists themselves. Near the end of his *Plaine and Easie Introduction to Practicall Musicke* of 1597, Thomas Morley offers a taxonomy of genres descending in seriousness from sacred motets through lighter madrigals, ending with *villanellas, balletti, vinate*, and *giustiniane*. Of the *vinata*, Morley writes:

> The slightest kind of musick (if they deserve the name of musicke) are the *vinate* or drincking songes, for as I said before, there is no kinde of vanitie whereunto they have not applied some musicke or other, as they have framde this to be sung in their drinking, but that vice being so rare among the Italians, & Spaniards: I rather thinke that musicke to have bin devised by or for the Germains (who in swarmes do flocke to the Universitie of Italie) rather then for the Italians themselves.[53]

In the third volume of his *Syntagma Musicum* of 1619, Michael Praetorius offers a similar catalog of musical genres, indebted in various places to Morley's *Introduction*.[54] Praetorius devotes a chapter to songs sung by workers and peasants in which he writes of the *vinata* in surprisingly similar terms: "Vinettas or vinata is a ditty by a wine-grower or vintner who works in the vineyard, for vinetto means vintner or wine-grower.... Vinatas are drinking songs or, to use the proper title, boozing songs, which are neither unusual here in Germany nor uncommon. It is my belief that there is no vanity or triviality found in the world that has not been set or sung to music."[55]

The correspondence of the comments on vanity and music is revealing, since the phrase has no intrinsic connection to drinking songs per se, confirming (along with other significant correspondences) that Praetorius drew directly on Morley's influential treatise. But to what pieces were Morley and Praetorius actually referring? In 1597, when Morley's *Introduction* was published, the only pieces to have been printed with the label *vinata* were the two in *Selva* from seven years earlier, and it seems likely that they were Morley's only source for the term. He certainly knew Vecchi's book, having borrowed the text of the aria "So ben mi c'ha bon tempo" for an Italian contrafactum of his own ballett "Now is the month of maying." Furthermore, in the *Introduction* Morley mentions an unusual *fantasia* by Vecchi based exclusively on a single contrapuntal subject that can only be the one in *Selva* (no. 24). Praetorius conflates two distinct functions of the *vinata:* to Morley's description of a drinking song he adds the description of a vintner's work song. This aligns the genre with Praetorius's subsequent definition of the *giardiniero* as a gardener's song, apparently based on another misreading of Vecchi, this one of the song "O giardiniero" from *Convito musicale* (see chapter 6). Vecchi's evocations of popular traditions in his *vinate* were realistic enough for both theorists to read them as quasi-ethnographic transcriptions.

Despite their diverse styles, the *capricci* in *Selva* are united in depicting characters marked as rustic by their language, their actions, and the tunes they sing. As a unit within the book they separate the madrigals from the dances—two groups that share a more courtly milieu, the former in its literary guise of Petrarchan introspection and pastoral sociability, the latter seemingly in the more functional vein of music used in social dancing.

The Dances

Although Vecchi's five-voice dances return to more familiar terminology than the *capricci*, they are just as unconventional in relation to printed music of the period. They are the earliest known pieces printed with five polyphonic parts and lute tablature and the only multivoice pieces with lute to be identified as specific dance types.[56] As such, their function as music for actual social or theatrical dancing is questionable, and they seldom conform to the formal requirements of dance choreographies. The large majority of sixteenth-century dances to appear in print are "stylized" pieces for solo lute or keyboard, although dances for instrumental consorts more suited to accompany dancing were not unknown. Dances for vocal ensemble are relatively rare except for generically "dance-like" pieces such as Giovanni Giacomo Gastoldi's *Balletti* of 1591; labeling vocal polyphony with specific dance types was entirely novel. The instruction "per sonare e cantare insieme" (to play and sing together) suggests a variety of performance possibilities both for using the lute with some or all of the vocal parts and for doubling the voices with other instruments. The third dance, titled "Saltarello detto Trivella," is without text and carries the rubric "per sonare con gli strumenti da corde a 5" (to play on stringed instruments in five parts), so that if the dances are performed as a set, the availability of instruments to double or replace voices elsewhere must be assumed.

The dances' return to a pastoral setting after the urban humor of the *capricci* invites a comparison to the madrigals that begin the book. Like the introductory "Se desio di fuggir," the first dance, "Gitene ninfe" (no. 9), is a pastoral invitation exhorting shepherds to leave their flocks. The strophic text draws together Damon and Clori and celebrates their love, and the final line explicitly addresses the rubric "per cantare e sonare insieme," printed at the head of the piece:

Gitene Ninfe sù gl'herbosi prati,	Venture forth, nymphs, to the grassy fields,
E voi Pastori amati,	and you, loving shepherds,
E ghirlandette de piu vaghi fiori	and weave garlands of the prettiest flowers
Teset'à la mia Clori	for my Clori,
Poi che le died' Amori	since Love gave her
Bellezza tal che pò rapire il core	such beauty that can ravish the heart,
E di dolcezz'ancor trar l'alma fuore.	and draw out the soul with sweetness.
E tu Damone lascia i cari Armenti, herds,	And you, Damon, leave your dear
E al suon de nostr'accenti,	and at the sound of our songs
Prendila e seco men'alte carole,	take her and do many lively dances with her,
Che te sol bram'e vuole,	for she desires and longs for you alone.
E noi farem'intanto	And meanwhile we will make
Per allegrezza risonar le valli	the valleys resound with happiness
Al dolce suon de pletri canti e balli.	to the sweet sound of plectra, songs, and dances.

The piece's generic status as a *passamezzo* is problematic.[57] Vecchi employs neither the *passamezzo antico* nor *moderno* bass pattern, the most common harmonic frameworks for such dances, and the three strains, which in a *passamezzo* should be eight breves long, instead have nine, nine, and ten breves, respectively. The piece thus refers to the dance described in the poem more readily than it admits actual dancing.

"Gioite tutti" (no. 10) carries the rubric "saltarello detto il Vecchi," referring both to the composer and to the character given voice in the poem. The title might imply that the piece, or at least the tune, was already in circulation and perhaps that it was associated with Vecchi himself. However, the pastoral text exhorting lovers to dance and make love reveals itself, in the last stanza, as the warning of an old man whose youth is lost:

Gioite tutti in suoni e in canti e in balli,	Rejoice, everyone, with music, songs, and dances,
Poi che la vaga Primavera è giunta,	since the lovely spring has arrived,

E fioriscon le valli,	and the valleys are in flower,
E fuor la rosa spunta.	and the rose blooms forth.
Scherzan gli Amori,	Cupids frolic
E van spargendo fiori.	and go scattering flowers.
Prendete Ninfe i vostri almi Pastori,	Nymphs, take your dear shepherds,
Che la stagion novella invita al ballo.	because the new season invites you to dance.
Hor sfogate gli ardori	Now give vent to your passions
Senza porv' intervallo.	without pause;
Liete calcate	happily trample
Le verdi herbetti e grate.	the green and pleasant grass.
Passa la Primavera e'l Verno viene,	The spring passes and winter comes,
Però d'Amor godette il frutto ò Amanti,	therefore, lovers, enjoy the fruits of love;
Che le luci serene	for the clear lights
E d'Angeli i sembianti	and the angelic faces
Tost' hanno fine,	will soon be gone,
Come s'imbianca il crine.	as the hair turns white.

The theme of an exhortation to embrace love before time runs out is one that also appears in *Selva*'s six-voice canzonetta "Affrettiamoci tutti" (no. 27) and in the canzonetta from Book IV titled "Trista novella" (see chapter 2). Besides enacting Vecchi's stated desire to elicit pleasure with music, this favored theme creates a poetic persona derived from a pun on his own name. As a forty-year-old unmarried author of amorous and erotic poetry and music, Vecchi may have seen the old man as an apt pastoral alter ego.

No such biographical explanations are available for the title of the textless "Saltarello detto Trivella" (no. 11). *Trivella* can refer to an auger or drill but also to a battering ram or other war-machine used to breach walls. Vecchi's music, while possessing the vigorous mixed-meter rhythms characteristic of the *saltarello* (much more so than "Gioite tutti"), does not at first seem to depict any particular imagery. The key to this title only becomes clear in a reading of the dances as a complete series, concluding with "Mostrava in ciel" (no. 12), labeled *tedesca*, or allemande. The poem is an *alba* depicting a lover's departure at dawn, with the conventional association of "parting" with sexual climax:

Mostrav'in ciel l'Alba di gigli e rose	In the sky, Dawn was displaying her lovely hair,

Coronat'il bel crin quando s'unio	crowned with lilies and roses, when I joined
La mia bocc'à la bocca del ben mio.	my mouth with the mouth of my beloved.
Restai priv'all'hor di vita,	I then remained deprived of life,
Meschino me,	miserable me,
Quando sentii doppiarsi la ferita,	when I felt the wound redoubled,
O sventurato me.	oh, unlucky me.
Spuntava fuor da l'oceano i raggi	Out of the ocean the lovely sun
Lucidissim'il bel sol, quando s'udio	sprouted brightest rays, when I heard
Ragionarmi pian pian cosi il cor mio:	my heart speaking to me softly thus:
"Fa contento le tue voglie,	"Content your desires,
Beato te,	blessed one,
Che del servir'il frutt'al fin si coglie,	for you have at last reaped the fruits of your service,
O fortunato te."	oh, you fortunate one!"

As is typical of this poetic type, Vecchi contrasts the beauty of dawn with the anguish of the narrator at leaving his beloved, but the plea for him to remain is ambiguously attributed to the speaker's heart ("cor mio"), which refers to his own conscience or, aphoristically, to the female lover. This ambiguity maps onto the central double entendre of the poem.

The narrative of the four dances as a group becomes clear. "Gitene ninfe" is an invitation, calling a pair of lovers together to enjoy music and dancing in a pastoral setting. The "Saltarello detto il Vecchi," conversely, tells lovers participating in this celebration to go and enjoy love. Since the final *tedesca* is a postcoital *alba*, we can infer that the intervening textless "Saltarello detto Trivella" discreetly represents the physical union of the pair. This reading explains the meaning of *trivella* as an instrument of penetration and the "redoubled wound" of "Mostrava in ciel" as an urge for a sexual rematch.

Where the madrigals narrate the anguish of frustrated love, the dances depict a happier consummation, encouraged by Vecchi himself in the saltarello that bears his name. These two groups thus mirror the Battle of Love and Scorn that ends *Selva*. The *capricci* do not participate in this dialectic but suggest a different world altogether from the courtly pastoral milieu of the other groups. Thus both the narrative elements of each group and their musical forms and textures exemplify Vecchi's principle of variety through their contrast of the serious, humorous, and dance-like in music.

Order and Contrast

The remaining twenty-five pieces in *Selva* are arranged in groups according to number of voices and within each group by genre, with more established and serious genres preceding more innovative and humorous ones (see table 3.1). Of the three- and four-voice groups, none of the genre names are entirely new, though several are employed in novel ways. Vecchi's three-voice arias are in the new "alla romana" style of three-voice *villanelle* scored for a trio of two high voices and bass that was first employed by Luca Marenzio in his five books of *villanelle* published between 1584 and 1587.[58] Giustiniani described this style as an adaptation of accompanied solo song, and Vecchi provides for this possibility by including lute accompaniments in *Selva*. The musical and poetic forms of the *arie* resemble Vecchi's canzonettas: they are all binary forms setting strophic poems. The first two (nos. 13 and 14) are both addressed to mythological deities: "Se glie vero Himeneo" is a hymn to the god of marriage celebrating a pastoral wedding, while "Amor, opra che puoi" addresses Cupid. The second pair (nos. 15 and 16) are more pessimistic, employing Petrarchan paradoxes and lists of attributes in describing the speaker's suffering and his beloved's coldness.

These four *arie* are balanced by the three *giustiniane*, three-voice works without lute written in Venetian dialect for a trio of closely spaced voices. Setting the words of a comical *vecchio* of the kind exemplified by Pantalone of the *commedia dell'arte*, the old man's unrequited pleas for love are depicted through stuttering effects using repeated syllables and parallel triads (or, in a less "rustic" variant, parallel 6–3 sonorities). The *giustiniana* had been cultivated in the 1570s by Venetian composers, principally Andrea Gabrieli and Vincenzo Bellavere, and Vecchi's revival of it in *Selva* and in *Convito musicale* offers a sharp contrast to the pastoral and Petrarchan tone of his more "literary" poems. No. 17, "Sanitae allegrezza, e bezzi assai," makes the contrast of genres especially clear by parodying a wedding celebration. Here praises for the newlyweds are voiced in the first-person plural by a group who describe themselves as boatmen but whose stuttering effects confirm that the imitation is still of comic old men: "Semo qui traghettai / sol per vede-ne-ne-ner / coppia cusi zentil" (We are boatmen, here / just to s-s-s-see / such a fine couple [lines 3–5]). For recreational singers, the imitation of comic types of lower social status constituted a kind of play similar but opposite to the imitation of idealized Petrarchan lovers and pastoral shepherds in madrigal poetry.

The three canzonettas for four voices in *Selva* are notable among Vecchi's previous pieces in the genre only in the provision of lute tablature, a tacit acknowledgment of a performance practice that was widespread for the canzonetta already. Yet since skilled lutenists could accompany singers without the aid of tablature, its inclusion in *Selva* indicates once again the book's appeal to the aspirational qualities of some book buyers, catering to players who cannot improvise their own accompaniments but wish to mimic those who can. The question of musical and social status is also central to the four-voice aria "So ben mi ch'hà bon tempo" (no. 23), a cynical critique of courtly *sprezzatura* in a much simpler musical style than the canzonettas and employing a "fa-la" refrain (see chapter 6). This style became better known in the widely reprinted five-voice *balletti* published by Gastoldi in 1591, though the poetry of those works does not partake of Vecchi's biting social satire.[59] The four-voice "Fantasia senza parole" (no. 24) may likewise be read as a satirical display of compositional virtuosity. It exhaustively treats a single imitative subject to the widest possible range of techniques: stretto, multiple countersubjects, reharmonization, augmentation at three different levels, inversion, and changes of meter. This is the piece Morley referred to when he wrote of composers who "would take upon them to make a whole fancy of one point," "And in that also you shall find excellent fantasies both of *maister Alfonso, Horatio Vecci,* and others. But such they seldom compose, except it either bee to shewe their varietie at some odd time to see what may be done upon a point without a dittie, or at the request of some friend, to shew the diversitie of sundrie mens vaines upon one subject."[60]

The larger-scale works in *Selva* for six or more voices include pastoral madrigals and dialogues of a more conventional courtly nature, as well as more experimental pieces that depict bawdy songs, an allegorical lottery game, and the cacophonous street scene Vecchi labels "A diversi linguaggi." Some of these pieces, particularly the polychoral dialogues for eight and ten voices, seem intended for staged performance, but their inclusion in this recreational collection recasts them as material for social singing. The consistent juxtaposition of contrasting poems and musical genres could have appealed to readers even if they could not always muster the resources to sing the larger works.

Vecchi's confidence that the variety of *Selva* would be enjoyable prompts the question of why such varied collections were not more common. One answer may lie in the systems of patronage that supported the production of music books and the way in which Vecchi took advantage of his place outside it. Composers may have been constrained to associate their high-status dedicatees with literary madrigals, while books of light genres could be dedicated to more minor patrons, indirectly enforcing a segregation of genres in print that did not reflect recreational singing practices. This system was continually reinforced by the structure of the book market, in which patrons often financed the books dedicated to them and could therefore associate themselves with genres befitting their rank: the dedication, though ostensibly written in the obsequious tones of a composer or printer, was an especially public venue for self-fashioning; Vecchi himself observed this rule in his dedications for single-genre books in the 1580s. In *Selva*, however, he is less concerned with the dedicatees' fame than with the book's function in the market for printed music. He combines disparate genres not only to demonstrate an aesthetic position but to provide for private music making in which higher- and lower-status music could be enjoyed together without concern for public glory.

Convito musicale

After a seven-year hiatus Vecchi returned to print in 1597 with no fewer than four new books: the *Canzonette a tre voci* were dedicated on March 20, *Sacrarum Cantionum Liber Secundus* on April 10, *L'Amfiparnaso* on May 20, and finally *Convito musicale* on August 20. *Convito musicale* is a varied collection returning in many respects to the style of *Selva*. Einstein surmises that *Convito* was composed before *L'Amfiparnaso*, supporting a view that all of Vecchi's large-scale collections were conceived as unitary artworks, progressing teleologically toward *L'Amfiparnaso*: "[T]he *Convito*, already announced in the preface to the *Amphiparnaso*, was presumably the first to be written and is in any case the link between the *Selva* and the *Amphiparnaso*."[61] Considering the gap in Vecchi's publishing between 1590 and 1597, it is reasonable to assume that *Convito* was compiled from pieces composed over a longer period, as *Selva* had undoubtedly been (and indeed, one madrigal in *Convito* had been published fifteen years earlier in the Ferrarese anthology *Il lauro secco*). However, despite thematic or quasi-narrative links among groups of pieces within each book, *Selva* and *Convito* are heterogeneous books unified by their titular metaphors and aesthetic ideas rather than the theatrical plot of *L'Amfiparnaso*. Vecchi himself describes *Convito* as a sequel to *Selva* in the dedication to Ferdinand II, archduke of Austria, writing that he had heard that the archduke had previously enjoyed "strolling by the feet of his refined hearing [*i piedi del suo purgato udito*] through my FOREST of varied recreation" and that, having tasted those "wild fruits" (*frutti Selvatici*), "he will enjoy even more these meats seasoned with the salt of civil harmony."[62]

The front matter of *Convito musicale* separates this dedication from a more expansive preface (addressed "Ai lettori" [to the readers]) describing the book in terms of its titular metaphor. However, whereas in *Selva* Vecchi writes explicitly about the book and the meaning of its title, in the preface to *Convito musicale* he writes only about the imagined banquet itself: the metaphorical equivalency of musical works with various dishes is taken as self-evident. This fictive perspective allows Vecchi to expound his theory of balance, variety, and pleasure in terms of anti-Epicurean philosophy rather than poetics:

> The proper spice for food is hunger, says Socrates; therefore let him who is about to sit down to my Banquet bring a good appetite with him, so that each dish, however tasteless it may be, may seem to him sweet and savory. I say this because it would be no wonder (in view of the great abundance of music going the rounds today) if the ears of many, grown satiated and through this satiety weak, were in the condition of the sick, who have no more than tasted one thing than they call fastidiously for another. . . . But if the appetites of the guests are well disposed, it cannot be doubted that they will derive nourishment from even the slightest dish.[63]

Einstein believed that this is a critique of Gesualdo's avant-garde madrigals, but Vecchi's complaint is not about the contemporary musical style but rather the sheer quantity of music circulating in print. The opening sentence paraphrases the aphorism "Cibi condimentum esse famem, potionis sitim" (The best seasoning for one's food is hunger, and the best flavoring for one's drink is thirst), attributed to Socrates in book 2 of Cicero's *De finibus bonorum et malorum*, which presents Cicero's refutation of Epicurean philosophy.[64]

Cicero characterizes Epicureanism as a hedonistic philosophy in which pleasure is understood as the highest good. The Epicurean view distinguishes between "kinetic" pleasure, in which pleasant sensation replaces or relieves pain, and a higher form of "static" pleasure, which is the complete absence of pain. In attacking this distinction, Cicero addresses the issue of variety in a way that resonates with Vecchi's aesthetics:

There may be variation [*varietas*] in a poem or a speech, in one's behaviour or fortune, and pleasure too is often said to involve variation in the sense that quite different things may produce quite different pleasures. If that is the variation you were speaking of, I would understand it—I understand it even though you are not speaking of it. The variation you are speaking of is rather unclear: you say the height of pleasure is to be free from pain, and that when we taste those pleasures which give the senses a sweet sensation, then we experience "kinetic" pleasure. It is this sort of pleasure, you claim, which brings variation, but fails to add to the pleasure of being free from pain, though why you call the latter pleasure at all is a mystery to me.[65]

Cicero and Vecchi thus agree that only a variety of sensations or styles can produce pleasure, not merely a static surfeit of sensations of a single kind, however sweet. The ill-disposed and feminized constitutions Vecchi describes in *Convito* resemble Epicurean victims of an excessive diet of relatively undifferentiated pieces. He extends the metaphor to propose a kind of musical therapy that is also another defense of including various genres in a single book:

[I]f the appetites of some should be so badly adjusted that they need some allurement in the way of an appetizer, let them not give it a thought. For here there will be prepared a pie of banished ass from which they may perhaps derive the same appetite that jaded women do from charcoal, spleen, gypsum, and other things of the sort. And if this bait is not enough to captivate their ears, they will find to their taste a little ragout of canzonette, villotte, giustiniane, and other ingredients that will whet their sluggish appetites for them. Thus they will be able to apply themselves the more readily to the more substantial dishes, for let all be advised that although this is all one banquet, many tables are set, of which some are served with three, four and five plates and others with six, seven, or eight.[66]

The prescription of "a pie of banished ass" (a reference to "Il bando del asino," one of the game-like pieces in *Convito musicale*) is intended to restore the appetite by balancing the humors in accordance with Galenic medicine, like the compounds he describes as given to "jaded women."[67] In contrast to *Selva*, more extreme forms of variety are now not only a source of pleasure in themselves but the remedy to a declining demand (i.e., appetite) for music. Vecchi offers a sequence of musical "courses" that balance different humors—shifting between *grave* and *piacevole* affects as well as between larger and smaller ensembles with more flexibility than he had in the more systematically ordered *Selva*. Although the fluid organization of *Convito* is conspicuous to the reader, the book was not intended, either practically or ideally, for complete performances; Vecchi is quite clear that singers should choose whichever pieces suit their humors at any given moment.

In the closing passage of the preface, Vecchi returns to his anti-Epicurean stance, praising the pleasures of a simple and moderate diet before ending with a surprising comment that suggests a segue from this imagined speech directly into the music of the book:

> With all this, if it should seem to some glutton, overly greedy for musical spices, that this banquet is sparingly provided with dishes, let him learn now that when the stomach receives food in moderation, it digests it the more readily. In a word, let these preparations be measured, not by their multitude or by the sweetness of the foods, but by the liberality of the host, who is lavishly spending what he finds in the purse of his feeble wit. For men of discretion praise a simple, familiar banquet as much more apt to call for serenity of spirit than one that by an excessive number of dishes fills the stomach and the ears to overflowing without satisfying it. But it is enough to have talked so much, for I see that the tables are now set and the dishes prepared.[68]

The deictic final sentence locates the speaker amidst the preparations for the banquet, not only describing the tables but emphasizing that he *sees* them, vividly evoking the imagery of the book's central metaphor. This invitation "to the Readers" extends into the sung *proemio*.

The Music of *Convito musicale*

The imagined move from the forest of *Selva* to the feast of *Convito musicale* that Vecchi suggested for Ferdinand in the dedication continues in the *proemio*, which addresses the singers.

Voi che già stanchi sete	You who are already tired
Di mirar l'alto abete,	of contemplating the high fir tree,
Il verdeggiant'allor, l'ombrosio faggio,	the evergreen laurel, the shady beech,
Et altre piante nel fiorito Maggio,	and other plants of the flowering May,
Per la selv'hoggimai non v'aggirate,	do not go about through the forest henceforth,
S'altro piacer bramate,	if you wish other pleasure,
Mentre vi chiam'e invito,	while I call and invite you,
Per ristorarvi al Musical Convito.	to restore yourselves at this Musical Banquet.[69]

The poem both refers to the forest of *Selva* and mirrors the invitational mode of that book's own *proemio,* especially its last line, "venite à ricrearvi in questa SELVA." Readers must understand the intertextual reference for the poem to make sense.

Convito continues in a manner somewhat similar to *Selva,* though with more pieces in most of the voice groups and more flexibility in their juxtapositions (table 3.3).[70] In contrast to the explicit genre labels in *Selva,* here they are mostly absent, though there is little ambiguity. The five-voice *proemio* is followed by eleven madrigals (not labeled as such) for five voices and three for six voices. In all of these, Vecchi eschews the pastoralisms that had come to dominate in his 1589 *Madrigali a cinque voci* and in *Selva,* as though the metaphorical shift from the forest to the courtly banquet entailed a shift toward internalized Petrarchan speech as well. One of these pieces, "Fummo felici un tempo" (no. 11), had in fact been Vecchi's contribution, fifteen years earlier, to the distinctly Petrarchan Ferrarese anthology *Il lauro secco.*[71] Another, no. 10, "Veder beltà divina," is a slight variation of the sestet to Petrarch's sonnet "In qual parte del ciel," and two other poems, no. 5, "Corre la nave mia colma di gioia," and the final six-voice madrigal of this group, no. 18, "Vanne la nave mia pront'e sicura," likewise allude to the maritime imagery of Petrarch's *sestina* "Chi è fermato di menar sua vita," which Vecchi gives an austere four-voice setting later in *Convito.*

Two final unlabeled six-voice pieces, nos. 16 and 17, "Felice schiera di leggiadr'e belle" and "Non più pen' e tormenti," mark both a poetic and a musical shift toward the canzonetta style. The poetic tone shifts from Petrarchan to pastoral, with references to shepherds singing in "Felice schiera di leggiadr'e belle" and a first-person-plural declaration of joy in "Non più pen' e tormenti." As in Vecchi's six-voice canzonettas, the settings are mostly homophonic and use triple meter liberally. In "Felice schiera," Vecchi even repeats the first and last sections in the manner of the *villanesca* and his early canzonettas. These canzonettas thus form a transition to the two *villotte*—identified as such— that follow (see chapter 6). The decision to give the *villotte* explicit generic labels reflects the relative rarity of the rustic style by this late date, as well as Vecchi's having mentioned *villotte* among the lighter genres in the preface.

The more unusual pieces continue with two depictions of games: the rustic drinking-scene "O Giardiniero!," which combines elements of the *villotta* and *vinata,* and the "Bando del asino." This two-part piece, still for six voices, depicts two imitative games played in precisely the style prescribed by

Table 3.3. Contents of *Convito musicale*

	INCIPIT	GENRE OR TITLE	VOICES	CLEFS	SIGNATURE/ FINAL
1	Voi che gi's stanchi sete maggior meraviglia	Proem [madrigal]	5	g2/c1/c3/c3/f3	♭/F
2	Che nova Cintia/Ma	[Madrigal]	5	g2/c1/c3/c3/f3	♭/F
3	Ahi tormentosi abissi	[Madrigal]	5	g2/c2/c3/c3/f3	♭/F
4	Ti die natura	[Madrigal]	5	c1/c2/c4/c4/f4	♭/G
5	Corre la Nave mia	[Madrigal]	5	g2/g2/c2/c3/f3	♮/G
6	Questo legato in oro	[Madrigal]	5	g2/g2/c2/c3/c4	♮/G
7	Lunghi danni (Petrarch)	[Madrigal]	5	c1/c3/c4/c4/f4	♮/D
8	Augellin, che la voce/ O soave cagion	[Madrigal]	5	c1/c3/c4/c4/f4	♮/D
9	Candida d'oriente perla	[Madrigal]	5	g2/g2/c2/c3/f3	♭/G
10	Veder beltà divina (Petrarch)	[Madrigal]	5	c1/c3/c3/c4/f4	♮/D
11	Fummo felici un tempo (Tasso)	[Madrigal]	5	c1/c1/c3/c4/f4	♭/G
12	Se la luce vital	[Madrigal]	5	g2/c1/c3/c3/f3	♭/G
13	Donna, se voi m'odiate	[Madrigal]	6	g2/g2/c1/c3/c4/c4	♮/A
14	Io ardo e'l celo/Hor che farem	[Madrigal]	6	g2/g2/c2/c3/c3/f3	♭/G
15	Vanne la nave mia	[Madrigal]	6	c1/c3/c4/c4/f3/f4	♮/D
16	Felice schiera	[Madrigal]	6	c1/c1/c3/c4/c4/f4	♮/D
17	Non più pene	[Madrigal]	6	c1/c2/c3/c4/c4/f4	♮/D
18	Non mi toccare	*Villotta*	6	g2/c1/c2/c3/c3/c4	♮/C
19	Sapete voi Bifolci	*Villotta*	6	g2/g2/c2/c3/c3/f3	♮/G
20	O Giardiniero/Hor prendi/Quest'è un altra	Giardiniero [*Vinate*]	6	c1/c2/c3/c4/c4/f4	♮/D
21	Questa ghirlanda/ Ciascun di voi	"Bando del asino"	6	g2/g2/c2/c3/c3/c4	♮/D
22	O Bacco Bacco	[*Vinate*]	6	g2/g2/c2/c3/c3/f3	♮/G
23	Hor ch'ogni vento	[Madrigal]	6	c1/c1/c3/c4/c4/f4	♭/F
24	Miri e stupisca	[Madrigal]	6	g2/g2/c2/c3/c3/c4	♮/A
25	Chi è fermato (Petrarch) /L'Aura soave/Chiuso gran tempo/Come lume di notte/Non perch'io sia /S'io esca vivo	*Canzone* (in Tavola), *sestina* (in headings)	4	g2/c2/c3/c4	♮/C
26	Angioletta fugace	*Madrigale*	4	g2/c2/c3/f3	♭/G
27	Amor se tu vedrai	*Madrigale*	4	c1/c3/c4/f4	♮/D
28	O bella Primavera	*Madrigale pastoreccio*	4	c1/c3/c4/f4	♮/D
29	Felice e liete piaggie	Canzonetta	4	g2/g2/c2/c3	♭/G
30	Chi vuol goder' il mondo	*Privilegi della corte*	4	c1/c3/c4/f4	♭/G

Table 3.3. Contents of *Convito musicale* (cont.)

	INCIPIT	GENRE OR TITLE	VOICES	CLEFS	SIGNATURE/ FINAL
31	Pastor tutti correte	[Canzonetta]	4	g2/g2/g2/c3	♭/G
32	Sott'un ombrogio faggio	[Canzonetta]	4	g2/g2/c1/c3	♭/F
33	Buon dì e buon anno	L'anno novo [Canzonetta]	4	g2/g2/c1/c3	♭/F
34	O cara bocca	*Dialogo* [Canzonetta]	4	c1/c2/c3/f4	♭/G
35	Più cantar non vogliamo	*Moresca de schiavi*	4	c1/c3/c4/f4	♭/D
36	Non basta contentarmi	[Canzonetta]	4	g2/g2/c2/c3	♭/G
37	Gode la terra/Gioisce l'aria e'l cielo/E per maggior dolcezza/ O vago canto	Canzonettas	3	g2/c1/c3	♮/G
38	Ingrat'Aminta	*Dialogo*, Aminta e Clori [Canzonetta]	3	g2/g2/c4	♮/C
39	Chi vi mira	Canzonetta	3	c1/c1/f4	♮/A
40	Tibrina	*Dialogo*, Tibrina e Aminta [Canzonetta]	3	c3&g2/c3&g2/f3&c3	♮/C
41	Non mi stornir	*Giustiniana*	3	c4/c4/f4	♭/F
42	Semo tre vecchietti	[*Giustiniana*]	3	c2/c3/c4	♮/C
43	Servo a un'ingrata	[*Giustiniana*]	3	c3/c3/c4	♮/A
44	Co vedo la mia Dona	[*Giustiniana*]	3	c2/c3/c4	♮/D
45	Non v'accorze	[*Giustiniana*]	3	c2/c3/c4	♮/D
46	E vorave saver	[*Giustiniana*]	3	c1/c3/c4	♮/C
47	Quando penso	[*Giustiniana*]	3	c3/c3/c4	♮/C
48	O gramo Pantalon (Croce?)	*Dialogo in Echo* [*Giustiniana*]	6	c2/c3/c4//c2/c3/c4	♮/C
49	Amor e foco	*Dialogo*	7	c1/c2/c4//c3/c3/c4/f4	♭/G
50	In questa piaggia	[*Dialogo*]	8	c1/c3/c4/f4//c1/c3/c4/f4	♭/F
51	Coppia reale	[*Dialogo*]	8	c1/c3/c4/f4//c1/c2/c3/c4	♭/F

Girolamo Bargagli in his treatise on Sienese games, which was to be a more explicit influence on Vecchi's *Veglie di Siena* of 1604 (see chapter 5). The six-voice group is completed with three shorter pieces that may originally have had theatrical functions. No. 24, "O Bacco, apportator de l'allegrezza," is a hymn to Bacchus in the form of a *vinata*, while no. 25, "Hor ch'ogni vento tace" (whose quotation of Petrarch in the incipit can only be a joke), is a call for nymphs and shepherds to sing in honor of "my" Licori. The first-person subject of the poem thus places itself within a company of participating singers. No. 26, "Miri e stupisca il mondo," is a more formal piece lacking in first-person terms altogether, focusing instead on Nichea, who is announced

Example 3.3. (*above and facing*) Vecchi, "Chi è fermato," *sesta parte,* mm. 38–47.

44

la.

la, l'af - fan - na - ta ve - la.

fan - na - ta ve - - - la.

la, l'af - fan - na - ta ve - - - la.

as being visibly present in the opening couplet: "Let the world gaze and marvel, / let heaven marvel too: this is Nichea." The celebrations of fictive characters in these three pieces suggest staged spectacles, but once they are recontextualized in *Convito musicale* as a sequence of dishes at a metaphorical banquet, this function drops away.

The centerpiece of *Convito*, at least in terms of intellectual seriousness, is the four-voice setting of Petrarch's *sestina* "Chi è fermato di menar sua vita." Vecchi's archaically contrapuntal four-voice setting underscores the *gravità* of Petrarch's text; it resembles Marenzio's four-voice madrigals from his unusual collection of self-consciously *grave* poems (including several Petrarch settings), the *Madrigali a quattro, cinque e sei voci.*[72] The retrospective musical style is particularly clear in the final part, "S'io esca vivo de dubbiosi scogli," which opens with imitation in paired voices and continues in a persistently imitative style, including an inverted point on the phrase "Ch'io sarei vago di volta la vela" (How pleased I would be to change sail), which vividly portrays the desire to change direction. The piece ends with an extended cadence reminiscent of Arcadelt (example 3.3).

The *sestina* is followed by a set of four-voice songs in progressively lighter genres that return to more up-to-date styles: two madrigals; a rustic *madrigale pastoreccio*, including instrumental imitations; a canzonetta; and a piece criticizing courtly pretension titled "Privilegi della corte" (no. 30) that is clearly modeled on "So ben mi c'ha bon tempo" (see chapter 6). The next group exemplifies the style of Vecchi's four-voice canzonettas (including the unusually high *voci pari* range) but resonate with the cynicism of "Privilegi della corte" by inverting typical pastoral tropes. The four stanzas of no. 33,

"Pastor tutti correte," begin as a typical call for shepherds and shepherdesses to hear the playing of pipes, but in successive stanzas, farmers, scholars, and finally singers are likewise urged to leave their usual occupations and take pleasure in music with others of their own class—note the use of "nostro" in the fourth line of each stanza:

Pastor tutti correte,	All shepherds, run,
Correte pastorelle,	run, shepherdesses,
Frà gl'arbori odoriferi	through the fragrant trees
Al suon de nostri Pifferi.	to the sound of our pipes.
Ta na na no. [etc.]	
Signor tutti lasciate	All gentlemen, leave
Il vostro toppa, e massa,	your patch, and large farms,
E'l vostro para, e dicoli	and your shelter, I tell them,
Al suon de nostri Agricoli.	for the sound of our farmers.
Ta na na no. [etc.]	
Dottor tutti venite,	All doctors, come,
Lasciate i vostri testi,	leave your texts
Se voi volete ridere,	if you want to laugh
Al nostro dolce stridere.	at our sweet tones.
Ta na na no. [etc.]	
Cantor tutti lasciate	All singers, leave
Il vostro dolce canto	your sweet song,
Pomposo e maestrevole,	ceremonious and masterful,
E udite il dilettevole.	and hear the amusing one.
Ta na na no. [etc.]	

By addressing a notional audience of contemporary professionals, including singers, the song parodies pastoral conventions by evoking urban life and even the immediate context of recreational music making.

The four remaining four-voice pieces, all in canzonetta-like musical styles, likewise extend the poetic conventions of the style: an archaic New Year's song; a simple dialogue in which the lovers' questions and answers are associated with Canto-Alto-Tenore and Alto-Tenore-Basso textures; a *moresca de schiavi* with yet another text incipit, "Piu cantar non vogliamo / Come già solevamo," that invokes Petrarch (here the *canzona* "Mai non vo' piu cantar com' io soleva") before continuing in an earthier fashion; and a final piece in the first-person singular that openly begs for sexual gratification, "Non basta contentarmi di parole." All of these pieces are in some sense parodistic, giving recreational singers the opportunity to enact attitudes and desires far from those they would ordinarily display.

The three-voice pieces return to the light genres mentioned in Vecchi's promised "ragout," namely, canzonettas and *giustiniane*. Vecchi expands the strophic canzonetta text of no. 39, "Gode la terr' e 'l mare," into a through-composed setting, though each section is in the binary form by now typical of the three-voice canzonetta. This elaboration of the form is prompted by the poem, a celebration of music that provides special opportunities for text depiction. The last of the group, no. 42, "Tibrina, bella Tibrina," introduces another innovation: the depiction of a male-female dialogue with clef changes in all three parts that suggest an alternation between conventional and falsetto singing. This idea was subsequently developed further by Adriano Banchieri in his three-voice adaptations of *L'Amfiparnaso* (see chapter 4). Banchieri writes that such a setting could ideally be performed by six singers to represent the two characters, implying that the more usual practice was the use of *alla bastarda* (falsetto) singing. The fact that Vecchi feels no need to provide such an explanation suggests that this use of falsetto was common enough to be self-evident from his notation—had he intended "Tibrina, bella Tibrina" to be sung by six singers, he could simply have distributed the parts among the first six part books of *Convito musicale*.

This was in fact precisely how Vecchi notated the six-voice *giustiniana* "in echo" (no. 50, "O gramo Pantalon, mal'arivao") that concludes the following group of *giustiniane*. These retain the poetic style, narrow total vocal range, and stuttering effects of the *giustiniana* in *Selva*, but five of them use the strophic texts and binary forms associated with the canzonetta. The echo piece, "O gramo Pantalon," is a resetting of a text used by Giovanni Croce in his *Triaca musicale* (1595).[73] It enacts the usual parody of the Venetian *vecchio* by placing him in the context of an echo dialogue, a normally serious genre in which a solitary lover's words are echoed back to him, usually with the final sonority of each echoed line forming a new word. Such poems had their renaissance model in Poliziano's "Che fai tu, Ecco, mentr'io ti chiamo?—Amo" (What do you do, Echo, when I call you?—I love) and continued to influence scenes of lament in operas of the seventeenth century.[74] Croce and Vecchi satirize the genre by replacing the lover with a *vecchio* who fails to recognize the echo for what it is until the end of the piece, notwithstanding the banality of most of the echo's responses.[75] Pantalone's ineloquence is reflected also in occasional spoken lines, which are notated in all three of the part books (Canto, Tenore, and Basso) that carry the main text. Although echo dialogues are ordinarily associated with theater, Vecchi's parody belongs to the realm of recreational song, since *giustiniane* are less susceptible to adaptation for solo singers than canzonettas are.

The introduction of a larger ensemble by way of "O gramo Pantalon" prepares us for the final three works for seven and eight voices, which are all polychoral but do not set dialogic texts. Like the eight- and ten-voice works in *Selva*, they all seem likely to have been written for theatrical functions. The seven-voice "Amor' è foco" (no. 49) is in the pastoral mode and depicts a plural "we" declaring love's treachery and finally forswearing it, much in the manner of a theatrical act-ending chorus. Nos. 50 and 51, "In questa piaggia" and "Coppia reale e bella," serve ceremonial functions. The latter is a wedding piece, and the former suggests a knightly investiture or similar ritual:

In questa piaggia amena	In this delightful slope,
Ove giamai non verna,	where it is never winter,
Ma dolc'aria serena	but sweet serene air
Fa Primavera eterna,	makes spring eternal,
Pose la gran Zirfea	the great Zirfea
La gloria di Nichea.	laid the glory of Nichea.
Sù Cavalieri invitti,	Rise, invincible knights,
Che vi son Mill'honor ivi	because a thousand honors are prescribed
prescritti.	for you there.[76]

Compared to the vivid contrasts of register and affect in *Selva* and its strict ordering of ensembles from small to large (excepting the opening five-voice group), a sequential reading of *Convito musicale* moves more subtly between high and low genres, with certain pieces or groups serving a transitional function, and ensemble sizes shifting somewhat more freely. This arrangement does not argue for performing *Convito musicale* as a complete work, much less as constituting a dramatic unity: Vecchi's clear indication in the preface is that singers should choose the songs most suited to their taste (and to their available resources). His modest claim that he is "lavishly spending what he finds in the purse of his feeble wit" can only be meant ironically: the fifty-one pieces in *Convito* obviate the practicality of a complete performance in any typical social setting, far exceeding those of the twelve in the *Corona di dodici sonetti* (1586, to which Vecchi contributed the last work) or the fourteen of *L'Amfiparnaso* (1597), books whose poetic unity and consistent ensemble size strongly recommend integral performance. Yet as with any book of polyphony, *Convito musicale* must have been browsed sequentially by singers choosing what to sing, and it might have been read in this way for its own sake by silent readers.

The more subtle organization of *Convito musicale* develops the poetics of variety and pleasure that Vecchi first enunciated in the dedication to *Selva,* balancing them against the practical considerations of singing from separate part books. Despite the book's seeming overabundance, the ordering tacitly endorses Cicero's anti-Epicurean argument in *De bonorum et malorum finibus:* mere satiety is less enjoyable than the ever-shifting stimulus (or "kinetic pleasure") of works in different styles, genres, and registers.

4 *L'Amfiparnaso*
Picturing Theater and the Problem of the "Madrigal Comedy"

In *The Italian Madrigal* Alfred Einstein complained of the "oceans of ink" that had been spilled over *L'Amfiparnaso,* and indeed in the two centuries preceding his study, virtually all writing on Vecchi centered on this book and on its status as an operatic, proto-operatic, or dramatic work.[1] It may be surprising, then, that the earliest historical writer to mention Vecchi, Filippo Picinelli, in his *Ateneo dei letterari milanesi* (1670), lists fourteen editions of music by the composer, and *L'Amfiparnaso* is not among them.[2] Yet by the early twentieth century this book had become both Vecchi's best-known work, appearing in two different editions, and the defining example of a genre, the so-called madrigal comedy.

In this chapter I read *L'Amfiparnaso* on its own terms and in relation to Vecchi's contemporaneous publications rather than through the ahistorical lens of its relation to the development of opera. An explication of Vecchi's aesthetics of variety and imitation clarifies the book's literary hybridity and contextualizes its idiosyncratic visual presentation, particularly the woodcut illustrations and printed texts that appear at the heading of each piece. Finally, I review the reception history of *L'Amfiparnaso* and other works to show how the genre of madrigal comedy was theorized to define what was generally understood as a teleological dead end.

"Almost All the Actions of the Private Man"

L'Amfiparnaso's fourteen constituent pieces, labeled as scenes within a three-act structure with a prologue, imitate theatrical dialogues and monologues in settings for five voices. While the book traces a narrative typical of sixteenth-century *commedia dell'arte* scenarios, some elements of the plot are more

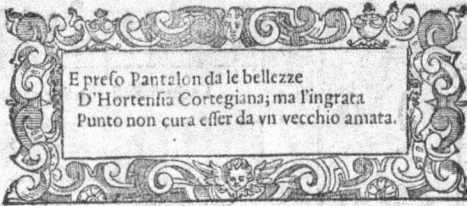

Figure 4.1. *L'Amfiparnaso*, Canto part book, 8: act 1, scene 1.

clearly associated with conventions of pastoral literature, allowing Vecchi to offer some of the poetic and musical variety that characterizes *Selva* and *Convito*. Adding to this novelty is an unprecedented degree of paramusical visual adornment. In the part books, each piece is preceded by a three-line verse *argomento* summarizing (and often augmenting) the action depicted in the

L'Amfiparnaso 133

PROLOGO, LELIO.

Figure 4.2a. *L'Amfiparnaso,* Tenore part book, 4: woodcut for prologue.
© The British Library Board. All rights reserved. Shelfmark K.2.b.1.

music, a custom-made woodcut illustration of the characters and situation represented in the piece, and a complete presentation of the sung text (see, e.g., figure 4.1).

The most novel visual elements of the *L'Amfiparnaso* print, the woodcut illustrations for each scene, have received scant attention from scholars who assumed an audience-directed theatrical or pseudotheatrical performative function for the book.[3] Indeed, readings that assume that *L'Amfiparnaso* is primarily intended for audience-directed performance would have little reason to investigate a visual element in the print that no audience member could see. Gino Roncaglia cited the woodcuts as evidence that Vecchi had

Figure 4.2b. Trapolini, *Antigone, tragedia* (Padua, 1581), act 1.
By permission of the Folger Shakespeare Library.

"theatrical tendencies" even if *L'Amfiparnaso* could not actually be called a theatrical work: "*L'Amfiparnaso* is not yet theater; it is a *dramatic madrigal,* though closer to theater than those works by Striggio and Croce, which were not [dramatic], but [*L'Amfiparnaso* was] not conceived for a staged performance. And this is despite the vignettes that adorn the sixteenth-century book, which undoubtedly make one sense in its author a scenic tendency and make one think instinctively of the theater."[4]

The presence of illustrations, despite their small size and sometimes rough execution, for each piece in a music print or even each scene in a printed play was virtually unprecedented. The *L'Amfiparnaso* woodcuts were carefully planned, skillfully executed, and by no means a haphazard addition to the print—as attested by their preservation and reuse in Gardano's 1610 reprint of the book.[5] Far from functioning as indications of how the work had been or should be performed, they belong to a tradition of illustrating printed plays that were meant primarily for private reading. Vecchi's image for the sung prologue (figure 4.2a), in particular, draws on the style of illustrations for the prologues of Girolamo Parabosco's *Il pellegrino* (1552) and Giovanni Paolo Trapolino's *Antigone* (1581) (figure 4.2b).[6] These images depict an actor (often an allegorical figure but in *L'Amfiparnaso* the *innamorato* Lelio) addressing a visible audience in front of the stage. The stage sets depicted in these woodcuts follow the principles of single-point perspective established in the first published treatise on scenography, a short passage at the end of book 2 of Sebastiano Serlio's *L'Architettura* (1545).[7] As T. E. Lawrenson and Helen Purkis observe, the influence of Serlian set design on book illustrations in the later sixteenth century makes the role of such images ambiguous: they can be read either as prescriptions for performance or as a prompt for readers to imagine both a fictive story and a theatrical performance.[8]

Following the examples of these prologue images, Vecchi's woodcuts employ realistic set designs in ways not seen in later composite illustrations for printed editions of pastorals such as Vincenzo Panciatichi's *Gli amorosi affani* (Venice, 1606) and Giovanni Battista Guarini's *Il pastor fido* (Venice, 1602).[9] Those images appear at the beginning of each act and each one includes vignettes from several different scenes, often depicting the same characters multiple times. Likewise, the depiction of figures in a perspectival set distinguishes the *L'Amfiparnaso* woodcuts from sixteenth- and seventeenth-century series of *commedia* images such as the engravings in the *Recueil Fossard* and Jacques Callot's *Balli di Sfessania* series, which to varying degrees depict characters in more naturalistic settings.[10]

As was his usual practice, Vecchi almost certainly wrote the texts for *L'Amfiparnaso* himself and was also responsible for the work's large-scale organization, artistic program, and complex visual presentation.[11] The dedication of the book to Alessandro d'Este, illegitimate cousin to Duke Alfonso II of Ferrara and half-brother to Cesare d'Este, the future duke of Modena, suggests that Vecchi may have for the first time benefited from the patronage of the powerful and cultured family of which, as a Modenese citizen, he was a subject. The dedication refers to Alessandro having heard and praised a performance of *L'Amfiparnaso,* and he would also have been in a position to underwrite the expenses of producing such an extraordinary print.[12]

Despite the subtitle *Comedia harmonica, L'Amfiparnaso* does not merely paraphrase scenes from a *commedia dell'arte* play; rather, it interpolates into a comic plot situations—specifically two scenes of attempted suicide—that were characteristic of the relatively new literary genre of pastoral tragicomedy.[13] These scenes are distinguished by their poetic subject matter, their musical style, and their visual depiction in the woodcut illustrations. They reflect a poetics of generic mixture that echoes contemporary literary developments—particularly Guarini's theorizing of tragicomedy and the pastoral—while realizing them in a specifically musical form.[14] For Vecchi, such eclecticism emerges from his idiosyncratic views of printed music books as sites of generic intermingling (reflected also in his other secular collections of the 1590s; see chapter 3) and of recreational singing as a game-like form of *imitatio*.

Vecchi's preface seems to anticipate or react to criticism of the book—a rhetorical trait typical of the prefatory texts in his other metaphorically titled books. The preface to *L'Amfiparnaso* is not a description of a new form of theater but rather a defense of the aesthetic of variety that occupied Vecchi's prefatory texts to *Selva* and *Convito* as well, here using the language of literary criticism in a largely metaphorical way. His opening distinguishes between the all-too-common *passatempo buffonesco* and more elevated comedy constructed according to "the proper rules":

> The excessively immodest and too-frequent jests that one sees in today's comedies, included more as meat than as sauce, have made it such that when one says "Comedy" one seems to mean a foolish pastime. And yet they are wrong who give to such a gracious poem a title of such little esteem, since if it is made by the proper rules—if one considers well its substance—it represents in its various characters almost all the actions of the private man, which as a mirror of human life has as its purpose usefulness no less than delight, and not merely the provocation of smiles, as some might believe and would make of this my Musical Comedy, not perceiving its true purpose.[15]

Vecchi's goal is the Aristotelian (and Guarinian) one of eliciting pleasure through successful imitation, the range of which encompasses both ridiculous and serious characters. Yet his assertion that such an imitation can be characterized as belonging to the "private man" is problematic. *L'uomo privato,* a person lacking noble rank, was understood to be the proper subject for comedy as classically defined: Guarini describes the instrumental purpose of comedy as being "to imitate those actions of private men which by their deficiency move us to laughter."[16] This is a paraphrase of Aristotle's *Poetics,* which describes "those who are worse than ourselves" rather than "private men."[17]

However, Lodovico Castelvetro restricts comic characters to commoners in his 1571 commentary on Aristotle not because inferior people are inherently risible but because comedies, unlike tragedies, must be entirely fictitious: "[The poet] is able to shape a happening he has invented in all its parts, and therefore it should concern a private person of whom and of the things that have happened to him no one has any recollection, nor will they be given to the memory of the future through history or fame."[18] Guarini likewise argues that the plot and characters of tragicomedy should be fictional, but in order to accommodate the mixture of comic and tragic elements, he creates "private" characters whose actions are not entirely laughable, namely, pastoral shepherds.[19] While Guarini's reasoning is something of an ex post facto justification for *Il pastor fido,* it conveys the sense in which Vecchi uses the term *l'uomo privato.* Though the four *innamorati* in *L'Amfiparnaso* are not shepherds and shepherdesses, their representation as speakers of quasi-pastoral poetry and, more precisely, the attempted suicides by two of them mimic both the style and plots of contemporary pastoral plays. Vecchi's interpretation of "almost all the actions of the private man" therefore encompasses both comic and serious scenes, as does Guarini's in his pastoral tragicomedy.

The claim that *L'Amfiparnaso* aims for both usefulness and delight reflects contemporary commentaries on Aristotle and Horace, but again Vecchi's poetic priorities resonate more with those of Guarini. The question of utility and moral instruction underlies Vecchi's subsequent apology for the lack of explicit moral conclusions in *L'Amfiparnaso:* "And it is true that its benefit will be somewhat remiss, and less than that of a simple Comedy, because since I had to direct the singing more to the emotions than to morality, it was best that I be greatly sparing of *sententiae.*" This defense espouses the terminology and values of classicist literary criticism while in fact adhering to up-to-date humanist poetics. The principle that Aristotelian *sententiae,* or maxims, carry the moral force in poetry is taken as a given, but the unique power of music to move the affections prompts Vecchi to take a position more consistent with Guarini's in *Il verato secondo:* "[The poet's] end, then, is not to imitate the good, but to imitate well, whether the mores be good or bad; and if he imitates badly what is good, he will not be a good poet, but if he imitates well what is bad, he may be called a good poet."[20]

Vecchi also apologizes for the incompleteness of the plot, blaming the slow pacing of sung text and the lack of opulent staging. Though the scenes do not therefore form a self-sufficient narrative, the reader familiar with dramatic conventions can infer the connections between them to imagine a coherent story:

And then the action is shorter than it should be because, bare speech being quicker than singing with words, it was better not to include certain details of the story so that the hearing would not tire before reaching the end, and this also because the music is not interspersed with visual spectacle such that one sense might relieve the changeability of the other. But whoever desires more action in this may refer every lack to what is assumed and implied within, and not outwardly expressed, and thus one may form in the mind a complete play.

This comment is properly understood as evidence that *L'Amfiparnaso* was not conceived with staging in mind, but I would go further and suggest that by referring to plot elements "sottointeso di dentro, e non espresso di fuori" (implied within, and not outwardly expressed), Vecchi refers not merely to a listening audience's knowledge of theatrical conventions—which logically need not be "implied" to be known—but to specific information conveyed by the woodcut images and *argomenti,* elements available only to singers holding the part books.[21]

This recreational, nontheatrical function admits not only the mixture of comic and tragicomic plot elements but also the inclusion of scenes that exceed the boundaries of either style. Tragicomic suicide scenes like Vecchi's were not staged even in pastoral plays but only narrated. The story imagined by the singers thus constitutes an imitation not only of a theatrical performance but also of life itself. Literary convention lends *L'Amfiparnaso* an organizational structure of acts and scenes that make it superficially resemble a theatrical work, but this formal device is to some extent merely a metaphor to accommodate a heterogeneous variety, like the imagery of the forest and the banquet in *Selva* and *Convito musicale.*

The framing device of the prologue image in *L'Amfiparnaso* confirms for the singers that with their first words addressing the "spettatori illustri" they are envoicing an imaginary figure addressing an imaginary audience, the scenario depicted in the books they are holding in their hands. They are already in the world of an imagined play, which shifts at the words "but meanwhile" to address the reality of the unstaged performance as "Lelio" explains that the play is primarily aural rather than visual:

Benché siat'usi, o spettatori illustri,	Illustrious spectators, although you are
solo di rimirar tragici aspetti	accustomed to see only tragic expressions
o comici apparati	or comic contrivances
in varie guise ornati,	in various ornate manners,
voi però non sdegnate	do not therefore disdain

questa comedia nostra	this our comedy,
se non di ricca e vaga scena adorna	which, if not graced with a rich and lovely stage,
almen di dopia novità composta.	is at least composed of a double novelty.
E la città dove si rappresenta	The city wherein is presented
quest'opre è 'l gran teatro	this work is the great theater
del mondo, perch'ognun desia d'udirla.	of the world, so everyone wants to hear it.
Ma voi sappiat'in tanto	But meanwhile, know
che questo di cui parlo	that this spectacle of which I speak
spettacolo si mira con la mente,	is beheld by the imagination,
dov'entra per l'orecchie e non per gl'occhi.	which it enters through the ears, not the eyes.
Però silenzio fate	Therefore be silent,
e 'n vece di vedere ora ascoltate.[22]	and instead of seeing, now listen.

The sung prologue's framing function thus works on two levels: within the imagined play the visible character Lelio addresses the "spectators" seen at the bottom of the woodcut, but to the real "audience"—that is, the singers or listeners—Vecchi reiterates (as he had in the preface) that the spectacle is not seen but heard. This dual subjectivity helps to clarify the otherwise enigmatic analogy of lines 8–11: "The city wherein is presented this work is the great theater of the world, so everyone wants to hear it." The play is imagined as occurring in a world that is itself a theater, since the actual singers imagine both the actors and the viewing audience addressed by Lelio. Vecchi's invocation of the *teatro del mondo* is thus more complex than the conventional metaphor for theater as an imitation of the real world. Both levels of representation play out in the minds of the singers, who draw on the textual and visual cues in the part books along with their prior knowledge of actors and conventions of the *commedia dell'arte* to create, as Vecchi promises, "a tale completed in the mind."

Of course, *L'Amfiparnaso* should not be read as the direct product of poetic theorizing any more than Guarini's *Il pastor fido* should be. The theatrical styles on which it draws—and from which it sometimes departs—are those of the contemporary *commedia dell'arte* companies that performed both semi-improvised comedies and up-to-date literary plays. Vecchi's texts for *L'Amfiparnaso* include four serious poems set as musical madrigals (including the prologue, a dialogue, and the two suicide monologues) and ten comic dialogues set in the novel contrapuntal style that Vecchi had introduced in the *capriccio* "Tich-toch" in *Selva*. The explicit plot consists of two main strands—one purely comic, one mostly serious—that never intersect until the final scene (see table 4.1) and whose relationship, though easily inferred, is never made explicit. The first is a stereotypical urban comedy involving foolish *vecchi* and *zanni* characters and conforming to conventions familiar from the earliest and largest anthology of *commedia dell'arte* scenarios, Flaminio Scala's *Il teatro delle favole rappresentative*.[23] In three scenes (nos. 4, 10, and 11) the Venetian Pantalone conspires to marry his daughter to the Bolognese Dottore Graziano, while in other scenes Pantalone tries to woo the courtesan Hortensia (no. 2), and one of his servants attempts to do business with some Jews, who sing in mock Hebrew from inside their house (no. 12).[24]

The more serious plot involves the trials of love among the four *innamorati* and Capitan Cardon, one iteration of the Spanish captain who functions in various scenarios as a comic character, an *innamorato*, or both.[25] The *secondi innamorati*, Lelio and Nisa, are featured in just one scene (no. 3), though Lelio is also named as the speaker of the prologue, and both characters reappear in the finale. These are the kind of "partially visible" characters that Vecchi compares in the preface to figures in a crowded painting, extending his argument that much of the play is left to the imagination.[26] The *primi innamorati*, Lucio and Isabella, are more fully depicted and give *L'Amfiparnaso* its partially tragicomic character. Lucio's apparent suicide (no. 6) is followed by Capitan Cardon's comic scenes, first with his servant and then with Isabella (nos. 6 and 7). Immediately upon the captain's departure Isabella laments Lucio's death and prepares to stab herself, only to be interrupted by Lucio's servant, Frulla, with the news that Lucio is alive (nos. 8 and 9). The fulfillment of this reversal is delayed until the lovers' recognition scene (no. 13), which segues into their wedding celebration in the finale (no. 14). This plotline includes some elements (notably the captain's intrusions) that would not be out of place in a comedy, but it turns on the two attempted suicides, events typical of pastoral plots. The comic and tragicomic threads are united only by the presence of all the characters in the final scene, as shown in table 4.1.

Not only are the two groups of characters restricted to separate scenes, but they also never refer to each other in any way. The identification of Isabella as Pantalone's daughter, though highly conventional, is only implicit: she is never actually named as Gratiano's intended bride. In the Scala scenarios

Table 4.1. Scene summary of *L'Amfiparnaso*

NUMBER	ARGOMENTI	ACTION DEPICTED IN SUNG TEXT	SPEAKERS
1. "Benche siat'usi" (prologue)		An explanation that this drama does not appear on a richly adorned stage but enters the mind aurally.	Lelio
2. "O Pierulin" (act 1, scene 1)	È preso Pantalon da le bellezze D'Ortensia cortigiana; ma l'ingrata Punto non cura esser da un vecchio amata.	Pantalone argues with his servant, Pedrolino, and then calls Hortensia, who rejects him.	Pantalone Pedrolino Hortensia
3. "Che volete voi dir" (act 1, scene 2)	Lelio non è sicure che la sua Nisa L'ami, e dal don ch'ella gli diè d'un fiore Geloso, egli argomenta poco amore.	Lelio questions the meaning of a narcissus given him by his beloved, who answers that she loves only herself.	Lelio Nisa
4. "Or per vegnir" (act 1, scene 3)	Promete Pantalon di dar sua figlia Al Dottore e di lui, qual rozzo, prende Piacer, che mal risponde e peggio intende.	Pantalone agrees to let Dottore Gratiano marry his daughter. Their dialogue is marked by malapropisms	Gratiano Pantalone
5. "Misero che farò" (act 2, scene 1)	Lucio per gelosia ch'ha d'Isabella Che non ami Cardone il Capitano Si va a precipitar, d'amor insano.	Lucio, believing that Isabella loves another, vows to go to a high mountain and throw himself off.	Lucio
6. "Viene a qua Zanico" (act 2, scene 2)	Grida Cardon con Zanni, che vorebbe Esser inteso a cenni, e lo confonde Ché mai per dritto senso gli risponde.	Cardon, speaking comical Spanish, commands Zanni to knock on Isabella's door. She appears (silently).	Cardon Zanni
7. "O ecco il capitano" (act 2, scene 3)	Finge Isabella arder di vero amore Con lo Spagnuol, per dar più grave crollo, Morendo, al suo desio non mai satollo.	Isabella flirts with Cardon, who rejoices that she loves him. (The *argomento* confirms that she is feigning.)	Isabella Cardon
8. "Ecco che più non resta" (act 2, scene 4)	Partito il Capitan, tosto Isabella Sfoga il dolor di Lucio e con ardire Il ferro stringe, e vuol di vita uscire.	Isabella laments Lucio's death and prepares to stab herself.	Isabella

Table 4.1. (*cont.*) Scene summary of *L'Amfiparnaso*

NUMBER	ARGOMENTI	ACTION DEPICTED IN SUNG TEXT	SPEAKERS
9. "Ah! Isabella che fai?" (act 2, scene 5)	Frulla impedisce che non abbia effetto / Il colpo d'Isabella, e le dà nova / Che Lucio amante suo viva si trova.	Isabella's suicide is interrupted by Lucio's servant, who tells her that Lucio's suicide was prevented by shepherds.	Frulla / Isabella
10. "Daspuò ch'ho stabilio" (act 3, scene 1)	Or che fra Pantalone e Graziano / Stretto è 'l partito del accasamento / Non lasciano di darsi ogni contento.	Pantalone discusses the wedding guests with Francatrippa, who lists his comical family. Then Gratiano prepares to sing.	Pantalone / Francatrippa / Gratiano
11. "Ancor ch'a parturire" (act 3, scene 2)	Canta il Dottore un madrigal gentile / Sotto 'l balcon de la sua cara sposa / Con voce soavissima e amorosa.	Gratiano serenades his bride and is praised by Pantalone. Francatrippa reports that the bride has invited them inside.	Gratiano / Pantalone / Francatrippa
12. "Tic tac tic toc" (act 3, scene 3)	Va a gli Ebrei Francatrippa a por'un pegno; / La porta forte scuote e una Babelle / S'ode di voci e orribili favelle.	Francatrippa knocks on the Jews' door; he wants to pawn a "hammock" but is refused because it is the Sabbath.	Francatrippa / Jews (inside)
13. "Lassa, che veggio?" (act 3, scene 4)	Trovansi a sorte i duo fedeli amanti / E fatto ch'hanno l'allegrezze insieme / Dansi la fede insino a l'ore estreme.	Isabella and Lucio meet and rejoice. Lelio arrives (silently), and they greet him, noting his suffering on their account.	Isabella / Lucio
14. "Rallegratevi meco" (act 3, scene 5)	Ogn'un s'allegre e gode, e si pon fine / Ai bramati Imenei con varî doni / E dentro fansi feste, nozze e suoni.	Everyone celebrates the wedding and presents Isabella and Lucio with gifts that carry symbolic or erotic associations.	[Lucio / Lelio / Isabella / Pantalone / Nisa / Cardon / Pedrolino / Gratiano]

Pantalone is frequently presented as a father plotting for his daughter to marry against her will, and the precise configuration of Pantalone's conspiring to marry his daughter (or, in one case, ward) to Gratiano occurs in five of the forty comedies in Scala's collection. In each case this marriage plan is thwarted, and the daughter marries for love.[27] The relationship between Pantalone and Isabella is confirmed in works by Adriano Banchieri that were modeled on *l'Amfiparnaso*. In *La pazzia senile* (1598, revised 1599), for example, the *innamorata* Doralice is explicitly identified as Pantalone's daughter.[28]

Vecchi's Comic Dialogues

We have already seen the novel musical technique of the five-voice comic dialogues in *L'Amfiparnaso* adumbrated in Vecchi's earlier music, including not only the *commedia*-influenced *capriccio* "Tich-toch" from *Selva* but also dialogues like "Quella ch'in mille selv'e 'n mille fratte" from the *Madrigali a cinque* and the even earlier "L'hore di recreatione" from the *Madrigali a sei* of 1583. The musical technique of Vecchi's comic dialogues stands apart both from polychoral dialogues, which require large-scale performing forces and identify individual character voices with distinct self-sufficient vocal groupings, and from madrigals depicting multiple speakers in which the full ensemble (with occasional text-depictive exceptions) sings the words of both or all the poetic voices.[29] Vecchi's intimate comic dialogue style delineates characters by shifting between subsets of the five-voice ensemble, most often using three-voice textures in the increasingly popular canzonetta texture of paired upper voices moving in parallel thirds or sixths over a more independent lower line and only occasional use of polyphonic counterpoint. As we have seen, Vecchi used this texture in three-voice arias in *Selva* and *Convito* and more exclusively in the *canzonette a tre voci* he coauthored with Gemignano Capilupi and published just two months before *L'Amfiparnaso*. The less comical dialogue scenes for the *innamorati* (nos. 3 and 13) consistently use the full five-voice texture, and the most serious scenes of all—the suicides—are monologues, which Vecchi sets as thoroughly up-to-date madrigals. The distinctions between poetic registers are thus mirrored by stylistic distinctions in the music.

Most crucially for the function of *L'Amfiparnaso* as a recreational work, specific voice groupings in the comic dialogue style are seldom firmly tied to a single character; instead, the shifts of texture themselves indicate changes of "speaking" voice. This can be seen clearly in the Zanni-Magnifico dialogue "O Pierulin, dov'estu?" (see table 4.2), in which individual singers frequently continue singing when the character-voice shifts, and some three-voice combinations represent different characters at different points (e.g., the combination Canto-Alto-Tenore represents each of the three characters at various points in the piece). Furthermore, some changes in voicing do *not* coincide with changes of speaker, as in Pantalone's lines beginning "Si pianta rave," in which the texture shifts twice during his speech. The subtlety of this technique makes the full printed texts in each part book—where each character's lines are labeled—essential for the singers to understand what is going on, since no individual sung part has the complete text. More than any other musical feature, this comic dialogue style exemplifies the "coupling of music and comic poetry" for which Vecchi takes credit in the preface. However, the full effect of *L'Amfiparnaso* depends on the imaginative synthesis by the reader/ singer of its visual as well as musicopoetic presentation.

As encapsulated in the *scenarii* of Flaminio Scala, the improvised urban comedies for which professional *commedia dell'arte* companies were best known could accommodate most of the scene types presented in *L'Amfiparnaso*, including both the comic scenes described above and some of the *innamorati* scenes. Lelio's complaint on the narcissus in no. 3, "Che volete voi dir," for example, is the sort of stock speech an actor might have kept in his repertoire for use in any appropriate scene, whereas the recognition scene between Isabella and Lucio in no. 13, "Lassa, che veggio?," represents the kind of peripeteia on which practically all *commedia* plots draw. Likewise, the woodcuts depict the conventional urban sets prescribed by Serlio for comedies, with a variety of buildings of different sizes and styles (as opposed to the more ordered rows of large houses appropriate to tragedy). All of the characters who should be "visible" in each scene are depicted in appropriate poses or locations: Hortensia and Nisa appear in elevated windows in nos. 2 and 3, and in no. 11 Gratiano plays a lute while his betrothed listens from a window (though she does not speak). Conversely, the Jews to whom Francatrippa speaks in no. 12 remain hidden behind a door, though we hear them singing from within. While these scenes are all broadly consistent with comic conventions, the specificity with which the woodcuts match these precise configurations is a striking contrast to other illustrations used in Venetian prints of comedies.[30]

Table 4.2. Text distribution and character representation in no. 2, "O Pierulin, dov'estu?"

VOICES*	SPEAKERS	SUNG TEXT	TRANSLATION
T	Pantalone	O Pierulin, dov'estu?	O Pedrolino, where are you?
		Dov'estu Pierulin?	Where are you, Pedrolino?
5	Pedrolino	Messir no' poss' vegni che su in Cusina.	Sir, I can't come, I'm up in the kitchen.
CAT	Pantalone	Ah laro ah can' che fastu in Cusina?	Rascal, dog, what are you doing in the kitchen?
CT5B	Pedrolino	A m'imp'u'l gargatù de cert cotai	I'm stuffing my throat with
CAT5B		Che canta tucch'u'l dì,	certain things That sing all day,
		Pi pi ri pi	Pi pi ri pi
		Cu cu ru cu	Cu cu ru cu
ATB	Pantalone	Ah bestia ti vol dir	O brute, what you mean to say
5B		E Galett'e Pizzon'.	Is chickens and pigeons.
		hor sù vien fora	Quickly, come here!
CAT	Pedrolino	Chem commandef messir Piantalimù?	What do you wish, Sir Lemon-Planter?
5B	Pantalone	Si pianta rave,	One plants radishes,
T5B		e no piantalimon.	not lemons.
A5B		Sù chiama Hortensia pezzo de poltron.	Call Hortensia, you poltroon!
CAT	Pedrolino	Hortensia Hortensia!	Hortensia, Hortensia!
5B	Pantalone	Che disela?	What does she say?
CAT	Pedrolino	La dis ch'andè in bon' hora!	She tells you to go away!
A5B	Pantalone	Ah porco aspetta che la chiama mi.	Pig! Wait, I'll call her myself.
		Hortensia, Horten-en-en-en-sia! en-sia!	Hortensia, Horten-en- en-sia!
CAT	Hortensia	E ch'è quell'importun che chiama Hortensia?	What pest keeps calling Hortensia?
A5B	Pantalone	Un vostro servior.	Your servant.
CAT	Hortensia	Che servitore? Vatene in mal'hora!	What servant? Go get lost!
		Vecchiaccio ribambito,	Childish old fool,
		Credi ch'io sia una Donna da partito?	Do you think I'm a lady to be had?
T5B	Pantalone	Pian pian cara Madonna.	Softly, softly, dear woman.
		Voleu che ve diga	Would you permit me to say
		Una parola sol da vù e mi?	Just a word between you and me?
CAT	Hortensia	No ch'io non voglio no,	No, I would not, no!
CAT5		S'io'l so s'io'l so?	Do I know it or do I know it?
		Flo flo flo flo.	Run along now!
		Mira che garbo	Look at his manners!
		Mira che fusto	Look at his figure!
		Havrei ben gusto.	I'd have a good time!
		Flo flo flo flo.	Now run along!
CAT5B	Pantalone	O povero Pantalon, ah Donna ingrata	O poor Pantalone, O ungrateful woman.
		Quando po ti vorrà mi no vorrò.	Next time you want it, I won't want you!

*C = Canto, A = Alto, T = Tenore, B = Basso, 5 = Quinto.

Lucio's Lament

Though Renaissance literary theorists unanimously rejected the portrayal of death in comic plots (reserving it for tragedies), "false deaths" occupy a more ambiguous position. Comic plots sometimes turn on feigned or mistaken death and allow for scenes of lamentation (played for humorous or pathetic effect), but the comic Scala scenarios do not include suicides, whether completed or not.[31] Even allowing for the possibility that some improvising actors might talk of killing themselves in such scenes (as they surely did in tragicomic ones), comic plots never depend on sincere attempts at self-slaughter.[32]

The suicidal shepherd is, on the other hand, a defining motif of the pastoral style, from its earliest sixteenth-century Ferrarese examples up through its best-known specimens, Tasso's *Aminta* (performed in 1573) and Guarini's *Il pastor fido* (completed by 1585 but not published until 1590). Although an explicit theory of tragicomedy emerged only in Guarini's writings, culminating in his *Compendio* (1599), the uncompleted suicide is a feature of most *cinquecento* pastoral plays and the classical eclogues on which they were in some respects modeled. Shepherds (and, more rarely, nymphs) may openly express the desire to die either in the face of unrequited love or in the belief that a lover is dead. These constraints on motivation are consistent with Giuseppe Gerbino's characterization of Arcadia as a place where internal emotions are translated into physical action as a matter of routine: "By relocating the inner life of the Petrarchist lover in the collective dimension of the pastoral community, Petrarch's introverted individualism was recontextualized as a social fact. The 'Arcadianization' of the discourse on love adapted the solitary and introspective psychologism of the *Canzoniere* to the social structure of the court."[33]

Of course, to restrain the pastoral plot from straying irretrievably into the realm of tragedy, the suicide must fail—either through accident or interruption—enabling the lovers' eventual reunion. Yet the threat of imminent heartbroken tragedy is one of the pastoral's most powerful and distinctive features. Both of the interrupted suicides in *L'Amfiparnaso* depart drastically from the prevailing comic tone in their poetry, music, and visual styles.

The shift from comic to pastoral is immediately evident in Lucio's suicide attempt, depicted in no. 5, "Misero che farò," in which the comic dialogue style of the preceding scenes is replaced by a musically sophisticated madrigal. The opening line introduces chromatic motion in the Alto (example 4.1a) and a particularly harsh simultaneous G/G♯ cross-relation between Alto and Canto (m. 3). The piece continues in the most up-to-date madrigalian style, featuring avoided and evaporated cadences, chromatic motion, and text setting that responds to both poetic imagery and affect, culminating as Lucio describes hurling himself from a clifftop in downward arpeggios on "col precipizio mio" (example 4.1b) that probably predate Luca Marenzio's well-known use of a similar device in *Solo e pensoso* (published in 1599).

The complete poem, however, is not so straightforward a depiction of a death as the music might suggest:

Misero che farò, Lucio infelice,	Miserable, what shall I do, unhappy Lucio,
s'ogni mio ben è tolto?	if all my joy is gone?
Ah, finto amore, e stolto,	Ah, false and foolish love,
ah, crudel Isabella,	ah, cruel Isabella,
che per novell'amor mi sei rubella!	since a new love has robbed me of you!
Ma nel più alpestre mont'i vad'or ora,	But into the wildest mountains I am now going,
perché ne l'ultim'ora	so that in my final hour
fia sazio il tuo desio,	your wish will be granted,
donna crudel, col prezipizio mio.	cruel lady, with my fall.

If this monologue were staged, Lucio would not yet have gone to the mountains, and his "final hour" would clearly still lie ahead. In this sense, the melodic plunges on "precipizio mio" are mere word painting, not a musical representation of action happening as Lucio speaks. In the imagined form of *L'Amfiparnaso,* however, the poem's meaning is more ambiguous. The emphasis on movement away from "here" in the line "Ma nel più alpestre mont'i vad'or ora" can be read either in the present tense with future meaning ("I am going now," i.e., in just a moment) or in the progressive aspect ("I am now going," i.e., in this moment). The latter reading defies the logic of a visible stage and places Lucio's final spoken lines at the clifftop itself, so that the descending arpeggios can be taken not merely as a madrigalism for his words "precipizio mio" but as a musical depiction of Lucio's actual suicide attempt.

The contrast with the limitations of stage action is highlighted by a comparison of Vecchi's language with that of the title character in Tasso's

Example 4.1a. Vecchi, *L'Amfiparnaso*, no. 5, "Misero, che farò," mm. 1–6.

Aminta, one of the most influential *cinquecento* pastorals. Aminta, preparing to kill himself over the believed death of his beloved, Silvia, has asked Nerina and Dafne to give him Silvia's bloodied veil; their refusal spurs his final departure, but this can only be conveyed onstage by his sudden exit and the remaining characters' description of the speed with which he runs away—a sight that they must describe, because it is invisible to the audience:

Example 4.1b. (*above and facing*) Vecchi, *L'Amfiparnaso,* no. 5,
"Misero, che farò," mm. 30–41.

AMINTA: Crudel, sì picciol dono
mi nieghi al punto estremo?
E 'n questo anco maligno
mi si mostra il mio fato. Io cedo, io cedo:
a te si resti: e voi restate ancora,
ch'io vo per non tornare.

Oh, harsh! You do deny
so small a gift, my last
request? My cruel fate
in this too shows itself. I yield, I yield:
you keep it then. And also stay back.
I go and won't return.

DAFNE: Aminta, aspetta, ascolta ...   Aminta, wait, and hear ...
Ohimé, con quanta furia egli si parte!   Alas, he left in such a maddened state!

NERINA: Egli va sì veloce,   He goes so swiftly
che fia vano seguirlo.   that it would be vain to follow him.[34]

Aminta's final speech at the clifftop itself is reported only in secondhand narration in act 4, scene 2, by Ergasto, who also describes Aminta's suicidal leap. By analogy with these stage conventions, Vecchi's musical and poetic representation of Lucio's speech could therefore be interpreted as a parallel to the earlier scene in *Aminta,* but with Lucio narrating his own departure for the mountains. However, the illustration in the *L'Amfiparnaso* print contradicts this scenario, complicating the singers' understanding of what their singing actually imitates.

The woodcut accompanying this madrigal, in comparison with the others in the book, is unusually ambitious (figure 4.3). Although the artist depicts the grand buildings that convey both an urban setting and a tragic Serlian scene, the foreground is dominated by a wild clifftop from which two men restrain a third from leaping. The artist shows an unusually precise concern for perspective, and the sky is ornamented, uniquely among the *L'Amfiparnaso* woodcuts, with shading that suggests clouds. Moreover, the three figures are shown in a moment of tension, whereas the other illus-

L'Amfiparnaso 151

ATTO Secondo. Scena Prima. Lucio ſolo.

Figure 4.3. *L'Amfiparnaso,* Tenore part book, 14: woodcut for act 2, scene 1.
© The British Library Board. All rights reserved. Shelfmark K.2.b.1.

trations, with their more theatrical aspect, depict static poses and conventionalized gestures. The dramatic energy of this vignette is approached only once more in *L'Amfiparnaso,* in the parallel scenes of Isabella's lament and interrupted suicide. The artist seems to have understood the generic differences between comic and tragicomic scenes and to have given special care to the latter. The exceptional content and artistic quality of this image not only exceed what would normally be possible in *commedia* performances, which are necessarily constrained to the generic stage floor used elsewhere in *L'Amfiparnaso,* but also mark a shift from the urban locale of the rest of the book to a quasi-pastoral landscape in which the required clifftop rises before the ever-present buildings.

Most striking of all, however, is the radical disjunction between the text and the image. Although the rubric labels the piece "Atto secondo, scene prima. Lucio solo" and the text suggests that Lucio makes his speech either before or during his ascent to the mountains, the woodcut shows him on the clifftop with the two shepherds who, we are later told, *heard* his lament and came to save his life. The illustration is therefore not the scene depicted in the poem and music but rather the one described by the servant Frulla in act 2, scene 4, in which he interrupts Isabella's suicide with the news that Lucio is alive:

FRULLA: È vero che che volea precipitarsi,	It's true that he wanted to leap,
ma certi pastorelli	but certain shepherds
ch'erano quivi intorno,	who were near there
uditi I suoi gravosi alti lamenti,	heard his sad and loud laments
fur sì presti al soccorso	and rushed quickly to his aid
che non seguì l'effetto	so that he did not effect
del folle suo desio.	the madness of his intent.

A useful comparison can made with an illustrated edition of *Aminta* published in 1589.[35] Here a woodcut is provided for each act rather than for each scene, and these depict multiple vignettes, showing various scenes from the act. The act 4 woodcut (figure 4.4) depicts scene 2 in the foreground, with Ergasto relating his tale to Dafne and Silvia. In the upper right corner, however, we see the event he is describing: Ergasto atop the cliff watching Aminta in mid-fall. Like the *L'Amfiparnaso* woodcut, this image shows a scene that is not enacted on the stage, but unlike it, nothing in the *Aminta* image assures the reader that the suicide will be averted. The Tasso illustration thus works in conjunction with the text to develop dramatic tension that will only be resolved in act 5, when Elpino reports that Aminta's fall was not fatal, whereas the music, text, and woodcut in *L'Amfiparnaso* conflate Lucio's departure for the mountains, his suicide attempt, and his last-minute rescue.

Isabella Interrupted

In contrast to the complicated presentation of Lucio's suicide attempt, Isabella's equivalent scene, no. 8, "Ecco che piu non resta," is clearly depicted in its woodcut as an onstage monologue. The *argomento* specifies that the scene follows directly from the previous one, a comic dialogue between Isabella and Capitan Cardon: "As soon as the captain is gone Isabella / relates her pain over Lucio and ardently / seizes the blade and would end her life." As

ATTO QVARTO.

SCENA PRIMA.

Dafne. Siluia. Choro.

Figure 4.4. Tasso, *Aminta* (Venice: Aldo Manucci, 1589), 72: woodcut for act 4.
© The British Library Board. All rights reserved. Shelfmark 11715.a.71.

with Lucio's "Misero che farò," both the music and the woodcut for this scene reveal an altogether more serious and ambitious plan than the comic scenes in *L'Amfiparnaso*. The music resembles the generally homophonic and harmonically advanced "heroic" rhetorical style associated with settings of poetry from Tasso's *Gerusaleme liberata* from the 1580s and 1590s by Giaches de Wert and Monteverdi.[36] The piece also matches the chromati-

Example 4.2. Vecchi, *L'Amfiparnaso*, no. 8, "Ecco che più non resta," mm. 18–24.

cism of "Misero che farò" and may refer to it more specifically with a similar cross-relation in m. 20 (example 4.2), in which a move from E major to E minor on the lines "Chiaro vedrai ch'io vissi a te fedele. E tu fosti crudele" (You will see clearly that I was faithful to you, and you were cruel) refers to Lucio and resembles the cross-relation to which he spoke his own name (see m. 3 of example 4.1a).

ATTO Secondo. Scena Quarta. Isabella sola.

Figure 4.5. *L'Amfiparnaso,* Alto part book, 22: woodcut for act 2, scene 4.
© The British Library Board. All rights reserved. Shelfmark K.2.b.1.

The woodcut's visual seriousness again mirrors the musical style. The groups of large houses on each side of the set form a pair of unbroken façades receding in perspective from the lower corners of the frame, resembling Serlio's *scena tragica* more clearly than any other image in *L'Amfiparnaso* (figure 4.5). Isabella's pose vividly "stages" her impending suicide: her weight is on both feet, her outstretched right hand holds the knife, and her tense left arm, with its stiffly angled wrist, suggests that she is braced to stab herself. The face is also by far the most ambitiously expressive among all the woodcuts, though the artist may have exceeded the detail that could be expected from the technology: only a perfectly printed copy can convey the details of her anguished mouth and eyes.[37]

The scene segues into the comic dialogue "Ah! Isabella, che fai?," for which the woodcut shows the servant Frulla rushing onstage from the left to inter-

Figure 4.6. *L'Amfiparnaso*, Tenore part book, 24: act 2, scene 5.
© The British Library Board. All rights reserved. Shelfmark K.2.b.1.

rupt Isabella's suicide attempt (figure 4.6). The visual vocabulary of this image reverts abruptly to the comic style. The background set has returned to its usual jumbled, comic appearance, and Isabella's costume—shown "seconds before" in the previous woodcut with her veil loosened and her collar open at the neck to receive the blade—has returned to the buttoned-up appearance of her previous scene with Capitan Cardon, ruff collar and all. Her posture, though superficially similar to that of "Ecco che piu non resta," is more theatrical in "Ah! Isabella, che fai?," her weight shifted to the left foot and her arms held higher in a position at once more fluid and more conventionalized.

The musical contrast between the two scenes is similarly striking. "Ecco che piu non resta" ends with a fully developed "serious" point of imitation on "E la trist'alma accogli" (and receive my sad soul), marked melodically by a harsh falling minor sixth (example 4.3). Frulla's interruption is also imitative but within the comic three-voice canzonetta style, with the ini-

Example 4.3. (*above and facing*) Vecchi, *L'Amfiparnaso,* no. 8,
"Ecco che più non resta," mm. 59–67.

tial entries outlining a major triad (example 4.4, mm. 1–12). Isabella's first
response ("Deh, lasciami morire") attempts to maintain her pathetic style
with a return to slower rhythms, but the texture is a simple fauxbourdon.
The elided cadence at the end of this phrase leads into an energetic sticho-
mythic exchange of hemistichs in which the news of Lucio's survival begins
to emerge:

FRULLA: Non farai!	Don't do it!
ISABELLA: Farò sì.	I'll do it, yes.
FRULLA: Depon giù l'armi!	Put down the weapon!
ISABELLA: L'armi ministre fien de la mia morte.	This weapon shall be the bringer of my death
FRULLA: E Lucio fia ministro di tua vita.	And Lucio shall be the bringer of your life!
ISABELLA: E come stanno insieme morte e vita?	And how can they be together, death and life?
FRULLA: Non stanno insieme no, ma vita e vita.	They are not together, no, but life and life!

The three-voice canzonetta texture here is used both to signify a shift from tragicomic to comic style and as a convenient vehicle for the rapid dialogue. Uniquely among the dialogues, it uses stable voice groupings for each character throughout: Isabella is always represented by the Canto, Quinto, and Alto voices (until her final lines, sung *tutti*), while Frulla's lines are always sung by the Alto, Tenore, and Basso. This stability mirrors the serious tone of the poetic parallelisms, capturing the scene's emotional affect while also articulating a stylistic break from the previous scene and allowing a return from the pathos of Isabella's lament to the comic style of the work's denouement.

Example 4.4. (*above and facing*) Vecchi, *L'Amfiparnaso*, no. 9, "Ah! Isabella, che fai?," mm. 1–12.

Vecchi makes no explicit claim that *L'Amfiparnaso* is a tragicomedy, but the variety of actions represented in its poetry, music, and illustrations resonates with the mixed genre theorized by Guarini in the *Compendio* (and in its earlier formulations *Il verrato* and *Il verrato secondo*). It would be dogmatic to attempt to classify Vecchi's musical collection according to theatrical genres, but an understanding of *L'Amfiparnaso*'s eclecticism is essential to reframe the book's convoluted reception history.

la - scia - mi __ mo - ri - - - re. Fa-rò sì.

la - scia-mi mo - ri - - - re. Fa-rò sì.

la - scia-mi mo - ri - re. Non fa-rai! Fa-rò sì.

Non fa -rai!

Non fa -rai!

L'ar-mi mi-ni-stre fien de la mia mor - te.

L'ar-mi mi-ni-stre fien de la mia mor - te.

De-pon giù l'ar - mi! L'ar-mi mi-ni-stre fien de la mia mor - te.

De-pon giù l'ar - mi!

De - pon giù l'ar - mi!

The Historiography of *L'Amfiparnaso* and the "Madrigal Comedy"

Despite Vecchi's insistence that *L'Amfiparnaso* is not a staged spectacle, the emergence of Florentine musical theater in the years around 1600 relegated the book's early historiography to the periphery of narratives about the growth of opera. Whether they identified the work itself as an opera or not, scholars before the twentieth century proposed for it an essentially theatrical function. Later writers (and a few early ones) critiqued this view, citing as the most obvious and persuasive evidence Vecchi's explicit description in the book's preface and the sung prologue of *L'Amfiparnaso* as a purely aural work that is only completed as "theater" in the imagination of the listener. The propagation of this view was accompanied in the last century by the coinage of a new genre, the so-called madrigal comedy, which has variously encompassed *L'Amfiparnaso* and Vecchi's other metaphorically titled books, Banchieri's books of canzonettas and madrigals, and a somewhat arbitrary range of other music that sets dialect texts or alludes to theatrical practices. Casting *L'Amfiparnaso* as the paradigmatic exemplar of this genre has led to overgeneralization and mischaracterization of books that, to a sixteenth-century reader, would have had only incidental similarities.

Until the mid-nineteenth century most writers assumed, explicitly or implicitly, that *L'Amfiparnaso* was an opera, and views differed only on the quality of its "libretto" and whether it was in fact the first opera, or perhaps only the first comic opera. Evidence in this debate was found in Vecchi's comment in the preface that he knew of no previous attempt to combine music and comedy: "I say that if there should be in my work some things that fail to satisfy the experts, they must reduce its imperfection to match their perfection; especially since this coupling of Comedy and Music has not been made before by others—as far as I know—and perhaps not even imagined, many other things may easily be added to perfect it."

Vecchi's remark, recognizable in context as a modest acknowledgment of the book's novelty, was mythologized as fact in an inscription on a tombstone erected in 1607 in the Carmelite church in Modena: "Orazio Vecchi . . . first joined together harmony and comedy, drawing the admiration of the whole world."[38] The unknown author of the inscription must have had Florentine opera in mind when thus paraphrasing Vecchi's comment, but this reveals nothing of Vecchi's meaning from a decade earlier. In 1706 the Modenese literary historian Lodovico Antonio Muratori took the inscription at face value in crediting Vecchi with composing the first opera, though Muratori apparently did so without knowledge of *L'Amfiparnaso* itself: "One such invention, at least regarding instrumental music, should be credited to the Modenese Orazio Vecchi. . . . This gentleman, before Rinuccini, taught the way to represent the aforesaid dramas, and full of years and glory he died in his homeland in 1605. A true witness to the fact remains in the Carmelite church of this city, carved in marble, that is, the funerary inscription made for him."[39] Muratori frames this comment as a discussion of concerted music, intending to encompass both Rinuccini's and Peri's Florentine operas and Vecchi's more idiosyncratic *comedia,* apparently assuming that all these works employed similar forms of accompanied singing. He had evidently consulted Apostolo Zeno on this matter while he was preparing his history, as shown by a letter in which Zeno discusses early Florentine opera but admits to having "not the least knowledge" of Orazio Vecchi of Modena.[40] Muratori also translates the inscription's Latin *comica* into Italian as *dramma,* rather than restoring Vecchi's original *comedia,* thereby obscuring the contrast between Vecchi's work and the tragedy-inspired operas of Peri and Rinuccini.

The first writer on Vecchi to cite *L'Amfiparnaso* by name was Scipione Maffei, in 1723. His account positions Vecchi as the first to assign sung lines to individual characters rather than solely to the chorus—a narrative seemingly influenced by Aristotle's account of Thespis as the first actor: "In the sixteenth century, we can be certain, choirs many times sang written music, portraying the rest [i.e., the crowd or chorus]; and finally in 1597 the Modenese Orazio Vecchi set a new example with his *L'Amfiparnaso,* making the actors sing too, not excepting Pantalone, Zanni, Doctor Graziano, and the Spanish captain, who all performed their parts in verse and music."[41] Although Maffei seems to have known the plot of *L'Amfiparnaso,* the polyphonic texture of the music eludes him. He apparently never saw the part books themselves, and he may have known the work from an edition of the poetry printed without music in Bologna in 1647.[42]

In the mid-1700s writers increasingly identified *L'Amfiparnaso* by name and made specific reference to the preface and the music. Giuseppe Ottavio Pitoni and Francesco Saverio Quadrio, writing in the 1740s, both describe the music of *L'Amfiparnaso* and note Vecchi's declaration of artistic priority in the preface. Quadrio, in book 3 of his *Della storia e della ragione d'ogne poesia,* reads it as an attempt to take credit for the invention of opera: "In the year 1597, in which the first opera (a beautiful work for music made by Ottavio Rinuccini) was performed in the house of Jacopo Corsi, Angelo Gardano in Venice actually published an opera in verse by Orazio Vecchi of Modena, with written music, titled *L'Amfiparnaso, Commedia Harmonica a 4* [sic], in the dedication of which the author boasts of this being his new invention. But as made, the opera is an insipid work of no account. It is, however, accompanied by music from the same Vecchi, who did this very well."[43]

In his manuscript "Notitia de' contrapuntisti e compositori di musica," Pitoni—the first of these authors whose main topic was music rather than poetry or theater—explicitly interprets Vecchi's claim as referring only to the combination of comic texts with *polyphonic* music, making no reference to the development of monody or opera: "[Vecchi] was the first to set comedies to music with multiple parts, as can be seen in his comedia titled *Anfiparnaso* [sic] a 5, printed in Venice in 1597 on May 20, set to music with great art and industry, where in the letter to the readers he tells of having been the first to adorn comedy with music."[44] Pitoni's manuscript seems to have had little influence on subsequent historians, though Giambattista Dall'Olio made a similar argument in 1790 as part of a wide-ranging argument against reading *L'Amfiparnaso* as an opera, particularly attacking literary historians' misunderstandings of the work:

> The words *armonica* from the frontispiece of the book, and *harmonium* from the marble tombstone, were in those places adopted in a technical sense. Our writers, who are wholly ignorant of these matters and little versed in musical learning, believed that *armonia,* which is a specific term, and *musica,* which is a general term, mean the same thing. But *armonia* in its technical sense indicates, as Padre Martini says on page 175 of Book I of his *History of Music,* a *simultaneous agreement of diverse melodies,* whereas *music,* according to Rousseau's Dictionary, means in general the art *of combining sounds in a manner pleasing to the ear.* Thus I explain the riddle: *L'Amfiparnaso* is a work of harmony, that is, one composed of diverse simultaneous melodies.[45]

Though Dall'Olio cites anachronistic sources in making his distinction between *armonia* and *musica,* they agree with Zarlino's definition of harmony as encompassing both the sounding of simultaneous tones and the ways in which consonances and dissonances change over time.[46]

By 1790 Dall'Olio was opposing a considerable scholarly consensus. In *Le rivoluzioni del teatro musicale italiano dalla sua origine al presente* (1783), a critique of recent trends in opera, Stefano Arteaga summarizes the comments of Muratori, Maffei, and Quadrio, and although he grants *L'Amfiparnaso* the status of *opera buffa,* he goes further than Quadrio in criticizing both the poetry and the music of *L'Amfiparnaso:* "Neither the music nor the poetry would deserve mention, if the circumstance of their being the first of their genre did not oblige me to give them a place in this history."[47] Arteaga goes on to describe the juxtaposition of languages and dialects as creating a "harmonic mess" (*armonico guazzabuglio*), citing in particular the scenes with

Isabella and Capitan Cardon (which apparently wounded his Spanish pride) and with Francatrippa and the Jews, whose fake Hebrew he also regards as self-evidently worth censure. His only comment on it is to add, "By saying that the music does no injury to poetry like this, I have rendered due justice to both."[48] These criticisms—and the way they relate linguistic issues to musical ones—are of a piece with Arteaga's larger theme.

Girolamo Tiraboschi, in his history of Modenese authors written in the 1780s, was the first writer to scrutinize directly Muratori's claim that Vecchi wrote the first opera, but he did so not by questioning L'Amfiparnaso's status as an opera but by considering then-current beliefs about the genre's chronology:[49]

> L'Amfiparnaso is the work to which the aforementioned tomb inscription refers in giving Vecchi the honor of having first joined music with theatrical poetry [Poesie Teatrale]. But to tell the truth, while he may be among the first, one cannot affirm that he was the first. In the prefatory letter to Euridice by Ottavio Rinuccini, printed in Venice in 1600, Jacopo Peri says: Although Signor Emilio del Cavaliere, before any other of whom I know, enabled us with marvelous invention to hear our kind of music upon the stage, nonetheless as early as 1594, it pleased Signors Jacopo Corsi and Ottavio Rinuccini that I should employ it in another guise and should set to music the fable of Dafne, written by Signor Ottavio to make a simple trial of what the music of our age could do. Therefore Rinuccini's Dafne was written and set to music as early as 1594, though published only many years later; and so it seems that to this collaboration, before all others, goes the title of Drama in Music.[50]

Tiraboschi does grant Vecchi the lesser distinction of being the first composer to have a music-drama published, but in any case the romanticizing historical imagination of some nineteenth-century writers was not to be swayed by chronological hairsplitting like Tiraboschi's, and by 1835 Vecchi was named as the inventor of opera in a semifictional tale published by Stéphen de la Madeleine in Gazette musicale.[51] By the end of the century, Romain Rolland would cast Vecchi as a kind of composer-hero of the new music, placing him on par with Peri and Rinuccini:

> The most interesting and the most complete of the champions—still awkward, but powerful—of the new art, wanting nothing of the ancients, and thinking only of faithfully expressing the spirit of his age, was Orazio Vecchi, of Modena. . . . The characteristic trait of [Vecchi's] secular works is that they are all comedies or scenes from comedies, as opposed to the Florentine school,

which wrote only tragedies. This is not to say that Orazio had difficulty with pathetic and passionate sentiments; some pages of his comedies demonstrate that he was capable in the tragic style. The sorrow of Isabella at the news of the death of her lover is as delicate a sentiment as the despair of the Florentine Orphei, and as noble a tragic drama.[52]

In the first edition of his *Biographie universelle des musiciens* (1844), François-Joseph Fétis reinscribed the debate over priority, taking Vecchi's claim of originality as evidence that *L'Amfiparnaso* was both composed and performed in 1594. Nevertheless, Fétis betrays some doubt as to whether the work is properly an opera at all: "The work that made Vecchi's popular reputation is a kind of comic opera [*une sorte d'opéra-comique en musique*] entitled *L'Amfiparnaso, commedia harmonica,* which was performed at Modena in 1594 and published in Venice three years later. According to Muratori, Vecchi's first essays preceded those that came from Florence around the same time to create serious opera, and this invention forever immortalized his name."[53] In the second edition Fétis substantially rewrote the entry on Vecchi to reflect information from Angelo Catelani's *Della vita e delle opere di Orazio Vecchi* (1864) but retained this passage (to which Catelani would surely have objected), only changing *opéra-comique* to *comédie en musique*.[54] Catelani's book, the first full-length study of the composer, was explicitly intended to shift discourse about *L'Amfiparnaso* away from opera:

> The last case [i.e., men famous in life but forgotten in death] is confirmed in Orazio Vecchi, but with this difference: just as legitimate as the renown he enjoyed in life as a composer of sacred and secular music was the injustice of the obscurity into which his memory fell after his death, despite the exaggerated efforts and erroneous opinions of those writers who wanted to attribute to him the principal honor of having created the first comic opera. Such exaggerations and errors necessarily give rise, sooner or later, not to denial of acknowledged positive merits but rather to that species of uncertainty or doubt that the absence of an incontrovertible truth is surely wont to produce in men and in human affairs.[55]

German scholarship in the second half of the nineteenth century follows Catelani in refraining from calling *L'Amfiparnaso* an opera, though at the expense of characterizing it instead as a problematic "transitional" work. The fourth volume of August Wilhelm Ambros's *Geschichte der Musik,* published posthumously in an edition by Gustav Nottebohm in 1878, discusses Vecchi's work as an example of comical music but describes comedy as the antithesis of the musical sublime, which is characterized by the style of Pale-strina.[56] The 1893 revision by Otto Kade acknowledges the criticisms of past authors: "Orazio Vecchi has come to be known not for his excellent church music, but rather for his *Amfiparnasso* [*sic*]. Writers have freely cited this work in general, only (like Arteaga) to anger themselves over its aesthetics. A comedy-dialogue in noisy five-voice madrigals!"[57] Kade defends this "comedy-dialogue" (*Comödiendialog*) by comparing it to the antiphonal choruses heard in court-theater intermezzi and Venetian polychoral church music. Kade describes *L'Amfiparnaso* in some detail, along with *Le veglie di Siena* and some of Adriano Banchieri's books. Finally, in the 1909 revision of Ambros, Hugo Leichtentritt transforms Kade's *Comödiendialog* into *Madrigal-komödie* and offers a list of examples of this newly identified genre. After a discussion of fourteenth- and fifteenth-century *mascherate* known only from literary sources, the text continues:

> We are somewhat better informed concerning the sixteenth-century madrigal comedy, since at least the main works to be considered have been preserved, even if only a small part thereof is available in score.
> The most important works of the transitional period from madrigal to musical drama may perhaps be the following:

Alessandro Striggio	*Il cicalamento delle donne al bucato*, 1567
Giovanni Croce	*Triaca musicale*, 1596
Orazio Vecchi	*Amfiparnaso*, 1597
Adriano Banchieri	*La pazzia senile*, 1598
	Il metamorfosi musicale, 1601
	Il zabaione musicale, 1603
Orazio Vecchi	*Le veglie di Siena*, 1604
Adriano Banchieri	*La barca di Venezia per Padova*, 1605
	La saviezza [*sic*, recte *prudenza*] *giovenile*, 1607[58]

In fact, only *Il cicalamento* and two editions of *L'Amfiparnaso* had been edited in the first years of the twentieth century.[59] The term "madrigal comedy" therefore emerged at a moment when the music of *L'Amfiparnaso* was becoming more widely known, the assumption that it was a comic opera was finally fading, and, most importantly, historians drawing connections to related books by Banchieri and others were positing a category of works in apparent need of a unifying label.

The notion of the madrigal comedy as a distinct genre—and of *L'Amfiparnaso* as its paragon—endured throughout the twentieth century, notably in Einstein's *The Italian Madrigal*, which brought the term into general use in English. As Leichtentritt's phrasing implies, the madrigal comedy was perceived from the first as a transitional genre lying at the cusp of the Renaissance and the Baroque as traditionally described; its history is thus necessarily circumscribed, and its definition carries the seeds of its own obsolescence. An early example of this is detectable in Nicola D'Arienzo's 1895 essay on the origins of comic opera, which characterizes *L'Amfiparnaso* as an *opera scenica* but suggests that Vecchi was falling out of step with advances being made in Florence:

> Vecchi, perhaps knowing nothing of, or perhaps not accepting, what the Florentine Camerata was doing in attempting to research the musical form of melodrama, adapted to a scenic action the polyphony of the madrigal, then very much in vogue. Following the example of the Flemish school, he concerned himself only with the conduct of the single parts in counterpoint, giving little thought to the characters, believing he could signal in the score [*nella partitura*] that the words were meant to be a man or a woman singing, Pantalone or else Hortensia.
>
> Many people strongly doubt that *L'Amfiparnaso* could have been staged [*rappresentato*], being unable to believe in the good will and indulgence of the spectators to hear five voices singing to represent one single character or more. Some believe that the character in the scene stood on the stage to sing his part, and simultaneously the others sang theirs behind the set. I am more inclined to the hypothesis that onstage there were pantomimers who accompanied in gestures music that was sung out of the sight of the audience.[60]

D'Arienzo's description exemplifies the enduring view of *L'Amfiparnaso* as a "problem" by assuming that it must be a form of staged work even though it is not an antecedent of opera, comic or otherwise.

Twentieth-century writers on *L'Amfiparnaso* have often addressed this "problem" either by dismissing the work as a simple failure (allowing it only isolated moments of charm) or by attempting to refine the scope and meaning of the madrigal comedy, its putative genre. The former approach was vividly exemplified in 1902 by C. Hubert H. Parry, who like D'Arienzo assumed that the action was to be mimed:

> Horazio Vecchi, one of the foremost composers of the old style, attempted to bring the mature art of choral music into the service of the stage by composing the music for a kind of play called *Anfiparnasso* [*sic*] in a madrigal style; setting the words, even the dialogue, for many voices to sing in parts unaccompanied, while the action was carried on apparently in dumb show. As this work is a

curiosity, and served as an excellent proof of the unfitness of the old style for dramatic purposes, some illustrations are worth considering. It begins with a kind of prologue for five voices, which is really a crude attempt to use vocal part-music for the purposes of recitation.[61]

Parry continues in this tone, examining several pieces in L'Amfiparnaso primarily to point out awkwardnesses and absurdities, and concludes his discussion with a wholly unsupported suggestion that the work might in fact have been influential as a negative example to the development of opera: "This work was but a kind of instructive parenthesis, and could not produce any kind of conviction in the minds of those seeking for dramatic expression; and it possibly helped to the decisive acceptance of the methods of the new school, infantile as they were, by suggesting at least the direction which could not profitably be followed in the search for secular ideals."[62]

A more evenhanded approach to the work was taken by Edward Dent in a pair of articles from 1906 and 1911.[63] In the first of these, Dent addressed for the first time the function of the woodcut illustrations in the part books, proposing an entirely nontheatrical performance context:

> It is possible—though I think hardly probable—that the partbooks were intended to serve as programmes: but the explanatory woodcuts and the separate printing of the words would still be more necessary as an assistance to the singers in properly interpreting the music. And, indeed, it is not really necessary to take the hypothetical audience into consideration at all. We know from Morley, from Benvenuto Cellini and others, how common was the practice in educated society in England and Italy of passing round the music-books after a supper-party. Why should not the "Amfiparnaso" have been designed to be sung in this way by a circle of friends sitting round a table with no other purpose than their own artistic enjoyment?[64]

Nevertheless, for some writers, like Henry Prunières in his study of Monteverdi, Vecchi continued to personify an historical dead end: "Polyphonic music [in Monteverdi's fifth book of madrigals] appears in unwonted forms of almost monstrous beauty. The art of the madrigal reaches its supreme expression. The way is closed. Monteverdi was not long in issuing from the impasse in which a man like Orazio Vecchi obstinately remained."[65] A spirited effort to overturn this view was mounted at a conference held in Modena in 1949 to commemorate the four-hundredth anniversary of Vecchi's birth, the proceedings of which were published the following year to coincide with the anniversary itself. Gino Roncaglia in particular tried to reposition

Vecchi as a *precursore* to the birth of opera in a series of articles around this time.[66] However, his focus on the composer's occasional use of individual voices in dialogue reinscribes an evolutionary view in which Vecchi's value is essentially dependent on his status as a harbinger of things to come. Despite the efforts of Roncaglia and his fellow conferees, the accepted view of late *cinquecento* musical developments continued to leave Vecchi in the margins.

This view derives in large part from Alfred Einstein, whose treatment of Striggio, Vecchi, Banchieri, and Giovanni Croce in *The Italian Madrigal* as purveyors of "music as entertainment" has led subsequent writers to isolate them from broader trends. The organization of Einstein's book collects small groups of composers under shorthand categorizations for each chapter. Thus Lasso, Monte, and Wert are "The Three Great Oltremontani"; Marenzio, Gesualdo, Monteverdi, and Marco da Gagliano are "The Great Virtuosi"; and so on. Vecchi and the other aforementioned composers are described under the heading "Music in Company," by which Einstein refers to what I have called the recreational function of this music. Confusingly, however, Einstein argues for this function on behalf of the madrigal generally before focusing on what he regards as a distinct subgenre:

> In the sixteenth century the several forms of secular music—the madrigal and the various classes related to it—are neither public nor private, but occupy an anomalous position halfway between the two. Solitary and completely intimate art, such as that of the Preludes and Fugues of the "Well-Tempered Clavichord" or certain sonatas of Mozart, Haydn, and Beethoven, is unthinkable. It would stand in complete contradiction to the function of sixteenth century music, whose aim is not emotion, not edification, uplift, or self-improvement, but to serve as entertainment at best. . . . What public music the age brings forth in the way of festival motets and festival madrigals is strictly segregated in its style and attitude from the great mass of the production—the chamber madrigal. But the chamber madrigal requires no audience. The four, five, or six singers are as self-sufficient as two chess players or a group at a card-table, where "kibitzers," although they may stand by, are uninvited and a general nuisance. For the madrigal this character of companionable entertainment is essential. Only after the foundation of the *accademie* do we begin to meet with "art for art's sake" and with the Horatian hatred of the *profanum vulgus*.
>
> But it is precisely these same *accademie* that create and cultivate the madrigal as a social game. Within the great general category of "madrigal as entertainment" a whole series of works embodies in the most striking manner the joys of singing and playing in company. These works have their roots in the arrange-

ments of folksongs from the turn of the century, in the quodlibet, in the dance song, and in the musical parody. They are a residue and at the same time a continuation of everything that the sentimental madrigal of 1535 excluded.[67]

Einstein thus characterizes the madrigal comedy as simultaneously exemplifying the social essence of the madrigal and standing apart from the best of its musical tradition. The implied value judgment is exposed when Einstein discusses an unusually scenic text set by Marenzio, "Passando con pensier per un boschetto": "All the naïve description, all the realism that Marenzio can command are in their right place here; everything is full of musical life and musical refinement. . . . Uncritically considered, the piece might also be assigned to another context, namely to convivial music, somewhere between Striggio's *Cicalamento* and *Gioco di primiera* and Vecchi's *Convito musicale*. But its level is much higher. It lacks the elements of self-parody, 'entertainment,' and fun. It is rather a work of the purest and noblest grace and the purest and noblest poetry."[68] In fact, the poetry, a fourteenth-century *caccia* poem, is in an unusually light style, and the music would not be out of place in any of Vecchi's madrigals. It would seem, rather, that Einstein resists identifying one of his "great virtuosi" with mere entertainment. This equivocation resurfaces as he, too, sums up *L'Amfiparnaso* as a dead end: "The madrigal and the lighter forms of sixteenth-century music have met as though by appointment and have made merry at one another's expense against what appears to be a dramatic background. It is an end. But Vecchi is so gay, so light, so impudent, so fascinating a companion, that we prefer to see his work as a golden sunset and not as a foreshadowing of the coming night. After Vecchi there is plenty of comedy in Italian music, but little gaiety that is as pure as his."[69] Einstein does not dismiss Vecchi as uninteresting, merely as historically inconsequential and outside the virtuosic madrigal tradition. He does not fall into the habits that characterize most other discussions of madrigal comedies: overemphasis on *L'Amfiparnaso* and a failure to contextualize the music adequately. On the first of these points Einstein repeatedly laments the attention lavished on *L'Amfiparnaso* at the expense of other works: "I shall give no further examples [of Vecchi's canzonettas], since a number of these canzonette have been reprinted and since Italian scholars are about to stop concentrating their whole attention on the *Amphiparnaso* and are now planning an edition of Vecchi's complete works."[70]

Einstein's strongly hierarchical view of musical styles likewise relegates "lighter genres" to the margins: he name-checks Vecchi in connection with

Andrea Gabrieli's *giustiniane,* Girolamo Conversi's *canzone,* and Gastoldi's *balletti.* The Gastoldi reference is of particular interest, since in it Einstein suggests that the category of madrigal comedy need not be as circumscribed as it usually is:

> Since Burney, Kiesewetter, Becker, Schneider, and Torchi were satisfied to publish single numbers from Gastoldi's print [of *balletti,* 1591], it has never been noticed that the print is an organic whole. It is a forerunner—the most important forerunner—of the *Amphiparnaso* of Orazio Vecchi and the other so-called madrigal comedies by Vecchi and Banchieri, and it might therefore have been as appropriately discussed in another chapter and in another context. (Vecchi's own *Selva,* which appeared four months before Gastoldi's balletti, is, in spite of its opening number, a mere potpourri.) But it is not always possible to separate the lines of development exactly, since toward the end of the century they often cross. To understand Gastoldi's work one must suppose that a merry company has come together to sing, to play, and to dance, and that the revelry has begun to take on the character of a comedy, in that the participants endeavor to represent in imagination every conceivable character.[71]

Einstein's reading of Gastoldi's *balletti* as an "organic whole" is problematic, but the "lines of separation" between genres cross even more than Einstein acknowledges: recent studies by Massimo Ossi and Mauro Calcagno, among others, have emphasized how narrative frameworks helped shape madrigal books by Wert, Marenzio, and Monteverdi (see chapter 3). But writers in the decades following Einstein continued to treat the madrigal comedy as a distinct genre defined by its theatrical or quasi-theatrical quality. Nino Pirrotta, for example, discusses works by Vecchi and Banchieri solely in terms of their dramatic function, in keeping with his larger project of relating musical and theatrical practice.[72]

Cecil Adkins, in his 1977 edition of *L'Amfiparnaso,* attempted to define the madrigal comedy as a coherent genre, a project that usefully draws attention away from questions of these works' relation to early opera. Yet while notionally locating *L'Amfiparnaso* within a broader tradition, the four categories of Adkins's "Genealogical Table of the Madrigal Comedy" (see table 4.3) in fact create an explicit hierarchy within the notional genre in which *L'Amfiparnaso* is the founding example of the most advanced type. All the others are seen as less fully unified efforts or (in the case of four works by Banchieri) imitations. The other works Adkins includes are exclusively those mentioned in Einstein's chapter "Music in Company." Adkins's typology provides the madrigal comedy, and *L'Amfiparnaso* in particular, with a "usable

Table 4.3. The categories of Cecil Adkins's
"Genealogical Table of the Madrigal Comedy"

Category 1 "Continuity provided only by the title"	1590	Croce, *Mascarate piacevoli et ridicolose per il carnevale*
	1590	Vecchi, *Selva di varia ricreatione*
	1595	Croce, *Triaca musicale*
	1597	Banchieri [*sic*, Vecchi], *Convito musicale*
	1599	Banchieri, *Il Donatio... [sic, 1598, Il Donativo...]*
Category 2 "Continuity provided by title and use of same characters throughout"	1567	Striggio, "Il cicalamento delle donna al bucato"
	1604	Vecchi, *Le veglie di Siena*
	1605	Banchieri, *Barca di Venetia per Padova*
	1608	Banchieri, *Festino nella sera del Giovedi Grasso avanti cena*
	1630	Banchieri, *Trattenimenti in villa [sic, da villa]*
Category 3 "Like 2, but all based on pastoral themes"	1594	P. Balsamino [*sic*, Simone Balsamino], *Aminta musicale*
	1600	Torelli, *I fidi amanti*
	1604	Banchieri, *Zabaione musicale*
	1614	Banchieri, *Tirsi, Filli, e Clori*
Category 4 Continuity provided by plot and character development	1597	Vecchi, *L'Amfiparnaso*
	1598	Banchieri, *La pazzia senile*
	1600	Banchieri, *Il studio dilettevole*
	1601	Banchieri, *Il metamorphosi musicale*
	1607	Banchieri, *La prudenza giovenile*
	1628	Banchieri, *Saviezza giovenile* [revision of *Prudenza giovenile*]

Source: Cecil Adkins, "Vecchi and the Madrigal Comedy," in Orazio Vecchi, *"L'Amfiparnaso":
A New Edition of the Music with Historical and Analytical Essays,* ed. Cecil Adkins
(Chapel Hill: University of North Carolina Press, 1977), 7.

past"—a history of nascent forms, preliminary experiments, and subsequent developments. However, the wholly abstract nature of his descriptions obscures the similarities and differences of the works in each category. In particular, the description of books in categories 2 and 3 as using "the same characters throughout" generalizes about collections in which individual character names only rarely recur within a book but whose general goal is to imitate the activities of an arbitrarily large group of people at a social gathering.

Yet even putting aside Adkins's four categories, the relation of many of these works to a coherent tradition is tenuous. Particularly striking in this regard is Alessandro Striggio's "Il cicalamento delle donne al bucato" of 1567, by far the earliest work in the list and the only one not published as an independent book. It is worth noting that the first edition of "Il cicalamento" was published in an edition by Giulio Bonagiunta along with Striggio's similarly imitative "La caccia" and Cipriano de Rore's setting of Dido's lament from the *Aeneid*.[73] As an independent work within a book—even a book to which it gives its title—"Il cicalamento" therefore functions differently from the other titles in Adkins's list. Circulating in printed form in the decades around the turn of the century, these works are best read in terms that were familiar to sixteenth-century creators, buyers, and users of music books, with particular attention to the musical genres and ensemble sizes employed, the specific theatrical styles or social situations imitated, and the visual presentation of the print itself.

Giovanni Croce's *Mascarate* (1590) and *Triaca musicale* (Musical panacea, 1595) are both fairly small collections of dialect songs.[74] The six *mascarate* are all distinctly Venetian both in language and in subject-matter, while in the seven works in *Triaca musicale* the Venetian-dialect pieces are interspersed with the Bolognese "Mascherata dei Graziani" and two pieces in Tuscan Italian: the "Canzon del cucco e rossignuolo con la sentenza del papagallo" (a fanciful singing contest among birds) and "Il gioco dell'oca" (a representation of noble men and women playing a board game; see chapter 5). Except for this last piece, all the music in both books imitates lower-status Venetians, foreigners, or animals, yet nothing links the pieces or suggests that the books benefit from complete performance. Donna Mae Gustafson argues that the *mascarate* may have been composed for some kind of theatrical performance at the Venetian monastery of the Knights of Saint John of Malta in 1585, but the dedication of the 1590 print (signed by the printer, Vincenzi) to the Venetian nobleman Leonardo Sanudo says that the pieces had been performed at different times under Sanudo's patronage and are only in the print being collected together: "Having at the insistence of many curious people gathered these little masquerades of Mr. Giovanni Croce of Chioggia, which have been performed several times with so much pleasure, it is an illustrious thing, and in particular to your Illustrious Lordship, who has been the one on various occasions to yield them to the world."[75] It therefore seems clear that even if, as Gustafson proposes, these six songs were composed for a single event, they were also performed separately prior to their publication and could of course function that way in print as well. *Triaca musicale,* similarly, bears no indication that its pieces constitute a complete work. As miscellaneous collections of dialect songs, then, Croce's books are better considered in relation to the *giustiniane* and *greghesche* of Croce's Venetian compatriots Andrea Gabrieli and Vincenzo Bellavere, Lasso's *Villanelle e moresche* of 1581, and Vecchi's *Selva* and *Convito,* which, I have argued, are best read as miscellanies rather than as "unified" collections. Simone Balsamino's *Novelette* and Torelli's *I fidi amanti* are musical settings of preexisting pastoral literature: two extended excerpts of Tasso's *Aminta* in the former case and a complete small-scale *Favola pastorale* by Ascanio Ordei in the latter.[76] As such they may be seen within the broader tradition of pastoralism in the late *cinquecento* madrigal and also in relation to the more circumscribed field of madrigal books setting or adapting excerpts from Guarini's *Il pastor fido:* Marenzio's seventh book for five voices and Monteverdi's fifth book.

In drawing these connections, my purpose is not to exclude books by Croce, Balsamino, and Torelli from a more narrowly defined madrigal comedy, of course, but to reject the usefulness of the term itself, which serves principally to relegate Vecchi's and Banchieri's books to the periphery of histories centered on courtly, literary madrigals and audience-directed and increasingly monodic performance at the end of the century. Reading *L'Amfiparnaso* on its own terms, and particularly with regard to the interaction of its extramusical texts and woodcut images, reveals a more complex engagement with contemporary literary theories, even while demonstrating the book's independence from music in theater.

5 Competition and Conversation
Games as Music

An overarching theme of this book is the way in which music by Orazio Vecchi and some of his contemporaries reveals how singing from printed music could function like a game in Italian courts, *ridotti,* academies, and more intimate private gatherings. The social acts of choosing music, singing it, and then discussing the pieces and their execution all mirror the phases of game playing as described in contemporary documents. This game-like process might remain relatively informal and implicit, as in the conversation with music depicted in Doni's *Dialogo,* though the social activity of reading and singing Doni's book itself would take on a game-like function as singers negotiated the various kinds of pieces the book contains, including at least one instance of an intentionally notated mistake.[1] In other cases, madrigal anthologies that consist of multiple settings of the same or related texts (such as *Sdegnosi ardori, L'amorosa Ero,* and *I fidi amanti*) suggest a kind of competition among composers that would, in recreational performance, give rise to a game-like sense of formalized turn-taking.[2] But indeed, any music book or selection of pieces available at a given social gathering could function in the same way. As the participants selected various pieces to sing, their choices of one composer or another, pieces of greater or lesser *gravità,* and genres of contrasting musical or poetic style provided opportunities for the self-fashioning performance of identity essential to much early modern gaming. As I have argued, Vecchi's unusually varied collections *Selva di varia ricreatione* and *Convito musicale* catered specifically to this social practice.

If I have thus far considered music as a game, in this chapter I consider games presented as music, that is, musical works that depict social groups playing games. Such pieces give a vivid—if simplified—impression of how social game play proceeded, but in an important sense they undermine the fundamental principle of gaming: as fully notated and "scripted" pieces, their outcome is predetermined. The appeal of such pieces, therefore, resides not only in their approximation of the experience of playing a game but in their mostly subtextual cues depicting the meaning of game playing and the social codes that surround it. I do not mean, of course, to overstate the broad importance of this music; only a handful of such pieces were published in Italy from the mid-sixteenth century through the early seventeenth century, and their reprint history suggests at best only modest popularity. Yet the relative consistency with which depictions of games continued to be published and the features they have in common (despite the wide range of games represented) suggest a coherent function for them. The games imitated range from gambling with cards or dice to displays of skill that might be quite frivolous or more intellectual.

The latter type culminates, in this sense, in Vecchi's *Le veglie di Siena* (1604), an idealized depiction of the recreational activities of the Accademia degli Intronati of Siena as described by Girolamo Bargagli in his *Dialogo de' giuochi che vegghie sanesi si usano di fare*, published in 1572.[3] The Intronati, along with all other Sienese academies, had been disbanded in 1568 by the order of Cosimo I de' Medici, so Bargagli's treatise was already a project of idealizing memorialization when it was first printed, although the printer claims that it was written some years before.[4] As has recently been shown, Vecchi lived in Siena from 1571 until ca. 1574, singing in the cathedral choir under his teacher Salvatore Essegna.[5] During this time he must have heard firsthand recollections of the Intronati, and he may have known Bargagli's treatise when it was still new. He almost certainly knew it by 1590, when he borrowed the terminology of Bargagli's game "Cicirlanda" for one of the drinking songs in *Selva di varia ricreatione*, though the structure of that piece is apparently derived from a different tradition (see chapter 6). The games depicted in "Il bando del asino" in *Convito musicale* are likewise derived from Bargagli, one of them taking its name from his treatise.

The *Veglie*, however, are more directly modeled on elements of Bargali's treatise, not only in its title and in references to the Intronati in its texts, but also in the way games of different kinds are juxtaposed. Bargagli's influence is also detectable in Vecchi's use of the term *veglie* for a book exclusively depicting games, since—as Laura Riccò has argued—references to *veglie* among the Intronati and other Sienese academies in the 1560s referred to a wider range of recreational activities that might include theater, storytelling, and music.[6] Girolamo and Scipione Bargagli were particularly concerned with mythologizing the Intronati as an academy specializing in games, a process that culminated in Scipione's *Oratione in lode dell'Accademia degli 'ntronati,* penned in 1603 (though not published until 1611) in honor of the academy's revival. Scipione claims that the Intronati's delightful evenings were constituted of new forms and manners, "not of formerly unseen dances, or of unheard singing or [instrumental] playing, but rather in the manner of Games not previously known or understood."[7] However, it seems unlikely that Vecchi's *Le veglie di Siena,* published a year after Scipione's speech was given but long before its publication, was inspired by the Intronati's revival, to which Vecchi never refers. The debt Vecchi owed to Girolamo Bargagli's treatise, on the other hand, is well known.[8] Yet, as I argue, this nostalgic view of the Intronati stands in tension with Vecchi's own defense of the *Veglie* in the dedication and the preface as a work embracing a variety of modern musical genres and poetic registers. Vecchi's argument is in the same spirit that had informed his monographic books since 1590, but here it reflects a concern for the questions of expression and musical novelty that surround emerging debates over the *seconda prattica*—a concern hinted at in Vecchi's subtitle, *I varii humori della musica moderna* (The various humors of modern music).

Gambling in Music: Cards, Dice, Lotteries, and the Performance of Virtue

Cards and Corruption

Bargali's *Dialogo* explicitly excludes games of cards, dice, and other forms of gambling from consideration, preferring games of wit or skill (characterized by various terms) that promoted conversation between the male members of the academy and their female guests. Musical depictions of gambling are particularly instructive both because the activity was seen to entail moral hazard and because—unlike conversational games—gambling requires relatively little to be said by the players. The scripts that musical imitations of gambling provide can therefore present side-talk, bluffing, and kibitzing among the players, as well as verisimilar lapses of decorum that imply authorial commentary on the risks of such games.

As with several other types of musical imitations, gambling makes its first appearance in *cinquecento* music in the work of Alessandro Striggio, the Mantuan nobleman who spent his courtly career in the service of the Medici court, though not in officially musical positions. His "Gioco di primiera" appeared in 1569 in a book that reprinted two earlier imitative cycles, "Il cicalamento delle donne al bucato" and "La caccia."[9] The first edition of this book had been published in 1567 and included Cipriano de Rore's setting of Dido's lament from Virgil's *Aeneid*.[10] Rore's learned and musically austere Latin-texted lament, a depiction of female eloquence *par excellence*, is strikingly juxtaposed with Striggio's imitation of unruly female speech and behavior in "Il cicalamento" and an imitation of courtly sport in "La caccia," a contrast perhaps not lost on the book's editor, Giulio Bonagiunta. The lament must not have been seen as a popular part of the book, however, since in Scotto's reprint editions of 1569 and 1584 it was omitted in favor of "Il gioco di primiera."

The card game *primiera*, or primero, had developed by the second quarter of the sixteenth century, its first descriptions appearing in a *capitolo* by Francesco Berni published in Rome in 1526 and a manuscript by the mathematician Gerolamo Cardano penned around the same time.[11] An antecedent of modern poker, the game uses a deck of cards from which the eights, nines, and tens are removed. After the initial ante, hands of four cards are dealt to the players, who then bid, declaring what type of hand they hold or hope to acquire. Bids are matched or raised, and players may discard and draw one or more cards in an effort to attain a winning hand. Briefly, the types of winning hands in ascending order of value are *numerus* (two or three cards of one suit), *primero* (one card from each suit), *supremus* (the ace, six, and seven of a single suit, plus one additional card), *fluxus* (four cards of one suit, not necessarily sequential), and *chorus* (four cards of the same rank, one from each suit). Between two hands of the same type the winner is determined by a complex system of points allotted to each card in which the seven is the most valuable, but a higher-ranking hand type will always beat a lower one. Additional rules govern how bids are matched or raised, how cards are exchanged, what kind of bluffing is allowed, and when the hands are revealed to determine a winner. These particulars are not clearly described in the sixteenth-century accounts, which assume a basic understanding of the game and focus instead on strategy (in Cardano's treatise) and elaborate rhetorical praise of the game (in Berni's *capitolo* and the commentary thereon).[12]

In any case, Striggio's piece does not enact the precise details of the game, partly because it presents only the players' spoken remarks without extraneous identifications of the imagined "visible" cards, but also because anxieties about the social decorum and moral hazards of gambling encouraged some ambiguity in this area. Striggio deflects this in his five-voice setting in two ways: first, although he identifies the five singers with five card players, he avoids associating individual singers uniquely with individual players, particularly during the betting phase of the game. Second, he depicts the game's conclusion as descending into disorderly behavior before harmony is restored by a new diversion—specifically, a dance. We have already seen this strategy in Vecchi's "L'hore di ricreatione," where an argument over a ball game is cut short by the proposal of another song (see chapter 1).

Despite Einstein's claim that in the "Gioco" "one has the illusion that each of the five players is an individual," the text distribution only rarely differentiates particular players.[13] The *prima parte* presents a generalized company out of which only two individual speakers can be identified: a senior male who calls for the cards, and the boy who brings them:

CA5T	Al vago e incerto gioco di primiera	The merry and uncertain game of primero—
CA5TB	Chi vuol giocar, dui scudi per piacere.	who wishes to play, two scudi please.
CT	Trov'il denaro e pongasi a sedere.	Find your money and take a seat.
CA5TB	Siamo qui in cinque.	There are five of us here.
AT	O là, ragazzo, presto, Arreca qui le carte!	Hey there, boy, quick, bring the cards!
C5B	Eccole qui signor, polit'e belle.	Here they are, sir, nice and clean.
CA5TB	Mescolatelle a un tratto, E poi faccia a chi tocca il primo sette, Con patto che si faccia al perditore Una dolc'e solenne tombettata.	Mix them at once, and then let's see who gets the first seven, provided we agree the loser gets a nice and solemn trumpet call.[14]

Most of the lines are sung *tutti,* but smaller subsets can represent individual players, whether their identities are defined or not. Thus line 3, "Find your money and take a seat," sung by the Canto and Tenore alone, implies a generic individual voice, whereas the exchange between the *ragazzo* and the *signore* in lines 4–6 individuates two players and defines a relationship of age and rank between them. The voices used here, Alto and Tenore for the *signore* and Canto, Quinto, and Basso for the *ragazzo,* are not obviously meant to depict this relationship, but they are combinations that will recall these two characters later in the piece. The regular line lengths (*settenari* and endecasillabi) of the opening define a kind of social speech outside the realm of the game itself; the *seconda parte* commences the game play, and irregular lineation is accompanied by more varied vocal textures. The dealing and betting phases of the game are particularly marked by textures that suggest dialogue without clearly identifying characters:

C5	Facciasi.	Fine, let's go.
AT	Hor date fuor.	Deal now.
C5B	Di' che caviamo	Say that we draw
A5B	de' grossi.	for the highest,
	E 'l grosso stesso il vada sia.	and let the highest open.
C	Passa.	Pass.
A5TB	Vad'il mio grosso.	Here is my high card.
CA5TB	Il voglio.	I'll take it.
CA5T	Ed io entro,	And I come in;
C	dattemi quattro.	give me four.
B	Datene quattro.	Give four of them.
T	Passa.	Pass.
A5B	I' scarto.	I discard.
AT	Primier'haggio scartato.	I discarded *primero*.
C5TB	Mal haggia chi di qella fu inventore!	Damn the one who invented it!
A5	Mi gioca tutto questo.	I'll play all of this.
CB	E a me gioca il mio resto.	And I'll play the rest of mine.
C5T	Passate.	Pass.
B	Passa.	Pass.
5T	A monte.[15]	Pass.
C5B	A monte.	Pass.
5T	Vada.	Here goes.
CAB	Vada il resto mio.	Here goes the rest of mine.
5T	Il voglio	I'll take it.
C5TB	Il voglio anch'io.	I want it too.
CA5TB	Tutti scartiam,	Let's all discard.

Although this passage has some moments of clear dialogue, such as the Canto's bidding and requesting four new cards, which are then ordered up by the Basso, the details of play here seem deliberately obscure. The comment sung by the Alto and Tenore, "I discarded *primero*," is not formally part of the game but rather a boast—or a bluff—to intimidate the other players. If a player holds *primero* and is bold enough to discard, he may hold three of a kind and be hoping for *chorus*, or at least a higher-scoring *primero*. The response "Damn the one who invented it!" suggests that this side-comment had its intended effect, and Striggio's use of the Alto-Tenore pair here may have some relevance. This combination also represented the *signore* in the *prima parte,* and in the remainder of the *seconda parte* a clearer sense of dialogue emerges between two players: one represented by the Alto-Tenore pair and the other by a Canto-Basso combination, which represented the *ragazzo* who fetched the cards in the *prima parte.* This dialogic organization is blurred somewhat by the Quinto, who sometimes joins either pair to add variety to the musical texture. The two players vie with each other in their final draws and discards, one attempting to make *primero* and the other *fluxus* (here, *flusso*); the lines are numbered to indicate Player 1 (the *signore*) and Player 2 (the *ragazzo*):

AT	**1** Vo a flusso.	I'm going for a flush.
C5B	**2** Ed io a primiera.	And I for *primero.*
AT	**1** Cinquanta, chi ha più punto è vincitore.	Fifty, whoever has the most points wins.
C5B	**2** Voglio far manco . . .	I'd like to go for less . . .
A5T	**1** No.	No!
C5B	**2** Farò primiera.	I'll make *primero.*
AT	**1** No, fatel'a piacer vostro.	No, do as you please.
C5B	**2** Eccola quivi.	Here it is.
AT	**1** Ventura che sian vivi,	We're lucky we're still alive,
A5T	**1** Vo a flusso.	I'm going for a flush.
	1 Che volete che facciamo?	What do you want us to do?
C5B	**2** Nulla, tirate suso.	Nothing; draw.
A5T	**1** Farò flusso.	I'll make a flush.
C5B	**2** Non vel vieto, su presto.	I won't stop you; hurry up!
A5T	**1** Adaggio un poco; che dite?	Slow down; what did you say?
CB	**2** Non m'havete inteso ancorsa?	Haven't you understood me yet?
C5B	**2** Hai piedi potran gir!	You have feet, they can go!
A5T	**1** Eccovi flusso.	Here's my flush.
C5B	**2** Cancar'a flusso e alla primier'insieme!	To hell with your flush and with *primero* too!
C5TB	**2** Ahi putanazza sorte, ahi ciel traverso,	Oh whorish fate, oh crooked heavens,
	2 Ahi carte ladre, fate ch'io fo buono!	Oh thievish cards, let me make it!
CA5TB	No no no no, facciasi prima	No, no, no, no, first let's do it:
	Al perditor del resto stampita.	For the loser the rest do an estampie.
	Facciasi allegramente:	Let's do it joyfully:
	Tipi tipi tap tipi tipi tap tap tap.	Tipi tipi tap tipi tipi tap tap tap.

The *signore* is both a skilled player and a somewhat manipulative one: the comment "Fifty, whoever has the most points wins" is a bluff, suggesting that if neither player makes the hand bid, he still has a high-scoring *numerus* hand (as is likely if he has bid a flush). The *ragazzo* is eager to win but unsportsmanlike when he loses: he makes his bid of *primero* and then becomes impatient for the hand to finish. Ultimately the *signore* wins, drawing out his immature opponent's impatience longer than is strictly necessary; the *ragazzo* is vividly identifiable as a younger and less skilled player. After the hand is won, however, the musical identities of the two players blur as the Tenor, previously associated with the *signore*, joins in the curses hurled by the *ragazzo*, who is eager for a rematch. The full ensemble, voicing a generalized group as it had in the opening, puts a stop to this tantrum and begins the dance.

"Il gioco di primiera" thus enacts both the pleasure and the danger of gambling, a ubiquitous social activity that invariably provoked anxieties not only about financial risk but also about the comportment of the players. Games of chance are mentioned in courtly literature from Boccaccio to Castiglione and beyond (including to Vincenzo Giustiniani) primarily as counterexamples of virtue: respectable women never gamble, and gentlemen do so only in moderation, and only for small stakes. In *Il cortegiano*, book 2, chapter 31, Castiglione has Frederico Fregoso explain that gambling with cards and dice is acceptable for the courtier as long as he does not play so eagerly as to neglect other matters or in such a way as to display avarice. Federico actually equates an excessive desire to win with cheating if one plays "non per altro che per vincer denari, ed inganasse il compagno" (for no other reason than to win money and cheat his partner). Upon losing, such a player also risks a loss of the self-control central to courtly *sprezzatura*: "Perdendo mostrasse dolore a dispiacere tanto grande, che fosse argomento d'avarizia" (When he loses, [he] is so dismayed and angry as to prove his avarice).[16]

Even Cardano's *Liber de ludo aleae*, which acknowledges the benefits of gambling, describes its moral hazard precisely as the threat to self-control enacted in Striggio's "Gioco":

> As advantages to well-managed play we obtain relaxation from anxiety and a pleasure from which we arise ready and eager for serious business.... It is also a means of gaining friendship, and many have risen from obscurity because of the friendship of princes formed in play.... But the losses incurred include lessening of reputation if one has formerly enjoyed any considerable prestige; to this is added loss of time, vain words, including on occasion curses against the gods,

the neglect of one's own business, the danger that it may become a settled habit, the time spent in planning after the game how one may recuperate, and in remembering how badly one has played. There are also disputes and, often, which is worst of all, provocation to anger; for then a man is carried away into playing for high stakes and into feelings of enmity, so that he no longer has control of his own mind. As a result he throws out large sums of money and may be said to abandon them instead of playing for them. Play is a very good test of man's patience or impatience. The greatest advantage in gaming comes from not playing at all. But there is a very great utility in it as a test of patience, for a good man will refrain from anger even at the moment of rising from the game in defeat.[17]

Striggio's losing player exhibits several of these negative traits: impatience, anger, cursing, and a reckless eagerness for a rematch. The other players' intervention with music and dancing restores social harmony, confirming the general belief in music as a more worthwhile pastime, a belief shared by Cardano: "As for the excuse made by some that [gambling] relieves boredom, this would better be done by pleasant reading, or by narrating tales or stories, or by one of the beautiful but not laborious arts. Among these latter, playing the lute or the virginals, or singing, or composing poetry will be more useful."[18] On the social function of gambling, Cardano affirms that games should be played within appropriate circles of friends or relations and not in public places: "Your opponent should be of suitable station in life; you should play rarely and for short periods, in a suitable place, for small stakes, and on suitable occasions, as at a holiday banquet. Your opponent might be the king, or a prelate of outstanding character, or a relative by blood or by marriage. To play with professional gamblers is most disrespectful and, as I have said, dangerous. The most respectable place is at home or at the house of a friend, where there can be no public scandal."[19]

There is little in Striggio's card game to suggest who is playing or where, though the nameless forms of address used for the *ragazzo* and *signore* in the *prima parte* imply a more public place, like the inn where Castiglione's gamblers play in book 2, chapter 86 of *Il cortegiano,* an episode ending with a practical joke that strains the limits of etiquette.[20] Cardano's warning against playing with professional gamblers, and the corrupting influence of cheating more broadly, brings to mind the scene of corruption in Caravaggio's *The Card-Sharps* (1594, figure 5.1). The upper-class boy on the left receives advice from an older but shabbily dressed man, the holes in the fingertips of whose gloves may facilitate reading cards marked with notches or scratches along the edge, another technique mentioned by Cardano.[21] This older man is actu-

Figure 5.1. Caravaggio (Michaelangelo Merisi), Italian (1571–1610). *The Cardsharps,* ca. 1595. Oil on canvas, 37 $^{1}/_{16}$ × 51 $^{9}/_{16}$ in. (94.2 × 130.9 cm), AP 1987.06. Kimbell Art Museum, Fort Worth, Texas.

ally an accomplice to the boy on the right, whom we see retrieving a card hidden in his belt. The cheater is also armed with a dagger, alluding to the threat of violence that may ensue. Although we do not see enough cards to know exactly how the hand is proceeding, the concealed cards are identifiable as a seven of hearts and a six of clubs, two of the highest-scoring cards in primero. The innocence of the victim, with his soft features and naive two-handed grip on his cards, contrasts most obviously with the older man's menacing expression and partly hidden face. The young cheater himself is already corrupted—presumably by the older man—but not beyond redemption; Lorenzo Pericolo reads his intent gaze at the victim and sensually open mouth as suggesting a homoerotic fascination that may mitigate his ill intent.[22]

The most important work modeled on Caravaggio's painting, Georges de La Tour's *The Cheat with the Ace of Diamonds* (ca. 1635, figure 5.2), depicts a similar contrast of class, though here the upper-class male victim (on the right) is more flamboyantly dressed than the cheat, and the narrative intrigue is more focused on the female player and the serving girl, whose glances be-

Figure 5.2. Georges de La Tour, *The Cheat with the Ace of Diamonds,* 1635. Oil on canvas, 106 × 146 cm. Louvre Museum, Paris.

tray suspicion and perhaps conspiracy. However, La Tour makes the details of the game more explicit: besides the ace the cheater (on the left) is concealing, we see that he already holds the six and seven; adding the ace will give him an almost unbeatable *supremus* or *fluxus* hand.[23] These paintings are set against a neutral or dark background, but the class mixing depicted in each is suggestive of an inn or tavern. Striggio's card game is set in a similar site of intermingling, thereby occupying an intermediate space in Striggio's book between the working-class women of "Il cicalamento" and the male nobility of "La caccia."

Virtue and Victory: Il gioco dell'oca

A different—and more precisely reconstructible—gambling game appears in Giovanni Croce's *Triaca musicale* of 1596, a book of comic and *mascherata*-like imitations discussed already (see chapter 4).[24] This is *Il gioco dell'oca* (the game of the goose), a dice-based board game that emerged in the mid-sixteenth century in Italy and remained popular well into the twentieth cen-

Figure 5.3. Board for *Il gioco dell'oca* (the game of the goose), (reverses to chessboard), northern Italian, sixteenth century, ebony, ebonized wood, ivory, green-dyed ivory, horn, gold wire, 43 × 41.9 cm. Metropolitan Museum of Art, New York.

tury; boards have been published with a variety of visual themes, seldom altering the game's underlying structure.[25] Early surviving examples of the game may reflect a less developed form (as in the inlaid board now in the Metropolitan Museum of Art, figure 5.3) or an alternate version with substantially different rules (such as the game *Filosofia cortesiana de Alonso Barros,* figure 5.4), but from the 1580s a standard layout appears in most printed game boards. This structure appears in the 1598 version by Luchino Gargano, *Il nuovo et piacevole gioco dell ocha* (figure 5.5), and, with monkeys in comical or obscene poses replacing the usual geese, in the *Gioco della scimia* by Altiero Gatti (1588, figure 5.6).

Figure 5.4. Mario Cartaro, *Filosofia cortesana de Alonso Barros* (Venice, 1598).

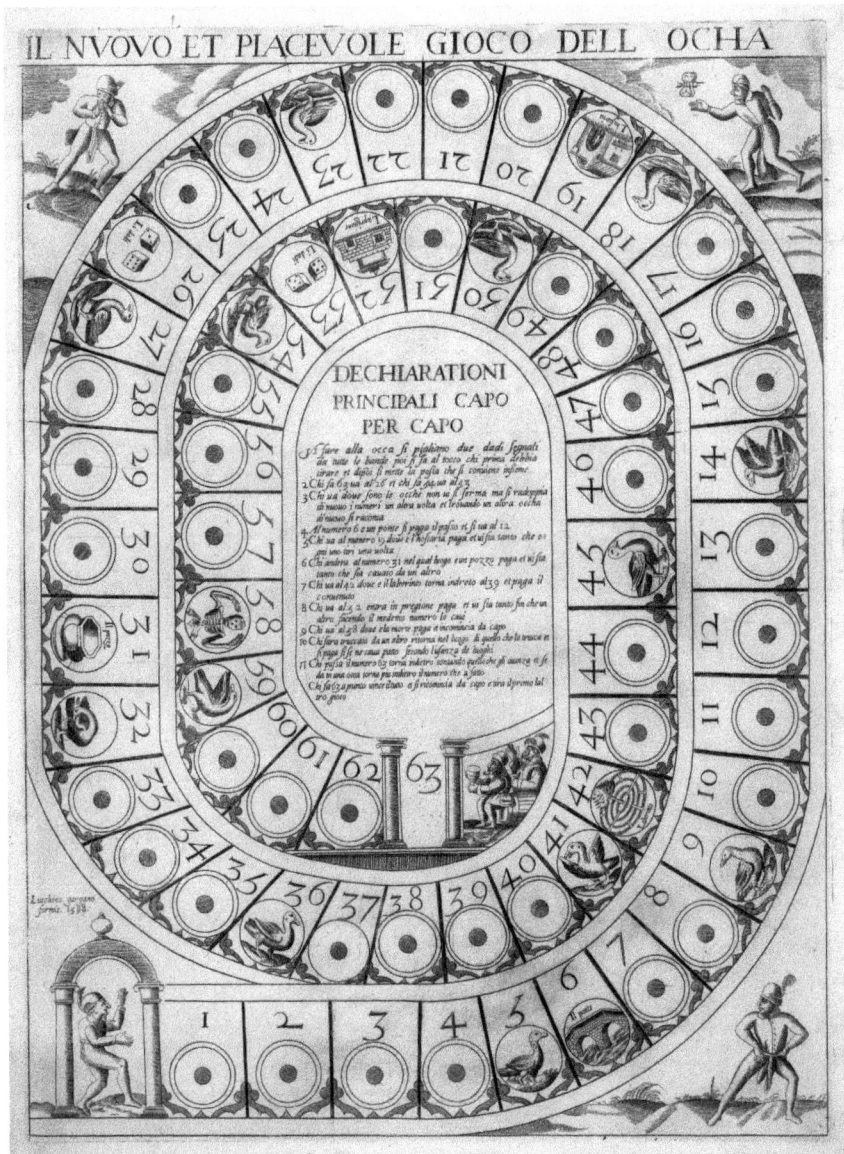

Figure 5.5. Luchino Gargano, *Il nuovo et piacevole gioco dell ocha* (1598).
© Trustees of the British Museum. All rights reserved.

Competition and Conversation 189

Figure 5.6. Altiero Gatti, *Il novo bello e piacevole gioco della scimia* (1588).

A track of sixty-three numbered spaces spirals inward to the central area, with geese pictured on two series of spaces, one on every ninth space (9, 18, 27, 36, 45, 54) and the other on every ninth space beginning with five (5, 14, 23, 32, 41, 50, 59). Each player rolls two dice and advances his token along the track; landing on a Goose entitles the player to continue moving by the same number as had been rolled. By this rule a player rolling a nine on the first move would immediately win the game, since the token would continue from Goose to Goose all the way to space 63. To prevent this, a special rule applies to nines rolled on the first move: if the dice roll produces a six and a three, the token moves directly to space 26, while a roll of four and five moves directly to space 53. (These spaces are usually illustrated with pairs of dice showing these combinations.) Other spaces along the track depict obstacles that delay a player's progress and, usually, require an additional payment into the pot. The first player to reach space 63 by an exact roll wins; a move that would overshoot space 63 must reverse itself and move backward to complete the number of the dice roll. These rules were apparently widely enough known to require no explanation except sometimes a brief indication on the decorated spaces, but the Gargano board of 1598 prints the rules in the center of the board.

The surviving visual evidence and the relatively simple rules make Croce's musical "Gioco dell'oca" much easier to reconstruct than Striggio's "Gioco di primiera"; Croce also identifies the players explicitly with the six singers by giving highly individuated lines to solo voices, using polyphony for comments in the dialogue that might be attributed to any individual or to the group as a whole. As in Striggio's piece, the *prima parte* depicts the proposal of the game, but the setting is now identified as a "noble place," and courtly formality is observed by the men (represented by the two tenors and the bass) asking the women to choose the game, and two of the ladies (the Alto and Canto Secondo) then deferring to the Canto, addressing her as "Signora," suggesting the highest-ranking lady present.

tutti	Or che siam qui d'intorno in cosi nobil loco, facciam, facciam un gioco.	Now that we are gathered here in such a noble place, let's play a game.
T^1T^2B	Dite voi, dame, a che giocar vogliamo, che qui pronti noi siamo.	You, ladies, say what game we should like, for we are here, ready.
C^2A	A voi, Signora, tocca.	Your Ladyship must choose.

C¹	Giochiam, giochiamo all'Occa.	Let's play the game of the goose.
C¹C²A	E pria che il gioco si cominci poi,	And before the game can begin,
	il premio ponga ciaschedun de noi.	each one of us must ante up.
tutti	Eccoci tutti uniti,	Here we all are, together,
	lieti, pronti, et arditi.	happy, ready, and eager.
T¹T²	Ecco il gioco,	Here is the game,
tutti	ecco i dati [dadi],	here are the dice,
	e i premi sian delli più fortunati.²⁶	and the prize will go to the luckiest.

The game itself commences in the *seconda parte,* with the *signora* again given the honor of the first turn. In a stroke of luck consistent with her station, she rolls a six and a three but modestly allows the others to state the significance of this roll: she moves ahead to space 26. The first Tenore and the Basso then each take a turn and experience worse luck: the former lands at the Inn (space 19) and must pay before his next turn, while the latter lands in the Well (space 31), which not only requires payment but also keeps the player there until someone else lands on the space.²⁷ Neither of these two moves is mathematically possible on a first move; Croce evidently preferred to highlight some of the more interesting potential results and, as we shall see, throw the diverse fates of lucky and unlucky players into sharp contrast:

AT¹T²B	A voi, Signora, tocca il primo tiro.	Your ladyship, take the first turn.
C¹	Sei e tre, s'io non erro, è quel ch'io miro.	Six and three, if I'm not mistaken, is what I see.
C²AT¹T²B	Dite il ver;	You tell the truth,
C²AT²B	or passate al ventisei.	now move to [space] 26.
T¹	Io qui tirar vorrei.	I'd like to play now.
C¹C²AT²B	Tirate	Take a turn.
T¹	Eccovi il punto	Here is the space.
C¹C²AT²	Affè, che sete giunto nell'Osteria, Signore;	Alas, you have arrived at the Inn, my lord;
C²AT²	qui vi convien pagar, per uscir fuore.	here one must pay to get out.
B	Ecco che tiro anch'io	Here, I'll play too.
C¹AT¹T²	O buon, per Dio!	O good, by God!
C¹C²A	Nella Cisterna entrate,	You land in the Well,
T¹T²	et il premio pagate,	and pay the penalty,
tutti	e state tanto poi,	and remain there until
	ch'altri venga per voi.	another comes for you.

The game continues with the other players taking their turns, beginning with the Alto. Although this voice had represented one of the ladies in the *prima parte*, this player is male (he will later be addressed as "Signore"), exhibiting some of the same lack of refinement as the Alto in the *gioco di primiera*: he seems first unready to take his turn and then to be wasting time "aiming" the dice. The result is another unlucky move: he lands in the Labyrinth (space 42, another impossible first move) and must move back to space 39. The Canto Secondo, now also addressed as "Signora," comports herself better, seeming to be unsure when to play or what her roll means, but in fact it is the best possible opening: the five-four combination that moves the player all the way to space 53. Finally, the second Tenore, addressed as "signor Conte," takes his turn and rolls a six, which correctly moves him to the Bridge. Croce's rule here is inconsistent with extant sixteenth-century versions of the game: normally the Bridge (space 6) is a lucky move, entitling the player to move ahead to space 12, though payment into the pot is still required. Here along with the payment the player must move back to the beginning; again, Croce's variant on the rules makes the men's bad luck as severe as possible.

AT^2B	Chi tocca dietro, tiri	Whose turn it is, take it
T^1T^2B	senz'altro indugio e miri.	without further delay and aiming.
$C^1C^2T^2$	Pagate, se volete.	Pay up, if you please.
A	Perchè?	Why?
$C^1T^1T^2B$	Perchè nel Laberinto sete.	Because you are in the Labyrinth.
$C^1C^2T^1T^2B$	Ecco il punto;	Here is the space;
C^1C^2	or pagate	now pay
$C^1C^2T^1T^2B$	e indietro poi tre punti ritornate.	and then return three spaces back.
C^1AT^1B	Tocca a voi il tir'or ora.	Now it's your turn.
C^2	A me?	Mine?
$C^1AT^1T^2$	Sì, sì Signora.	Yes, yes, my lady.
C^2	Cinque e quattro.	Five and four.
$C^1AT^1T^2B$	Vedete?	Do you see that?
	Cinquantatre di punto fatto avete.	You've made it to space fifty-three!
$C^1C^2AT^1$	Tirate, signor Conte.	Take your turn, signor Count.
T^2	Sei.	Six.
C^2AT^1B	Voi sete al Ponte;	You are on the Bridge;
C^1AT^1B	pagate, e dopo poco	pay, and then
$C^1C^2AT^1T^2B$	ritornerete a cominciar il gioco.	return to the beginning of the game.

The second round of turns begins with another lucky move for the Canto Primo: she lands on a Goose, moves ahead, and lands on a blank space carrying no further penalty. The first Tenore thinks his luck is changing when he too lands on a Goose, but the extra spaces he moves leave him in the Boat (a typical variant of the Prison on space 52), requiring another payment. The Basso, still stuck in the Well, loses his turn, and the Alto hopes for luck before rolling the dice ("Ecco il tiro e la sorte"). This mildly uncourtly oath is repaid with the worst possible luck: he lands on Death (space 58), obliging him to pay and return to the beginning. The Canto Secondo, who on her first turn had leapfrogged all the way to space 53, now rolls a ten to land on space 63 and win the game. Once again, although she knows the result, she leaves it to the others to confirm it, specifically the second Tenor, who has no need to take his next turn, since the game has been won.

C^1	A me tocca tirare.	It's my turn.
T^1T^2B	Ecco che vi convien l'occa passare.	Here you must [continue] past the Goose.
C^2A	Or qui fermate il segno	Now here your piece rests
$C^2AT^1T^2B$	senza poner il pegno.	without paying a price.
T^1	A me tirar pur occa.	I too got the Goose!
$C^1C^2AT^2B$	Olà!	Hooray!
C^1C^2A	Passate l'Occa	Pass the Goose
C^1AT^2B	e nella Barca entrate,	and arrive at the Boat,
$C^1C^2AT^2$	et ivi state et il premio pagate.	and here remain and pay the price.
B	Perd'il mio tir or ora perchè nella cisterna io fò dimora.	I lose my turn now since I'm still stuck in the Well.
A	Ecco il tiro e la sorte.	Here is my turn and my luck.
$C^1C^2T^1T^2B$	Pagate pur, Signor, che sete in Morte;	Pay up, sir, for you landed on Death
T^2B	et vi convien tornare	and must return
C^2AT^2B	dal principio del gioco e cominciare.	to the beginning of the game and start over.
C^2	Ora tirar vogl'io; quattre sei, per mia fe', che il gioco è mio!	Now I want my turn. Four and six, by my faith, the game is mine!
C^1AT^1B	Fate, Signor, el conto.	My lord, add up the total.
T^2	Sessantatré di punto.	Sixty-three spaces.
tutti	Signora vinto avete: or gli premi prendete.	My lady, you've won: now take the prize.

E noi per farle onore	And now in your honor
cantiamo a tutte l'hore:	we'll forever sing:
Viva, viva l'amore.	long live love!

Croce's piece thus depicts a game of chance that in fact inscribes the hierarchies of courtly society: the women remain somewhat aloof from the game (they seem to roll the dice themselves but not to advance their tokens on the board), have extraordinary luck, never pay a penalty, and in one case win the game in only two moves, the fewest in which a victory is mathematically possible. Their good fortune is affirmed by their moves' agreement with the layout of the standard *gioco dell'oca* board while also concluding the game before it becomes tedious for the singers. The men have worse luck, have to pay on every single move, and usually receive other penalties like a lost turn or backward movement on the track; the Alto, representing a younger man who flouts the etiquette of game playing, has the worst luck of all. That the men's moves are for the most part *not* mathematically possible doesn't interfere with the verisimilitude of the game, since the second Canto's winning moves, which set boundaries on the length of the piece, are technically plausible.

As in Striggio's "Gioco di primiera," Croce's depiction concludes with the players joining together in music making, but here this is framed not as a consolation for the loser but as a song in honor of the winner, "Viva l'amore," set in a brief triple-meter passage. The good fortune—and virtuous behavior—of the women has been rewarded not only with victory in the game itself but with a song in praise of love. The contextualization of a game of chance as a site for the veneration of female virtue is at odds with condemnations of gambling by Cardano and others, even given the noble setting and apparently inconsequential stakes. Yet in a musicalized—and therefore idealized—game, singers are granted imaginary access to an otherwise suspect activity, just as singing erotic madrigal texts allows them to envoice passions and model emotional experiences within a safely bounded conceptual realm.

The Lovers' Lottery

The metaphorical signification of a game of chance is carried further in Vecchi's "Lotto amoroso," a game for seven voices included in *Selva di varia ricreatione*. This "lottery of love" follows procedures similar to those described as early as 1448 for a public lottery in Milan.[28] Each player pays an ante for a numbered ticket on which is written his or her name or, as here, an associated motto; these are placed in a box or barrel. In a second box are tickets for each of the available prizes plus enough blank tickets to make up equal numbers with the first box. Tickets are drawn in pairs, one from each box, and the name or motto on the first is read out before the second ticket is revealed to indicate either a prize or a blank ticket. Vecchi's lottery is played out not in public but among a learned group, and the allegory of love determines most aspects of the game: the proposal in the *prima parte* is a polychoral dialogue between a four-voice *primo choro* (the proposer) and a three-voice *secondo choro* (the potential players). The ante is "one tear and one sigh," described in the dialogue as a small price, and the prizes available are Venus's face, Apollo's golden hair, and Mercury's wit. The game is to be conducted by the allegorical figures Honesty, Justice, and Fate.

The lottery begins in the *seconda parte* with no further preliminaries. The ten mottoes read are all reflections on luck; most are identifiable as quotations from Petrarch or mottoes that may have been in wider circulation (table 5.1).[29] The winning mottoes express the most dispassionate views of fortune, stoically accepting fate while modestly hoping for good luck; the other eight mottoes tend toward either avaricious wishes for luck or pessimistic dismissals of hope. The first motto, "Each has his destiny from the day he is born," which is the final line of Petrarch's "Amor, che meco al buon tempo di stavi," is sung by the Canto and Alto and answered by the full seven-voice texture with the words "Gratia ventura!" indicating that a winning ticket has been drawn from the second box. The rest of the mottoes are sung by the three-voice *secondo choro* and are answered by the four-voice *choro primo* with "Bianco, bianco!" indicating a white ticket. Finally the last motto, "The luck that one least expects is the best," provokes another exclamation of "Gratia ventura!" indicating another winner. There is no need to imagine representing individual players here: the contents of each ticket are announced by those running the lottery, not by the players themselves. Yet the erudite mottoes, which would have been chosen by each player, evoke the more elevated style of *giochi di spirito* described by Bargagli (see below). In a real game of wit, of course, we would expect that the most appropriate and learned mottoes would be chosen as winners, but here, as in Croce's "Gioco dell'oca," the correspondence between wit and luck is depicted as purely coincidental.

The third and final part of the lottery announces that, the prizes of Venus's face and Apollo's hair having been won, only Mercury's wit remains. The

Table 5.1. Sources of mottos in "Lotto amoroso," *seconda parte*

MOTTO (WINNERS INDICATED)	SOURCE AND COMMENTS
Sua ventura hà ciascun dal di che nasce (Each has his destiny from the day he is born) WINNER	Petrarch, poem no. 303, "Amor, che meco al buon tempo di stavi," line 14
A sorte s'indovina (Leave Fate to the fortune-teller)	
La speranza mi pasce (Hope nourishes me)	Related to Dante, *L'Inferno* 8.106–108, "Ma qui m'attendi, e lo spirito lasso / Conforta e ciba di speranza buona, Ch'io non ti lascierò nel mondo basso" (But you wait here for me, and feed and comfort your tired spirit with good hope, for I will not abandon you in this low world)
Gratie ch'à pochi il ciel largo destina (Grace, which generous heaven grants to few)	Petrarch, poem no. 213, "Grazie ch' a pochi il Ciel largo destina," line 1
Mie venture al venir son pigre e tarde (My luck is late and slow in coming)	Petrarch, poem no. 57, "Mie venture al venir son tarde e pigre," line 1
Sors bona nihil aliud (Good luck and nothing else)	Latin proverb of unknown origin; taken as a personal motto around 1652 by Hungarian poet Miklós Zrínyi
A i Lotti non do fede (I don't put my faith in lotteries)	
S'acquistan per ventur' e non per arte (One wins by luck, not by skill)	Petrarch, poem no. 261, "Qual donna attende a gloriosa fama," line 14
Nemo sua sorte contentus (No one is content with his fortune)	Latin proverb, from Horace, *Satires* 1.1.1–3: "Qui fit, Maecenas, ut nemo, quam sibi sortem / seu ratio dederit seu fors obiecerit, illa / contentus vivat, laudet diversa sequentis?" (How comes it, Maecenas, that no man living is content with the lot that either his choice has given him or chance has thrown in his way, but each has praise for those who follow other paths?)
Piu ne giova quel ben che men s'aspetta (The luck that one least expects is the best) WINNER	

game play now progresses somewhat differently. The mottoes, such as they are, are now sung by solo voices (including the Settimo part, abbreviated as 7 in the analysis below) rather than by the *choro secondo,* and the replies of "Bianco, bianco!" are now given to various combinations of voices drawn from both choirs. Moreover, the solo statements are no longer poetic quotations but rather imitations of various Italian dialects and foreign languages. Following the traditional rules of this type of lottery, of course, it is implausible that the tickets randomly drawn from the barrel would suddenly all have a different style of motto. Instead, it would seem as though individual players each draw tickets from the second box, and the declarations are more informal and spontaneous comments on luck. Once again, ten tickets are drawn; the final prize goes to the last one:

choro primo (675B)	Hora che 'l crin de l'oro De l'auriga celest'in premio è dato, Sol vi riman del Messagier allato La facondia.	Now that the golden hair of the celestial charioteer has been awarded, there remains only the wit of Mercury.
tutti	Hor veggiam di chi la sia.	Now let's see whose it will be.
C	Si mi estreglia me ghia, De sta vez seras mia.	If my star guides me, this time you will be mine.
675B	Bianco, bianco!	White! White!
A	O assortao, mi Pantalon, Se me busco sto boccon!	Dear Pantalone, may fate grant me this morsel!
C75B	Bianco, bianco!	White! White!
6	Le visage di Vener, par ma foi, Je suis bien sert que sera de moi.	The face of Venus, by my faith, I am sure will be mine.
CAT5	Bianco, bianco!	White! White!
B	A su pur ach merlot S'à crez d'havi sto lot!	I am such a fool if I think I'll win this lottery!
675T	Bianco, bianco!	White! White!
T	Frate, se'l luotto mi buorrà toccare, Chisso e chillo e chillautro hà da spantare!	Brother, if I win the lottery, this, that, and the other one will have to look out!
CA5B	Bianco, bianco!	White! White!
7	Io havid da saver che sta ventura L'hà da tuccar à qualche creatura.	One must understand that the luck must go to someone.
6ATB	Bianco, bianco!	White! White!
5	Se mi toccer sentur da compagnon, Mi follere far un trinchere col fiascon.	If I hear it goes to a friend, I would offer a toast from my flask.
67TB	Bianco, bianco!	White! White!
A	Fasil'intmè cascher à la Romegna, Se no cha digh iet si chencher'i. megna	Let it be sent off right away to Romagna, or else I say it will be eaten up here by the pox.
C75B	Bianco, bianco!	White! White!

T	Vuot una ruzla de sulcizza fina,	I want a string of fine sausage
	E fa cla tocca à la me Mudnina.	and to have it go to my Modenese girl.
C75B	Bianco, bianco!	White! White!
6	Il dì che costei nacque eran le stelle	The day she was born the stars
	Che producon fra noi felici effetti.	produced happiness among us.
tutti	Gratia ventura!	Congratulations!
choro primo	Facciam s'innanzi gli tre fortunati.	Have them come forward, the three lucky ones.
	Ecco i premii bramati.	Here are the much-valued prizes.
choro secondo	Siamo qui Guiderdon 'apparecchiati.	We here, the Rewarders, are prepared.
choro primo	Dica ciascuno il numero del motto.	Each one say the number of the motto:
C	Trenta,	Thirty,
A	quaranta,	forty,
T	e'l mio novanta otto.	and my ninety-eight.
tutti	Hor prendete,	Now take it,
	Eccov'il lotto, onde felici sete.	the lottery there, and thus be happy.
	Gratia ventura!	Congratulations!

After a string of stereotypical (and often indecorous or obscene) comments in various dialects, the winning ticket goes to the only Tuscan motto, another from Petrarch, "The day she was born the stars produced happy effects among us."[30] The erudition of the quotation is matched by a highly embellished cadence on "effetti" that functions both as text painting and as a reference to the vocal virtuosity of the solo singers connected to the most important Italian courts (example 5.1). Since the players were established in the first two *partes* as learned participants in polite social play, the rest of the mottoes in this part should not be read as indicating that they come from the wide range of places and social levels represented but rather that they are now taking turns imitating various linguistic types. The mottoes are thus always in a sense comic, portraying a cultural "other" defined as alien to the social sphere of the players; the background function of the "Lotto amoroso" is therefore to reinforce social norms through negative example.

The crucial difference between Vecchi's negative examples and Striggio's or Croce's is that Vecchi's imagined players know they are imitating humorous stereotypes, while the angry outbursts of the young man (voiced

Example 5.1. Vecchi, "Lotto amoroso," mm. 150–155 (Sesto).

by the Alto) in the other *giochi* are (within the imagined world of the poem) "real" losses of composure that must be regained through the more regulated (and therefore regulating) activity of musical performance at the end of each piece. Vecchi's game, in which no such outbursts occur, does not end with a call for music but only with a repetition of the congratulatory cry, "Gratia ventura!" The *terza parte* of the "Lotto amoroso," while still depicting a game of chance like Striggio's and Croce's *giuochi,* in which the winners' virtue is essentially allegorical, moves closer to representing a game of skill in which the players entertain one another through imitations.

Comic Imitations: "Il bando del asino"

Vecchi's first depiction of a game in the "Sienese" style described in Bargagli's *Dialogo* is found not in *Le veglie di Siena* itself but in the *Convito musicale* of 1597. "Il bando del asino" is mentioned in the preface to *Convito* as "a pie of banished ass"—one of the nutritionally outlandish dishes to tempt weak appetites (see chapter 3). This six-voice piece in two parts depicts a courtly group playing two games of imitations. Both games are in the style Bargagli classes as *giuochi di scherzo,* whose goal is to prompt laughter, as opposed to the more intellectual *giuochi di spirito.* Yet in the context of *Convito* the pastoral setting of the "Bando" identifies it as an idealized and elevated entertainment, particularly in contrast to the piece that precedes it, "O Giardiniero," which depicts an unidentified visitor (*passagiero*) strolling by a cultivated garden. The gardener encourages him to taste various wines, mimicking the structure of a rustic drinking game, until he exhibits their intoxicating effects in both words and music (see chapter 6). The games in the "Bando," however frivolous, are played out according to the formal structure of courtly games by players who demonstrate imagination and skill with imitations of both musical sounds and chaotic noise.

Following the initial greeting, the first game is announced as the *gioco de'*
stromenti, in which each player is asked to "play" an instrument. This being
a game, no further comment is required to explain that the players are imitating their chosen instruments vocally, singing syllables suggestive of instrumental timbres. After each player has taken a turn, all the instruments
join together to play simultaneously, prompting laughter. This game has no
exact parallel in Bargagli's *Dialogo,* but in form it resembles his "Giuoco del
gridare un'arte," in which each player imitates a street cry, first individu-
ally and finally all at once.[31] The crucial difference between these games,
of course, is that the street cries will yield only cacophony, while the instruments playing together in Vecchi's game produce a pleasing harmony—an
effect that would be impossible in a "real" game of instrumental imitations
(except perhaps among a group of musicians highly trained in *contrapunto
alla mente,* which Vecchi's seem not to be).

The depiction of individual characters in the first phase of the game follows some of the principles we have observed in other musical games: shifting two-, three-, and four-voice textures represent the voices of different
players, but not in such a way as to identify them with particular singers.
In brief exchanges of dialogue, the players ask each other what instruments
they "play" and prompt them to demonstrate. The effect can be seen in the
first extended exchange of this kind (following the *proposta*), as the game's
king, or leader, and another player imitate a harpsichord and a violone:

tutti	Questa ghirlanda che di noi facciamo,	This ring that we make of ourselves,
	O come mi diletta.	O how it pleases me.
	Hor che di tanto ci aletta	Now since it delights us so much
	Lo star qui assisi	to be seated here
	Fra l'herbett'e fiori,	among the grasses and flowers,
	Passiam l'hore noiose.	let's pass the weary hours.
	Hor sù, signori, tutti uniti,	Now up, gentlemen, all together,
	O che cantiamo	either let us sing,
	Over giochiamo.	or let us play.
C6A5	Voi set'il nostro Re, così vogliamo.	You will be our king, that is our wish.
5TB	Presto si faccia il gioco di stromenti.	Quickly, play the game of instruments.
tutti	Eccoci tutti intenti.	Here we are, all ready.
5TB	Qual stromento sai tu sonare?	What instrument do you know how to play?

C6A	So sonar'il mio Arpicordo.	I know how to play my harpsichord.
5TB	Sona un poco il tuo Arpicordo.	Play your harpsichord a little.
C6A	dingu dengu la dingu	dingu dengu la dingu
5TB	Bon per mia fe!	Good, by my faith!
C6A	E tu, che sai toccare?	And you, what do you know how to play?
5TB	So toccare il mio violone.	I know how to play my viol.
C6A	Tocca un poco, quel tuo violone.	Play it a bit, that viol of yours.
5TB	lirum lirum li	lirum lirum li
C6A	Buon per mia vita!	Good, by my life![32]

This pattern continues with different vocal combinations as other players imitate a lyre, crumhorn, and lute. The association of individual singers with players changes when all the instruments play together, since in this passage each voice imitates a different instrument (example 5.2). Table 5.2 indicates the vocal groupings that initially sing each imitation and the solo voices that take up the equivalent vocables in the "instrumental" *tutti* passage.[33] Logically enough, in the *tutti* passage each instrument is imitated by one of the voices previously associated with it. Since only five instruments are described in the first phase of the game, however, one voice—the Alto—is left without an instrument to imitate. Its vocables, "tincu tin trenco trenca tren," have not previously been heard, so it would seem that this voice is here representing a new, unnamed instrument. One wonders whether the singers of "Il bando del asino" might have noticed this and speculated about what instrument this new sound might represent. In any case, the passage of collective imitations comprises two identical statements of a four-breve passage in six-voice counterpoint in which each voice's melodic style remains faithful to that of the instrument it represents. More importantly, the players themselves find the result successful, exclaiming, "O che grata sinfonia" (What a pleasing *sinfonia*!). One of their number (voiced by the Alto, Tenore, and Basso) now takes on the role of leader, promising that the next game, "The Devil's Music" will be even more humorous.

The "Giuoco della Musica del diavolo" described by Bargagli is in fact a game based on imitations of animal sounds, and Vecchi's game is derived from his description: "[Of games] with imitation one may mention that of the Music of the devil, each player making the cry of an animal and, when the pestle [a symbol of the leader's authority] is thrown down, everyone making his noise at once."[34] Of course, this is the same general procedure prescribed for the "Giuoco del gridare un'arte" and played out in Vecchi's

Table 5.2. Vocal textures and instrumental imitations in "Il bando del asino," *prima parte*

INSTRUMENT	FIRST IMITATION	VOCABLES	*TUTTI* IMITATION (MM. 89–96)
harpsichord	CSA (mm. 37–45)	dingu denga la dingu	Canto
violone	5TB (mm. 51–54)	lirum lirum li	Basso
lyre (*lira*)	CSAT (mm. 60–66)	lira lira lira	Tenore
crumhorn (*cornamusa*)	CS5 (mm. 72–75)	vion vion vo	Sesto
lute	CS5B (mm. 79–85)	tren tren tirin tren tin tirin tren	Quinto
?	—	tincu tin trenco trenca tren	Alto

gioco de' stromenti. However, the pattern is varied somewhat in the version played in the second half of "Il bando del asino": six players (represented by solo voices) claim two animals each, a bird and a land animal. The contrast here with the instrumental imitations of the *gioco de' stromenti* is significant: as the leader says, the players must now exchange "song" for "voice and sound." The turn-taking portion of the game does not include the imitations themselves but only the players claiming their animals; this alone is enough to provoke unanimous laughter:

ATB	Ciascun di voi s'elegga duo animali,	Each of you should select two animals,
	Volatil' un, l'altro terrestre sia.	one winged, the other terrestrial.
C65	E poi c'abbiam da fare?	And then what would we have to do?
ATB	Havet'il versi lor'a contrafare.	You have to mimic their voices.
C65	Questo sarà difficil d'imitare.	This will be difficult to imitate.
ATB	Quello ch'esprimer non si puo al canto,	That which cannot be expressed in song
	Supplisc'invece sua la voc'e'l suono.	must instead be supplied by voice and sound.
tutti	O buon'o buono!	Oh good, oh good!
T	Io prendo dunque la Cornachia e'l Cane;	I'll take the crow and the dog.
C	Io la Gallina e'l Grillo;	I the hen and the cricket.
A	Io la Pecora e'l Cuco;	I the sheep and the cuckoo.
B	L'Anitra vogl'e'il Toro;	I want the duck and the bull.
6	Io 'l Lusignuolo e'l Gatto;	I the nightingale and the cat.
5	Io l'Asino e'l Colombo.	I the ass and the dove.
tutti	Ah, ah, ah! Mo chi non riderebbe, d'esta musica nova?	Ha ha ha! Now who would not laugh at this new music?[35]

Example 5.2. (*above, facing, and overleaf*) Vecchi, "Il bando del asino," mm. 89–96.

92
din - gu, di, din-gu, din-gu, din-gu, din-gu, din - gu,
- on, vo, vi - on, vo, vi-on, vi, vi-on, vo,
- cu, tin, tren - - - - co
ti - rin, tren, tron, tren, ti - rin, tren,
li-ra, li - ra, li - ra, li-ra, li -
- rum, li, li - - - - rum,
94
din - gu, din - gu, la din - gu, din - gu,
vi - on, vi, vi - on, vo,
tran - ca, tren - ca,
ti - rin, ti - rin, tren, ti - rin, ti - rin,
ra, li - ra, li - ra, li -
li - rum, li - rum,

The *tutti* imitations follow, first with the bird sounds and then with the land animals. Although the imitations are sung, the leader's instruction that something other than "expression in song" is required to imitate these sounds is still relevant: for nine breves the music reiterates a single harmony almost without interruption (example 5.3). Such harmonic stasis had frequently been used to imitate nonmusical noise in *battaglie* and *caccie* since the middle of the century, and here it stands in contrast to the somewhat comical but still "musical" imitation of instruments in the *prima parte,* which featured harmonic movement in a clear and repeating pattern. As participants in social music making, the performers are, in fact, singing, but as imagined players in a game of imitations, they produce something recognizable as noise.

Within this "noisy" understanding of the animal imitations, the condemnation of the ass (Quinto) for a contrapuntal error takes on a parodistic quality, since the Quinto does not actually commit a musical solecism (at worst, he is guilty of doubling the chordal third).

Hor fermat'il concerto,	Now stop the concert,
Che l'asino inesperto	for the inexpert ass
È callato tre voci.	is lowered by three notes.

Example 5.3. (*above and following three pages*) Vecchi,
"Il bando del asino," *seconda parte*, mm. 30–45.

34
dà, cot co-dà, cot co - dà, co co co co co cot co-
di le di le di le di le di pi-o pi-o pi-o pi-o pi - o.
cu cu cu cu cu cu cu cu cu cu
umb umb umb umb
cra cra cra cra cra cra cra cra
qua qua qua qua qua
36
dà. Gri gri gri
Gnau gnau gnau gnau
cu cu. Be be be be
umb. An o - gnhan
cra cra.
Bau bau bau bau bau bau
qua. Muon un muon

38
gri gri gri gri gri gri gri gri
gnau re - gnau gnau gnau gnau gnau
be be be be be be be be
an o - gnhan an
bau bau bau bau bau bau bau bau bau bau bau
muon un muon un
40
gri gri. Hor fer - ma - t'il con -
gnau gnau.
be - e - e - e - e. Hor fer - ma - t'il con -
an an.
bau bau bau. Hor fer - ma - t'il con -
muon. Hor fer - ma - t'il con -

cer - to, è cal - la -

cer - to, Che l'A - si-no in - es - per - to è____

cer - to, Che l'A - si-no in - es - per - to

cer - to, Che l'A - si-no in - es - per - to è cal -

to tre vo - - ci.

cal - la - to tre vo - ci.

è cal - la - to tre vo - ci.

la - to tre vo - ci.

The mistake can best be explained as one of imitation rather than counterpoint: the voice of the ass has been established in mm. 36–39 as confined to the pitches b and c′, but in m. 40 it falls to g and e; the move to g avoids forming parallel octaves with the Sesto (the cat). This shift to a lower vocal register does not compromise the contrapuntal texture so much as highlight the comic timbre of the ass's "voice"—a quality that Vecchi cannot convey in notated music but that singers could readily play to the hilt.

The remainder of the *seconda parte* is a much longer exaggerated condemnation pronouncing the ass's banishment, from which the piece's name is taken, replete with imitations of trumpets, a "public" instrument not heard among the courtly ensemble of the *prima parte*. Each statement in this section is first sung by the lowest three voices and immediately repeated by the upper three in the manner of a public proclamation. The ass is banished in perpetuity, and all animals are commanded not to sing in his company, "because he does not know the style of modern singing." Although this section of the piece corresponds to the final "judgment" portion of a game, in which winners are announced and penalties are levied, "Il bando del asino" pronounces punishment not on the player but on the animal itself, playfully blurring the distinction between the imitation of a game and the imitation enacted within that game. Only the final line, "Vivan gli spensierati" (Long live the carefree), provides a brief return to a *tutti* homophonic musical texture and to the framing social setting. The term *spensierati* could well be intended to evoke the kinds of names used by academies, similar to the Intronati, that were Bargagli's source.[36]

Giuochi di spirito and *di scherzo:* Games and Variety

In Bargagli's *Dialogo*, the leader of the conversation, Sodo (the academic pseudonym of Marcantonio Piccolomini, though here ventriloquized by Bargagli), offers his most concrete definition of the sorts of games under discussion only after the conversation is well under way and various games have been described. His central tenet is that games are a means of fostering conversation, particularly between men and women, and for this reason he rejects physical sport, gambling, and chess—games that exclude women in polite society or do not encourage conversation. He also omits jokes (*burla e scherzo*) that are sometimes called games, "except insofar as in our games we desire pleasure [*piacevolezza*]."[37] Sodo's approved games have pleasure as their goal precisely because they are to be played among mixed-gender groups to nurture desire: "Among the most ingenious and learned men in the world, if there were no women to be found, they would never play anything other than wicked and insipid games, and even among women and men together, if there is not some spark of honest passion, the games will always proceed with coldness and melancholy."[38] The pleasure of games, therefore, is a manifestation of erotic pleasure, and the contention involved in such games is ultimately the competition for love. This emphasis, which echoes Castiglione's general comments on all aspects of courtly behavior, is not to be overlooked in Sodo's subsequent "official" definition of games as "a festive activity of a happy and amorous company [*lieta e amorosa brigata*], in which, upon a pleasant or ingenious proposition [*piacevole od ingegnosa proposta*] made by one person acting as author or guide of the game, the others all do or say something different from each other, and this is done for the purpose of delight and entertainment [*di diletto e d'intertenimento*]."[39] Bargagli's description of the group as *amorosa* here is significant, as are the terms used to describe the games themselves: all games have as their goal *diletto* and *intertenimento,* qualities for which Bargagli elsewhere uses *piacevolezza.* Here, however, he distinguishes games based on propositions that are *piacevole* from those that are *ingegnosa.* Although this classification of games into ever more subtly delineated categories leads him to recycle terminology in potentially ambiguous ways, the contrasts he draws between games of greater and lesser degrees of seriousness are congruent with Vecchi's poetics of variety, particularly in his division of *Le veglie di Siena* into two parts, which he labels "Piacevole" and "Grave."

The Games of *Le veglie di Siena*

At the lightest end of Sodo's spectrum are activities whose very identity as respectable games is contested. One of the interlocutors, l'Attonito (the pseudonym of Lelio Maretti), suggests that the game of tongue twisters (*bisticci*) should be included in the definition of games: "I like your definition of the game together with your defense of it. My only doubt is that some games (that really are games) are not covered by this definition, such as the game of *Bisticci,* since if I have proposed this *bisticcio* . . . [he recites two examples], everyone must say the same words quickly without changing anything, and changing it in error he would be punished."[40] Sodo replies that since the difference of action in such a game is the result of error rather than choice, he would consider *bisticci* to be "simple jests [*scherzi*] rather than games . . . and almost *intermezzi* to true games."[41]

Bargagli's distinction between true games involving conversation and *bisticci*, which are in a sense fully "scripted," draws a striking parallel to music and points up the most crucial difference between playing games and recreational singing: the first goal of singing polyphony must be to sing one's own part correctly so that the contrapuntal fabric remains intact. Deviations from the written music may be allowable in the form of embellishments, but if these are elaborate, they require prior preparation and rehearsal—conditions that were common for audience-directed performance by professional groups such as the Ferrarese *concerto* and its imitators but were less suited to amateur recreational singers.[42] If sung correctly, a polyphonic song will always sound substantially the same, and the enjoyably game-like quality of recreational singing (as distinct from the aesthetic quality) lies in the challenge of getting it right, just as it does for tongue twisters.

Musical settings of *bisticci* therefore pose a double challenge: both the music and the text must be negotiated correctly by the singers. We have already seen such a piece, Vecchi's canzonetta "O donna ch'a mio danno I ciel ti denno" (see chapter 1), in which the challenge of the *bisticcio* is emphasized by the relatively consistent contrapuntal texture, requiring each singer to negotiate the difficult text independently. However, a different challenge faces the singers of a piece that itself imitates a *game* of tongue twisters, such as the one sung in *Le veglie di Siena* at the conclusion of the first part. This piece not only adapts one of the *bisticci* recited by Attonito in Bargagli's *Dialogo* but also is placed—like an intermezzo—between more substantial games, *La caccia d'Amore* (the hunt for Cupid, another game described by Bargagli) and "the humors of modern music" represented in the second part of the book. Only three of the six singers actually perform the *bisticcio,* but they must do so twice:

ATB	A chi di voi dà il core,	Whoever among you has the courage,
TB	con lingua sciolta, libera, e spedita,	with limber, free, and quick tongue,
ATB	Di dir com'io dirò, nè faccia errore,	to speak as I shall speak, without error,
AT5B	Havrà plauso d'honore.	will be honored with applause.
tutti	Hor comenciate [*sic*], e 'l gioco n'inesgnate.	Now begin, and learn the game.

A5B	Al pozzo de messer Pazzin de' Pazzi	At the well of Mister Pazzin de' Pazzi
	V'era una Pazza, che per gran pezzo	there was a madwoman who always
	Mangiava pizza, lavando pezze,	ate pizza while washing rags.
	Ma sopragiunse Pazzin de' Pazzi,	But Mister Pazzin de' Pazzi came,
	Prese la pazza la pizz'e le pezze,	took the madwoman, the pizza, and the rags,
	E le gittò nel pozzo.	and threw them into the well.
tutti	O stravagante gioco!	What a funny game!
	Tornatelo a ridire.	Go back and say it again.
ATB	Per questa volta sola.	Just this one time.
tutti	Ma ditelo a parola per parola.	But say it word by word.
A5B	Al pozzo de messer Pazzin de' Pazzi	At the well of Mister Pazzin de' Pazzi
	V'era una Pazza, che per gran pezzo	there was a madwoman who always
	Mangiava pizza, lavando pezze,	ate pizza while washing rags.
	Ma sopragiunse Pazzin de' Pazzi,	But Mister Pazzin de' Pazzi came,
	Prese la pazza la pizz'e le pezze,	took the madwoman, the pizza, and the rags,
	E le gittò nel pozzo.	and threw them into the well.
TB	Siate la prima voi,	You shall be the first one,
ATB	Signora Margherita.	Signora Margherita.
CS	Eccomi, eccomi	Here I am, here I am,
CSA	Pronta a'cenni suoi,	ready for your signal,
	Che la legge del gioco a ciò m'invita.	as the rules of the game ask of me.
T5B	O che dama compita!	O what a gracious lady!
	Mi date pur la vita.	She'll enliven me.
CSA	Al pozzo de messer Pazzan dal Pozzo ...	At the well of Mister Pazzan dal Pozzo ...
tutti	Un pegno, Signora!	A forfeit, Signora!
	Un pegno, chè avete errato.	A forfeit, since you have erred.
CSAT	Basta, basta; perchè quest è un bisticcio	Enough, enough; for this tongue twister
	Che troppo ha del capriccio.	is too frivolous.
SA5B	Non più, non più, mutiamo gioco,	No more, no more, let's change games,
tutti	Chè ogni facetia è bella per un poco.	for every pleasure is only amusing for a bit.

Certain characters can be distinguished by their vocal textures, though as with other games these identifications are not always precise: the proposal for the game is voiced by the Alto-Tenore-Basso trio, saying that the others must "speak as I shall speak," yet the *bisticcio* itself is sung by a slightly different trio of Alto, Quinto, and Basso. Signora Margherita is unambiguously represented by the three upper voices (Canto, Sesto, and Alto), while the three lower ones respond as another member of the company, using the first-person singular in "Mi date pur la vita."[43]

The piece begins in a **c** mensuration, indicating an evenly divided semibreve *tactus*, but the *bisticcio* sections switch to triple meter signed with **3** and written in perfect semibreves. By the end of the sixteenth century there was no standard notational practice to suggest a tempo relationship between these signs, but it is clear from the text that the triple-meter *bisticcio* is to be sung quickly—very likely as quickly as possible.[44] This question of tempo is significant, because when the players (now back in **c** mensuration) ask for the *bisticcio* to be repeated slowly ("ma ditelo a parola per parola"), they sing in a syncopated rhythm that mimics a slower version of triple meter, only to have the leader recite it again with exactly the same mensural shift as before (example 5.4).

Does the notation suggest that the leader playfully ignores the request for a slower performance of the *bisticcio* and sings it just as quickly as before, or did Vecchi simply reuse the same notation for a repetition that can or should be sung at a slower tempo? Clearly, the singers themselves might choose either option, interpreting how players in a game might behave; the leader's desire to help the players learn the words competes against the temptation to show off the speed of which he is capable. Signora Margherita's brief attempt at the *bisticcio* likewise uses triple meter, the rhythmic style of which by this point clearly distinguishes performance of the tongue twister from ordinary speech. In the end the players dismiss the game as too frivolous ("troppa ha del capriccio"), echoing Bargagli's comment that *bisticci* are simple jests (*scherzi*) that are at best diversions to be enjoyed among other "true" games. This is precisely how the *gioco de' bisticci* is situated within *Le veglie di Siena*, where it is included among games conforming to Bargagli's strict definition.

As Bargali's treatise continues, Sodo broadens his categories of *ignegnosi* and *piacevoli* in a way that complicates their relationship with the usual poetic binarism (used by Vecchi in *Le veglie*) of *grave* and *piacevole*: "But having said what a game might be, let us look at what sorts of games there are. In truth, it seems that all games of the kind we are speaking about and as we have defined them can be reduced to this general division: they are games either of wit and ingenuity [*di spirito e d'ignegno*] or of jest and pleasure [*di scherzo e di piacevolezza*]."[45] The meaning of *giuochi di scherzo* here is distinct from

Example 5.4. (*above, facing, and overleaf*) Vecchi, "A chi di voi d'al core" ("Bisticcio"), from *Le veglie di Siena*, mm. 976–1007.

Paz - zi V'e - ra u - na paz - za, che per gran pez - za Man -

Paz - zi V'e - ra u - na paz - za, che per gran pez - za Man -

Paz - zi V'e - ra u - na paz - za, che per gran pez - za Man -

gia - va piz - za, la - van - do pez - ze, Ma so - pra -

gia - va piz - za, la - van - do pez - ze, Ma so - pra -

gia - va piz - za, la - van - do pez - ze, Ma so - pra -

997
giun - se Paz - zin de' Paz - zi, Pre - se la paz - za la
giun - se Paz - zin de' Paz - zi, Pre - se la paz - za la
giun - se Paz - zin de' Paz - zi, Pre - se la paz - za la
1002
piz - z'e le pez - ze, E le git - tò nel poz - zo.
piz - z'e le pez - ze, E le git - tò nel poz - zo.
piz - z'e le pez - ze, E le git - tò nel poz - zo.

the simple *scherzo*, the latter having already been rejected from the kinds of games under discussion. As the dialogue continues, in fact, the two types of games are consistently described as *di spirito* and *di scherzo*. When the interlocutor Frastagliato objects that even games of jest may require a degree of wit, Sodo replies that although this is true, and that games of wit should likewise entail pleasure, the difference lies in the game's intended effect. Games of wit should provoke "more of a serious hilarity, so to speak, than open laughter," whereas games of jest should make people bold and cheerful, "even though this must be accompanied by the grace and skill of the players."[46] Vecchi's characterization of the two parts of *Le veglie di Siena* as *piacevole* and *grave* conforms more to Bargagli's continuum of *scherzoso* and *spiritoso* than to Pietro Bembo's terminology for poetic styles.

The tension between the imitative subject of *Le veglie*—evenings of entertainment in the Accademia degli Intronati—and Vecchi's by now familiar goal of combining various musical styles in a single book is immediately evident. The latter intent is declared on the title page, which announces that the book contains *I varii humori della musica moderna* and is divided into two parts, one light (*piacevole*) and the other serious (*grave*). The first part is described very briefly as including "gli humori faceti" (the comic humors), which emphasize Bargagli's *scherzoso* style while also requiring a measure of "grace and skill." To the second is attributed a list of fourteen distinct humors, many of which are enigmatic, and some of which are arguably more light than serious:[47]

LE VEGLIE
DI SIENA,
OVERO I VARII HUMORI
Della Musica Moderna
D'HORATIO VECCHI
A Tre à 4. à 5. & à 6. Voci composte
E divise in due parti Piacevole e Grave
Nel piacevole s'havranno gli humori faceti.
E nel grave se n'havrà,

L'HUMOR GRAVE.	L'HUMOR GENTILE.
L'HUMOR ALLEGRO.	L'HUMOR AFFETUOSO.
L'HUMOR UNIVERSALE.	L'HUMOR PERFIDIOSO.
L'HUMOR MISTO.	L'HUMOR SINCERO.
L'HUMOR LICENTIOSO.	L'HUMOR SVEGGHIATO.
L'HUMOR DOLENTE.	L'HUMOR MALENCONICO.
L'HUMOR LUSINGHIERO.	L'HUMOR BALZANO.

In fact, the first part depicts three games played over two nights: a game of linguistic imitations on the first night, and the games of *La caccia d'Amore* and the *bisticci* (discussed above) on the second. The book's second part represents a single game in which the fourteen named "humors" are demonstrated through a series of as many madrigals. Although a "Prencipe," or leader, introduces each of the games, the musical representations of the games themselves vary in their fidelity to the kinds of activities described in Bargagli's *Dialogo*.

The game of imitations that comprises the first evening's entertainment has been compared to Bargagli's *giuoco delle lingue,* but there are important differences.[48] Bargagli's game emphasizes the mixture of languages in each player's speech and culminates (like the *Musica del diavolo*) in a moment of chaotic noise when all the players speak simultaneously in different languages or dialects:

> "The variety of languages," Mansueto now said, "would give occasion, as I see it, to making a game called the Game of Languages, in which, proposing to imitate the era of the Tower of Babel, one would order that each person would speak some words or say some motto in a language, each different from the others, and then putting them into conversation, speaking his own language and that of another. And when the pestle is thrown down, everyone would have to speak his chosen language at once."[49]

Whereas Vecchi elsewhere takes the titles of his games directly from Bargagli, the first *proposta* that opens *Le veglie di Siena* refers not to a *gioco delle lingue* but to a game of imitations (*De gli* IMITATI *il gioco,* from the *argomento*) or impersonations (*contrafare,* in the sung text). Moreover, Vecchi's series of imitations lacks the second and third phases of Bargagli's game, in which the players mingle different languages and finally all speak at once. The second phase is not fully explained in Mansueto's speech, since it closely resembles other games described in the treatise: the speakers play a kind of "verbal tag," each intermingling his or her own assumed language with that of another player, signaling that the second player must then do likewise.[50]

Vecchi's game consists more simply of a series of imitations of national types by the members of the company, each preceded by a *proposta* and followed by an *applauso*. Both women and men are included in the company, the latter all having pseudonymous academic names taken from interlocutors in Bargagli's *Dialogo* ("Signor Giocoso," a name absent from the *Dialogo,* being the only exception). The *proposte* all begin with a three-voice combination representing the leader, who chooses the next player and assigns the nationality to be imitated, with the rest of the company then joining in to express their anticipation of the performance. The imitations are also usually represented by a trio of voices, and in two cases the chosen player comments within the *proposta*, though there each player is represented by a vocal trio different from the one that performs the imitation itself. The *applauso* praising each imitation is, in every case, sung by all six voices; in the *applausi* for the Spanish and French songs, the company replies in the foreign language, as though to demonstrate its understanding of the speech. In the latter case, however, they also request a repetition of the imitation in Italian, for which Vecchi provides a translation printed in the music beneath the French.[51]

As shown in table 5.3, the distribution of singing voices in groups representing individual players is far less equitable than in the other games examined in this chapter.[52] Most notable is the presence of the Basso voice in every imitative section (and most of the trios within the *proposte*), a consistency that could accommodate an instrumental accompaniment improvised from the Basso part, and that in any case typifies the polarized treble-bass relationship that by 1604 had become standard in three-voice canzonettas and other styles increasingly identified as modern.[53] This texture is especially evident in the imitations performed by the female players Laura and Emilia, which are voiced as high duets over the considerably lower bass (even though Emilia imitates a male voice). The pieces in which male characters are represented by the narrower ambitus of the Tenore-Quinto-Basso trio sometimes use the newer treble-bass style, but they also employ the older equal-voiced texture typical of the *giustiniana,* particularly for the comic imitations of the Sicilian, the "Italianized German," and of course the Venetian.

The vocal distributions in this extended game imply not only potential instrumental accompaniment but also the kind of audience-directed performance with which the new texture was increasingly associated. The ubiquitous presence of the Basso and the relatively sparse use of the Sesto and Alto (who sing in only three imitations each) argues against the primarily recreational function of earlier musical games, or indeed of most of Vecchi's earlier music books, since these two singers would have considerably fewer opportunities to "play" at the two levels of imitation (of Sienese Intronati or of national types) on offer in the book. This is especially true if we assume that the game of imitations is to be performed as a complete series of seven

Table 5.3. Imitations and vocal textures in the game of imitations in *Le veglie di Siena*

TURN	SPEAKER(S) IN THE *PROPOSTA*	PLAYER CHOSEN	*IMITATIONE*	VOICES IN THE *IMITATIONE*
1	CATB (leader)	Stordito	Siciliano	T5B
2	T5B (leader)	Laura	Villanella	CAB
3	T5B (leader)	Frastagliato	Tedesco	T5B
4	ATB (leader)	Sodo	Spagnuolo	C6AB
5	ATB (leader)			
	C65 (Emilia)	Emilia	Francese	C6B
6	C6AT (leader)			
	AT5B (Giocoso)	Giocoso	Venetiano	T5B
7	C6B (leader)	Giulia	gli Hebrei	T5B/6AB (in dialogue)

sequences of *proposta–imitatione–applauso.* In any case, bass-dominated textures are not a constant feature of Vecchi's style in *Le veglie di Siena:* in longer pieces with more frequent changes of speaker (such as the game of *bisticci* and *La caccia d'Amore*), Vecchi allows more passages without the Basso, and in the final fourteen madrigals representing "the humors of modern music," he treats the voices relatively equally in five- and six-voice polyphony.

Reading the game of imitations as a "realistic" representation presents some ambiguities when the levels of imitation blur together. As in other musical games, Vecchi's polyphonic music represents speech both in the *proposte* and *applausi* that frame each imitation and nominally in the imitations themselves. Yet the imitations gain their national or regional character not only from the language used but also from their musical style. Sodo's imitation of a Spaniard, for example, employs the triple meter, syncopations, and predominantly homophonic texture of the contemporary *villancico,* though in a binary form without the repetition of the opening that might suggest the distinction between *estribillo* and *copla.* While the real singers and audience can therefore recognize the performance as musically "Spanish," the imagined players hear Sodo's imitation simply as a speech imitating a foreign language. Stordito's impression of a Sicilian is more ambiguous, since it includes a song-like passage of vocables (framed by a repeated passage of text and music) that would not make sense in a purely spoken imitation:

Tuttu lu tiempu, tuttu lu iornu,	All the time, all day long,
Tuttu le chiatu, tuttu lu cuori,	all my breath, all my heart,
Tuttu lu tiempu, ly iorno, lu chiatu,	all my time, my day, my breath,

Lu cor'haiu spisu con l'amurusa mea!	my heart I have spent on my love!
Ch'Amuri è un truffariellu,	For love is a little trickster,
Pizzicariellu,	a little pincher,
Ch'a chis'e qhill'a chill'autru	who strikes now this one, now that one,
Dà martiellu.	now another.
Lu crappiciusu, spissu mi fa chiangiri;	He is so capricious he often makes me cry;
Ma dicere lu voglio à la mamma!	how I would like to tell my mama!
Tra na nai na, la tra na nai na.	Tra na nai na, la tra na nai na.
Ch'Amuri è un truffariellu,	For love is a little trickster,
Pizzicariellu,	a little pincher,
Ch'a chis'e qhill'a chill'autru	who strikes now this one, now that one,
Dà martiellu.	now another.
Lu crappiciusu, spissu mi fa chiangiri;	He is so capricious he often makes me cry;
Ma dicere lu voglio à la mamma!	how I would like to tell my mama!

By separating a repeated musical unit, the vocables "tra na nai na, la tra na nai na" function as markers of musical form and might be interpreted as imitations of an instrument or as a vocal refrain such as those used in Gastoldi's *balletti* and related genres. Stordito's impersonation seems to take the form not of a speech but of a song, yet in the *applauso* the others remark, "Very good, *for he has spoken well*" ("che *dice* buono"). Vecchi seems to be playing his own game here, allowing the musical form of his imitation to penetrate the allegedly spoken form of the imagined game itself.

In the following imitation of a *villanella*, the ambiguity of the term—suggesting both a rustic girl and a form of rustic song—is hinted at in the *proposta* itself, which begins:

E voi Signora Laura,	And you, Signora Laura,
Che si v'aggrada	so that the sweet air of this villa
De la villa la dolce aura,	may be pleased,
Imitate una rozza villanella,	imitate a coarse *villanella*
Che quando al ballo va,	who, when she goes to the dance
S'e'n va cantando:	goes singing:
Fa la la la!	Fa la la la!

Laura, of course, obliges with a song featuring just such a refrain set in an up-to-date binary form and "modern" trio texture rather than the ternary form of the older faux-rustic *villanella*. Once again, however, the *applauso* praises Laura in terms that do not necessarily imply that she has been singing; her imitation is called a "nimble tale" ("sciolta favella"), and she is complimented for the grace of her "gestures, speech, and face" ("Ai gest'ai dett'al viso"). Laura has clearly given a performance, but not a musical one.

The most complex blurring between levels of imitation in Vecchi's game comes in the final turn, when Giulia is commanded to imitate Jews "realistically." The request is unusual, since the previous *proposte* have specifically requested performances of stereotypes: a lovesick Sicilian, a brazen peasant girl, an amorously steadfast Frenchman, and so on. Even more strange is the request that Giulia should imitate a plural group (*gli hebrei*) in her monologue and that she subsequently does so by depicting a dialogue of lamenting Jews whose geese have been stolen and eaten by Christians. The preceding exotic and humorous imitations of love-struck foreigners and peasants fulfill Bargagli's rule that games should be played by mixed-gender groups as a means of expressing or arousing desire. Giulia's imitation is compatible with this kind of erotic discourse only if we allow that the victimized Jews are simultaneously laughable and realistic; this assumption stands behind the enigmatic linkage in the *proposta* between Giulia's capacity for love and her ability to imitate well:

C6B	Signora Giulia, dove alberga Amore,	Signora Giulia, wherever Cupid lodges,
	Indi s'esprime ciò che detta il core.	there the heart's command is expressed.
	Però, se questo vale,	However, if this is true,
	Imitate gli hebrei del naturale.	imitate the Jews realistically.
tutti	O che riso, che riso!	Oh what a laugh, what a laugh!

In describing Cupid as residing in Giulia's heart, the leader picks up on a similar comment by Signor Giocoso in the previous *proposta*.[54] Giulia's imitation of the Jews, exceptionally, employs five of Vecchi's six voices, making possible a clearly constructed dialogue within Giulia's "solo" performance:

T5B	Corrit, corrit, Messer Aron!	Run, run, Mister Aron!
SAB	Chè gli Goi, chè gli Goi	Oh, the goyim, the goyim
	Hanno ucciso lo Peper'e 'l nostro Ochon,	have killed the gander and our goose:
	E'l nostro Peper'e 'l nostro Ochon.	it's our gander; it's our goose!

T5B	Badanai se l'han traffughet,	Oh my god, they've stabbed them,
	Affagatet,	they've strangled them,
	se l'hanno pelet.	they've skinned them.
	Merdochai,	Oh shit,
	se l'han, se l'han papet!	they've, they've gobbled them up![55]
	[the piece repeats from the second line]	

Don Harrán has read the opening line as a taunt from the Christian thief, who is now chasing Aron.[56] However, Vecchi's return to the Tenore-Quinto-Basso texture in the fifth line clarifies that the dialogue is between two Jews, just as the *proposta* had ordered. The "realism" of the portrayal can be accounted for in two ways. First, it makes only very limited use of the fake Hebrew language that characterizes comic depictions of Jews in music and theater of the period, notably in the scene between Francatrippa and the Jews in *L'Amfiparnaso*.[57] More insidiously, this scene of victimization is framed as the most humorous and also the most virtuosic performance of the evening. In the *applauso*, Giulia is declared the game's winner in lofty poetic language that strongly contrasts with the Jews' complaint and—uniquely among these imitations—describes her performance as *singing*. In a shift of voicing, the leader notes that the group enjoys this kind of performance, and then he begins to suggest another game before the party finally breaks up for the night:

tutti	Com'in Cielo ha più splendore	As in heaven the Great Comet[58]
	Stella Giulia fra le stelle,	has the greatest splendor among the stars,
	Così voi, fra queste belle,	so you, among these beauties,
	V'acquistat'il primo honore	take the first honor
	Di cantare, d'imitare,	for singing, and for imitating,
AT5B	Con manier'a noi si care.	in the manner dear to us.
	Vorrei proporv'un gioco assai più bello.	I'd like to propose an even lovelier game.
tutti	Ma, ma,	But, but,
CSA5	Odi che cant'homai	don't you now hear that
	Il vigilant'augello?	the unsleeping bird is singing?
tutti	Habbiam vegghiat'assai;	We have stayed up so long,
	Ecco le torce accese.	here are the lighted torches.
	Giten'in grembo a Endimion cortese.	Go to the lap of Endymion.

As in Croce's "Il gioco dell'oca" and Vecchi's "Lotto amoroso," a beautiful woman wins the game, confirming the hierarchy of an idealized social gathering, whether courtly or—as here—academic. This victory also reinscribes codes of social exclusion by emphasizing that although all the imitations are presented as laughable, that of the Jews is the most "realistic" because of Giulia's virtuosity.

This division of the book's *prima parte* into two separate evenings hints at various performance options: if the game of imitations (depicted as a separate, self-sufficient evening) is sung as a complete unit, the final *applauso* creates a satisfying ending, and the players bid each other good night. On the other hand, if the singers (or silent readers) continue through the book, the references to Cupid in the last two *proposte* of the first night link the game of imitations to *La caccia d'Amore.*

La caccia d'Amore

Although "The Hunt for Cupid" takes its name and much of its detail from Bargagli, Vecchi's four-part piece expands on the game described in the *Dialogo,* following the precedent of earlier musical hunts by Janequin and Striggio. The first part begins by contextualizing the game of imitations as having been enjoyed the previous night by the Intronati and their female guests. Although the academic names Stordito, Frastagliato, and Sodo used in the previous game are taken from the *Dialogo,* this is the only explicit reference in the sung text to the Intronati as a group. The beginning of the leader's proposal for the game directly paraphrases Bargagli's description of it:

> BARGAGLI: Come vagamente introdurebbe il **giuoco della Caccia d'Amore,** chi cominciassse a dire come, atteso che **questo animale d'Amore fa tanti gran male** e ch'egli è una fiera tanto **indomita** e velenosa . . .

> How lovely it would be to introduce the game of the Hunt for Cupid, beginning by saying how this animal, Cupid, does great harm and that he is a wild beast so indomitable and poisonous . . .

VECCHI: Tal fu il piacer che noi prendemm' hiersera	Such was the pleasure that we had last night
De gl'Imitati,	in the Imitations,
Cortesi donne e voi, sagg'Intronati,	courteous ladies and wise Intronati,
Ch'hora non men si spera	that now no less gracious a favor
Da voi grato favore	is expected of you
Al **gioco detto La Caccia d'Amore.**	in the game called "The Hunt for Cupid."
E chi non sa ch'**Amor'è un animale**	And who does not know that Cupid is an animal

Che fa infinito male?	that does infinite harm?
È indomit'e sfrenato,	He is indomitable and wild,
E di lascivia nato.	and born for lust.

The game-play Bargagli describes combines *spiritoso* and *scherzoso* elements in a way that Sodo praises: the players are to propose bodily locations where Cupid hides in a particular member of the company; that player must then make a denial by claiming that Cupid is to be found in someone else, continuing the game. The turns taken in this way may include literary allusions and erotic innuendo, both aspects of Bargagli's *giuochi di spirito*. The *scherzoso* aspect of the game derives from the imitation of an actual hunt: Sodo commands that the players must make noise, bark like dogs, and cry out to one another "All'Amore! All'Amore!" and similar shouts.

The party having agreed enthusiastically to the game, the imitation of the hunt begins in the second part. Vecchi's point of departure here is not Bargagli's description of the game, however, but Alessandro Striggio's musical imitation of a hunt that was first published, as we have seen, in 1567 along with his "Cicalamento delle donne al bucato" (and, in later editions, with his "Gioco di primiera"). Striggio's "Caccia," which is directly addressed to the hunting-mad Mantuan court of Guglielmo Gonzaga, includes just the kind of noises Bargagli calls for: imitations of horns, barking dogs, and the excited cries of the hunters. Vecchi frequently sets these effects to extended static harmonies that, as we have already seen in Vecchi's "Bando del asino," were emblematic of chaotic and specifically nonmusical noise in sixteenth- and seventeenth-century music.

The *spiritoso* (or *ingegnoso*) aspect of the game begins only in the third part as the "hunters" claim to have seen Cupid hiding in the bodies of other players. These declarations by individuals, as we might by now expect, are set as trios drawn from the six-voice ensemble, and each is followed by a *tutti* refrain. Unlike the trios in the previous game of imitations, which stand as self-sufficient pieces and always include the Basso, the voicings here are, with one exception, unique to each character (table 5.4). The names in *La caccia d'Amore* are all different from those used in the previous game of imitations, and only one of them, "Materiale," is associated with the Intronati: it was Bargagli's own academic pseudonym. The poetry involves mildly erotic allusions that culminate in a humorous attempt to capture Cupid between Angiola's breasts: the final three lines begin with gentle falling intervals and minim rhythms to suggest the quietness of "Pian pian, pian pian," but the increasing rhythmic activity and extensive repetitions of "prendasi" suggest that the hunt grows louder by the end.

After this game the hunters conclude that Cupid is a spirit, not a body, and cannot be captured. Beyond the plural opening exclamation, "Miseri noi, s'è di novo smarrito" (Unhappy we, for he is lost again), Vecchi here eschews first-person forms altogether, and the poem and music unfold in a chromatically expressive madrigalistic style with no elements of dialogue or character identification. The opening line includes irregularly resolved dissonances and a striking augmented-sixth harmony that exceeds the harmonic range of anything else in the book thus far, anticipating the more experimental and forward-looking harmonic style of the madrigals from the book's second, "grave" part. Bargagli's description of *La caccia d'amore* does not suggest how the game should end, so the general admission of defeat is likely Vecchi's invention. The final line of the text, "Chè non si prend'Amor se non fuggendo" (One captures Cupid only by fleeing), is a paraphrase of Bembo's "Non si vince amor se non fuggendo" (from the sonnet "Alma, se state fossi in pieno accorta").[59] The overtly madrigalistic—and thus, self-consciously "sung"—style of this conclusion suggests that, just as in Striggio's and Croce's gambling games (and Vecchi's "L'hore di recreatione") the frustration of unsuccessful players is dissipated by the charms of music.

But not entirely. The following piece bears an *argomento* suggesting that it functions mainly as a transition to the more diverting game of *bisticci:* "The indignant company wants vengeance on Cupid, but now they set aside their anger and play the game of *bisticci*." This call for vengeance plays out as yet another game in which the various players describe the physical mutilations they would inflict on Cupid in order to reduce the damage he causes. The characters in this dialogue are not named, but shifting trio textures represent them clearly enough. This gruesome discussion is not named as a game (and has no relative in Bargagli's *Dialogo,* where such a severe deprecation of love would be out of place), but the opening phrase by the Alto-Tenore-Basso trio addresses the players and functions as a *proposta,* even if it does not exactly specify what each player should do: "Let us begin, you players [*vegliatori*]! Wake up, all of you, let's have vengeance on Cupid for a thousand offenses." Various punishments are suggested and then criticized or approved: plucking out Cupid's eyes would be pointless, for example, since he is already blind, but cutting off his lips would prevent his false and flattering smiles. The transition to the game of *bisticci* is accomplished in the final punishment,

Table 5.4. Vocal textures and characters in "La caccia d'Amore," *terza parte*

VOICES	CHARACTER		
C6AT		E dov'è questo ribello?	And where is this rebel?
Tutti		Séguilo, seguilo! Véllo, véllo!	Follow him, follow him! See him, see him!
		Ahi, chè l'habbiam smarrito!	Alas, we have lost him!
C6T5		O buoni cacciatori, e dov'è gito?	Good hunters, where has he gone?
A5B	[Affumicato?]	Ecco, ecco, che se n'è gito	There, there, he has gone over there
		La, in quel bel seno	into that lovely breast
		Di Leonora,	of Leonora,
		U' si ristora.	where he is refreshing himself.
Tutti	[refrain]	Dalli, dalli, a l'Amor, a l'Amor!	Get him, get him, after Cupid, after Cupid!
		A la caccia! A la caccia!	To the hunt! To the hunt!
C6T	Leonora	Entro il mio seno	In my breast
		Non è mai stato,	he has never been,
		Ma s'è veduto	but he was seen
		In un orecchio dell'Affumicato.	in one of Affumicato's ears.
Tutti	[refrain]	Dalli, dalli...	Get him, get him...
A5B	Affumicato	Ne le mie orrechie	Into my ears
		Non è volato;	he has never flown;
		Costì saltella	he is dancing there,
		Negli occhi d'Isabella.	in Isabella's eyes.
Tutti	[refrain]	Dalli, dalli...	Get him, get him...
C6A	Isabella	Amor non è in quest'occhi	Cupid is not in these eyes,
		Nè gli ha mai tocchi.	nor has he ever touched me.
		Veggi'o parmi,	It seems that I see
		Che scopre l'ale	that his wings are showing
		Sot'il capello	under the hair
		Del Materiale.	of Materiale.
tutti	[refrain]	Dalli, dalli...	Get him, get him...
T5B	Materiale	Nel mio capello,	In my hair,
		Non è già ello;	he certainly is not;
		Ma sta ne volto	but in the face
		Di Giglia accolto.	of Giglia he is welcomed.
tutti	[refrain]	Dalli, dalli...	Get him, get him...
C6A	Giglia	Non l'ho nel volto,	I don't have him in my face,
		Ma sta a covile,	but he is in his lair,
		Fra le mammelle d'Angiola gentile.	between gentle Angiola's breasts.
T5B	[Materiale?]	Or siate presti senza far rumore.	Now be quick, without making noise.
tutti		Pian pian, pian pian,	Quietly, quietly,
		L'è qui, l'è qui Signore,	he's there, he's there, Sir,
		Prendasi, prendas'il traditore!	get him, get the traitor!

in which a punning transformation of Cupid's name suggests the language of the tongue twister:

Più non si nome, Amor per nome,	No more will Cupid be called by his name,
Ma lo chiamate, amaro humore.	but you shall call him Bitter Humor.
Hor diamo loco a la vendetta à l'ira	Now let's set aside our vengeance and anger
E da quel vostro nome amaro humore,	and from this name, Bitter Humor,
Piacciavi fare de'bisticci il gioco.	enjoy playing a game of tongue twisters.

Of course, the description of love as a "bitter humor" refers also to the subtitle of *Le veglie di Siena, I varii humori della musica moderna. La caccia d'Amore* is thus drawn, with all the musical styles it encompasses, into the book's larger project of imitating life, and the links between successive games throughout the book depict the spontaneous selection of varied games in an imagined academy.

The Humors of Modern Music

The *seconda parte delle veglie* begins with a proem in which a new game is proposed that appropriates the title page's description of the complete book. As the *argomento* summarizes it, "The leader introduces a new game, 'The humors of modern music,' which moves people to marvel and delight." We are still in the imagined world of a game in the Academia degli Intronati, since the *proposta* (given by the Alto-Quinto-Basso trio) declares that each singer will choose his or her own style, despite the variety of tastes and opinions present, and that in the resulting game the winner will be the one who most moves the affections:

Hor sù, dunque da i vostri disparei	So come now, from your differing ideas
Questo gioco traremo:	we shall make this game:
Che chi di voi più desterà gli affetti,	whichever of you most arouses the emotions
Col suo lodato modo,	with his praiseworthy style
Quell'havra premio di memoria eterna.	shall have the prize of eternal fame.
E lo potrem chiamare:	And we shall call it
Gli humori di musica moderna.	"The humors of modern music."

This proposal implies that each of the ensuing performances is a solo and that there are therefore fourteen imagined singers present. Vecchi's madrigals are for five and six voices in polyphony, so a distinction must still be kept in mind between the imagined singer-players and the real singers. The point bears emphasis, since after the proem no further references to the game appear: there are no individual *proposte* and *applausi,* as in the game of imitations, nor is each madrigal headed with a textual *argomento* (as in the *prima parte*). The game is not mentioned again until the final piece, which, as we shall see, functions only imperfectly as a "judgment" and more overtly as a comment on modern music by Vecchi himself.

The madrigals—the term is applicable here as it is not in the rest of *Le veglie di Siena*—are labeled with the fourteen humors listed on the title page (reproduced above), though the ordering has been changed in one case: the *humor malenconico* is not the penultimate piece but the eighth. The names of humors assigned to each piece are often enigmatic, and many of them defy unambiguous translation.[60] Massimo Privitera and Anthony Newcomb have proposed categorizing the pieces as either *piacevole* or *grave,* and while the insights gained by these projects are revealing, nothing in Vecchi's own descriptions either in the book's front matter or in the texts themselves suggests that such a strict binarism is inherent to the madrigals or their ordering.[61] Newcomb's study draws particular attention to the way in which the pieces he classifies as *grave* tend to be written for five voices and to set poems already known in settings by other composers (these works are marked in bold in table 5.5).

The only six-voice pieces Newcomb identifies as *grave* are no. 1, "Si grav'è il mio dolore," and no. 6, the two-part setting of Petrarch's "Hor che'l ciel'e la terr'e 'l vento tace," the most iconically *grave* text in the book. The composers who had previously set the five-voice pieces are notable for being of a younger generation than Vecchi and distinctly identifiable with progressive trends. Newcomb cites several instances where Vecchi quotes these settings and shows how various details of his resettings demonstrate the kinds of "errors" decried by Giovanni Maria Artusi in *L'Artusi, ovvero delle imperfettione della moderna musica.*[62] Considering that such devices (including irregularly treated dissonances, prohibited intervals, and accidentals resolved incorrectly) are not at all common in Vecchi's earlier music, the composer seems to have been aligning himself, at least in these pieces, with the burgeoning public debate over what was to become known as the *seconda prattica.* While Newcomb confines his study to these poetic resettings, Vecchi's "modern" tendencies appear in some settings of poems presumed to be his own. The "*Humor Grave,*" "Si grav'e 'l mio dolore," includes several moments to which Artusi would have objected, including leaps of a diminished fourth in the

Table 5.5. Madrigals in *Le veglie di Siena, seconda parte*

HUMOR	INCIPIT AND POET (IF NOT ASSUMED TO BE VECCHI)	VOICES	PREVIOUS SETTING(S)
1. Grave	Si grav'è il mio dolore	6	
2. Allegro	Liete piagge e gradite	6	
3. Universale	Tra mille fiamme e tra mille cathene	6	Vecchi, 1583
			Monteverdi, 1587
4. Misto	La mia cara Licori	6	
5. Licentioso	Di marmo sete voi (**Marino**)	5	**Gagliano, 1602**
6. Dolente	Hor che 'l ciel'e la terr'e 'l vento	6	
	tace (**Petrarch**)		
7. Lusinghiero	Alma ben gentil ben nata	6	
8. Malenconico	Le mie lagrim'amare (**Vecchi**)	5	**Vecchi, 1604**
9. Gentile	Vieni Flora gentil, apr'il thesoro.	6	
10. Affetuoso	Era l'anima mia (**Guarini**)	5	**Pallavicino, 1600**
			Monteverdi, by 1603
			Fontanelli, 1604
11. Perfidioso	Ritrosetta Amarilli	6	
12. Sincero	Copr'il candido seno (**Arlotti**)	5	**Nenna, 1603**
			Fontanelli, 1604
			Gesualdo, ?
13. Svegghiato	Viva la gioia (Vecchi)	5	Vecchi, 1604
14. Balzano	Hor che lieta stagion gli	5	
	huomini invita		

point of imitation on "Che'l cor mio si vien men di pass'in passo" (For my heart grows faint, step by step; example 5.5a) and, in the final passage, an unresolved sharp in the Sesto (m. 90) and an augmented second in the Alto (m. 92, example 5.5b).[63] Similarly forward-looking devices appear, as one might expect, in Vecchi's setting of "Hor che'l ciel," whose harmonically static opening Newcomb sees as a snub to Artusi's criticism of Monteverdi's "Era l'anima mia," a gesture of support that Monteverdi was to repay years later with his own setting of Petrarch's sonnet.[64]

The implication that Vecchi was trying to position himself among composers of *musica moderna* is confirmed by his reuse of three of his own poems from other settings. These are no. 8, "Le mie lagrim'amare," and no. 13, "Viva la gioia" (both extracts from the *Mascherata della Malinconia et Allegrezza* of 1604), and no. 3, "Tra mille fiamme e tra mille cathene," a six-voice expansion of a five-voice madrigal printed in 1583 that had already been reset by Claudio Monteverdi in his first book of madrigals (1587).[65] Vecchi's *Mascherata della Malinconia et Allegrezza* is a ten-voice polychoral work performed as part of an outdoor procession in 1604 for the wedding celebrations of

Example 5.5a. Vecchi, "Si grav'è il mio dolore" ("L'humor grave"),
from *Le veglie di Siena,* mm. 66–71.

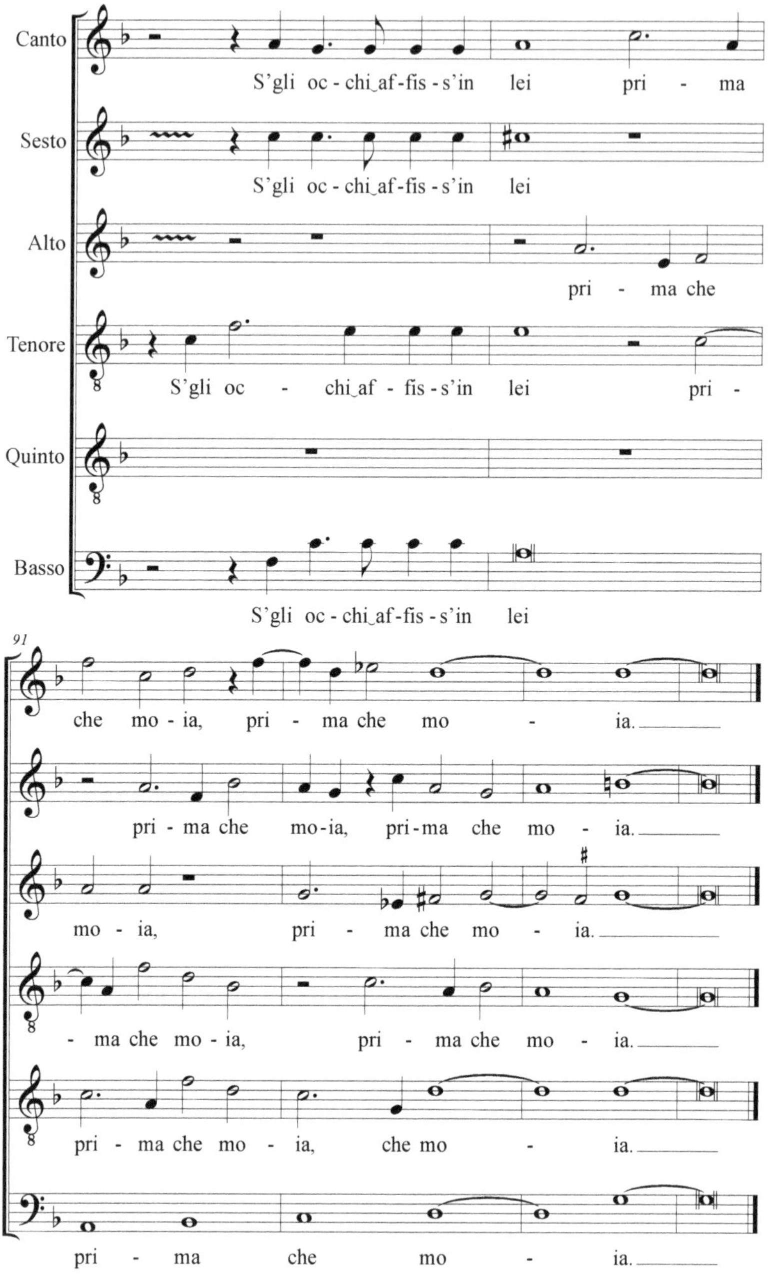

Example 5.5b. Vecchi, "Si grav'è il mio dolore," mm. 89–94.

Cesare d'Este's daughter Laura to Alessandro Pico della Mirandola.[66] "Le mie lagrim'amare" (the "humor malenconico") is a direct transcription of the first three speeches by the chorus representing Melancholy, with some changes to the text. The change to the first line, "Queste lagrim'amare," reflects the general principle of rendering the first-person-plural voice of the *mascherata* as first-person singular in the madrigal, but Vecchi makes only very minor adjustments to the music. "Viva la gioia" is a more thorough adaptation of music sung by the opposing choir, representing Happiness, with most of the text completely changed.

David Nutter assumes that the madrigals in *Le veglie* are the original versions; we cannot be absolutely certain about this, but the opposite direction of adaptation may be suggested by the anomalous ordering of *humori* listed on the title page. Whereas the opposing affections that are juxtaposed in the *Mascherata della Malinconia et Allegrezza* could have been drawn from any of the contrasting madrigals of the final part of *Le veglie*, the placement of the *svegghiato* and *malinconico* adjacent to one another on that book's title page could reflect their common derivation from the *mascherata*. The melancholy humor, "Le mie lagrim'amare," is the only piece in the book that appears out of order relative to the title-page list. As Newcomb notes, the rearrangement could also have been intended to intensify the turn in the last few pieces toward lighter, canzonetta-like madrigals.[67] "Viva la gioia" and the final "Hor che lieta stagion gli huomini invita" certainly fulfill this function not only in their celebratory texts but with frequent shifts to dance-like triple meter and, especially in the last section of "Hor che lieta stagion," sectional repeats in the manner of a canzonetta or *ballo*.

Vecchi's most progressive piece in *Le veglie* may, however, be the final framing piece that concludes "the humors of modern music" and the entire book. It carries the rubric "compliments of the leader to the company," but it hints at Vecchi's own attitude about how listeners should approach different musical styles:

Qual honor, qual degna lode	What honor, what worthy praise
Che pareggia 'l vostro canto,	to equal your song
Vi darem, cigno canori?	could we give, you singing swans?
No'l so io, no'l sa chi l'ode,	I don't know, nor do those who hear it,
A chi debba dars'il vanto	to whom should be given the merit
Di sì dolci e varii humori.	for such sweet and varied humors.
Questo so: che tai concenti,	I know this: that such harmonies

Tutti sono, in sua natura,	are all, in their nature,
Fabricat'al suo diletto.	made for your pleasure.
Ma se'l gusto de le genti	But if the tastes of the people
Ama quest'e quel non cura,	like this one, and don't care for that one,
Ciò non è d'arte difetto.	it is not a defect of the art.
Ma perchè già tarda è l'hora,	But since the hour is already late,
Vi ringratio, o vegliatori,	I thank you, O players,
Chè temp'è di far partita.	for it is time to depart.
Ecco homai la vaga Aurora,	Here, now, is the lovely dawn,
Che dal mar vuol uscir fuora:	ready to come up from the sea:
Sia la veglia qui finita.	may the evening now be ended.

The second stanza as a whole might be taken as a direct jab at Artusi were not such comments already typical in Vecchi's prefatory texts as early as 1590. Yet the poetic form they take here, of a strophic canzonetta written entirely in *ottonari,* is one that would soon be associated, at least by proximity, with the most substantial surviving defense of the *seconda prattica,* Giulio Cesare Monteverdi's "Dichiaratione della lettera," published in his brother Claudio's *Scherzi musicali* in 1607.[68] Although Vecchi's poem serves an imitative and didactic function far removed from the light Chiabreresque poetry of Monteverdi's *scherzi,* Vecchi's rhythmic treatment of it is clearly in the same style (see example 5.6). Condensed for three voices rather than six and provided with a suitable ritornello, "Qual honor, qual degna lode" would not be much out of place among Monteverdi's *Scherzi musicali* or the canzonettas in *L'Orfeo.* It thus points in two directions, completing the game of the Intronati imagined from almost four decades earlier and embracing a musical style that was to become an essential feature of seventeenth-century music. Vecchi's madrigals may allude to Artusi's complaints, but here he seems to be aesthetically in stride with developments that would move well beyond the terms of that debate.

Le veglie di Siena and the Seconda prattica

Just as in *L'Amfiparnaso* Vecchi had subsumed different dramatic and musical styles under the imprecise title "Comedia Harmonica," in *Le veglie* his priority is to present a wide range of musical genres and imitations rather than to evoke "realistically" a series of documented games. The prefatory texts to the book are notable for making almost no reference to the historical games of the Intronati.

Example 5.6. (*above and following two pages*) Vecchi, "Qual honor, qual degna lode" ("Complimenti del Prencipe a Vegliatori"), from *Le veglie di Siena*, mm. 922–933.

926
— ca - no - ri? No'l so io, no'l sa chi l'o -
— ca - no - ri? No'l so io, no'l sa chi l'o -
gni ca - no - ri? No'l so io, no'l sa chi l'o -
— ca - no - ri? No'l so io, no'l sa chi l'o -
— ca - no - ri? No'l so io, — no'l sa chi l'o -
— ca - no - ri? No'l so io, no'l sa chi l'o -
928
de, A chi deb - ba dar - s'il van - to
de, A chi deb - ba dar - s'il van - to Di sì
de, A chi deb - ba dar - s'il van - to
de, A chi deb - ba dar - s'il van - to Di sì
de, Di sì dol - ci‿e
de, Di sì

930
Di sì dol-ci‿e va-rii‿hu-mo - ri,
dol-ci‿e va-rii‿hu-mo - ri, Di sì dol-ci‿e va-rii‿hu-
Di sì dol-ci‿e va - rii‿hu - mo - ri,
dol-ci‿e va-rii‿hu-mo - ri, Di sì dol - ci‿e va-rii‿hu-
va - rii‿hu - mo - ri, Di sì dol-ci‿e
dol-ci‿e va-rii‿hu-mo - ri, e va -
932
Di sì dol - ci‿e va - rii‿hu - mo - ri.
mo - ri, e va - rii‿hu - mo - ri.
Di sì dol-ci‿e va - rii‿hu - mo - ri.
mo - - - - ri.
va - rii‿hu - mo - ri.
rii‿hu - mo - ri.

The dedication to King Christian IV of Denmark follows the pattern of those dedications I have called "aspirational" in the context of books printed up until 1597. Although he never traveled to Denmark or met the king, Vecchi's reputation there was sufficient that in 1600 Danish envoys came to Modena to meet him, but he was in Rome at the time as part of Cardinal Alessandro d'Este's entourage.[69] In the dedication to *Le veglie di Siena* of four years later, Vecchi explains that he knows that Christian has heard his music, and so he offers the book to him in thanks. The language here is unusual in suggesting that Christian did not merely know Vecchi's previously published music (as Vecchi claimed about Archduke Ferdinand in the dedication to *Convito musicale,* for example) but had heard at least some of the music in *Le veglie* itself: "If I had thought that *these* musical exercises of mine should ever have come within the hearing of Your Majesty, as I have been assured they have, I would have applied myself with as much effort as I could, enough to deserve your royal grace, through the willingness of my spirit if not the excellence of the notes" (emphasis added).[70] Vecchi confirms that he had begun composing the songs of *Le veglie* prior to deciding to dedicate them to Christian and with a more purely artistic purpose in mind: "I found it expedient to address to Your Majesty these songs entitled LE VEGLIE DI SIENA, inventions that I have undertaken willingly, so as to have the opportunity to vary and play with all the genres on music."

In a final echo of the rhetorical strategies used in his previous aspirational dedications, Vecchi mentions one of Christian's own musicians, Melchior Borchgrevinck, who had been in the service of the court since 1587 (a year before Christian IV's own coronation at age eleven). By 1604 Borchgrevinck had made two extended trips to Venice (in 1599–1600 and 1601–1602) and had been elevated to the post of principal instrumentalist at the Danish court in 1603.[71] Borchgrevinck had studied with Giovanni Gabrieli in Venice, and it seems to be only through Gabrieli that Vecchi knew of the Danish musician. More importantly, this passage describes potential challenges that the work might present, and that Borchgrevinck would be able to overcome: "And I am reassured to believe that whatever might be difficult to perform in order to fully enjoy these our Italian pieces, you will be helped by Signor Melchior Borchgrevinck, truly worthy musician of Your Majesty's, he being unique in this profession, as is confirmed by the authority of Signor Giovanni Gabrieli." The suggestion that Italian compositions would present special challenges to a court widely known to be enthusiastic about music from south of the Alps is surprising. Vecchi may be referring here to the pieces in *Le veglie* that use non-Tuscan Italian dialects or depict cultural stereotypes that might be unfamiliar in the north—that is, elements typically absent from conventional printed collections of madrigals or canzonettas. Furthermore, the dedication never characterizes either the music or the imitative project of the book in terms of games or offers any explanation of the title—an exceptional departure from Vecchi's practice in his other metaphorically titled books.

The preface addressed to the readers likewise downplays the contextual frame of the Intronati's games, referring to it only elliptically in the final sentences: "And if I have chosen the games of Siena, it is not without reason, since Aristotle defined music as nothing other than a game or jest.[72] I shall not tell you the title of the work, since it is well known; you need only know that the Materiale Intronato and his brother have written abundantly about it, and most judiciously, as that most ancient and virtuous city has found." Vecchi is of course referring to the *Dialogo* and to *I trattenimenti*, published by Girolamo's brother Scipione Bargagli in 1587, though the games imitated in *Le veglie* are drawn only from the *Dialogo*.[73] However, the rest of the preface makes it clear that for Vecchi the framing function of Sienese-style gaming is only a pretext for compiling a book of music in which Vecchi can, as stated in the dedication, "vary and play with all the genres of music."

Specifically, the preface addresses the question of combining humorous and serious music in a single book, a practice that, as we have seen, Vecchi had defended as early as 1590 in the dedication to *Selva di varia ricreatione* but that he claims had come in for special criticism over *L'Amfiparnaso*: "It would be no great thing if the appearance of my *Veglie di Siena* were to stir up a few opinions or judgments, as not long ago my *Amfiparnaso, Comedia musicale* did, about which it was said that one does not keep decorum by mixing humorous [*ridicola*] music with serious [*grave*], for then it is rendered hardly praiseworthy, and the profession even less worthy of esteem." *L'Amfiparnaso* may well have caused confusion when it was published in 1597, but the presence of such defensive language in Vecchi's writings as early as 1590 prompts some skepticism about his claim that *L'Amfiparnaso* was singled out in this manner; certainly no other evidence of *L'Amfiparnaso*'s having been criticized in his lifetime has come to light.

The defense of *Le veglie* that Vecchi offers, moreover, is in no way based on a claim that he is faithfully imitating or evoking the activities of the Intronati.

Such a claim, supported by the evidence of Bargagli's *Dialogo,* could in fact have constituted a more effective argument for the intermingling of *piacevole* and *grave* games than the hodge-podge of references that Vecchi offers instead. He cites Aristotle's *Poetics* and the misattributed *Rhetoric for Theodore and Alexander* as claiming that both the best and the worst can be imitated, though Aristotle uses this contrast to distinguish tragedy from comedy, not to propose an intermingling of the two.[74] A reference to the long discussion of humor in book 2 of Castiglione's *Il cortegiano* is more relevant to the context of social music making but is undercut by the citation of Homer and Virgil as writing both epic and lighter works.[75] Such examples support the validity of contrasting genres but not their juxtaposition in a single book. Vecchi's quotation of four lines from the opening of Tasso's *Gerusalemme liberata* is more apt as a defense of intermingling serious matter with pleasant verse, especially if read in the context of Tasso's previous octave (Vecchi includes only the last four lines quoted here):

O Musa, tu che di caduchi allori	O Muse, you who do not string a garland of
non circondi la fronte in Elicona,	the fading laurel frond of Helicon,
ma su nel cielo infra i beati cori	but far in heaven among the blessed choirs
hai di stelle immortali aurea corona,	wreathe deathless stars into a golden crown,
tu spira al petto mio celesti ardori,	breathe into my heart the fire of heavenly love,
tu rischiara il mio canto, e tu perdona	illuminate my song, and if I have sewn
s'intesso fregi al ver, s'adorno in parte	embroideries of the truth in any place,
d'altri diletti, che de' tuoi, le carte.	I ask forgiveness for their lesser grace.
Sai che là corre il mondo ove più versi	You know the world delights in lovely things,
di sue dolcezze il lusinghier Parnaso,	for men have hearts sweet poetry will win,
e che 'l vero, condito in molli versi,	and when the truth is seasoned in soft rhyme
i più schivi allettando ha persuaso.	it lures and leads the most reluctant in.[76]

Whereas in *Selva* Vecchi had claimed that variety was a source of delight, here he reiterates the idea introduced in *Convito* that it is also useful. Having again expounded the aesthetic of variety, he now places all four of his eclectic collections in this context, though using syntax that emphasizes the metaphorical nature of the titles given to his late books: "Let it not be any wonder, then, if I have gone now with Forests [*Selve*], now with Banquets [*Conviti*], now with Comedies [*Comedie*], and most recently with the Evening Games of Siena [*Veglie di Siena*], luring the tastes of others with the bait of variety and the net of my inventions, disdaining to give myself entirely to a single form, with which I could no doubt please only a few." Intriguingly, given the self-proclaimed "modern" style of the madrigals in the *seconda parte,* in the continuation of this passage Vecchi refers to the problem of matching poetic affect to musical style—the issue at the core of Monteverdi's defense of the *seconda prattica* in the polemic begun in 1600 by Giovanni Maria Artusi:

> And I know this to be true and proven beyond a doubt: that whoever would remain always serious, his music would lose much of its beauty and variety—as is the case with others who always repeat the same harmonies for different matters [*le consonanze istesse per cose diverse*], so that their music, though its words may change or its poems be new, yet its form and the character of its inflections may as well be utterly the same, for they have the same flavor of invention, the same aroma of conceits, and the same colors of harmonies.

Artusi's famous attacks on the "imperfections of modern music" had been published in 1600 and 1603, and from the latter we also have evidence of an early response, from a Ferrarese correspondent using the pseudonym L'Ottuso Academico. Whereas Artusi's criticisms of various musical passages from as-yet-unpublished madrigals by Monteverdi had suppressed the words and considered only the handling of dissonance in counterpoint, L'Ottuso introduced the notion that while the offending passages did depart from classical practice, they were intended to produce new expressive effects: "The purpose of this new movement of the parts is to discover through its novelty new harmonies and new affections, and this without departing in any way from good reason, even if it leaves behind somehow the ancient traditions of some excellent composers."[77] Vecchi's condemnation of repeating the same harmonies for different matters, and particularly of keeping musical style constant even for changed words and new poems, corresponds closely to L'Ottuso's advocacy of "new harmonies and new affections." Of course, this line of reasoning prefigures the definition of the *seconda prattica* eventually articulated by Giulio Cesare Monteverdi in the *Dichiaratione.* There is no reason to suppose that Vecchi was more than a spectator to the debates between Artusi and L'Ottuso, especially considering that his innovations in *Le veglie* are in fact more poetic and imitative than contrapuntal (a few exceptional passages notwithstanding), but in his eclectic defense of generic mixture he is eager to draw on contemporary debates as well as classical authority.[78] Vecchi's own priority of presenting a widely varied book is linked to the terms of Artusi's argument most explicitly in the book's full title, *Le veglie di Siena, overo i varii humori della musica moderna.*

It is within this wide-ranging defense of musical variety that we should understand Vecchi's most succinct (and often-quoted) description of his goals in *Le veglie:*

> And therefore I represent characters with dramatic poetry for no other effect than to imitate better the matters of life. And whoever does not understand these benefits will likely be put off by tedium and the singers' fatigue. Now the first part I call Pleasing, which if it may find some opponents will also find many who praise it. The second part I call Serious; in it there are fourteen humors all of different natures, which with long study I have made as realistic as possible; for these are not those humors in Garzoni's hospital for the mad, but of wise men who have a place at the tables of Princes.

Vecchi emphasizes the realistic depiction of humors and matters of life (*cose al vivo*), for which the imagined Sienese academy is at best a stand-in. *L'ospedale de' pazzi incurabili* of Tomaso Garzoni, published in 1586, is a satirical treatise purporting to catalog all the varieties of madness, but it takes its title from a game described by Girolamo Bargagli in the *Dialogo.*[79] Bargagli's game requires each player to explain how he has been driven mad by love and then to perform an act of madness. Vecchi's game of "the humors of modern music"—which as Haar points out has no direct model in the *Dialogo*—is thus implicitly a kind of *risposta* to Bargagli's game, presenting forms of normative (i.e., courtly) emotional experience rather than madness.

The imitation of courtly humors and academic amusements in *Le veglie di Siena* thus constitutes a script for correct behavior no less than Striggio's and Croce's depictions of gambling do. Like the structured conversations of Bargagli's games, the dialogues and soliloquies played out in recreational singing here model—and thus regulate—social decorum. This musical depiction of the Sienese games does not include the unpleasant behavior we witness in musical imitations of games of chance, because the games themselves entail less moral risk, and the company is depicted as ideally virtuous. Instead, Vecchi transforms Bargagli's nostalgic memorial of conversations among the Intronati into his own contribution to a public conversation—one might even say his own turn in a game—about modern music.

6 Representation and Identity in Musical Performance

In chapter 5 we saw how musical depictions of games inscribe standards of polite behavior in courtly and academic contexts through both positive and negative examples. While depictions of game playing may be the most metasocial form of recreational music, other imitations of courtly and non-courtly life can also reflect and critique the social structures in which they circulate. In this chapter I examine depictions of hierarchical social levels both consistent with and distinct from those of the singers (at least as the fictive character's identity is construed in the poetic voice of the song). I am particularly concerned here with the means of imitation such music employs and the commentary it offers on class, frequently through its depiction of sexuality.

While discourses on sexuality can be difficult to parse at four centuries' remove, a word is in order about two broad categories to which I refer, the *erotic* and the *obscene*. Roger Thompson and David O. Frantz have situated these terms within a lexicon that also includes the "pornographic" and the "bawdy," but since their distinctions depend largely on how a reader responds to text, I have preferred to use only two categories.[1] Thompson distinguishes between the "bawdy," which is primarily humorous, and the "obscene," which is intended to elicit shock and disapprobation, while acknowledging the frequent use of the latter in satire. "Pornography" refers specifically to material that prompts or assists literal physical arousal, but many kinds of discourse might potentially be put to this use, including the "erotic," that is, the expression of sexuality within an approved context of love. The vast majority of sexually allusive poetry set to music in the sixteenth century partakes of the erotic in this way, but depictions of lower-class or nonnormative sexuality instead function as shockingly—and therefore also laughably—obscene.

Singing Social Hierarchies

The four-voice aria "So ben mi c'ha bon tempo," from Vecchi's *Selva di varia ricreatione,* represents one of the most up-to-date styles in that wide-ranging book. Its short stanzas, persistent homophony, and fa-la refrains closely resemble the *balletti* in Giovanni Giacomo Gastoldi's book published the following year.[2] Like Gastoldi's influential and often-reprinted pieces, "So ben mi c'ha bon tempo" became one of Vecchi's most promiscuous songs, its adaptability to different performance situations enhanced by his provision of a lute accompaniment in the *Selva* print.[3] The song was copied, along with two of the three-voice arias from *Selva,* into Cosimo Bottegari's personal lute manuscript within a few years, notated for solo voice with a simpler lute accompaniment.[4] Bottegari (1554–1620) was active at the courts of Bavaria in the 1570s and in his native Florence after 1580. Although the earliest pieces in the manuscript were copied in the mid-1570s, various dedications for individual pieces confirm that music was added to the book over the next several decades, and the songs from *Selva* show signs of having been copied from the 1590 print.[5] In Bottegari's copy of "So ben mi c'ha bon tempo," the music and intabulation, with the first two-line stanza of text underlaid, are followed by eight more stanzas copied in two columns identical to the layout in *Selva,* but Vecchi's tenth stanza, centered between the two columns in the *Selva* print, is absent in the manuscript, and three of the stanzas included in the manuscript were subsequently struck out (figure 6.1). These variants suggest that Bottegari had both initial doubts and additional second thoughts about how best to perform Vecchi's song.

The style of Gastoldi's *balletti* was to prove popular among English composers in the early seventeenth century, and, as Joseph Kerman demonstrated, "So ben mi c'ha bon tempo" itself was a model for the rhythms of Morley's ballett "Now is the month of maying" (1595).[6] "So ben mi c'ha bon tempo" was also included in *Le gratie d'Amore* (1602), a treatise on dance and comportment by the Milanese Cesare Negri.[7] This book presents the music as a wordless monophonic tune and in a simple lute intabulation, and it provides a triple-meter galliard variation on the melody. Negri's dance is dedicated to Isabella Borromea, countess of San Secondo, who is named earlier in *Le gratie d'Amore* in lists of women whose dancing was known in courtly Milanese circles.[8] In short, "So ben mi c'he bon tempo" was a kind of epitome of courtly music suited not only to the recreational-singing model that has been the main focus of this book but also to a variety of performance

Figure 6.1. "So ben mi c'ha bon tempo" in Bottegari's lute book, Biblioteca Estense Universitaria Mus.C.311, fol. 5. By permission of the Ministero dei bene e delle attività culturali e del turismo.

contexts for separate audiences, including accompanied solo singing, instrumental performance, and courtly dance.

The poem of "So ben mi c'ha bon tempo," however, is a cynical denunciation of courtly life and its amorous intrigues (asterisks indicate the stanzas struck out in Bottegari's lute book; a dagger indicates the stanza omitted):

1. So ben c'ha bon tempo, fa la la   I know well who has good fortune,
   Al so mo basta mo. fa la la   I know, but enough.
2. So ben ch'è favorito, fa la la   I know well who is the favorite;
   Ahimè no 'l posso dir. fa la la   alas, I cannot say.
3. O s'io potessi dire, fa la la   Or, if I could say
   Chi và, chi sta, chi vien, fa la la   who goes, who stays, and who comes,
4. La ti darà martello, fa la la   It would make you jealous,
   Per farti disperar.[9] fa la la   cause you to depair.
5. Saluti e baciamani, fa la la   Greetings and hand kissing
   Son tutti inderno à fè. fa la la   are all in vain.

6. *Non giova fare il Zanni, fa la la	Don't play at being the Zanni,
Andando sù e giù. fa la la	pacing up and down.
7. *Al puo ben impiccarsi, fa la la	One could hang himself;
Ch'al non sarà nient'. fa la la	it would be for nothing.
8. Passeggia pur chi vuole, fa la la	Stroll some more, whoever wants to,
Che 'l tempo perderà. fa la la	it will be a waste of time.
9. *O parli, ò ridi, ò piangi, fa la la	Whether you talk, or laugh, or weep,
Non troverai pietà. fa la la	you'll find no pity.
10. †Dice il proverbio antico: fa la la	So says the ancient proverb:
Chi hà fatto suo bon prò. fa la la	Whoever has good luck makes his own.

The song lays bare the essence of courtly *sprezzatura:* courtiers are performers and flatterers, comparable to theatrical clowns, and advancement
is gained through subterfuge that must not be openly acknowledged. The
paradoxical nature of "the art of concealing art" is undermined through ex-
posure: in "performing" the idealized role prescribed in Castiglione's *Il cortegiano* and similar courtesy books, courtiers operate in a condition of bad
faith that Harry Berger, Jr., has described as "representation anxiety":

> The discussion of sprezzatura in Book 2 [of *Il cortegiano*] thus opens onto a pros-
> pect of apprehensiveness, distrust of hidden motives, fear of exposure, and a
> general sense of the weakness of the courtier's position. Both as observer and as
> observed, the courtier focuses his anxiety on the hidden "reality" of the unrepre-
> sented self produced by—and haunting—the culture of sprezzatura, with its em-
> phasis on self-misrepresentation. The problems that beset this culture are concen-
> trated in the interpretive combat between performer and spectators/auditors, a
> field of play charged with the tension between aesthetic *jouissance* and suspicion.[10]

Such anxiety, according to Berger, simmers just under the surface of all
courtly performance, nurturing an atmosphere of personal insecurity and
social surveillance. Rigidly encoded norms of courtly comportment require
both an illusion of spontaneity and a carefully policed banishment of true
unmediated behavior, underlining the subservience of the courtier's own
rank relative to his prince and other social superiors. The need to maintain one's own position within a competitive social network likewise fosters
vigilance against any possible error in the manners of others that might be
exploited in the symbolic economy of courtly decorum. As Berger demonstrates, this police state of etiquette forms the context for latter courtesy
books like Giovanni Della Casa's *Galateo* (1558).[11]

I believe that expressions of these anxieties were possible through the
more distanced metaperformative discourses of imitative games and music

making, activities in which indecorous behavior could be enacted within a bounded framework as an expression of courtly wit. In the case of dances like Negri's, the critique may be further abstracted by instrumental textures that suppress words known only to the cognoscenti. Within a courtly context, a sung or danced performance of "So ben mi c'ha bon tempo" thus proclaims a tension all courtiers experience but cannot acknowledge; the inability to speak openly is the particular subject of the first four stanzas, with their insistence on discretion. The rest of the song mocks the vanity of courtly behavior, comparing it to the comical bowing and scraping of a theatrical Zanni and ascribing to its practitioners a comparable degree of cunning self-interest. The Zanni reference alludes not only to *commedia dell'arte* performativity, however, but also to the broader category of the court jester, who moves within a courtly circle but has license to criticize both courtiers and, most importantly, the princes they serve.[12] As with the imitations performed in the first part of *Le veglie di Siena* and other works, "So ben mi c'ha bon tempo" affords a frame within which courtiers can transgress normal bounds of behavior, but here with the added frisson that these transgressions are critiques of the court itself. Of course, such transgressions still have limits in certain contexts; the stanzas crossed out in the Bottegari manuscript are precisely those that compare courtiers to pitiless theatrical fools. The canceled lines are still legible, so it is possible that Bottegari considered these stanzas acceptable for some occasions but not others. His positions at courts in Munich and Florence undoubtedly required performances in multiple social contexts that permitted various degrees of subversive rhetorical play.

Vecchi develops the anticourtly view further in "Chi vuol goder il mondo," a piece in *Convito musicale* labeled "Privilegi della Corte." A virtual sequel to "So ben mi c'ha bon tempo" in both poetic and musical rhythms and form, "Chi vuol goder il mondo" is even more pointed in its denunciation of the vanity, duplicity, and mendacity of courtiers:

1. Chi vuol goder il mondo	He who wishes to enjoy the world
E star sempre giocondo, fa la la,	and always to remain joyful
Diventi Cortigiano,	should become a courtier,
Di quei del baciamano, fa la la,	one of those hand-kissers,
Che gran piacer'havrà.	because he will have great pleasure.
2. Ma sempre la speranza	But hope always
Gli fa viver in danza, fa la la,	makes them spend their lives dancing,
E del passar de gli anni,	and from the passage of years

| Non hanno doglie, o affanni, fa la la, | they have no griefs or sorrows |
| che non pensan più in là. | who do not think too far ahead. |

3. Questo è di loro il fine, / This is their goal,
   Far bianc'in cort'il crine. fa la la, / to make their hair turn white at court.
   È un gaudio per godere / It is a joy to wish
   Mille tormenti havere. fa la la, / them a thousand torments.
   Questo ciascun la fà. / This is what everyone does.

4. Son sempre d'un'humore, / They are always in good humor,
   Mostrano a tutti il core. fa la la, / they show their hearts to all.
   Sono artificiosi, / They are artificial,
   Nè però son noiosi, fa la la, / thus they are not boring
   O in corte, o fuor do cà. / either in court or outside the house.

5. Son rettorici veri / They are the true rhetoricians
   (Udite i bei pensieri). fa la la, / (listen to their beautiful thoughts).
   Per colorir bugie, / To paint falsehoods
   Hanno più modi e vie. fa la la, / they have more means and ways
   Ch'arena il mar non hà. / than the sea has sand.

6. E'n questo hanno tal uso / And in this they have such facility
   Che'l ver sarebbe abuso, fa la la, / that the truth would be abuse.
   Ne do ciò son biasmate, / Nor are they blamed for this;
   Anzi, per saggi amati. fa la la, / rather, they are loved as wise people.
   Questo stupir mi fà. / This astonishes me.

7. La Corte gli fa accorti / The court makes them aware
   Da gl'inganni, e da i torti. fa la la, / of deceits and wrongs.
   Son pronti a le risposte / They are ready to reply
   A chi fa lor proposte. fa la la, / to whomever makes suggestions to them.
   Nessun gli abbatterà. / No one will defeat them.

8. Non temono il Tinello / They do not shun the dining-room
   Che l'aman da fratello. fa la la, / who love it like a brother.
   Leggete il Caporale / Read the heading
   Nel suo memoriale, fa la la, / in their memorial
   Che cronica ne fà. / who makes the current gossip of it.

9. Voi dite al vestir poi, / You say from their dress, then,
   Che son figli d'heroi. fa la la, / that they are the sons of heroes.
   Hanno oro e argento poco, / They have little gold or silver,
   Ma questo s'hanno a gioco. fa la la, / but this they have for play.
   Così la Corte dà. / Thus the court gives.

10. In somma, han privilegio, / In short, they have privilege,
    Che son'a tutt'in pregio. fa la la, / for they are esteemed by all.
    È ver che disse Corte / It is true that he who said "court"
    Errò; volse dir sorte. fa la la, / erred: he wished to say "fate."
    Cattiva a chi vi stà. / Ill will to whoever stays there.[13]

The opening stanzas appear relatively benign, but by the final lines courtiers are revealed as deceptive, gluttonous, and vain sophists, and the poetic speaker's open contempt is explicit. Yet "Chi vuol goder il mondo," like its predecessor "So ben mi c'he bon tempo," is in the very "lightest" form of the *balletto*, with simple repeating sections and fa-la refrains sublimating the inflammatory text in a musical style whose chief appeal is its lively rhythm and suitability for dancing.

Parallel to the associations (through dedications and later sources) of these two songs with high-status Florentine, Bavarian, Milanese, and Austrian courts, alternative readings of them are available in the wider contexts in which printed music books could circulate. Vecchi himself had only sporadic access to Italian courts, and the range of users of his books must have included not only courts but also bourgeois households whose attitude to the courtly world was marked by ambivalence and academies in which the urban merchant class and the landed aristocracy sometimes intermingled. For these upwardly mobile users, the divided identity required by the culture of *sprezzatura* was implicated in the fluidity of their own evolving social positions. Vecchi's critique of courtliness could express an outsider's view of courtly technologies of exclusion that nevertheless, if mastered, could also offer a way in, as Barbara Correll has described:

> In both court and city, early modern consolidation and regulation pushed toward restraint, toward defining status and boundaries. . . . [B]oth court and city sought to distinguish themselves in what was a competitive relationship and to encode competition through increased emphasis on consideration and sensitivity to what in personal behavior might offend. Significantly, in this point of transition, if the former court attempted to hold onto what it was, the urban bourgeoisie tried to codify and justify a less certain identity. In this respect, the modified precepts of the humanist and bourgeois etiquette specifying what one does—and especially what one does not do—expose what one is not yet and would like to become.[14]

For bourgeois readers and singers, performing Vecchi's *balletti* offers one way of negotiating the margins of the courtly realm, where aspirations to the trappings of nobility necessitate a fragmenting sense of "natural" identity. The need to perform an idealized courtly identity presumes, and therefore constructs, an alternate, concealed identity. Berger elucidates the problem in his commentary on Norbert Elias's *The Civilizing Process:* "The perception of self-division [is] at once registered and confused by the interdependence between the socially sanctioned 'nature' one has to learn and is supposed to proclaim and the repressed 'nature' everyone by the same token assumes is already there and must not be proclaimed. Since the two natures and their differences are produced simultaneously and are mutually implicative, the second is no less 'the product of education, effort, and artifice' [Elias's phrase] than the first."[15] Vecchi implies just this confusion of the natural and artificial in "Chi vuol goder il mondo," whose accusations of artificiality stake a claim to a more natural, authentic stance. Courtiers, despite pretending to express their true natures ("They show their hearts to all"), are in fact "artificial" and skilled at mendacity. Yet singing is itself one of the most artificial kinds of courtly performance, and the poetic voice of "Chi vuol goder il mondo" emanates from Berger's "learned nature," even if it covertly expresses anxieties proper to the "repressed nature." Vecchi's interest in imitating human nature falls into a kind of infinite regress in which layers of representation slide continuously over each other.

By engaging anxieties surrounding courtly representation, "So ben mi c'ha bon tempo" and "Chi vuol goder il mondo" open themselves up to more equivocal readings as well, since they trade in terminology relatable in sixteenth-century literature to nonnormative sexual practices. As Melanie Marshall has shown, texts sung or read in courtly and academic circles often participated in a lively tradition of verbal equivocation.[16] "So ben mi c'ha bon tempo" can easily be read as referring to a homosexual relationship between a courtier (the "favorito") and the male addressee of the poem, who is subject to jealousy ("La ti darà martello") and behaves like a Zanni, but the final stanzas further suggest that courtiers engage in sodomy. The juxtaposition of "sù e giù" (up and down) used in stanza 6 is one of many antonym pairs that can contrast vaginal and anal sex, and "impiccarsi" in stanza 7 can refer to phallic penetration.[17] As with all equivocal readings, readers and listeners may or may not have understood or acknowledged these potential meanings, but the stanzas just cited are among those crossed out in Cosimo Bottegari's lute book, as though he decided at some point after copying the poem that he should not sing certain parts of it, at least in some performances.

"Chi vuol goder il mondo" offers a clearer network of equivocal references to sodomy by referring explicitly to the court and the culture of *sprezzatura*. Both as a physical space and as a realm of artificial behavior, the term *corte* itself could allude to the anus, as in this tercet from Giovanni Della Casa's "Capitolo del bacio":

Trovansi baci al mondo di due sorte,	One finds in the world two kinds of kisses,
Parte ne sono asciutti e parte molli,	some are dry and some are soft;
I primi s'usan volentier in corte.[18]	the first is used willingly in the court.

Since *asciutto* and *molle* are, like *sù* and *giù*, identified with bodily orifices, the "dry kiss" preferred "in the court" suggests anal sex.[19] The "artificial" behavior of courtiers likewise plays into this reading, since sodomy and artifice are both contrary to "nature."[20] Once the possibility of such a reading is revealed, other themes of the poem can be seen to play into it: "lies" (*bugie*) and falsehoods generally also refer to "unnatural" sexual acts, and "loving the dining room [*tinello*] like a brother" suggests both hunger—sexual appetite—and perhaps a gender-inversion of "washtub" (*tinella*), a euphemism for the vagina.[21]

This reading multiplies the playful meanings available to both courtly and bourgeois singers of these pieces. As with sexual euphemisms in more literary poetry, the suggestions of sodomy in "So ben mi c'he bon tempo" and "Chi vuol goder il mondo" could be ignored by those who are unaware of them (or pretend to be), but alternatively they could be heard as amplifying the jester-like critique of courtly behavior. Accusations of flattery, vanity, and hedonism combine with suggestions of more "unnatural" acts. In some contexts—homosocial academies or other gatherings, presumably—these songs might acknowledge the reality of homosexual practices within courtly circles.[22]

Vecchi's *Villotte*: Performing the Obscene Other

"So ben mi c'ha bon tempo" and "Chi vuol goder il mondo" are notable not for their suggestions of sexual licentiousness per se but for situating it in a courtly context and representing it (at least potentially) as sodomitical. Other *cinquecento* genres participate in sexual discourses of various kinds: the erotic potential of madrigalistic poetry in the Petrarchan and pastoral modes is well attested. In other genres, including songs in *Selva* and *Convito*, sexual discourses are conveyed through a much clearer range of euphemisms and, more significantly, are depicted in rustic social settings distinct from those in which notated polyphony normally circulated. As we saw in chapter 3, *Selva* includes a *capriccio*, "Margarita dai corai," that playfully sets a nonliterate popular tune in a complex contrapuntal treatment. The poem, by engaging the recondite equivocal tradition in stanzas added by Vecchi, likewise participates in this juxtaposition of cultural registers.

Vecchi's more conventional depictions of rustic eroticism are labeled *villotta,* a term that appears to date back to the fifteenth century but has a more immediate predecessor in the four-voice *villotte* that first appeared in the 1520s and flourished in prints of the mid-*cinquecento. Villotte* are usually assumed to be derived from songs in a popular unnotated tradition, but this trend is better documented in the earlier sixteenth century than later.[23] Three types of *villotte* are generally recognized: the strophic *villotta piccola,* the monostrophic but musically more extended *villotta grande,* and the quodlibet *villotta,* which quotes multiple preexisting songs.[24] Other early features of the genre include passages of vocables (a feature known as a *lilolela*) and a closing section in triple meter (the *nio*), but these appear less frequently in later *villotte,* whose generic identity depended less on formal markers than on texture and text. The midcentury *villotta* was distinguished by its northern dialect, its formal flexibility (it might be strophic or through-composed, employ various line lengths, and intersperse triple-meter passages more freely), and its persistent depiction of rustic characters at a time when the *canzona villanesca* was gradually discarding this feature. In contrast to the earlier *frottola* and midcentury three-voice *villanesche,* the *villotta* seems from its earliest examples to have been intended for four voices to sing.[25]

By the late sixteenth century the term *villotta* had fallen out of common use as a generic descriptor, and the differences between the few prints in which it does appear suggest that it no longer conveyed a consistent meaning. The anonymous four-voice *Villotte mantovane* of 1583 (of which only the Alto and Tenore part books survive) are of the quodlibet type, each piece citing several other songs from the earlier *villotta* and *frottola* repertories.[26] The texts that frame these quotations, however, allude to the courtly world—often refracted through the pastoral lens—within which such songs circulated in their polyphonic forms.

Vecchi's three *villotte* follow a different model: their depictions of rustic characters are not mediated by framing text or by references to the text itself as a song. Like earlier four-voice *villotte,* Vecchi's six-voice pieces require all parts to be sung, as confirmed by a peculiar feature not seen in earlier *villotte* but shared by all three of Vecchi's: each of them culminates in a moment in which all the singers rapidly speak or sing a series of short solo statements. The consistency with which he uses this device suggests that, more than merely clarifying the depiction of a rustic social setting, such moments are, for Vecchi, a mode of imitation that distinguishes the *villotta* as a genre. The solo moments are also marked by particularly overt sexual innuendo within songs that already depict an unrestrained rustic sexual discourse that William Prizer has described (in reference to the earlier *villotta*) as "a kind of play of the elite with the popular culture through a distancing from the notions of *amour courtois*."[27] In another departure from earlier conventions of the *villotta*, Vecchi sets his in triple meter throughout, with only short passages in imperfect time or, in one case, unmeasured *falsobordone*. The emphasis on triple meter might allude to the *nio* sections that sometimes concluded older *villotte*, but it also reflects Vecchi's frequent association of triple meter with sexual expression.

Vecchi's first *villotta*, "O bella ò bianca piu che la cagiata" from *Selva di varia ricreatione*, trades both in the euphemisms of equivocal poetry and in more overt innuendo to depict a group of rustics who plead for sexual favors from a married girl, identifying themselves with aggrandizing, phallically suggestive names. The sixth voice shares a clef with the Alto rather than the Canto (the cleffing is c1/c3/c3/c4/c4/f4), possibly reflecting the imitation of an all-male plural poetic voice—not because low clefs imply male voices but because the disposition of the voices is unusually weighted toward the bottom of the piece's overall ambitus, emphasizing "lowness" regardless of the absolute pitch used. Italics indicate textual repetition with changed voicing:

CATB	O bella ò bianca piu che la cagiata,	O beauty, whiter than curds,
	O saporita piu che l'insalata,	O tastier than salad,
tutti	*O bella ò bianca piu che la cagiata,*	*O beauty, whiter than curds,*
	O saporita piu che l'insalata,	*O tastier than salad,*
	[the above section repeats]	
CAT5	Deh lasciati baciare.	now let yourself be kissed;
C6TB	*Deh lasciati baciare.*	*now let yourself be kissed;*
tutti	Non ti voler mostrare	you do not want to appear
CA5B	Si dispettosa,	scornful,
	Che sei la sposa	just because you are the wife
	Del Barba Ton.	of "Uncle Tony."
	La dindirin don,	La dindirin don,
	La dindirin don.	La dindirin don.
Tutti	*Deh lasciati baciare.*	*now let yourself be kissed;*
	Non ti voler mostrare	*you do not want to appear*

	Si dispettosa,	scornful,
	Che sei la sposa	just because you are the wife
	Del Barba Ton.	of "Uncle Tony."
	La dindirin don.	La dindirin don.
	La dindirin don.	La dindirin don.
T	L'è qui Tognon!	Here is "Big Tony"!
B	L'è qui Giandon!	Here is "Big Johnny"!
6	Barba Pedrazz!	"Uncle Peter"!
A	E 'l to Zanol!	And your "Little John"!
C	L'è qui Berton!	Here is "Big Bert"!
5	O buon, ò buon!	Oh good, oh good!
tutti	Andiam di compagnia	Let's go in a group
	Per la piu dritta via.	by the straightest route.

An equivocal reading of the curds (semen) and salad (the vagina and sexual activity in general) to which the addressee is compared contextualizes this *villotta* in sexual terms even before the entreaties begin.[28] The verb "kiss" implies intercourse, and the exhortation not "to appear scornful" has a quality of predatory wheedling. The vocable "la dindirin don" is related to the *lilolela* found in earlier *villotte* but is here also suggestive of a lute, as it is in Vecchi's "Margarita dai corai" and Lasso's "Matona mia cara." It thus evokes social singing, but with connotations of a (male) singer "touching" (*toccare*) or "playing" the curved, hollow, and therefore feminine lute. The final couplet, which on the surface suggests that the group is leaving the woman they address to cavort through the streets, is actually the initiation of group sex, "via" being a widely used metaphor for the vagina, through which the named men intend to go "di compagnia."[29] The final solo exclamation, "O buon, ò buon," may be the voice of the woman, enthusiastically consenting to have sex with her five suitors. Assuming that *villotte* like "O bella ò bianca" were likely to have been sung recreationally in homosocial settings (as Marshall argues for earlier *villotte*), the comic figure of the promiscuous lower-class woman is aptly depicted not by the highest-lying Canto voice but by a relatively lower tenor. Christina Fuhrmann describes a similar correlation of gender and class inversion in Striggio's "Cicalamento dell donne al bucato" (discussed in more detail below), in which the women's voices are distributed across the full vocal range. The effect is not merely comic; it plays into a network of reversals implicit in a courtly performance of such music: "In performance, *Il Cicalamento* would have facilitated exactly this type of inversion and freedom: men adopt women's voices, patrician citizens sing as lowly washerwomen, and all revel in a sexual license normally condemned."[30]

The two *villotte* in *Convito musicale* employ similar obscene innuendo and play with representations of rustic characters. "Non mi toccare" depicts a female voice resisting the advances of Barba Ton—a nice symmetry with the promiscuity of that character's wife in "O bella ò bianca." Despite her rebuffs, a degree of flirtation is evident as she describes her wedding dress in oppositional terms highlighted by dialogic alternations of three-voice groups. As Jean Toscan argues, these oppositions (long/short, narrow/wide) can accommodate a variety of suggestive readings, making her eventual invitation of the "whole company" to her wedding readable as an invitation to sex similar to the one in "O bella ò bianca." The women named—this *villotta*'s opportunity for a series of solo exclamations—are all associated with men who will be present at this eroticized "wedding."[31]

CA6B	Non mi toccare,	Do not touch me,
	Non t'accostare,	do not approach me,
	Lasciami stare,	let me be,
	O Barba Ton,	O Barba Ton,
Tutti	*Non mi toccare,*	*Do not touch me,*
	Non t'accostare,	*do not approach me,*
	Lasciami stare,	*let me be,*
	O Barba Ton,	*O Barba Ton,*
A65B	Che la Comare	because my godmother
	Me vuol provare	wants me to try on
	La mia stannella	my dress,
	Pulita e bella,	clean and pretty,
tutti	*Che la Comare*	*because my godmother*
	Me vuol provare	*wants me to try on*
	La mia stannella	*my dress,*
	Pulita e bella,	*clean and pretty,*
CA6	Se l'è curta,	if it is short,
T5B	Se l'è lunga,	if it is long,
CA6	Se l'è stretta,	if it is narrow,
T5B	Se l'è larga,	if it is wide,
tutti	Fa la la la.	Fa la la la.
CA6	Monna Riccia orlata l'ha	Mistress Riccia has hemmed it
T5B	Di grograno e taffettà.	of heavy silk and taffeta.
tutti	Hor venga a nozze tutta la brigata	Now to the wedding comes the whole company
	Del parentà de la nostra vallata.	of relatives of our valley.

T	V'è la Iacma de Zanon,	There is Iacma of Zanon,	
B	E la Togna de Piron,	and Togna of Piron,	
C	La sorella di Pedrazz	the sister of Pedrazz,	
5	E la Menghe de Buttazz,	and Menghe of Buttazz,	
A	La Tadea de Manganel	Tadea of Manganel,	
6	E l'Agnesa dal Sivel.	and Agnesa of Sivel.	
tutti	Che stasera havrò l'annello,	For tonight I shall have the ring,	
CA5	Havrò il gioiello,	I will have the jewel	
6TB	*Havrò il gioiello,*	*I will have the jewel*	
tutti	Che non s'è vist'il più bello.	for a more beautiful one has never been seen.	

The second *villotta* in *Convito musicale,* "Sapete voi, Bifolci," begins with a male peasant's description of his wife's beauty, referring to her as "la mia manza" (my heifer) and comparing her to "una rident'Agnella" (a laughing ewe)—descriptions that confirm his rustic identity but also give his speech the air of an auction. In its last section, he invites his companions to name her most beautiful body part in a simplified version of the "Giuoco delle belle parti" described by Bargagli.[32] The "turns" in this game progress from the innocuous to the erotic and provide this *villotta'*s solo exclamations, which are spoken rather than sung, with rubrics in the part books indicating in what order the lines are to be said, since conventionally notated rests would be of no use in a passage of unmeasured speech. Whatever humorous effect these spoken lines would have is part of a larger goal in this part of the song to imitate speech rhythms: the following *tutti* repetitions of the list, though sung, are notated in the style of *falsobordone,* with varying numbers of semi-breves divided by barlines to reflect the accentuation of the text (example 6.1).

No winner of this game (or auction) is named, but the song ends with the innuendo-laden observation that one member of the company is not present: "Ma vi manca Giandon, / col suo dirindon / Cioè col suo Pivon" (But Big Johnny is missing / with his "thing," / that is, with his big bagpipe). "Dirindon" is both a stand-in for the phallic reference and an opportunity for instrumental imitation, which Vecchi sets with an extended series of rep-etitions in the manner of a *lilolela* before concluding with a heavy-handed explanation of the double entendre. The implication, of course, is that the main speaker's "heifer" (a cow that has not yet bred) is at the very moment being deflowered by the well-endowed "Johnny."

Vecchi's *villotte* are thus a carnivalesque inversion of the arias "So ben mi c'ha bon tempo" and "Chi vuol goder il mondo": by depicting the cheerfully

Example 6.1. (*above, and following two pages*) Vecchi, "Sapete voi, Bifolci," mm. 53–70.

(Secondo:) Il collo.

(Primo:) Il naso.

(Terzo:) La bocca.

(Quinto:) Le poppe.

(Quarto:) Gl'occhi.

(Sesto:) La panza.

E vi - va_il na - so_il col - lo la boc - ca gl'oc - chi

E vi - va_il na - so_il col - lo la boc - ca gl'oc - chi

E vi - va_il na - so_il col - lo la boc - ca gl'oc - chi

E vi - va_il na - so_il col - lo la boc - ca gl'oc - chi

E vi - va_il na - so_il col - lo la boc - ca gl'oc - chi

E vi - va_il na - so_il col - lo la boc - ca gl'oc - chi

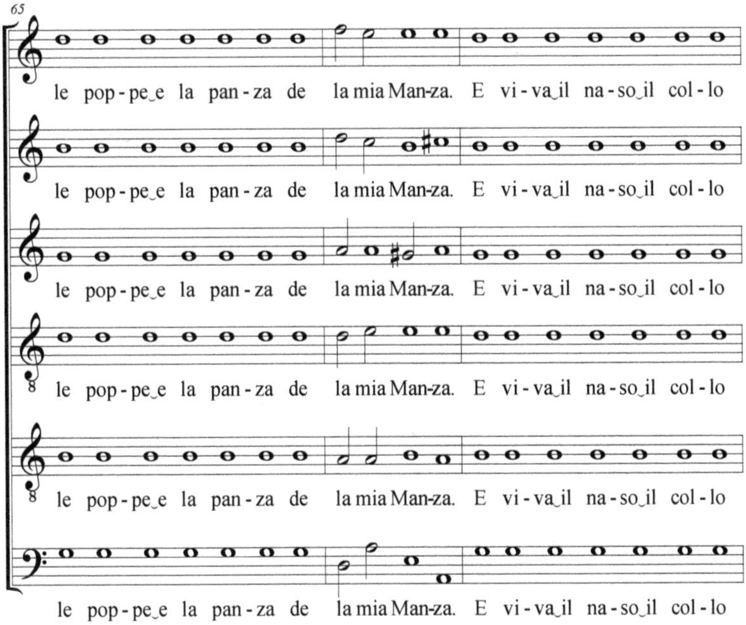
65
le pop-pe_e la pan-za de la mia Man-za. E vi-va_il na-so_il col-lo
le pop-pe_e la pan-za de la mia Man-za. E vi-va_il na-so_il col-lo
le pop-pe_e la pan-za de la mia Man-za. E vi-va_il na-so_il col-lo
le pop-pe_e la pan-za de la mia Man-za. E vi-va_il na-so_il col-lo
le pop-pe_e la pan-za de la mia Man-za. E vi-va_il na-so_il col-lo
le pop-pe_e la pan-za de la mia Man-za. E vi-va_il na-so_il col-lo

68
la boc-ca gl'oc-chi le pop-pe_e la pan-za de la mia Man-za.
la boc-ca gl'oc-chi le pop-pe_e la pan-za de la mia Man-za.
la boc-ca gl'oc-chi le pop-pe_e la pan-za de la mia Man-za.
la boc-ca gl'oc-chi le pop-pe_e la pan-za de la mia Man-za.
la boc-ca gl'oc-chi le pop-pe_e la pan-za de la mia Man-za.
la boc-ca gl'oc-chi le pop-pe_e la pan-za de la mia Man-za.

lascivious but "natural" behavior of a lower-class "other," they complement the critique of "artificial" life at court. This contrast of low and high registers is reflected also in the two genre's performance practices, the *villotte* requiring an all-sung texture in order to present the text complete, and the arias facilitating a wider range of up-to-date vocal, instrumental, and danced presentations.

There is little reason to conclude that Vecchi's *villotte* are arrangements of songs either from earlier *villotte* (as we find, for example, in the 1583 *Villotte mantovane*) or from an unwritten popular tradition. Vecchi occasionally did use popular songs (besides "Margarita," most notably the "Girometta" and "Franceschina" tunes that appear in his piece *a diversi linguaggi* "O Messir"), but he only approached the manner of the quodlibet in "L'hore di recreatione" from the *Madrigali a sei* of 1583 (see chapter 1). In his *villotte,* however, he was more concerned with imitating rustic characters—and their lascivious speech—than with adapting rustic songs.

"The Slightest Kind of Music":
Drinking Games, Real and Imagined

Another popular unnotated practice appears to have been the origin of the pieces that Vecchi labeled as *vinate.* This term, obviously derived from *vino,* is elusive in its musical application, having appeared in print first in *Selva* and later for a piece by Adriano Banchieri and in theoretical works by Thomas Morley and Michael Praetorius (see chapter 3).[33] Regardless of the term's rarity as a genre label, however, the drinking songs—or, more properly, drinking games—to which it is applied seem to imitate practices known in both courtly and lower-status circles.

The first *vinata* in *Selva,* "Cicirlanda," has a clear predecessor in "Berlinghin," from Giovan Ferretti's fifth book of *canzoni alla napolitana* for five voices of 1585. These pieces are also directly related to a song in Vecchi's *Convito musicale* of 1597 and to a piece labeled *vinata* in Adriano Banchieri's 1608 collection *Festino nella sera del giovedì grasso avanti cena.* Ferretti's "Berlinghin" is not listed in the 1585 print as a *vinata* but rather as "un brindes alla Marchiana," or "a toasting song of Marche," making a claim that the piece is an adaptation of a popular regional song.[34] However, "Berlinghin" is not merely a polyphonic elaboration of a vernacular tune but a semidramatic representation of a group of individuals engaged in both drinking and social play.

Like the later *vinate,* "Berlinghin" represents a drinking game in which players take turns asking their server—Berlinghin—about the origin of their wine. He offers various answers, and the players propose punning toasts on each answer (the first two turns are shown in example 6.2). At the end of the song, the Canto voice, which initiated the questioning at the beginning, has an instruction in the part book to finish his or her drink while the other voices sing a final toast in triple meter, recalling the *nio* of earlier *villotte.* Clearly, the song was intended to be sung by a group who were actually drinking, though Ferretti's text setting lacks verisimilitude: in the first stanza, the Canto voice both asks and answers the question, and subsequent stanzas are set for the full ensemble throughout, obscuring the dialogic nature of the text:

Canto	Berlinghin, Berlinghin, dove nasce 'sto bon vin?	Berlinghin, Berlinghin, where does this good wine come from?
tutti	Berlinghin, Berlinghin, dove nasce 'sto bon vin?	Berlinghin, Berlinghin, where does this good wine come from?
Canto	'Sto bon vin nasce dal monte.	This wine comes from the mountain.
tutti	Monte, montemolo, montemolo!³⁵	Raise, raise it up, raise it up!

tutti	Berlinghin, Berlinghin, dove nasce 'sto bon vin? 'Sto bon vin nasce dal basso. Basso, bassemolo, bassemolo!	Berlinghin, Berlinghin, where does this good wine come from? This wine comes from the lowlands. Down, down with it, down with it!
	Berlinghin, Berlinghin, dove nasce 'sto bon vin? 'Sto bon vin nasce dal braccio. Braccio, braccemolo, braccemolo!	Berlinghin, Berlinghin, where does this good wine come from? This wine comes from Braccio. Embrace, embrace it, embrace it!
	Berlinghin, Berlinghin, dove nasce 'sto bon vin? 'Sto bon vin nasce alla costa. Costa, costemolo, costemolo!	Berlinghin, Berlinghin, where does this good wine come from? This wine comes from the coast. Taste it, let's taste it, let's taste it!
	Berlinghin, Berlinghin, dove nasce 'sto bon vin? 'Sto bon vin nasce dal tiro. Tiro, tiremolo, tiremolo!	Berlinghin, Berlinghin, where does this good wine come from? This wine comes from Tiro. Pick it, pick it up, pick it up!
	[Canto part book has the rubric "Bevelo tutto et non cantare" (Drink it all and do not sing)]	
AT5B	Bevelo tutto, ch'el bon pro ti possa fare!	Drink it all, and may it do you good!

Example 6.2. (*above, facing, and overleaf*) Ferretti, "Berlinghin," mm. 1–13.

Vecchi's "Cicirlanda" follows a very similar pattern and has four of its five puns in common with "Berlinghin." Vecchi seems to have taken Ferretti as a textual model but not a musical one: his melody is distinct from Ferretti's and is handled with greater flexibility in the polyphonic passages (example 6.3). Vecchi also dramatizes the text more fully than Ferretti does, giving each singer a turn as the questioner and allowing the rest of the ensemble to answer each time. The punning toast is sung *tutti,* but with each round's questioner always leading the counterpoint. In the ending passage, the Quinto proposes the last toast and then drinks while the others sing, joining in only on the final repeat.

T	Cicirlanda!	Cicirlanda!
CA5B	Che commanda?	What do you command?
T	Dove nasce sta bevanda?	Where does this drink come from?
CA5B	Sta bevanda nasce al Monte.	This drink comes from the mountain.
tutti	Montemola, montemola!	Let's raise it up, let's raise it up!

A	Cicirlanda!	Cicirlanda!
CT5B	Che commanda?	What do you command?
A	Dove nasce sta bevanda?	Where does this drink come from?
CT5B	Sta bevanda vien da Costa.	This drink comes from the coast.
tutti	Costemola, costemola!	Let's taste it, let's taste it!
C	Cicirlanda!	Cicirlanda!
AT5B	Che commanda?	What do you command?
C	Dove nasce sta bevanda?	Where does this drink come from?

AT5B	Sta bevanda nasc'al Braccio.	This drink comes from Braccio.
tutti	Braccemola, braccemola!	Let's embrace it, let's embrace it!
5	Cicirlanda!	Cicirlanda!
CATB	Che commanda?	What do you command?
5	Dove nasce sta bevanda?	Where does this drink come from?
CATB	Sta bevanda nasce dal Tiro.	This drink comes from Tiro.
tutti	Tiremola, tiremola!	Let's pick it up, let's pick it up!
B	Cicirlanda!	Cicirlanda!
CAT5	Che commanda?	What do you command?
B	Dove nasce sta bevanda?	Where does this drink come from?
CAT5	Sta bevanda nasc'à la Bevagna.	This drink comes from Bevagna.
tutti	Bevemola, bevemola!	Let's drink it, let's drink it!
5	Brindes compagnia!	Everyone toast!

[Quinto part book has the rubric "Bevilo tutto, e poi canta la seconda replica a5" (Drink it all, and then sing the second time)]

CATB	Buon pro ti faccia,	May it do you good,
	Bevilo tutto.	drink it all.
	Che'l buon vin fa sempre frutto.	For good wine always bears fruit.
Tutti	*Buon pro ti faccia,*	*May it do you good,*
	Bevilo tutto.	*drink it all.*
	Che'l buon vin fa sempre frutto.	*For good wine always bears fruit.*

Vecchi's setting clarifies the song's identity as a *game*, a recreational genre that, as we have seen, served many of the same purposes in *cinquecento* society as secular music making: social recreation, the display of *sprezzatura*, and the transmission of cultural values. However, as attested by Ferretti, the game represented in "Berlinghin" has its origin not in a courtly game but in a rural toasting game or ritual (*brindisi*, Ferretti's term, is not otherwise associated with drinking songs in the sixteenth and seventeenth centuries). Vecchi's incipit, "Cicirlanda," appears as the name of one of the first games described in Bargagli's *Dialogo*. That book commences with Sodo, the principal interlocutor, arguing that the conversational games he will discuss were invented by the Accademia degli Intronati itself, to which another of the participants, Il Frastagliato, objects, pointing out that games of this kind had been known in other places and times.[36] He cites the games proposed in the opening of Castiglione's *Il cortegiano* at the Urbinate court and the one played in Alcina's company by the entranced Ruggiero in *Orlando furioso*. He

Example 6.3. (*above, facing, and overleaf*) Vecchi, "Cicirlanda," mm. 1–15.

goes on to claim that many of the games played by the Intronati themselves have their origins in rural customs, specifically citing "Cicirlanda":

> From what I understand, some games are to be seen in villages and castles that we play here in the city. And it does not seem possible to me that in so few years they have learned them from us, much less those in some wild and mountainous places where a nobleman's face has never been seen, so that it seems to me more as though we have taken some [games] from them, just as we have clearly

7

la, monte - mo-la, mon-te-mo - la!   Che com-man-da?

la, monte - mo-la, mon-te-mo - la! Ci-cir-lan - da!   Do-ve

te - mo-la, mon-te - mo - la!   Che com-man-da?

te - mo-la,   mon-te-mo - la!   Che com-man-da?

la, monte - mo-la, mon-te-mo - la!   Che com-man-da?

10

Sta be-van - da,   sta be-van - da   vien

na - sce sta   be-van - da?

Sta be-van - da,   sta be-van - da   vien

Sta be-van - da,   sta be-van - da vien   da

Sta be-van - da,   sta be-van - da   vien

taken many of their songs and dances. My belief in this is confirmed by the game of "Cicirlanda," which is much in use and which, if it were so modern, would never have a name that modern people do not understand. We should presume, then, that it is very old, having a very old derivation. So "Cicirlanda" ... is a word corrupted from "garland," since whoever had the privilege of questioning put one on, as is still done today in eminent places, and calling those who were around to listen and obey, said, "O ghirlanda!" and the circle responded, as they do today, "Che commanda?" and that which he wanted them to have to do, he commanded.[37]

Representation and Identity 269

13

da la co - sta. Co - ste-mo-la, co-ste-mo - la, co-ste-mo-la!

Co-ste - mo - la, co - ste-mo-la, co-ste - mo-la!

da la co - sta. Co - ste-mo-la, co-ste-mo - la, co-ste-mo-la!

la co - sta. Co - ste-mo-la, _____ co-ste - mo-la!

da la co - sta. Co - ste-mo - la, co-ste-mo - la, co-ste-mo-la!

If we take Frastagliato to be correct (as Sodo does not), the courtly academic game of "Cicirlanda" originates in an older rural game. Yet as he describes it, "Cicirlanda" does not specifically involve either drinking or wordplay as depicted in Ferretti's and Vecchi's music; the leader of the game might call for any sort of action. By substituting a name from Bargagli's treatise for Ferretti's rustic "Berlinghin," Vecchi does not raise the status of the game to that of the Intronati but the reverse: he confirms that his *vinata* depicts a rustic custom transformed for urban use. Yet Vecchi's "Cicirlanda" functions as a real drinking song to the extent that the singers are expected to have wine on hand while they sing it, as the instruction for the Quinto to finish his drink before the final refrain suggests. The other singers would likewise need wine to perform the toasts at the end of each turn as well. The spontaneity of a true game is missing, as it is in any musical depiction of a game, but the potentially intoxicating outcome is still present.

Vecchi is again playing with the limits of acceptable behavior among courtly or bourgeois circles: among the games played in such contexts, those leading to drunkenness were a particular anxiety. In his etiquette book *Galateo*, Giovanni Della Casa specifically inveighs against competitive toasting:

> It is also a barbarous habit to challenge someone to a drinking bout. This is not one of our Italian customs, and so we give it a foreign name, that is, "brindisi."

It has not yet become the practice in our lands, and so it should not be done. If someone should invite you to a drinking bout, you can easily refuse the invitation and say that you admit defeat, thanking him and tasting the wine out of courtesy without drinking more of it. Still, this "brindisi," as I have heard it claimed by several learned men, may have been an ancient custom in certain parts of Greece. . . . Whatever the ancient books may say about this, I thank God that with all the other plagues that have come to us from across the mountains, this most foul one of enjoying the act of getting drunk not only as a sport but also as a glory has not yet reached us. Nor will I ever believe that temperance can be learned from such teachers as wine and drunkenness.[38]

Although Della Casa's belief that the drinking bout is a northern practice (i.e., "from across the mountains") agrees with the received etymology of *brindisi* as deriving from a corruption of the German *bring' es dir* (I bring it to you), *Galateo* is concerned with policing class boundaries as much as geographical ones. If we grant any quasi-ethnographic authority to Ferretti's designation of "Berlinghin" as "un brindes alla Marchiana," drinking bouts were known (and perhaps known as *brindisi*) in the region of Marche, where Ferretti served as *maestro di cappella* at the cathedrals of Ancona and Loreto. When Della Casa's narrator claims that the practice "has not yet reached us," he taps into the anxiety encoded in the culture of *sprezzatura:* the danger of a drinking bout is not only the risk of drunkenness but also the contamination of Italian courts with foreign or rustic customs.

As he often did, Adriano Banchieri stretches Vecchi's imitative techniques even further. His "Vinata di brindisi e ragioni" is modeled on the general principle of rhyming toasts, but Banchieri maintains a clear and consistent association of singers with characters: not only is each game player represented by an individual singer, but so is the leader.[39] The Tenor, representing the barman, or *cantiniero,* initiates each round of the game with a toast to the other singers, addressed according to their voice parts as Canto, Falsetto, Alto, and Basso; this group then collectively ask the wine's name. In a twist new to Banchieri's *vinata,* the name by which the barman is addressed varies in each round, prompting him to give a rhyming name for the wine. An individual player then responds with the punning that is at the heart of the game and then drinks. In another innovation, Banchieri instructs each singer to drop out of the piece after his or her turn (the rubrics are shown below in italics), declaring "faccio ragione." The full ensemble only sings again in the final passage, which is explicitly labeled *applauso* in the part books:

	Canto, Falsetto, Alto, Tenore e Basso, col cantinier bevendo, hanno un bel spasso.	*Canto, Falsetto, Tenor, and Bass, drinking with the barman, have a good time.*
T	Brindesi: al Basso, Canto ed Alto, col Falsetto	A toast: to the Bass, Canto, Alto, and Falsetto.
C5AB	Che vino è questo, Messer Covello?	What wine is this, Master Cellarman?
T	Questo da noi vien detto vin chiarello.	Around here it's called claret.
C	Chiarello, buon chiarello, Io ti chiarisco mò: faccio ragione. *Quivi il Canto beve, nè canta più fina all'applauso.*	Claret, good claret, let me thin you down: now I'm in deep thought. *Canto drinks and doesn't sing until the applause.*
5AB	Bon prò! Bon prò! Bon prò!	Cheers! Cheers! Cheers!
T	Brindesi: al Basso, col Falsetto ed il Contralto	A toast: to the Bass, Falsetto, and Alto.
5AB	Che vino è questo, o cantiniero?	What wine is this, barman?
T	Questo da noi vien detto vin versiero.	Around here it's called versiero.
5	Versiero, buon versiero, Io ti riservo mò: faccio ragione.	Versiero, good versiero, I'll drink you now: now I'm in deep thought.
	Quivi il Falsetto beve, nè canta più fina all'applauso	*Falsetto drinks and doesn't sing until the applause.*
AB	Bon prò! Bon prò! Bon prò!	Cheers! Cheers! Cheers!
T	Brindesi: al Basso col Contralto, belli umori.	A toast: to the Bass and Alto, in high spirits.
AB	Che vino è questo, bon compagnone?	What wine is this, my good companion?
T	Questo da noi vien detto vin trincone.	Around here it's called toasting wine.
A	Trincone, buon trincone, Ecco ti trinco mò: faccio ragione. *Quivi il Contralto beve, nè canta più fina all'applauso.*	Toasting wine, good toasting wine, I toast you: now I'm in deep thought. *Alto drinks and doesn't sing until the applause.*
B	Bon prò! Bon prò! Bon prò!	Cheers! Cheers! Cheers!
T	Brindesi: al Basso galantuom e buon compagno.	A toast: to the Bass, a gentleman and good friend.
B	Che vino è questo, messer cotale?	What wine is this, Mr. So-and-So?
T	Questo da noi vien detto codriale.	Around here it's called cordial.

C	O dolce codriale,	O sweet cordial,
	Entrami in corpo mò.	Let's get you into me!
	Quivi il Basso beve mentre pausa.	*Bass drinks during a pause.*
	Applauso.	*Applause.*
T	Che ne dite di questo vino?	What do you think of this wine?
C5AB	È buono a fè, è buono a fè,	It's good indeed,
	Cantiniero gran mercè!	Barman, many thanks!
tutti	È buono a fè, è buono a fè.	It's good indeed.

Whatever its debt to Vecchi's and Ferretti's drinking songs, this *vinata* makes no textual or musical reference to rural practices. Like *Selva* and *Convito musicale*, Banchieri's *Festino* is a book of widely varying contents, but unlike Vecchi's books, it explicitly contextualizes the music as being sung at an imagined nonpastoral social gathering. The title refers to a party in a private urban home, and most of the comic songs (including a Venetian *giustiniana* and a pseudorustic *villanella*) are presented as masquerades performed by members of the company. In the *vinata*, the guests represent only themselves, as the naming of the singers by their voice parts suggests. In the previous song, ascribed to *li festinanti*, the party declares that they have no more masquerades prepared and are ready for dinner; the *vinata* is thus a final toast before the host dismisses the guests. While the social class of the participants is not made explicitly clear, they are neither peasants nor nobility; *Festino* probably represents a social setting not entirely unlike those with which Banchieri was familiar in his native Bologna and those where his published book would have found a ready market.[40]

From *Chanson à boire* to *Vinata*

Whatever its relation to a rustic game, the drinking bouts depicted in "Cicirlanda" and its relatives do not lead to any obvious musical depiction of drunkenness beyond the raucous *nio*-like triple meter of the final toast. The other *vinata* in *Selva*, however, dramatizes a preexisting *chanson à boire* by arranging it to suggest increasing intoxication. The earliest known source of "Je veu le cerf du bois salir" is a four-voice chanson by Pierre du Manchicourt (ca. 1510–1564) published by Pierre Attaignant in his *Tresiesme livre* (Paris, 1543) and then again in Tylman Susato's *Neufiesme livre* (Antwerp, 1545), a book comprised entirely of Manchicourt's *chansons*.[41] As these sources imply, the song includes features generally associated with both the Franco-Flemish

Example 6.4. (*above and facing*) Manchicourt, "J'ay veu le cerf du bois sallir," mm. 1–12.

Et boi - re' a la fon - tai - ne,

tai - ne, Et boi - re' a la

re' a la fon - tai - ne, Et boi - re' a

Et boi - re' a la fon - tai - ne, Et

and the newer "Parisian" styles, but its formal poetic rhetoric, pervasively imitative music, and *rondeau*-like refrain confirm ties to the older type:[42]

Manchicourt	Vecchi	
J'ay veu le cerf du bois sallir	Je veu le cerf du bois salir	I see the stag of the woods arise
Et boire'a la fontaine.	E boir a la fonteine.	and drink at the fountain.
Je bois a ty mon bel amy,	Je boy a toy mon bel amy	I drink to you, my good friend,
Et a ta souveraine,	E a ta soveraine.	and to your queen.
Si tu no fais ainsi que my	Si tu ne fais ainsi que mi	If you don't do as I do,
Tu pairas pinte plaine,	Tu paira pinte pleine.	your glass will remain full.
J'ay veu le cerf du bois sallir	Le cerf du bois je ne pas pris	I have not caught the stag of the woods,
Et boire'a la fontaine.	Mais on ira gran peine,	but I would take great pains,
	E boir a la fonteine.	and drink at the fountain.

Except for an almost literal repeat of the music for the refrain, however, Manchicourt's song is a through-composed elaboration of this melody, with no sectional cadences (example 6.4). The tune's near-contemporaneous circulation as a popular monophonic song is demonstrated by a *noël* contrafact printed without music in *La grand bible des noelz* (1554) under the rubric "Noel nouveau, sur la chanson, / J'ay veu le Cerf du boys saillir, Et boire à la fontaine."[43] This text runs to a total of ninety-six lines, arranged in quatrains rather than the original's couplets, beginning "J'ay veu ce qu'Isaye a dict /

Que le fils de Dieu le pere / Naistroit ça bas sans contredict, / Vierge seroit sa mere" (I have seen that which Isaiah foretold: that the son of God the father would be born here below without doubt; a virgin would be his mother). The *noël* refers to the original text both by beginning each quatrain with "J'ay veu . . ." and by quoting it at greater length elsewhere as it describes the gifts prepared for Jesus by various rustically named shepherds.

Le grand bible des noelz collects *noël* texts to be sung to a wide variety of musical sources, including plainchant, dance tunes, and tunes from polyphonic *chansons*. Manchicourt's "J'ay veu le cerf du boys sallir" might therefore have been the original source of the melody for "J'ay veu ce qu'Isaye a dict," or both may have been derived from a popular monophonic song on the former text. The tune had certainly taken on the quality of a popular character by the turn of the seventeenth century, as a different but still recognizable version of the text appears in a print in 1607, *Airs de Cour comprenans le trésor des trésors . . .*, without music but with performing indications (shown in italics below) that reflect the texture of Vecchi's setting and suggest a parallel to the drinking prescribed in the rubrics to Ferretti's "Berlinghin" and Vecchi's "Cicirlanda":[44]

L'un de la compagnie chantera seul.	*One of the company sings alone:*
J'ay veu le cerf du bois saillir,	I saw the stag of the woods arise,
Je bois à toy mon bel amy,	I drink to you, my good friend,
Et à ta souveraine	and to your queen,
Or verduron duree.	for a long time.
La compagnie doibt dire pendant qu'il boira.	*The company must say while he drinks:*
Le cerf du bois si n'est pas pris,	If the stag of the woods is not caught,
Il n'y faut pas boire a demy	he should not drink half
Pas ne luy faut l'haleine,	without needing a breath,
Or verduron duree,	for a long time.
Celuy qui avra beu dira.	*He who has drunk says:*
J'ay tant beu que i'ay veu le fons,	I have drunk so much that I see the bottom,
Or c'est à toy mon compagnon	but now it is up to you, my friend,
A en faire de mesme,	to do the same,
Or verduron duree,	for a long time.

The quatrains of this poem are metrically distinct from the couplets of the earlier poems (with syllable counts of 8, 8, 7, 7 instead of 8, 7), but the text emphasizes competitive drinking even more strongly. The performing indications are similar to those for other *chansons à boire* in the 1607 print and are clearly intended as instructions for recreational drinking songs, not as "stage directions" in an audience-directed performance of a faux-rustic song. Vecchi's setting from 1590 implicitly follows a similar pattern, with each couplet sung first by the Tenore (whose part has the rubric "Intonatione solo il tenore"), followed by a simple harmonization of the same text in five parts (labeled "Risposta a 5") with the melody in the Canto. This is followed by a long peroration on the final refrain "e boir a la fonteine," labeled "Chiusa" (closing), which is marked by gradually increasing contrapuntal complexity and rhythmic activity (example 6.5). It is ambiguous whether the *chiusa* is to be sung after each stanza or only at the end of the piece, where Vecchi's modified final couplet makes it syntactically obligatory. In either case, the accelerating musical pace in the *chiusa* vividly suggests increasingly raucous singing and intoxication. Singers hoping to maintain a consistent *tactus* must sing the opening sections (set in minims and semibreves) at quite a stately tempo in order to accommodate the long passages in semiminims and *fusae* that gradually emerge in the *chiusa*.

The archaic French text, while clearly appropriate for a *chanson à boire*, is made a subject of parody here. However, Vecchi also provides an Italian text for the song, accommodating users who either do not understand French or simply prefer Italian. The Italian text lacks the sense of alternating drinking implied by the French poem and by the musical form, emphasizing group drinking and the sensation of increasing intoxication instead:[45]

Ecc'il bon Bacco à noi viene,	See, good Bacchus comes to us:
Beviam per fargl'onore.	let's drink to do him honor.
Vedi il gotto ch'in man tiene	You see the goblet he holds in his hand
Per allegrarne il core.	to gladden his heart.
Sento già aprirsi le vene	I already feel my veins opening up
A cosi grato odore.	from such a pleasing aroma.
Questo al mondo ne mantiene,	This is what sustains us in this world:
Gustiam si buon liquore.	let us enjoy good liquor.
Gustiam si buon liquore.	Let us enjoy good liquor.

If, as Einstein surmised, Vecchi dedicated *Selva di varia ricreatione* to the Fugger brothers in Augsburg as part of a general (unsuccessful) campaign to seek Orlando di Lasso's position at the Bavarian court, this bilingual song might have been meant to demonstrate, however modestly, the command of multiple languages and national musical styles that was so closely identified with Lasso.

Example 6.5. (*above and facing*) Vecchi, "Je veu le cerf," mm. 15–23.

"O Giardinerio": Wine, Men, and Song

Vecchi used the wine-related wordplay of "Cicirlanda" again in a piece from *Convito musicale*, though without the label *vinata* or the formalized sense of game play. The six-voice "O Giardiniero," in three parts, has no genre label, but it appears in the book just after the two *villotte* discussed above, which resemble it textually, if not musically. "O Giardiniero" begins as a polyphonic depiction of a two-person dialogue in the "comic" style Vecchi used in *L'Amfiparnaso*. A passerby asks to see a gardener's vineyard and is invited inside; the ensuing praise for the plump grapes and the description of squeezing them to produce wine carries erotic overtones typical of Vecchi's *villotte*:[46]

T	[Pass.] O Giardiniero!	O gardener!
6	[Giard.] Che vuoi tu o Passaggiero?	What do you want, O passerby?
T	[Pass.] Vorrei veder'un poc'il tuo, Giardino	I would like to see a little of your garden,
	E quella vigna che fa si buon vino.	and that vineyard that makes such good wine.
tutti	[Giard.] Ben venga, entr'a tua posta,	Welcome, enter at your pleasure,
	Che nulla costa.	because it costs nothing.
CAT	Hor d'ogn'intorno mira,	Now everywhere around you, see
	L'uve dorate e l'uve purpurine.	golden grapes and purple grapes.
	Vagheggia i varii frutti;	Gaze at the various fruits;
	E fanne se ti par saggio di tutti.[47]	and if you like, taste them all.
tutti	[Pass.] O bel vedere,	O beautiful sight,
	O che piacere,	O what pleasure,
CATB	O bel giardino,	O beautiful garden,
	C'ha del divino.	that has something of the divine.
CA5	[Giard.] Mira	Look at
C5	che quel grappolino,	this little bunch of grapes;
CAT5	Se non sembra rubino?	is it not like a ruby?
65B	Vedi quella Rossetta	See this reddish one,
6T5B	Che spesso tra' da gl'occhi	which often draws from the eyes
tutti	Più d'una lagrimetta.	more than one small tear.
C65	Vè, vè che trà le fronde,	See, among the leaves
	Quella che là s'asconde;	that which is hiding there,
CAT5	Ch'espost'al sole ardente	which, exposed to the burning sun,
	Somiglia oro lucente.	resembles shining gold.
6B	Deh gusta un poc'o amico,	Pray, taste a little, O friend,
6T5B	Questa, via più del mel dolc'e del fico.	this one, sweeter than honey or the fig.
tutti	[Pass.] O com'è dolce, O com'altrui diletta,	O how sweet it is, O how it delights others.
	Com'è odorosa,	How aromatic,
	Com'è mustosa,	how like a young wine,
	Come rinfranca	how it refreshes
	La vita stanca.	the tired life.
CA5	Dei vini che tu premi	Of the wine that you press
	Da si dolci racemi,	from such sweet bunches of grapes,
	Fa ch'un sorso di tutt'almen n'accoglia,	take at least a sip of all of them gathered here.
tutti	[Giard.] Di gratia, volentier, di buona voglia.	With thanks, willingly, and with goodwill.

After the monophonic opening, the dialogic nature of the poem is frequently obscured by shifting textures within each speaker's speeches. As in Vecchi's other small-scale dialogues, this allows each singer to represent both speakers and partake equally in the equivocal humor of the piece. The obscene level of the discourse can be read from the premise itself: since garden imagery is frequently associated with female sexuality, the rustic male gardener's invitation to the urban visitor to enter his garden carries a suggestion of a homosexual encounter.[48] The grapes that he then invites the visitor to admire carry phallic associations, particularly in connection with revealing something hidden from sight, extracting juice, or provoking others to shed tears.[49] The visitor's enthusiastic responses are best read as a naive city-boy's failure to understand the lewd innuendo of his social inferior. "O giardiniero" thus presents an intermingling of social classes—possibly on an illicit level—not depicted in Vecchi's *villotte*.

Given the potential erotic overtones of the *prima parte,* the second and third parts of "O giardiniero" can likewise be read equivocally as depicting increasingly sexual contact between the two men. The gardener's vividly sensual descriptions of the various wines he offers to the visitor continue to allude covertly to bodily fluids and ejaculation, and the visitor in turn celebrates their taste and intoxicating effects in terms of physical arousal. On a more literal level, the *seconda parte* begins to resemble the kinds of toasting songs we have seen, as the gardener names the various wines he offers:

CAT	[Giard.] Hor prend'e fann'il saggio,	Now take it and taste it,
	Che men noioso ti parrà il viaggio.	so that your journey will seem less boring.
tutti	Bevilo allegramente,	Drink it cheerfully,
	Ch'io vengo col second'e più possente.	for I am coming with a second, stronger one.
CAT	[Pass.] O ponderoso vino,	O heavy wine,
	O nettare divino,	O divine nectar,
	Gentil più del claretto,	gentler than claret,
	C'ha'l leggiero, e lo scarico e'l tondetto.	which has lightness, ease, and roundness.
	Come si chiama?	What is it called?
65B	[Giard.] Quest'è Marzemino,	This is Marzemino,
	Quel che tanto s'appretia	that which is so much appreciated
	Ne inclita Venetia.	in glorious Venice.

tutti	[Pass.] Felice ch'ivi è nato,		Happy is he who was born there,
	E c'ha bon gustato		and who has tasted
	Sì buon licore		such good liquor,
	Ch'allegra il mesto core.		which gladdens the sad heart.
65B	[Giard.] Bevi, Quest'è la lagrima di Roma		Drink: this is the tear of Rome,
	Ch'ogni tantalea set'ammorz'e doma.		which quenches and tames every Tantalean thirst.
CAT	[Pass.] O come dolc'inaffia,		O how sweetly it wets,
	E vag'ispruzza,		how beautifully it sprays,
	Che l'appetito aguzza,		so as to sharpen the appetite,
	Salticchia e brilla,		it jumps and shines,
	Rid'e sfavilla,		it laughs and glitters,
	Mord' e rimord' e bacia, e tra di calci,		bites and bites again, and kisses, and kicks,
tutti	O benedetti tralci,		O blessed branch,
	O pretiosa vite,		O precious vine,
	Ch'altrui col tuo licor dai mille vite.		that with your liquor gives others a thousand lives.
65B	[Giard.] Hor t'apparecchia,		Now prepare yourself,
	Che quest'è vin polputo d'una orecchia.		for this is a wine as pulpy as an ear.
tutti	[Pass.] Lascia, ch'io prendi fiato,		Stop, that I might take a breath
	Ch'al tuo cortes'invito i farò grato.		so that I may enjoy your courteous invitation.

Vecchi's delineation of the characters through voicing is much clearer in this section, though not entirely consistent. With the exception of the opening two lines, the Canto-Alto-Tenore trio represents the visitor and the lower-pitched Sesto-Quinto-Basso voices the gardener. *Tutti* textures may or may not signal a change of speaker but tend to mark the moments of greatest enthusiasm or arousal. Envoicing the visitor at a higher pitch conveys both his "higher" social position as a city-dweller with leisure time to spare and also his youth—and thus his susceptibility to corruption by the lower-status (and lower-pitched) gardener. One is reminded again of the young men depicted in Striggio's "Gioco di primiera," Croce's "Gioco dell'Oca," or Caravaggio's *Cardsharps*.

The third part extends the questioning about each wine's name to the game-like conceit of rhyming each answer with the wine's description:

CAT	[Pass.] Quest'è un altra bevanda	This is another drink
CA6T	Che merita ghirlanda.	that deserves a garland.
65B	[Giard.] Tien dritto, ch'una goccia non si spanda.	Hold it straight, so that not a drop is spilled.
5B	[Pass.] E come si domanda?	And how does one ask for it?
CAT	[Giard.] Si chiam'il vin Roteglia, Perché'l perduto gust'arruota e sveglia.	The wine is called Roteglia, for it sharpens and awakens the lost taste.

The trios that represent each character are less sharply defined here, as the Sesto migrates from singing the gardener's lines to joining in one of the visitor's, but the depiction at this point is still clear, as is the equivocal reading of the text: the visitor now praises the pulpy—or "fleshy"—wine served to him at the end of the second part, and the gardener advises him to hold it straight—that is, erect—so that it does not spill. After a passage in praise of Bacchus (set in the completely homophonic style of the *villotta*) the game-like rhyming continues, but at this point new vocal combinations are used for every line, blurring the previously clear character distinctions (some poetic lines are divided to show shifts in voicing):

6TB	[Giard.] Quest'ultim'è Trebbiano,	This last is Trebbiano,
6B	Licor almo e sovrano,	lively and supreme liquor,
CAT5B	Ch'in pioggia d'oro	that in a shower of gold
tutti	piove.	rains.
CA6T	Questo fa gire altero;	This makes one turn proud:
tutti	è Secchia ed Arno.[50]	it is Secchia and Arno.
CA6T	[Pass.] Porgilo quà,	Offer it here,
tutti	Ch'a berlo, i mi ci incarno.	that in drinking it I immerse myself.
	[Giard?] Bevi si buon licor in sin'al fondo,	Drink such good liquor all the way to the bottom,
CT5	Che quest'è un di giocondo.	for this is a joyful day.
A65	[Pass.?] O vin brillante,	O brilliant wine,
T	O vin frizzante,	O sparkling wine,
CAT	O l'è galante.	O it is gallant.

The visitor's declaration "i mi ci incarno" might more literally be read as "I am penetrated," to which the gardener's reply to drink the wine "in sin'al fondo" (set over a bass that descends stepwise through an octave plus a sixth; example 6.6) continues the potential for a sodomitical reading of the poem.[51]

Example 6.6. (*above and facing*) Vecchi, "O Giardiniero," *terza parte,* mm. 45–53.

49
Che que-st'è‿un di gio - con - - -
O
si - n'al fon - do,
che que-st'è‿un di gio - con - - -
fon - do, Che que-st'è‿un di gio - con - do.
si - n'al fon - do,
51
do.
vin bril-lan - - - te,
O vin bril-lan - - te,
do. O vin friz-zan - te,
O vin bril-lan - te,

Indeed, in the ensuing passage, which concludes the piece, the visitor's cry that he will faint ("vengo meno") and that he is full of whims (*grilli*, literally, "crickets"), which might be taken as erotically evocative in any case, has an equivocal meaning that suggests sodomy.[52] After more potentially suggestive dialogue regarding the road to take (reminiscent of the *dritta via* mentioned at the end of Vecchi's "O bella ò bianca più che la cagiata"), the visitor finally bids farewell to the gardener with "ti lascio," a phrase associated with orgasm even in high-register literary poetry.

CA6T	[Pass.] Ohimè,	Alas,
CAT	ch'io vengo meno.	for I am fainting.
tutti	Di grilli ho colm'il seno.	My breast is full of whims.
CAB	[Giard.] Compagno, non temer,	Companion, do not fear,
CATB	ma ti conforte	but comfort yourself
	Che'l buon vin non da mai morte.	that good wine never causes death.
C6T5	[Pass.] Deh, mostrami la strada,	Oh, show me the road,
	Ch'è temp'homai ch'io vada.	for it is time at last that I go.
tutti	[Giard.] Camina sempre lungo questo rio,	Always follow this brook,
	Ne ti torcere mai,	do not ever stray
	Che tost' a la Città tu giungerai.	until you reach the city.
AT5B	[Pass.] Ti lascio,	I leave you,
C65B	hor vanne	now go,
T	Giardiniero,	Gardener,
CA6B	Addio.	farewell.
T	*Giardiniero,*	*Gardener,*
CA6B	*Addio.*	*farewell.*

Einstein calls this "the first representation of drunkenness in music" and proposes that the depiction of intoxication is a parody of Gesualdo's musical eccentricities. In fact, Vecchi's harmonic style here is never particularly unorthodox, though he uses the device of juxtaposing major triads on A and F twice to indicate a shift from the gardener's voice to that of the drunken visitor (mm. 70–71 and 77–78 in example 6.7). The second of these coincides with a striking juxtaposition of *villotta*-style homophony and more affective madrigalian polyphony in the crucial words "ti lascio." The visitor calls out twice more to the gardener, voiced by the solo Tenore in an exact quote of the piece's beginning. The farewell vividly mimics the topos of the lover's farewell but finally ends abruptly with a repeated off-beat cadence and a final weak plagal inflection. Depending on the singers' understanding of the piece,

Example 6.7. (*above and the following three pages*)
Vecchi, "O Giardiniero," *terza parte,* mm. 65–84.

Deh, mo-stra-mi la stra-da, Ch'è tem-p'ho-mai ch'io va-da. Ca-

Ca-

Deh, mo-stra-mi la stra-da, Ch'è tem-p'ho-mai ch'io va - da. Ca-

Deh, mo-stra-mi la stra-da, Ch'è tem-p'ho-mai ch'io va - da. Ca-

Deh, mo-stra-mi la stra-da, Ch'è tem-p'ho-mai ch'io va - da. Ca-

mi-

mi-na sem-pre lun-go que-sto ri-o, No ti tor - ce-re ma-i, Che to-st'a la Cit-

mi-na sem-pre lun-go que-sto ri-o, No ti tor - ce-re ma-i, Che to-st'a la Cit-

mi-na sem-pre lun-go que-sto ri-o, No ti tor - ce-re ma-i, Che to-st'a la Cit-

mi-na sem-pre lun-go que-sto ri-o, No ti tor - ce-re ma-i, Che to-st'a la Cit-

mi-na sem-pre lun-go que-sto ri-o, No ti tor - ce-re ma-i, Che to-st'a la Cit-

mi-na sem-pre lun-go que-sto ri-o, No ti tor - ce-re ma-i, Che to-st'a la Cit-

77
tà tu giun-ge-ra - i. hor
tà tu giun-ge-ra - i. Ti la - scio,
tà tu giun-ge-ra - i. hor
tà tu giun-ge-ra - i. Ti la - - - scio,
tà tu giun-ge-ra - i. Ti la - - scio, hor
tà tu giun-ge-ra - i. Ti la - - scio, hor
80
van - ne, van - ne, A Dio, a Dio, a
A Dio, a Dio, a
van - ne, van - ne, A Dio, a Dio, a
Giar - di - nie - ro.
van - ne, van - ne,
van - ne, van - ne, A Dio, a Dio, a

this might be sung with a diminuendo to suggest the visitor's disappearance down the path or else as a spluttering failure of his attempt at amorous speech in bidding farewell to the gardener. In the latter reading, the young man's corruption through drunkenness and perhaps sodomy is signaled by a loss of both verbal and musical eloquence.

The moral hazard depicted in "Giardiniero," whether one reads it as a coded homosexual encounter or simply as a drinking bout of the kind condemned by Della Casa, is of socializing across class boundaries. Vecchi's other musical settings of courtiers and peasants depict them as enclosed within their own social spheres, even when the view is parodistic or cynically critical. Drinking games played among peasants (or courtiers imitating peasants) are harmless fun, but when a young urban man crosses into a rural garden of delights, his honor and his dignity are at greater risk.

Music for Audiences Public and Private

Throughout this book I have emphasized the ways in which Vecchi's music engages its singers' imaginations. The new genres that Vecchi invented or adopted and the more idiosyncratic pieces not conforming to any established genre all lend themselves to this context of recreational singing, and such readings are of course available for his more conventional madrigal books as well, a perspective that encourages considering his music in the printed form in which it circulated. Vecchi was unusually concerned with the structure, meaning, and function of his music books—even though, like other composers, he derived little financial profit from the enterprise of printing and reprinting his music—because he was not beholden to courtly patrons. Vecchi's biography reveals that his direct patronage beyond the church was limited and that his attempts to promote his name to courts with large professional musical establishments were unsuccessful. His only secular appointment came in 1598, when he was named *maestro della musica* to the much-reduced Este court, newly relocated from Ferrara to Modena. This job included responsibility for teaching music to Cesare's children, but the compensation of 80 scudi per year was not sufficient for Vecchi to leave his position at the cathedral, where he is recorded in 1600 as receiving a salary of 120 scudi annually.[53]

Even before this appointment, Vecchi had occasional opportunities to compose large-scale works intended for a separate audience. As early as 1579 he had composed music for the festivities in honor of Francesco de' Medici's wedding to Bianca Cappello, providing one stanza to a collaborative setting of a sestina, "Sperar non si potea da si bella Alba," to which Tiburzio Massaino (who seems to have been responsible for the project and the book in which it was published), Andrea Gabrieli, Vincenzo Bellavere, Claudio da Correggio, and Baldassare Donati also contributed.[54] The large-scale polychoral pieces in *Selva* and in *Convito musicale* and Vecchi's contributions to Gardano's 1590 publication of dialogues were likewise probably composed for festive events, though in most cases the specific events have eluded identification.[55] Two of the dialogues in *Selva*, the eight-voice "Ecco nuncio di gioia" and the ten-voice "Ecco su 'l tauro," are clearly wedding pieces, the latter explicitly, declaring that "the handsome Favonio is taking the beautiful Flora to wife." *Convito musicale* ends with an eight-voice wedding dialogue, "Coppia reale e bella," though again the "royal couple" of the title is not identified.

One work from *Selva* can be tied to a particular event, the *Battaglia d'Amor' e Dispetto* (Battle of Love and Scorn), Vecchi's largest-scale secular work to survive. It was composed for the 1587 wedding celebrations in Sassuolo for Marco Pio di Savoia and Clelia Farnese.[56] The bride and groom are both named in the text, and Vecchi is known to have been present at the festivities, though there is no evidence that his *battaglia* was actually performed there. Composed for two choirs of four and six voices and set in four large sections, it makes an ideal finale for a large collection like *Selva*, embodying in its theme both the book's governing aesthetic principle of contrast and the specific conflict of many of the other pieces: love versus scorn. It also employs markers of the sixteenth-century *battaglia* style—imitations of triadic fanfares, calls to arms, and the tumult of battle—deployed in long passages of static harmony. This musical topos resembles depictions of nonmusical noise in *battaglie* and hunt-based *caccie* by Clement Janequin, Matthias Werrecore, Alessandro Striggio, and Andrea Gabrieli, as well as in other works by Vecchi that imitate the noise of a chaotic street scene ("Diversi linguaggi" from *Selva*) or a raucous game ("Il bando del asino" from *Convito*). Among other large-scale sixteenth-century battle pieces, the *Battaglia d'Amor' e Dispetto* is unique in its imaginative allegorical meaning, which forges links both between the imitative agendas of Vecchi's smaller-scale music and his polychoral spectacles, and between Renaissance *battaglie* and the Monteverdian *genere concitato* of the seventeenth century.[57]

We have fuller documentation for performances of spectacles by Vecchi for which the music itself does not survive. Spaccini describes presentations both outdoors and in courtly settings following Vecchi's appointment to Cesare d'Este's court. The most public of these were the *carozze* used in street processions during Carnival, such as the ones presented—despite inclement weather—on February 2, 1600, which included two different and highly contrasting scenes: "There was performed a *mascherata* of shepherds with Diana going to the hunt, with good music by Ercole Sforzini, a singer. It was not like the *mascherate* that were once possible, on account of the bad weather: it snowed continually. After that there were three carriages revealed to be full of puppets; in one of these there was good music by Orazio Vecchi, which they sang from the windows, and it was snowing very hard."[58] "Sforzini" is Ercole Biancolini, recorded (with his nickname "Sforcino") as a singer in the cathedral choir in 1584 and 1600.[59] It was typical for Vecchi to share his composing duties for such events with his subordinates and indeed to assign or allow them to provide music for the more serious scenes. On February 14, 1600, Vecchi shared a series of *mascherate* with Capilupi, and despite Spaccini's praise for Vecchi's seemingly unremarkable *giustiniana*, Capilupi's *mascherata* as described was more opulent both visually and musically:

There was performed a *mascherata* of Pantaloni, who rowed in gondolas, singing in the Venetian language of the antiquity of that city, and it was a composition of Orazio Vecchi, one of the most beautiful that was ever made. Another was performed of the Great Mother, who was on top of a chariot drawn by lions; she had on her head a crown of towers, and a garment woven of green grass and encircled with leafy branches. She had her sceptre in one hand and a key in the other, and around her were some empty seats, and there were resounding drums, and she was accompanied by certain priests with helmets on their heads, shields on their arms, and rods in their hands, and they played a great concerto, which was by Geminiano Capilupi.[60]

Vecchi's specialty seems to have been the comic *mascherate,* including one from 1599 featuring typically obscene *gramolatori di pasta*—"dough kneaders"—who handed out loaves and pastries to the crowd.[61] He produced them not only for public processions like those described here but also for private performances within the court. These sometimes featured the duke's children, whose musical education was Vecchi's responsibility, as in this performance following a ducal procession on January 30, 1600, to mark the beginning of the feast of San Geminiano: "Having reached the castle, in his chambers, he was met by two of the little princes and a lady graciously dressed with much adornment, where they sang a madrigal, and finally he cried, 'Masks, masks!' After this the princes reappeared dressed as Pantaloni and sang a very laughable *pantalona,* an invention of Orazio Vecchi, their singing master."[62] On March 5 (Carnival Monday) of the same year, a more formal performance was given of a *pastorella* that included the princes and other noble children. This seems to have been a more complex theatrical piece, since Vecchi is credited only with the *intermedi et musica.*[63] The more public performances, according to Spaccini's accounts, were taken over by Capilupi and by Giovan Battista Stefanini, a singer at the cathedral since 1593 who was eventually to become *maestro di cappella* there following Capilupi's death in 1616.[64]

Vecchi composed another large-scale work, the *Mascherata della Malenconia at Allegrezza,* for the wedding festivities of Cesare's daughter Laura d'Este to Alessandro Pico della Mirandola during Carnival in 1604. The *mascherata* is described in detail in Gismondo Florio's official account of the wedding festivities, and Spaccini quotes this account verbatim.[65] This piece is the unique example of a large-scale courtly work from Vecchi's period of service to the Este court whose music survives and can be identified, since it was printed as the final (and largest) piece in Vecchi's posthumous *Dialoghi* of 1608, edited by Paolo Bravusi. As we have seen in chapter 5, the very public *mascherata* is intimately tied to Vecchi's smaller-scale music for recreational use, since large sections of its music were adapted for—or adapted from—madrigals that were printed, according to Spaccini, some seven months later in *Le veglie di Siena.*

Vecchi remained as *maestro di capella* until the notorious incident on October 7, 1604, when he was suddenly dismissed by the bishop, Gaspare Silingardi, on the grounds, according to Spaccini, "che andasse a cantare alle Monache" (that he had gone to sing to the nuns) against the injunction of the bishop.[66] This infraction seems likely to have been a mere pretext within a power struggle between Vecchi and his student and former collaborator Geminiano Capilupi (described by Spaccini as Vecchi's "student and enemy in one"), who was named *maestro di cappella* following Vecchi's dismissal. A rift between teacher and student had opened a year earlier for reasons unknown, and on June 27, 1603, Vecchi had formally disinherited Capilupi, who had been named heir to Vecchi's musical possessions in wills dated 1588, 1592, and 1595.[67] Spaccini's sense of injustice at the dismissal is understandable, and his sympathies are clearly with Vecchi. Just two weeks earlier, on September 26, the chronicler had declared that with the recent publication of Vecchi's *Le veglie di Siena* and the *Hymni qui per totum annum in Ecclesia Romanum concinnuntur,* "it seems as though His Highness [i.e., Duke Cesare d'Este] will want to restore his music as his antecedents formerly had."[68] Spaccini's hope seems to have been groundless, however, since the town council's recommendation for the duke and the bishop to reinstate Vecchi was ignored.[69]

On February 17, 1605, Vecchi dictated a new will naming Paolo Bravusi as his musical heir, just days before his death on February 19 or 20. Spaccini's account of the deathbed scene is surprisingly detailed for one who was presumably not himself present, so we might read with a grain of salt his description of the remorseful bishop's belated offer to pay for Vecchi's burial and the family's indignant refusal, and likewise Capilupi's hypocritical wish to honor the mentor he had betrayed by directing the music at the funeral.[70] The mysterious enmity that arose between Vecchi and his student in 1603, its precise role in Vecchi's dismissal from his post as *maestro di capella* the following year, and its contribution to his final illness have all been amplified in the melodramatic fashion of much of Vecchi's subsequent biography. By 1607 Vecchi's reputation as a leading composer and source of civic pride had been restored, as attested by the laudatory tombstone erected that year in the Carmelite church.

Appendix:
Vecchi, "L'hore di recreatione,"
from *Madrigali a sei* (1583)

L'hore di recreatione

Orazio Vecchi
from *Madrigali a sei voci* (1583)

Canto (C1)

Hor che le piag - gie ri - don d'o - gn'_in-tor-no,

Quinto (C1)

Alto (C2)

Hor che le piag - - - gie ri - don d'o - gn'_in-tor-no,

Tenore (C4)

Hor che le piag - - - gie ri - don d'o - gn'_in-tor-no,

Sesto (C4)

Hor che le piag - gie ri - don d'o - gn'_in-tor-no,

Basso II (F3)

Hor che le piag - gie ri - don d'ogn'_in-tor-no,

Basso (F4)

Hor che le piag - gie ri - don d'o - gn'_in-tor-no,

4

E spun-tan fuor vi-o-le_e gi-gl'e ro-se,

E spun-tan fuor vi-o-le_e gi-gl'e ro-se,

E spun-tan fuor vi-o-le_e gi-gl'e ro-se, E gl'au-gel-let - ti per le val-l'om-

E gl'au-gel-let - ti per le val-l'om-

E spun-tan fuor vi-o-le_e gi-gl'e ro-se,

E gl'au-gel-let - ti per le val-l'om-

E gl'au-gel-let - ti per le val-l'om-

7
Leg - gia - dre, leg - gia -
Leg-gia - dre, leg-
bro-se, Can-ta-n'in sti - le‿a-dor - no Leg-gia - dre,
bro-se, Can-ta-n'in sti - le‿a-dor - no
Leg - gia - dre
bro-se, Can-ta-n'in sti - le‿a-dor - no
bro-se, Can-ta-n'in sti - le‿a-dor - no
10
dre, leg - gia - dre Can-zo-net-te‿e a-mo-ro - se Don-ne‿e don-
gia - dre, leg - gia-dre Can-zo-net-te‿e a-mo-ro - se Don-ne‿e don-
leg-gia - dre Can-zo - net-te‿e a - mo-ro - se Don-ne‿e don-
Don-ne‿e don-
Can - zo - net - te‿e a - mo - ro - se Don-ne‿e don-
Don-ne‿e don-
Don-ne‿e don-

13
zel - le leg - gia - dret - te‿e bel - le, leg - gia-
zel - le leg - gia-dret - te‿e bel -
zel - le leg - gia-dret - te‿e bel - le, leg - gia-dret - te‿e
zel - le leg - gia-dret - te‿e bel - le, leg - gia-dret - te‿e
zel - le leg - gia-dret - te‿e bel -
zel - le leg - gia-dret - te‿e bel - le, leg - gia-dret - te‿e
zel - le leg - gia-dret - te‿e bel - le, leg - gia-dret - te‿e
15
dret - te‿e bel - le, leg - gia - dret-te‿e bel - le, Ch'in
le, leg - gia-dret - te‿e bel - le, Ch'in
bel - le, leg - gia-dret - te‿e bel - - - le,
bel - le, leg - gia-dret - te‿e bel - - - le, Ch'in
le, leg - gia-dret - te‿e bel - le, e bel - le,
bel - le, leg - gia-dret - te‿e bel - - - le, Ch'in
bel - le, leg - gia-dret - te‿e bel - - - le,

17
gio - ia͜ a tut - te l'o - re Con gran pia -
gio - ia͜ a tut - te l'o - re Con gran pia - cer
Con gran pia-cer
gio - ia͜ a tut - te l'o - re
Con gran pia - cer
gio - ia͜ a tut - te l'o - re Con gran pia - cer in voi s'an-ni-d'A-
Con gran pia - cer in voi s'an-ni-d'A-
20
cer in voi s'an - ni - d'A - mo - - - re,
s'an - ni - d'A - mo - re, in
in voi s'an - ni - d'A - mo - re,
Con gran pia - cer
mo - re, in voi s'an - ni - d'A -
mo - - - re, Con

Measure 22:

s'an-ni - d'A-mo - - re. Deh,

voi s'an-ni-d'A-mo - re, s'an-ni-d'A-mo-re. Deh,

in voi s'an-ni-d'A-mo - re, Deh,

Con gran pia-cer in voi s'an-ni - d'A-mo-re.

in vois'an-ni-d'A-mo-re.

mo - re, s'an-ni-d'A-mo-re.

gran pia - cer in voi s'an-ni-d'A-mo - re.

Measure 25:

3

deh, deh tut-ti u-ni - ti in-sie - me: Can-tiam qual -

deh, deh tut-ti u-ni - ti in-sie - me: Can-tiam qual -

deh, deh tut-ti-u-ni-ti in-sie - - me: Can-tiam qual -

Deh tut-ti u-ni - ti in-sie - me: Can-tiam qual -

Deh tut-ti u-ni - ti in-sie - me: Can-tiam qual -

Deh tut-ti u-ni - ti in-sie - me: Can-tiam qual -

Deh tut-ti u-ni - ti in-sie - me: Can-tiam qual -

29
che bal - la - ta‿o Can - zo - net - ta!
che bal - la - ta‿o Can - zo - net - ta!
che bal - la - ta‿o Can - zo - net - ta!
che bal - la - ta‿o Can - zo - net - ta! Chi fa - rà‿il
che bal - la - ta‿o Can - zo - net - ta!
che bal - la - ta‿o Can - zo - net - ta! Chi fa - rà‿il
che bal - la - ta‿o Can - zo - net - ta! Chi fa - rà‿il
32
Chi fa - ra‿il Can - to? Chi
Ec - co-mi qua!
Chi fa-ra‿il Can - to?
Bas - - - so? Chi
Chi fa - ra‿il Can - to?
Bas - - - so? Chi
Bas - so? I - - - o! Chi

36
fa - ra l'Al - to? Del Te-nor' ve n'è cop -
I - o!
fa - ra l'Al - to? Del Te-nor' ve n'è cop -
Del Te-nor' ve n'è cop -
fa-ra l'Al - to? Del Te-nor' ve n'è cop -
fa - ra l'Al - to?
39
pia, or com-men-cia - mo!
or com-men-cia - mo! or com-men-cia - mo!
or com-men-cia - mo!
pia, or com-men-cia - mo! or com-men -
pia, or com-men-cia - mo!
pia, or com-men-cia - mo! or com-men -
or com-men-cia - mo! or com-men -

41
Chi mi-ra gl'oc-chi tuo-i E non so-spi-ra po-i, E non so-
Chi mi-ra gl'oc-chi tuo-i E non so-spi-ra po-i, E non so-
Chi mi-ra gl'oc-chi tuo-i E non so-spi-ra po-i, E non so-
cia-mo! Chi mi-ra gl'oc-chi tuo-i E non so-spi-ra po-i, E non so-
Chi mi-ra gl'oc-chi tuo-i E non so-spi-ra po-i, E non so-
cia-mo! Chi mi-ra gl'oc-chi tuo-i E non so-spi-ra po-i, E non so-
cia-mo! Chi mi-ra gl'oc-chi tuo-i E non so-spi-ra po-i, E non so-
44
spi-ra po-i, Chi mi-ra gl'oc-chi tuo-i E non so-spi-ra po-
spi-ra po-i, Chi mi-ra gl'oc-chi tuo-i E non so-spi-ra po-
spi-ra po-i, Chi mi-ra gl'oc-chi tuo-i E non so-spi-ra po-
spi-ra po-i, Chi mi-ra gl'oc-chi tuo-i E non so-spi-ra po-
spi-ra po-i, Chi mi-ra gl'oc-chi tuo-i E non so-spi-ra po-
spi-ra po-i, Chi mi-ra gl'oc-chi tuo-i E non so-spi-ra po-
spi-ra po-i, Chi mi-ra gl'oc-chi tuo-i E non so-spi-ra po-

47
i, E non so-spi - ra po - i, Cre - do che non sia vi -
i, E non so-spi - ra po - i,
i, E non so-spi - ra po - i,
i, E non so-spi - ra po - i, Cre - do che
i, E non so-spi - ra po - i, Cre - do che non sia vi - vo,
i, E non so-spi - ra po - i, Cre -
i, E non so-spi - ra po - i, Cre - do che non sia
49
vo, Cre - do che non sia vi - - - vo, O
Cre - do che non sia vi - vo, vi - vo, O
Cre - do che non sia vi - - - vo, O
non sia vi - vo, che non sia vi - - - vo, O
Cre - do che non sia vi - vo, O
do che non sia vi - vo, O di
vi - vo, Cre - do che non sia vi - - - vo, O

51
di giu - di - zio pri - vo, Cre - do che non sia vi -
di giu - di - zio pri - vo,
di giu - di - zio pri - vo,
di giu - di - zio pri - vo, Cre - do che
di giu - di - zio pri - vo, Cre - do che non sia vi - vo,
giu - di - zio pri - vo, Cre -
di giu - di - zio pri - vo, Cre - do che non sia
53
vo, Cre - do che non sia vi - - - vo, O
Cre - do che non sia vi - vo, vi - vo, O
Cre - do che non sia vi - - - vo, O
non sia vi - vo, che non sia vi - - - vo, O
Cre - do che non sia vi - vo, O
do che non sia vi - vo, O di
vi - vo, Cre - do che non sia vi - - - vo, O

55
di giu - di - zio pri - - - vo.
di giu - di - zio pri - - - vo.
Breve
di giu - di - zio pri - - - vo.
di giu - di - zio pri - - - - - - vo.
di giu - di - zio pri - - - vo.
giu - di - zio pri - - - - - - vo.
di giu - di - zio pri - - - vo.
57
Seconda parte
Non più, non più, non più, non
U - n'al - tra vol - ta, u - n'al - tra
U - n'al - tra vol - ta, u - n'al - tra
Non più, non più, non più,
U - n'al - tra vol - ta, u - n'al - tra vol - ta,
Non più, non
U - n'al - tra vol - ta, u - n'al - tra

61
più, non più, fac - cia - m'un bal -
vol - ta, sen - z'al - tr'in - ter - val - lo!
vol - ta, sen - z'al - tr'in - ter - val - lo!
non più, non più, fac - cia - m'un bal -
sen - z'al - tr'in - ter - val - lo! Non più, fac - cia - m'un bal -
più, non più, fac - cia - m'un bal -
vol - ta, sen - z'al - tr'in - ter - val - lo!
64
ø3
lo, non più, facciam'un bal - lo!
Non più, facciam'un bal - lo! Bal - la - re - stu fan -
Non più, facciam'un bal - lo! Bal - la - re - stu fan -
lo, un bal - lo! Bal - la - re - stu fan -
lo, non più, facciam'un bal - lo!
lo, non più, facciam'un bal - lo!
Non più, facciam'un bal - lo! Bal - la - re - stu fan -

Bal - la - re - ve ben

ti - na, Da la far - za tur - chi - na?

ti - na, Da la far - za tur - chi - na? Bal - la - re - ve ben

ti - na, Da la far - za tur - chi - na?

Bal - la - re - ve ben

Bal - la - re - ve ben

ti - na, Da la far - za tur - chi - na?

mi, sa sa - ves - se con chi! Bal - la - re - ve ben

Bal - la - re - ve ben

mi, sa sa - ves - se con chi! Bal - la - re - ve ben

Bal - la - re - ve ben

mi, sa sa - ves - se con chi! Bal - la - re - ve ben

mi, sa sa - ves - se con chi! Bal - la - re - ve ben

Bal - la - re - ve ben

1583: c'

308 *Appendix*

75
mi, sa sa - ves - se con chi! Non più, non
mi, sa sa - ves - se con chi! Non più, non più fre-
mi, sa sa - ves - se con chi! Non più,
mi, sa sa - ves - se con chi!
mi, sa sa - ves - se con chi!
mi, sa sa - ves - se con chi!
mi, sa sa - ves - se con chi!
78
più fre - na-te il ri - - - - - so!
na-te il ri - - - - - - so!
non più, non più fre - na - te il ri - so!
E, poi - ché dol -
E, poi - ché dol -
E, poi - ché dol -
E, poi - ché dol -

81
ø3
Can - ta - no gl'au - gel - let - ti,
Can - ta - no gl'au - gel - let - ti,
Can - ta - no gl'au - gel - let - ti,
ce - men - te Can - ta - no
ce - men - te Can - ta - no
ce - men - te Can - ta - no
ce - men - te Can - ta - no
85
can - ta - no gl'au - gel - let - ti, can - ta - no
can - ta - no gl'au - gel - let - ti, can - ta - no
can - ta - no gl'au - gel - let - ti, can - ta - no
gl'au - gel - let - ti, can - ta - no
gl'au - gel - let - ti, can - ta - no
gl'au - gel - let - ti, can - ta - no
gl'au - gel - let - ti, can - ta - no

*1583: f'-sharp

gl'au - gel - let - ti_ai no - str'ac - cen-ti, Piac-cia-vi di can-

gl'au - gel - let - ti_ai no - str'ac - cen-ti,

gl'au - gel - let - ti_ai no - str'ac - cen-ti, Piac-cia-vi di can-

gl'au - gel - let - ti_ai no - str'ac - cen-ti,

gl'au - gel - let - ti_ai no - str'ac - cen-ti, Piac-cia-vi di can-

gl'au - gel - let - ti_ai no - str'ac - cen-ti,

gl'au - gel - let - ti_ai no - str'ac - cen-ti, Piac-cia-vi di can-

ta - re Quel-la che sì di - let - ta,

Quel-la che sì di - let - ta, quel-la che sì di-

ta - re Quel-la che sì di-

Quel-la che sì di - let - ta, quel-la che sì di-

ta - re Quel-la che sì di - let - ta,

Quel-la che sì di - let - ta, quel-la che sì di - let - ta

ta - re Quel-la che sì di - let - ta

quel-la che sì di-let-t'a mio com-pa - re. Co-me si

let - ta a mio com-pa - re. Co-me si

let - ta, di-let-t'a mio com-pa - re. Co-me si

let - ta, di-let-ta a mio com-pa - re. Co - me si

quel-la che sì di-let-ta a mio com-pa - re.

a mio com - pa - re.

a mio com - pa - re.

chia-ma, che n'ab-biam ben cen - to? Or

chia-ma, che n'ab-biam ben cen - to? Or

chia-ma, che n'ab-biam ben cen - to? Or

chia-ma, che n'ab - biam ben cen - to? Non mi so-vie - ne.

Non mi so-vie - ne.

Non mi so-vie - ne.

Non mi so-vie - ne.

100
stia cia-scu-n'at-ten-to: Or va Can-zo - na mia, non du-bi-
stia cia-scu-n'at-ten-to: Or va Can-zo - na mia, non du-bi-
stia cia-scu-n'at-ten-to: Or va Can-zo - na mia, non du-bi-
Or va Can-zo - na mia, non du-bi-
Or va Can-zo - na mia, non du-bi-
Or va Can - zo-na mia, non du-bi-
Or va Can-zo - na mia, non du-bi-
103
ta - re, non du-bi-ta - re... Per-ché?
ta - re, non du-bi-ta - re...
ta - re, non du-bi-ta - re... Per-ché? quel-la ch'io vo-glio È
ta - re, non du-bi-ta - re...
ta - re, non du-bi-ta - re... Per-ché? quel-la ch'io vo-glio È
ta - re, non du-bi-ta - re... Fer-ma-te-vi! quel-la ch'io vo-glio È
ta - re, non du-bi-ta - re... Per-ché quel-la ch'io vo-glio È

Sì, sì, gliè ver, or di-te_al-le-gra-men-te, al -

Sì, sì, gliè ver, or di-te_al-

u-na Iu-sti-nia-na! Sì, sì, gliè ver, or di-te_al-le-gra-men-te, al -

Sì, sì, gliè ver, or di-te_al-le-gra-men-te:

u-na Iu-sti-nia-na!

u-na Iu-sti-nia-na! or di-te_al-

u-na Iu-sti-nia-na! or di-te_al-le-gra-men-te:

le-gra-men-te: Tut - to_il dì ti te

le-gra-men-te: Tut - to_il dì ti te

le-gra-men-te: Tut - to_il dì ti te

Tut - to_il dì ti te

Tut - to_il dì ti te

le-gra-men-te: Tut - to_il dì ti te

Tut - to_il dì ti te

stam - po - li   Che mi son un   pe - ta - go - lo

stam - po - li   Che mi son un   pe - ta - go - lo

stam - po - li   Che mi son un   pe - ta - go - lo

stam - po - li   Che mi son un   pe - ta - go - lo

stam - po - li   Che mi son un   pe - ta - go - lo

stam - po - li   Che mi son un   pe - ta - go - lo

stam - po - li   Che mi son un   pe - ta - go - lo

E che pa - r'un   co - ruo - go - lo

E che pa - r'un   co - ruo - go - lo

E che pa - r'un   co - ruo - go - lo

E che pa - r'un   co - ruo - go - lo

E che pa - r'un   co - ruo - go - lo

E che pa - r'un   co - ruo - go - lo

E che pa - r'un   co - ruo - go - lo

122
Con la coa tut - ta toc - co - li...
Con la coa tut - ta toc - co - li...
Con la coa tut - ta toc - co - li...
Con la coa tut - ta toc - co - li...
Con la coa tut - ta toc - co - li...
Con la coa tut - ta toc - co - li...
Con la coa tut - ta toc - co - li...
126
Or io mi sen - to rad - dol-ci - to‿il co - re,
Or io mi sen - to rad - dol-ci - to‿il co - re,
Or io mi sen - to rad - dol-ci - to‿il co - re,
Or io mi sen - to rad - dol-ci - to‿il co - re,

128
Doh, vi - va l'a - mo - re, doh,
Doh, vi - va l'a - mo - re, doh, vi - va l'a - mo - re, doh,
Doh, vi - va l'a - mo - re, doh,
Doh, vi - va l'a - mo - re, doh,
Doh,
Doh, vi - va l'a - mo - re, doh,
Doh, vi - va l'a - mo - re, doh,
130
vi - va l'a - mo - re, doh, vi - va l'a - mo - re!
vi - va l'a - mo - re, doh, vi - va l'a - mo - re!
vi - va l'a - mo - re, doh, vi - va l'a - mo - re!
vi - va l'a - mo - re, doh, vi - va l'a - mo - re!
vi - va l'a - mo - re, doh, vi - va l'a - mo - re!
vi - va l'a - mo - re, doh, vi - va l'a - mo - re!
vi - va l'a - mo - re, doh, vi - va l'a - mo - re!

133
Terza parte
Or - mai po - nia - mo fi - - - ne‿al no - stro can -
Or - mai po - nia - mo fi - ne‿al no - stro can -
Or - mai po - nia - mo fi - ne‿al no - stro can -
Or - mai po - nia - mo fi - ne‿al no - stro can -
136
to E‿a la pal-la fac-cia - m'u - na par - ti - ta!
Noi gio - ca -
Noi gio - ca -
Noi gio - ca -
to E‿a la pal-la fac-cia-m'u - na par - ti - ta!
to E‿a la pal-la fac-cia-m'u - na par - ti - ta!
to E‿a la pal-la fac-cia-m'u - na par - ti - ta!

138

D'un Giu-lio al gio - co. Fac-

rem ma di - te-ci di quan-to. È trop-po po-co!

rem ma di - te-ci di quan-to. È trop-po po-co!

rem ma di - te-ci di quan-to. È trop-po po-co!

D'un Giu-lio al gio - co. Fac-

D'un Giu-lio al gio - co. Fac-

D'un Giu-lio al gio - co. Fac-

141

ciam d'un quar-to e che non va - di il mar - zo!

Ci con - ten - tia -

Ci con - ten - tia -

Ci con - ten - tia -

ciam d'un quar-to e che non va - di il mar - zo!

ciam d'un quar-to e che non va - di il mar - zo!

ciam d'un quar-to e che non va - di il mar - zo!

144
Or-sù, chi bat-ter vuo-le? A l'a-mo-ra gio-chiam,
mo! A l'a-mo-ra gio-chiam, co-me si suo-
mo! A l'a-mo-ra gio-chiam, co-me si
mo! A l'a-mo-ra gio-chiam, co-me si
Or-sù, chi bat-ter vuo-le? A l'a-mo-ra gio-chiam,
Or-sù, chi bat-ter vuo-le? A l'a-mo-ra gio-chiam,
Or-sù, chi bat-ter vuo-le? A l'a-mo-ra gio-chiam,
147
cin-que, no-ve, tut-ti!
le. ot-to, cin-que, tut-ti! Or toc-ca a vo-
suo-le. cin-que, no-ve, tut-ti! Or toc-ca a vo-
suo-le. ot-to, cin-que, se-i!
set-te, quat-tro, se-i! Or toc-ca a vo-
ot-to, cin-que, se-i!
set-te, quat-tro, tut-ti! Or toc-ca a vo-

150
dia-mo prin-ci-pi'al gio-co! Ec-co-la qua!
i, Chi‿ha la pal-la di vo-i? Ec-co-la
i, Chi‿ha la pal-la di vo-i? Ec-co-la
dia-mo prin-ci-pi'al gio-co! Ec-co-la qua!
i, Ec-co-la qua!
Chi‿ha la pal-la di vo-i? Ec-co-la
i, Chi‿ha la pal-la di vo-i? Ec-co-la
153
Ec-co-la qua!
qua!
qua!
Ec-co-la qua! Fac-cia-m'a duoi a duo-
Ec-co-la qua! Fac-cia-m'a duoi a duo-i, Fac-cia-m'a
qua! Fac-cia-m'a duoi a duo-
qua! Fac-cia-m'a duoi a duo-i, Fac-cia-m'a

155
Bat - te - te! A vo - i!
Bat - te - te! Gliè fal la pri - ma vol -
Bat - te - te! Gliè fal la pri - ma vol -
i, Fac-cia-m'a duoi a duo - i. Bat - te - te! Gliè fal la pri - ma vol -
duoi a duo - i. A vo - i!
i, Fac-cia-m'a duoi a duo - i. A vo - i!
duoi a duo - i. Bat - te - te! Gliè fal la pri - ma vol -
158
Non gia, ch'io non l'ho col - to!
ta! Voi v'in-gan - na - te, che
ta! Non gia, ch'io non l'ho col-to! Voi v'in-gan - na - te, che gliè
ta!
Voi v'in-gan - na - te, che gliè fal - lo
Non gia, ch'io non l'ho col - to!
ta! Voi v'in-gan - na - te, che gliè

Non di-te_il ve - ro!

gliè fal - lo mar - zo! Fuor di qui ci

fal - lo mar - zo! Fuor di qui ci

Non di-te_il ve - ro!

mar - - - zo! Fuor di qui ci

Non di-te_il ve - ro!

fal - lo mar - zo! Fuor di qui ci

Fuordi qui ci par-le-re-mo, fuor di qui ci par-le-re-mo!

par-le-re-mo,fuordi qui ci par-le-re-mo! Si-gno-ri non gri-da-

par-le-re-mo,fuordi qui ci par-le-re-mo! Si-gno-ri non gri-da-

Fuordi qui ci par-le-re-mo, ci par-le-re-mo!

par-le-re-mo,fuordi qui ci par-le-re-mo! Si-gno-ri non gri-da-

Fuordi qui ci par-le-re-mo, fuor di qui ci par-le-re-mo!

par-le-re-mo,fuordi qui ci par-le-re-mo! Si-gno-ri non gri-da-

*1583: minim

166
Ma piut-tos-to‿a can-tar voi ri-tor-na - te A l'om-bra
te, A l'om-bra di quel fag - gio,
te, Ma piut-tos-to‿a can-tar voi ri-tor-na - te A l'om-bra di quel
A l'om-bra di quel fag -
te, A l'om-bra di quel fag -
Ma piut-tos-to‿a can-tar voi ri-tor-na - te
te, A
169
di quel fag - gio, a l'om-bra di quel fag - gio,
a l'om-bra di quel fag - gio, a l'om-bra
fag - gio, a l'om-bra di quel fag - gio, a
gio, a l'om-
gio, a l'om-bra di quel fag - - - gio,
A l'om-bra di quel fag - - - - gio, a l'om-bra
l'om-bra di quel fag - gio, a l'om-bra di quel fag - gio, a

a l'om-bra di quel fag - gio: Ben ven - ga

di quel fag - - - gio: Ben ven - ga Mag - gio,

l'om-bra di quel fag - gio: Ben ven - ga Mag - gio,

bra di quel fag - gio: Ben ven - ga Mag - gio,

a l'om-bra di quel fag - gio: Ben ven - ga

di quel fag - gio: Ben ven - ga Mag - gio,

l'om-bra di quel fag - gio: Ben ven - ga

Mag - gio, ben ven - ga Mag - gio, ben ven - ga

ben ven - ga Mag - gio, ben ven - ga, Mag - gio, ben ven - ga

ben ven - ga Mag - gio, ben ven - ga Mag - gio, ben ven - ga

ben ven - ga Mag - gio, ben ven - ga Mag - gio, ben ven - ga

Mag - gio, ben ven - ga Mag - gio, ben ven - ga

ben ven - ga Mag - gio, ben ven - ga Mag - gio, ben ven - ga

Mag - gio, ben ven - ga Mag - gio, ben ven - ga

Mag - gio, ben ven - ga Mag-gio! Ma piut-tos-to a can-tar voi

Mag - gio, ben ven - ga Mag-gio!

Mag - gio, ben ven - ga Mag-gio! Ma piut-tos-to a can-tar voi

Mag - gio, ben ven - ga Mag-gio!

Mag - gio, ben ven - ga Mag-gio!

Mag - gio, ben ven - ga Mag-gio! Ma piut-tos-to a can-tar voi

Mag - gio, ben ven - ga Mag-gio!

ri - tor - na - te A l'om-bra di quel fag -

A l'om-bra di quel fag - gio, a

ri - tor - na - te A l'om-bra di quel fag - gio,

A l'om-bra di quel fag - - - gio,

A l'om-bra di quel fag - gio, a

ri - tor - na - te A l'om-bra

A l'om-bra di quel

186
gio, a l'om-bra di quel fag - gio, a l'om-bra
l'om-bra di quel fag - gio, a l'om-bra di quel fag -
a l'om-bra di quel fag - gio, a l'om-bra di
a l'om-bra di quel
l'om-bra di quel fag - - gio, a l'om-bra
di quel fag - - - - gio, a l'om-bra di quel fag -
fag - gio, a l'om-bra di quel fag - gio, a l'om-bra di
188
3
di quel fag-gio: Ben ven - ga Mag - gio,
gio: Ben ven - ga Mag - gio, ben ven - ga
quel fag-gio: Ben ven - ga Mag - gio, ben ven - ga
fag - gio: Ben ven - ga Mag - gio, ben ven - ga
di quel fag-gio: Ben ven - ga Mag - gio,
gio: Ben ven - ga Mag - gio, ben ven - ga
quel fag-gio: Ben ven - ga Mag - gio,

192

ben ven - ga Mag - gio, ben ven - ga

Mag - gio, ben ven - ga Mag - gio, ben ven - ga

*

Mag - gio, ben ven - ga Mag - gio, ben ven - ga

Mag - gio, ben ven - ga Mag - gio, ben ven - ga

ben ven - ga Mag - gio, ben ven - ga

Mag - gio, ben ven - ga Mag - gio, ben ven - ga

ben ven - ga Mag - gio, ben ven - ga

196

Mag - gio, ben ven - ga Mag - gio!

Mag - gio, ben ven - ga Mag - gio!

Mag - gio, ben ven - ga Mag - gio!

Mag - gio, ben ven - ga Mag - gio!

Mag - gio, ben ven - ga Mag - gio!

Mag - gio, ben ven - ga Mag - gio!

Mag - gio, ben ven - ga Mag - gio!

*1583: f'

Notes

Introduction

The sources of the chapter epigraphs are Johan Huizinga, *Homo Ludens: A Study of the Play-Element in Culture* (Boston: Roy, 1950), 13–14; and Umberto Eco, *The Open Work*, translated by Anna Cancogni (Cambridge, Mass.: Harvard University Press, 1989), 9.

1. The sacred works are cataloged in *Einzeldrucke vor 1800*, Répertoire international des sources musicales (RISM), Series A/1, V 1004–1007. The *Motetti a otto voci* (1579) listed as V1003 appears to be a ghost. A documentary account of Vecchi's life is given in Evaristo Pancaldi and Gino Roncaglia, "Orazio Vecchi: La vita e le opere," in *Orazio Vecchi: Precursore del melodramma (1550–1605)* (Modena: Accademia di scienze lettere e arti di Modena, 1950), 9–56. Additions to his biography are included in Massimo Privitera, ed., *Theatro dell'udito, theatro del mondo: Atti del convegno internazionale nel IV centenario della morte di Orazio Vecchi, Modena-Vignola, 29 settembre–1 ottobre 2005* (Modena: Mucchi, 2010); see especially the contributions by Luca Colombini and Sauro Rodolfi.

2. The *Libro quinto delle Muse* included music by several composers associated with Siena: Andrea Feliciani, Ascanio Marri, and Essegna. Vecchi's two contributions to the book are "Amor m'ha posto come scoglio a'londa," a sonnet by the Perugian poet Francesco Beccuti (known as "Il coppetta") printed in 1580 that was itself modeled on Petrarch's "Amor m'à posto come segno al strale," and "Mentr'ebbi al bel camin l'aer sereno," which sets an excerpt (lines 80–90) of a *canzone* by Luigi Tansillo, "Amor se vòi ch'io torni al giogo antico." See Frank D'Accone, *The Civic Muse: Music and Musicians in Siena during the Middle Ages and the Renaissance* (Chicago: University of Chicago Press, 1997), 356–361.

3. Girolamo Tiraboschi, *Biblioteca modenese*, bk. 6, pt. 1 (Modena: Società tipografica, 1786), 205. Unless credited otherwise, all translations are my own.

4. These incidents are reported in Giovan Battista Spaccini, *Cronaca di Modena*, vol. 1 (1588–1602), ed. Albano Biondi, Rolando Bussi, and Carlo Giovannini (Modena: Franco Cosimo Panini, 1993).

5. Paul Schleuse, "'A Tale Completed in the Mind': Genre and Imitation in *L'Amfiparnaso* (1597)," *Journal of Musicology* 29 (2012): 101–153.

1. The Four-Voice Canzonetta as (and in) Recreational Polyphony

The source of the chapter epigraph is Vincenzo Giustiniani, *Discorso sopra la musica*, in *Discorsi sulle arti e sui mestieri*, edited by Anna Banti (Florence: Sansoni, 1981), 18, translated in Carol MacClintock, *Hercole Bottrigari: "Il Desiderio" & Vincenzo Giustiniani: "Discorso sopra la musica,"* Musicological Studies and Documents 9 ([Rome]: American Institute of Musicology, 1962), 67. For *esercizio del gioco*, MacClintock gives "gambling."

1. Anthony Newcomb, *The Madrigal at Ferrara, 1579–1597* (Princeton, NJ: Princeton University Press, 1980), 46–52.

2. Giustiniani, *Discorsi*, ed. Banti, 20–21, and MacClintock, *Il Desiderio*, 68, emphasis added; for *il gusto della musica*, MacClintock gives "the style of music."

3. The former in Newcomb, *Madrigal*, 48, and the latter in Ruth I. DeFord, "Marenzio and the *villanella alla romana*," *Early Music* 27 (1999): 535–552.

4. Giustiniani, *Discorsi,* ed. Banti, 21–22, and MacClintock, *Il Desiderio,* 69.

5. Newcomb, *Madrigal,* 48–49. Brancaccio, it should be noted, sang at the Ferrarese court until 1583, though never unambiguously in consort with the women of the *concerto.* See Richard Wistreich, *Warrior, Courtier, Singer: Giulio Cesare Brancaccio and the Performance of Identity in the Late Renaissance* (Aldershot, UK: Ashgate, 2007), 206.

6. Orazio Vecchi, *The Four-Voice Canzonettas,* ed. Ruth I. DeFord, Recent Researches in Music of the Renaissance 92–93 (Madison, WI: A-R Editions, 1993), 1:13. It is curious, perhaps, that Giustiniani never uses the term *canzonetta* in this description, but by 1628, when he wrote the *Discorso,* that term had come to denote a specifically soloistic genre.

7. For further evidence for the continuing popularity of polyphonic performance without continuo accompaniment during the period of which Giustiniani writes, see Tim Carter, "Music Publishing in Italy, c. 1580–c. 1625: Some Preliminary Observations," *Royal Musical Association Research Chronicle* 20 (1986–87): 19–37.

8. Vecchi is named as having suggested Forno to the printer Giacomo Vincenti as a suitable dedicatee for the latter's *De floridi virtuosi d'Italia il secondo libro de madrigali a cinque voci* (Venice: Vincenti & Amadino, 1585). See Emma Hilary Wakelin, "*De floridi virtuosi d'Italia:* A Study of Three Italian Madrigal Anthologies of the 1580s" (PhD diss., Royal Holloway, University of London, 1997), 57–58.

9. Donna G. Cardamone, *The Canzone villanesca alla napolitana and Related Forms, 1537–1570,* 2 vols. (Ann Arbor, Mich.: UMI Research Press, 1981), 67–92.

10. No. 19, "Quando mirai s'a bella faccia d'oro," which had been set by Marc'Antonio Mazzone in *Corona delle napolitane a tre & a quattro voci* (Venice: Scotto, 1578). Although both settings use binary form, they distribute the stanzas differently over the structural midpoint and are musically unrelated.

11. Cardamone, *Canzone villanesca,* 1:129.

12. Cardamone, *Canzone villanesca,* chap. 7, passim.

13. As Ruth DeFord points out, this makes modal assignment of the canzonettas problematic, even by the standards of Vecchi's own treatise on mode. See DeFord, "Orazio Vecchi's Treatise on the Modes and Its Application to His Four-Voice 'Canzonette,'" in *Theatro dell'udito, Theatro del mondo: Atti del convegno internazionale, nel IV centenario della morte di Orazio Vecchi, Modena-Vignola, 29 settember–1 ottobre 2005,* ed. Massimo Privitera (Modena: Mucchi, 2010), 335–356. The treatise is edited in Orazio Vecchi, *Mostra delli Tuoni della Musica,* ed. Mariarosa Pollastri (Modena: Aedes Muratoriana, 1987).

14. My numbering of the canzonettas (which is continuous through all four books) is taken from DeFord's edition.

15. For complete lists of Vecchi's canzonetta prints, see DeFord's edition, pp. 13–15.

16. "Essendo sparso per molti luochi [*sic*] d'Italia, la maggior parte delle presenti mie Canzonette, sotto nome di diversi autori; mi è paruto à proposito, di far sapere al mondo, co'l mezo della stampa, ch'elle sono le mie, come in effetto sono. Onde le hò richiamate alli loro primi Originali, rassettate, et riposte nell'esser di prima" (reprinted in Pancaldi and Roncaglia, *Orazio Vecchi,* 61).

17. "Hora mò per farle comparire piu contente, et liete in ogni luoco, tutti insieme: non lacerate et guaste, come fin a questo di sono andate à torno, ma ridotte nella loro natia sembianza, et adorni di bellissimi ornamenti di stampe" (Pancaldi and Roncaglia, *Orazio Vecchi,* 61).

18. All poems are as edited in Vecchi, *The Four Voice Canzonettas,* ed. DeFord. I have adapted DeFord's prose translations to reflect more literally the lineation of the poems.

19. Vecchi, *The Four-Voice Canzonettas*, ed. DeFord, 12.

20. Giovanni Domenico da Nola, *Corona delle napolitane a tre voci a tre et a quattro voci, di diversi eccellentissimi musici* (Venice: Scotto, 1570).

21. Gasparo Fiorino, *Libro Secondo Canzonelle a tre e a quattro voci* (Venice: Gardano, 1574), 165. DeFord erroneously cites the previous source as Fiorino's *Nobilità di Roma* of the same year in *The Four-Voice Canzonettas*, 25n14.

22. Cesare Tudino, *Canzon napolitane a tre voci, di L'Arpa, Cesare Todino, Joan Domenico de Nola, Et di altri musici...* (Venice: Scotto, 1566). Rosanna Dalmonte and Massimo Privitera identify Angelo Grillo, alias Livio Celiano (1557–1629), as the author of this poem, but the early date of Tudino's setting argues against this. Grillo's version of the poem, first published in 1587, is substantially different from the Tudino and Vecchi texts. See Dalmonte and Privitera, *Gitene, canzonette: Studio e trascrizione delle* Canzonette a sei voci d'Horatio Vecchi *(1587)* (Florence: Olschki, 1996), 16n7. Grillo's version is edited in Elio Durante and Anna Martellotti, *Don Angelo Grillo O.S.B. alias Livio Celiano: Poeta per musica del secolo decimosesto* (Florence: Studio per Edizioni Scelti, 1989), 319.

23. Warren Kirkendale, "Franceschina, Girometta, and Their Companions in a Madrigal 'a diversi linguaggi' by Luca Marenzio and Orazio Vecchi," *Acta Musicologica* 44 (1972): 181–235, reprint, Kirkendale and Kirkendale, *Music and Meaning*, 125–204. The text quoted is from *Cose notabili occorse in Roma dall'anno MDLXXVI fin' all' anno MDCXLVIIII di M. Antonio Valena*, Rome, Archivo Storico Capitolino, cred. XIV, t. 9, fols. 2v–3r, quoted and translated in Kirkendale, "Franceschina," 224 (in the reprint, 190).

24. Vecchi, *The Four-Voice Canzonettas*, ed. DeFord, 2:10–12.

25. On the likelihood that this work was in fact composed by Vecchi himself, see Paul Schleuse, "On the Origin of the Work 'A diversi linguaggi' Attributed to Luca Marenzio and Orazio Vecchi," in Privitera, *Theatro dell'udito*, 121–153.

26. Vecchi, *The Four-Voice Canzonettas*, ed. DeFord, 2:22–23.

27. This couplet quotes Lodovico Ariosto, *Orlando furioso*, canto 10, st. 4, presumably with satiric intent.

28. Mauro Calcagno identifies a similar relationship between textural variation and poetic subjectivity in madrigals by Arcadelt, Willaert, and Rore in *From Madrigal to Opera: Monteverdi's Staging of the Self* (Berkeley: University of California Press, 2012), chap. 5, "In Search of Voice: Musical Petrarchism in the Sixteenth-Century Madrigal," 109–144.

29. Vecchi, *The Four-Voice Canzonettas*, ed. DeFord, 2:42–45.

30. The introduction of *quinari* in lighter poetry is generally credited to Gabriello Chiabrera beginning in the 1590s, but as Vecchi's canzonettas attest, the five-syllable line was not unknown previously. They appear in seven of Vecchi's canzonettas, almost always in pairs. See Vecchi, *The Four-Voice Canzonettas*, ed. DeFord, 3.

31. Jane A. Bernstein, *Music Printing in Renaissance Venice: The Scotto Press (1539–1572)* (New York: Oxford University Press, 1998), 841.

32. Giuseppe Gerbino, *Music and the Myth of Arcadia in Renaissance Italy* (Cambridge: Cambridge University Press, 2009), 247.

33. "Se bene il dono di queste mie Canzonette non aggiunga ne alla grandezzza dell'animo mio, ne all'altezze dei meriti suoi, sò nondimeno che V. S. s'appagherà del mio buon volere" (reprinted in Pancaldi and Roncaglia, *Orazio Vecchi*, 61–62).

34. I use the convention of indicating *settenari* with lowercase letters and *endecasillabi* with capitals; lines of other lengths are indicated by superscript numbers. Lines are assumed to be *piano* except where indicated by an apostrophe before the letter to indicate *tronco* lines

and after to indicate *sdruccioli*. See Aldo Menichetti, *Metrica Italiana: Fondamenti metrici, prosodia, rima* (Padua: Antenore, 1993), 109.

35. On the musical imitation of high- and low-status social contexts and the cultural critique they imply, see chapter 6.

36. Girolamo Bargagli, *Dialogo de' giuochi che nelle vegghie sanesi si usano di fare* (Siena: Bonetti, 1572), modern edition by Patrizia D'Icalci Ermini (Siena: Accademia Senese degli Intronati, 1982), 72.

37. The music of this piece is missing from Orazio Vecchi, *Madrigali a sei voci,* ed. Mariarosa Pollastri, I Quaderni di *Musicaaa!* 19–20 (Mantua: I Quaderni di *Musicaaa!,* n.d.), available in PDF format by request from http://maren.interfree.it.

38. The voicing of each line is indicated in descending order of ranges, using C = Canto, 5 = Quinto, A = Alto, T = Tenore, 6 = Sesto, B² = Basso secondo, B¹ = Basso. Vecchi's cleffing for these parts is c1/c1/c2/c4/c4/f3/f4.

39. In *Il secondo libro de' Madrigali a quattro voci* (Venice: Gardano, 1557), in Cipriano de Rore, *Opera Omnia,* ed. Bernhard Meier, Corpus mensurabilis musicae 14 ([Rome:] American Institute of Musicology, 1969), 4:54–57.

40. "Ballarestu fantina," with the second line as "che te fesse ballar?," appears in Negri, *Affetti Amorosi a tre voci* (Venice: Gardano, 1608) and also in Nuvoloni, *Canzonette di Massimiliano Nuvoloni a tre . . . agiontovi alcuni Capricii, & Balletti di Alessandro suo Padre* (Milan: Tini & Lomazzo, 1608).

41. Giovanni Ferretti, *Primo libro delle villotte alla Napolitana a tre voci di diversi* (Venice: Scotto, 1565); and Ferretti, *Canzone alla napolitana a cinque voci* (Venice: Scotto: 1567). Vecchi's seven-voice setting is more closely based on the three-voice *villotta* than on Feretti's arrangement; see Bernstein, *Music Printing,* 704–705.

42. Vincenzo Bellavere, *Il primo libro delle Justiniane di diversi* (Venice: Scotto, 1570). The middle voice does not survive, and the dialect text has thus far eluded translation.

43. The repetition of "perché" distorts the meter of the poem but is essential to Vecchi's sense of question and answer in the setting. I have broken up the line in order to show the shifting vocal combinations to which it is set.

44. Angelo Poliziano, *Stanze, Orfeo, Rime, con il saggio Delle poesie toscane di messer Angelo Poliziano di Giosuè Carducci,* ed. Sergio Marconi (Milan: Feltrinelli, 1981), 160. Vecchi's setting of the opening line is musically unrelated to the popular Florentine *lauda* modeled on Poliziano's poem; see Patrick Macey, ed., *Savonarolan Laude, Motets, and Anthems,* Recent Reserches in Music of the Renaissance 116 (Madison, WI: A-R Editions, 1999), 61–62.

45. On larger-scale polyphonic dialogues, see David Nutter, "The Italian Polyphonic Dialogue of the Sixteenth Century" (Phd diss., University of Nottingham, 1977).

2. Intertextuality in Vecchi's Canzonettas and Madrigals, 1583–1590

1. Vecchi, *The Four-Voice Canzonettas,* ed. DeFord; Rossana Dalmonte and Massimo Privitera, *Gitene, canzonette: Studio e trascrizione delle* Canzonette a sei voci *d'Horatio Vecchi (1587)* (Florence: Olschki, 1996); Orazio Vecchi, *Madrigali a sei voci,* ed. Mariarosa Pollastri, I Quaderni di *Musicaaa!* 19–20 (Mantua: I Quaderni di *Musicaaa!,* n.d.), available in PDF format by request from http://maren.interfree.it; Orazio Vecchi, *Madrigali a cinque voci (Venezia, 1589),* ed. Mariarosa Pollastri (Bologna: Ut Orpheus, 1997).

2. Innocentio Ringhieri, *Cento giuochi liberali* (Bologna: Giaccarelli, 1551); Girolamo Bargagli, *Dialogo de' giuochi che nelle vegghie sanesi si usano di fare* (Siena: Bonetti, 1572), modern edition by Patrizia D'Icalci Ermini (Siena: Accademia Senese degli Intronati, 1982).

3. Baldessare Castiglione, *Il libro del cortegiano*, ed. Bruno Maier (Turin: Union typografico-editrice torinese, 1964); Antonfrancesco Doni, *Dialogo della Musica*, ed. Gian Francesco Malipiero (Vienna: Universal, 1964).

4. Claudio Sartori, "Orazio Vecchi e Tiburzio Massaino a Salò: Nuovi documenti inediti," in *Renaissance-Muzeik 1400–1600: Donum naticalum René Bernard Lenaerts*, ed. Jozef Robijns (Leuven: Kothlieke Universiteit Seminarie voor Muzeikwetenscap, 1969), 234–235.

5. Sartori, "Orazio Vecchi," 236.

6. Archivio Storico Comunale di Modena, *Partiti Comunale*, 1583–1584, no. 23, cited in Evaristo Pancaldi and Gino Roncaglia, eds., *Orazio Vecchi, precursore di melodramma* (Modena: Accademia di Scienze Lettere e Arte, 1950), 13.

7. Archivio Storico Comunale di Modena, *Partiti Comunale*, cited in Pancaldi and Roncaglia, *Orazio Vecchi*, 47.

8. The dedication is reprinted in Pancaldi and Roncaglia, *Orazio Vecchi*, 62–63.

9. Only two poems in the book, no. 46, "Mentre il cuculo," and no. 61, "Mi vorrei trasformare," had appeared previously, both in Giuseppe Caimo's *Secondo libro di canzonette a quattro* (Venice: Amadino & Vincenti, 1584).

10. Documents from the *Atti Capitolari* and the *Partiti Communale* cited in Pancaldi and Roncaglia, *Orazio Vecchi*, 48.

11. Ian Fenlon, *Music and Patronage in Sixteenth-Century Mantua* (Cambridge: Cambridge University Press, 1980), 23–24.

12. "Gravissimo dolore io ricevei, Sereniss[imo] Sig[nor], non essendomi trovato i Correggio quando all'Altezza V[ostra] piacque di honorar questa Città con la sua presenza, perche con quell'occasione, potevo pur una volta effettuare quello che già buon tempo fà, ardentemente hò desiderato, ch'è di scoprirmele per quel devoto Servitore ch'io li sono sempre stato da che hebbi alcuna cognitione della magnaminità dell'animo di lei, et delle Heroiche virtù delle quali ella è così riccamente adornata" (reprinted in Pancaldi and Roncaglia, *Orazio Vecchi*, 65).

13. Alfred Einstein proposes that Vecchi was angling to replace the aging and ailing Lassus at the Bavarian court (*The Italian Madrigal*, translated by Alexander H. Krappe, Roger H. Sessions, and Oliver Strunk [Princeton, NJ: Princeton University Press, 1949], 2:774).

14. See Newcomb, *Madrigal*, 1, 25–26, 26, 55. In some cases but not all, these copies included the music as well as the words.

15. Giovanni Battista Guarini, *Rime* (Venice: Ciotti, 1598), fol. 109v.

16. Giovanni Battista Strozzi, *Madrigali*, ed. Luigi Sorrento (Strasbourg: Heitz, 1909), 112–113.

17. Federico Ghisi, *Feste musicali della Firenze medicea (1480–1589)* (Bologna: Forni, 1939), xxxv–xl.

18. Another madrigal in the 1583 book, "Dolce cantava a l'appair del sole," also attests to Vecchi's Florentine connections, mentioning both the Arno and "Leonora," presumably Leonora de' Medici. Again, we cannot be sure for what occasion (if any) this madrigal was written, but it might have been intended for her wedding to Vincenzo Gonzaga, which had been under discussion since 1582, though it was not finally contracted until early 1584.

19. Jennifer L. King, "The *proposta e risposta* Madrigal, Dialogue, Cultural Discourse, and the Issue of *Imitatio*" (PhD diss., Indiana University, 2007), 19–23.

20. *Sdegnosi ardori* (Munich: Berg, 1585), edited in George Schuetze, ed., *Settings of* Ardo sì *and Related Texts,* Recent Researches in the Music of the Renaissance 78–81 (Madison, WI: A-R Editions, 1981).

21. King, "The *proposta e risposta* Madrigal," 66–71.

22. Ruth I. DeFord, "Musical Relationships between the Italian Madrigal and Light Genres in the Sixteenth Century," *Musica Disciplina* 39 (1985): 107–168.

23. Vecchi, *Gitene, Canzonette,* ed. Dalmonte and Privitera, 17. Dalmonte and Privitera cite these later, longer versions to argue Vecchi's having authored the original poems, discounting the possibility that they were expanded by other authors.

24. Three of the madrigals in the 1589 book had previously appeared in anthologies printed between 1584 and 1586.

25. Francesco Petrarch, *Petrarch's Lyric Poems: The* Rime sparse *and Other Lyrics,* trans. and ed. Robert M. Durling (Cambridge, MA: Harvard University Press, 1976), 531; Giambattista Guarini, *Opere,* ed. Luigi Fassò ([Torino]: UTET, 1950), 453.

26. Marco Giulini, ed., *I lieti amanti: Madrigali di venti musicisti ferraresi e non* (Florence: Olschki, 1990), 25. See also James Chater, "'Such Sweet Sorrow': The *dialogo di partenza* in the Italian Madrigal," *Early Music* 27, no. 4 (November 1999): 576–590.

27. François Lesure and Claudio Sartori, *Il nuovo Vogel: Bibliografia della musica italiana vocale profana pubblicata dal 1500 al 1700* (Pomezia: Staderini, 1977), nos. 98–147.

28. Doni, *Dialogo della Musica,* ed. Malipiero, 36.

29. James Haar, "Popularity in the Sixteenth-Century Madrigal: A Study of Two Instances," in *Studies in Musical Sources and Style: Essays in Honor of Jan LaRue,* ed. Eugene K. Wolf and Edward H. Roesner (Madison, WI: A-R Editions, 1990), 191–212, at 202.

30. Translation from Jacopo Sannazaro, *Arcadia & Picatorial Eclogues,* trans. Ralph Nash (Detroit, MI: Wayne State University Press, 1966), 99.

31. (Venice: Gardano, 1585), modern edition in Marenzio, *The Complete Four-Voice Madrigals,* ed. John Steele (New York: Gaudia, 1995), 118–142.

32. Laura Macy, "Speaking of Sex: Metaphor and Performance in the Italian Madrigal," *Journal of Musicology* 14 (1996): 1–34, 16.

33. Macy, "Speaking of Sex," 19–21. Macy's table 1 mistakenly lists Wert's setting as having been published in 1588 rather than 1581.

34. Vecchi, *Madrigali a cinque voci,* ed. Pollastri, vi.

35. Vecchi, *The Four-Voice* Canzonettas, ed. DeFord, 1:51, 2:104–106.

36. Vecchi, *The Four-Voice* Canzonettas, ed. DeFord, 1:53–54, 2:120–123.

37. Innocenzo Ringhieri, *Cento giuochi liberali et d'ingegno* (Bologna: Giaccarelli, 1551), fols. 4–5v.

38. In Ariosto, *Orlando furioso,* 10.1–34, Bireno, duke of Zeeland, proves himself false by abandoning his lover, Olimpia.

39. Giuseppe Caimo, *Il libro primo de madrigali* (Milan: Moscheni, 1564); see King, "The *proposta e risposta* Madrigal," 24–27.

40. Pancaldi and Roncaglia, *Orazio Vecchi,* 68.

41. Vecchi, *The Four-Voice* Canzonettas, ed. DeFord, 1:60, 2:152–154.

42. King, "The *proposta e risposta* Madrigal," 227. King discusses these seven canzonetta pairs in detail (226–257).

43. Geoffrey Chew, "A Model Musical Education: Monteverdi's Early Works," in *The Cambridge Companion to Monteverdi,* ed. John Whenham and Richard Wistreich (Cambridge: Cambridge University Press, 2007), 38–39. Chew's argument that Monteverdi's setting of "Raggi, dov'è il mio bene" draws on Vecchi's earlier setting is less convincing.

44. As Giussepe Gerbino points out, sorceresses are sometimes found in pastoral litera-ture, but in the examples he cites, such as Ercole Pasquini's *I fidi amanti* (1593), they function as adjuncts to the main characters only, providing potions or casting spells in the manner of a *dea ex machina,* not falling in love themselves (*Music and the Myth of Arcadia in Renaissance Italy* [Cambridge: Cambridge University Press, 2009], 248–249).

45. Ariosto, *Orlando furioso,* 7.11–13.

46. Guarini, *Opere,* ed. Fassò, 457–458. Vecchi's canzonetta may, of course, have been writ-ten for or in honor of a Barbara, though there is no evidence for any specific identification. One of the best-known candidates is Barbara Sanseverina, who was famous for her beauty and is believed to have been the lover of multiple Italian aristocrats, most notably Vincenzo Gonzaga. Despite the similarity of her reputation and the reading I am proposing here, it seems unlikely that Vecchi would have propagated such disrepute in a printed book. Giacomo Mori's *Gli encomii musicali* (Vencie: Vincenzi & Amadino, 1585), for example, includes pieces dedicated both to Barbara Sanserverina and to Barbara d'Este; both poems include the dedi-catee's name, but neither plays on its irony.

47. The other is no. 29, "Non ti fuggir da me," in Book II. On the use of *rime tronche,* see Menichetti, *Metrica italiana,* 102.

48. Ariosto does not give Alcina a speech to this effect, possibly because the relevant episode (in canto 10) begins with the extended scene of Olympia's lament, and a second set piece of this kind in the same canto would have been repetitive. Tasso's Armida has an ex-tended lament in canto 16 of *Gerusalemme liberata,* partly in dialogue with Rinaldo, partly in monologue.

49. Ariosto, *Orlando furioso,* 7.72–73, trans. Guido Waldman (Oxford: Oxford University Press, 1973), 68–69.

3. Forest and Feast

1. Pancaldi and Roncaglia, *Orazio Vecchi,* 20.

2. *Gemma musicalis* (Nuremberg: Gerlach, 1588) includes six of Vecchi's canzonettas, more than by any other composer. The second book of this series (1589) includes another four-voice canzonetta and a seven-voice dialogue.

3. Reprinted in Pancaldi and Roncaglia, *Orazio Vecchi,* 66.

4. Vecchi, *Selva di varia ricreatione* (Venice: Gardano, 1590), edited by Paul Schleuse, Recent Researches in Music of the Renaissance 157 (Middleton, WI: A-R Editions, 2012), xvii–xviii.

5. Robert Eitner, *Biographisch-bibliographisches Quellen-Lexikon der Musiker und Mu-sikgelehrten christlicher Zeitrechnung bis zur Mitte des neunzehnten Jahrhunderts* (Leipzig: Breitkopf & Härtel, 1898–1904; repr., Graz: Akademische Druck- und Verlagsanstalt, 1959), 7:445.

6. Wolfgang Boetticher, *Aus Orlando di Lassos Wirkungkreis* (Kassel: Bärenreiter, 1963), 119.

7. Einstein, *The Italian Madrigal,* 2:774

8. On Lasso's involvement in one *commedia*-style performance at the Munich court in 1566, see Martha Farahat, "Villanescas of the Virtuosi: Lasso and the *Commedia dell'arte,*" *Performance Practice Review* 3, no. 2 (Fall 1990): 121–137.

9. Vecchi, *Dialoghi a sette e otto voci* (Venice: Gardano, 1608).

10. On the evidence for a 1594 edition, see Richard Agee, *The Gardano Music Printing Firms, 1569–1611* (Rochester, NY: University of Rochester Press, 1998), 290.

11. Pancaldi and Roncaglia, *Orazio Vecchi*, 48.

12. Orazio Vecchi and Geminiano Capilupi, *Canzonette a tre voci* (Venice: Gardano, 1597), edited by Andrea Bornstein (Bologna: Ut Orpheus, 1997), iv. See also Marco Mangani, "Un'*alta impresa* di Vecchi e Capilupi: Le canzonette a tre voci del 1597," in Privitera, *Teatro dell'udito,* 315.

13. *Canzonette a tre,* ed. Bornstein, vi.

14. The dedication is reprinted in Pancaldi and Roncaglia, *Orazio Vecchi,* 69–70.

15. The date of 1594 for a premiere, first named by Fetis in 1844, is unsupported. See Schleuse, "'A Tale Completed in the Mind,'" 108–115.

16. Hellmut Federhofer, *Musikpflege und Musiker em Grazer Habsburgerhof der Erzherzöge Karl und Ferdinand von Innerösterreich (1564–1619)* (Mainz: B. Schott's Söhne, 1967), 57–60.

17. Paul Schleuse, "Genre and Meaning in Orazio Vecchi's *Selva di varia ricreatione* (1590)" (Ph.D. diss., City University of New York, 2005), 24–31.

18. Vecchi, *Selva,* ed. Schleuse, 3.

19. Papinius Statius, *Statius* vol. 1, trans. and ed. J. H. Mozley (Cambridge, MA: Harvard University Press, 1928).

20. Quintilian, *Institutioni oratoria,* trans. and ed. H. E. Butler (Cambridge, MA: Harvard University Press, 1922), 10.3.17.

21. Aulus Gellius, *The Attic Nights, Books I–IV,* trans. John C. Rolfe (Cambridge, MA: Harvard University Press, 1927), pref. 2–6.

22. Antonio Palau y Dulcet, *Manual de Librero Hispanoamericano,* 2nd ed. (Barcelona: Libreria Palau, 1956), 9:170.

23. "[S]elva (silva) que sin orden, como, según dice el autor, los árboles y las hojas en la selva, se agrupa todo el saber acumulado en sus lecturas, y que era el de su tiempo" (Palau y Dulcet, *Manual,* 9:170).

24. (Granada: Hugo de Mena, 1588). This may be a later edition of a *Selva de varios romances* printed in Barcelona in 1561.

25. Carlo Passi, *La selva di varia istoria di Carlo Passi, la quale avanti attorno stampata sotto nome finto di annotazioni dell'Infortunio, nella prima e secondo parte delle istorie di Mons. Paolo Giovio* (Venice: Altobelli Salicato, 1572).

26. (Valladolid: Fernandez de Cordova, 1547). See also John Griffiths, "Valderrábano, Enriquez de," *The New Grove Dictionary of Music and Musicians,* 2nd ed., ed. Stanley Sadie and John Tyrrell (New York: Grove's Dictionaries; London: Macmillan, 2001), 26:202–203.

27. (Rome: G. B. Robletti, 1617).

28. (Milan: Lomazzo, 1620), modern edition in Francesco Rongoni, *Selva de varii passaggi: 1620,* ed. Richard Erig (Zurich: Musik Hug, 1987).

29. See also Paolo Fabbri, *Monteverdi,* trans. Tim Carter (Cambridge: Cambridge University Press, 1994), 247–249.

30. Barton Hudson, "Storace, Bernardo," in Sadie and Tyrrell, *The New Grove Dictionary,* 24:441.

31. Gioseffo Zarlino, *Institutioni harmoniche* (Venice, 1558), bk. 4, pt. 32, trans. Oliver Strunk in *Source Readings in Music History,* rev. ed., ed. Leo Treitler (New York: W. W. Norton, 1998), 458.

32. Horace, *The Art of Poetry,* trans. Burton Raffel and James Hynd (Albany: State University of New York Press, 1974), 47, lines 86–98.

33. Guarini, *Il Verrato,* trans. in Bernard Weinberg, *A History of Literary Criticism in the Italian Renaissance* (Chicago: University of Chicago Press, 1961), 2:1081.

34. Jonathan Morgan, review of *"Gitene, canzonette": Studio e trascrizione delle "Canzonette a sei voci" d'Horatio Vecchi*, by Rossana Dalmonte and Massimo Privitera, *Music & Letters* 79 (1998): 103.

35. Vecchi, *Selva*, ed. Schleuse, 3.

36. See Dean T. Mace, "Pietro Bembo and the Literary Origins of the Italian Madrigal," *Musical Quarterly* 55 (1969): 65–86.

37. Martha Feldman, *City Culture and the Madrigal at Venice* (Berkeley: University of California Press, 1995), 145–147.

38. (Venice: Gardano, 1542), modern edition in Cipriano Rore, *Opera Omnia* 2, ed. Bernhard Meier (Rome: American Institue of Musicology, 1959). On the modal ordering of the book, see p. iii. On the understandings of mode implied by this and other modally ordered books, see Harold Powers, "Tonal Types and Modal Categories in Renaissance Polyphony," *Journal of the American Musicological Society* 34 (1981): 428–470.

39. Mauro Calcagno, *From Madrigal to Opera: Monteverdi's Staging of the Self* (Berkeley: University of California Press, 2012), 157–188.

40. Luca Marenzio, *The Secular Works* 14, ed. Patricia Myers (New York: Broude Bros., 1980); Claudio Monteverdi, *Opera omnia* 6, ed. Fondazione Claudio Monteverdi (Cremona: Athenaeum Cremonense, 1970). On the narrative organization of these books, see (on Marenzio) Myers's edition and Calcagno, *From Madrigal to Opera*, 161–171, and (on Monteverdi) Massimo Ossi, *Divining the Oracle: Monteverdi's "Seconda prattica"* (Chicago: University of Chicago Press, 2003), chap. 2, "Toward a New Conception of the Madrigal Book: Aspects of Large-Scale Organization in the Fourth and Fifth Books."

41. Ruth I. DeFord, "The Evolution of Rhythmic Style in Italian Secular Music of the Late Sixteenth Century," *Studi musicali* 10 (1981): 43–74.

42. (Venice: Vincenzi, 1588), modern edition in Luca Marenzio, *The Secular Works* 7, ed. Stephen Ledbetter and Patricia Myers (New York: Broude Brothers, 1977).

43. In *Madrigali libro primo a cinque voci* (Venice: Gardano, 1580), modern edition in Luca Marenzio, *The Complete Five Voice Madrigals* 1, ed. John Steele (New York: Gaudia, 1996), 42–47.

44. On the stylistic markers of various light genres of the sixteenth century, see Ruth I. DeFord, "Musical Relationships between the Italian Madrigal and Light Genres in the Sixteenth Century," *Musica Disciplina* 39 (1985): 107–168.

45. Giuseppe Giamberti, *Duo tessuti con diversi solfeggiamenti, scherzi, perfidie, et oblighi* (Rome: Balmonti, 1652), 8–9, modern edition in Duo 39, ed. Andrea Bornstein (Bologna: Ut Orpheus, 2001), 6; Marcello Conati, "Theatro dell'udito: Appunti su Orazio Vecchi e il suo tempo," *Ricerche musicali* 2, no. 2 (November 1978): 61.

46. F. J. E. Raby, ed., *Oxford Book of Medieval Latin Verse* (Oxford: Oxford University Press, 1959), 264, lines 29–36. In the previous century Landulf of Milan expressed a similar sentiment in his *Historiae Mediolanensis* (III.i): "Mediolanum in clericis, Papia in deliciis, Roma in aedificiis, Ravenna in ecclesiis" (Milan for clerics, Pavia for pleasures, Rome for buildings, Ravenna for churches). Landulphi Senioris, *Mediolanensis historiae*, ed. Alessandro Cutulo, Rerum Italicarum Scriptores, t. 4, pt. 2 (Bologna: Zanichelli, 1942), 82.

47. Trans. in Bette Talvacchi, *Taking Positions: On the Erotic in Renaissance Culture* (Princeton, NJ: Princeton University Press, 1999), 209.

48. See Jean Toscan, *Le carnaval de langage: Le lexique érotique des poètes de l'équivoque de Burchiello à Marino (XVe–XVIIe siècles)*, 4 vols. (Lille: Atelier Reproduction des Thèses, 1981), 1:455.

49. On equivocal readings of cooking, see Valter Boggione and Giovanni Casalegno, *Dizionario storico del lessico erotico italiano* (Milan: TEA, 1996), 11–15. On poverty, see Toscan, *Le carnaval de langage,* 3:993, 1025.

50. Concetta Assenza, *Giovan Ferretti tra* canzonetta *e madrigale, con l'edizione critica del Quinto libro di canzoni alla napolitana a cinque voci (1585)* (Florence: Olschki, 1989).

51. Paul Schleuse, *"Balla la mona e salta il babuino:* Performing Obscenity in a Musical Dialogue," in *Sexualities, Textualities, Art and Music in Early Modern Italy: Playing with Boundaries,* ed. Melanie L. Marshall, Katherine McIver, and Linda Carroll (Farnham, UK: Ashgate, 2014), 41–73.

52. Schleuse, "Performing Obscenity."

53. Thomas Morley, *A Plaine and Easie Introduction to Practicall Musicke* (London: Short, 1597), 180, modern edition ed. Alex Harman (New York: Norton, 1952), 295.

54. See Schleuse, "Italian Genres in Morley's *Introduction,"* in a volume of essays to accompany Thomas Morley, *A Plaine and Easie Introduction to Practicall Musicke,* ed. Jessie Ann Owens and John Milsom (Farnham, UK: Ashgate, forthcoming).

55. Michael Praetorius, *Syntagma Musicum III,* trans. and ed. Jeffery T. Kite-Powell (New York: Oxford University Press, 2004), 37.

56. Kevin Mason, "Accompanying Italian Lute Song," in *Performance on Lute, Guitar, and Vihuela,* ed. Victor Anand Coelho (Cambridge: Cambridge University Press, 1997), 81–84.

57. On the conventional features of the genre, see Giuseppe Gerbino and Alexander Silbiger, "Passamezzo," in Sadie and Tyrrell, *The New Grove Dictionary,* 19:194–196.

58. See Ruth I. DeFord, "Marenzio and the *villanella alla romana," Early Music* 27, no. 4 (November 1999): 535–552. DeFord proposes that Vecchi's own four-voice canzonettas, which increasingly isolate the upper voices from the bass in terms of range, may have influenced Marenzio's development of the texture (543).

59. Giovanni Giacomo Gastoldi, *Balletti a cinque voci* (1591), ed. Michel Sanvoisin (Paris: Heugel, 1968).

60. Morley, *A Plaine and Easie Introduction,* 162; in the edition by Harman, 271. See also Schleuse, "Italian Genres."

61. Einstein, *The Italian Madrigal,* 2:782.

62. Pancaldi and Roncaglia, *Orazio Vecchi,* 73.

63. Pancaldi and Roncaglia, *Orazio Vecchi,* 73–74, trans. in Einstein, *The Italian Madrigal,* 2:782–783.

64. Cicero, *De finibus bonorum et malorum,* bk. 2, chap. 28, ed. M. A. Rackham, Loeb Classical Library (London: Heineman; New York: Macmillan, 1914), 182; translation from Cicero, *On Moral Ends,* ed. Julia Annas, Cambridge Texts in the History of Philosophy (Cambridge: Cambridge University Press, 2001), 56.

65. Cicero, *On Moral Ends,* 29.

66. Trans. in Einstein, *The Italian Madrigal,* 783.

67. See Galen, *On the Properties of Foodstuffs (De alimentorum facultatibus),* translation and commentary by Owen Powell (Cambridge: Cambridge University Press, 2003). Galen addresses the problem of lost appetite throughout, and a range of remedies are suggested.

68. Trans. in Einstein, *The Italian Madrigal,* 783.

69. Orazio Vecchi, *Convito musicale* (Venice: Gardano, 1597); edition by William R. Martin (Rome: Edizioni de Santis, 1966), 231.

70. The numbers I assign to pieces differ from those in William Martin's edition because I have not numbered the sections of multipartite works separately.

71. *Il lauro secco* (Ferrara: Baldini, 1582). The poem is a variant version of Tasso's "Fummo un tempo felici."

72. (Venice: Vicenzi, 1588), modern edition in Luca Marenzio, *The Secular Works,* ed. Steven Ledbetter and Patricia Myers, vol. 7 (New York: Broude Brothers, 1977).

73. (Venice: Vincenti, 1595; repr., 1596), modern edition (based on the 1596 ed.) in Giovanni Croce, *Triaca musicale,* ed. Achille Schinelli, Capolavori polifonici del secolo XVI, vol. 3 (Rome: De Santis, 1942), 1–8. Croce had previously set a similar comic echo piece in his *Mascarate piacevole et ridicolose per il carnevale* (Venice: Vincenti, 1590), modern edition in Donna Mae Jenon Gustafson, "Giovanni Croce's *Mascarate piacevoli et ridicolose per il carnevale:* A Contextual Study and Critical Edition" (Ph.D. diss., University of Minnesota, 1993), 162–165, 190–215.

74. See Frederick W. Sternfeld, "Repetition and Echo in Poetry and Music," chap. 7 of *The Birth of Opera* (Oxford: Clarendon Press, 1993), 197–226.

75. Lasso also experimented with a comic echo piece in "O la, o che bon ecchо!," in his *Libro di villanelle, moresche, et altri canzone* (Paris, 1581), but the effect is achieved differently: the complete text sung by one four-voice ensemble is echoed at the distance of a semibreve by an equal second ensemble. Orlando di Lasso, *Sämtliche Werke,* ed. F. X. Haberl and A. Sandberger (Leipzig, 1894–1926; repr., New York: Broude, 1974), 10:140.

76. Vecchi, *Convito musicale,* ed. Martin, 248. I have not been able to trace the reference to Zirfea and Nichea.

4. *L'Amfiparnaso*

Some of the material on *L'Amfiparnaso* in this chapter appeared in an earlier form in my article "'A Tale Completed in the Mind': Genre and Imitation in *L'Amfiparnaso* (1597)," *Journal of Musicology* 29 (2012): 101–153.

1. Einstein, *The Italian Madrigal,* 2:794.

2. Filippo Piccinelli, *Ateneo dei letterati milanesi* (Milan: Vigone, 1670), 435–436. Picinelli lists nine prints (first editions and reprints) of Vecchi's canzonettas, a reprint of the *Madrigali a sei,* various editions of *Le veglie di Siena,* and three of Vecchi's sacred works. Picinelli also introduced the biographical error of claiming that Vecchi was Milanese, which reappeared in some later scholarship. Later writers also sometimes confuse Oratio with Orfeo Vecchi (ca. 1551–1603), who spent most of his career in Milan, but Picinelli does not.

3. The images are reproduced without comment in fifteen unnumbered plates between pp. 264 and 265 in Vito Pandolfi, *La commedia dell'arte: Storia e testo* (Florence: Sansoni, 1957), vol. 2. M. A. Katritzky, *The Art of Commedia: A Study of the Commedia dell'arte 1560–1620 with Special Reference to the Visual Records* (Amsterdam: Rodopi, 2006), likewise makes only passing reference to *L'Amfiparnaso.* The most thorough description of the woodcuts, though lacking critical interpretation, is in Bettina Lupo, "Scene e persone musicale dell' *Amfiparnaso,*" *Rassegna musicale* 11 (1938): 445–459.

4. "*L'Amfiparnaso* non è ancora teatro; è *madrigale drammatico:* ancora più prossimo al teatro di quello che non fossero le opere dello Striggio e del Croce, ma non concepito per una rappresentazione scenica. E ciò, malgrado le vignette che adornano il libretto del secolo XVI, e che indubbiamente ci fanno sentire nel suo autore una tendenza scenica e ci fanno istintivamente pensare al teatro" (Gino Roncaglia, "Orazio Vecchi e il 'madrigale drammatico,'" in Pancaldi and Roncaglia, *Orazio Vecchi,* 149).

5. Indeed, we can assume that since commissioning the woodcuts added considerable expense to the book's production, the project would not have been undertaken lightly. See Jane

Bernstein, *Print Culture and Music in Sixteenth-Century Venice* (Oxford: Oxford University Press, 2001), 47–57.

6. The Parabosco scene is reproduced in T. E. Lawrenson and Helen Purkis, "Les éditions illustrées de Térence dans l'histoire du théatre," in *Le lieu theatral a la renaissance*, ed. Jean Jacquot (Paris: Éditions du centre national de la recherche scientifique, 1964), plate 8, fig. 15; see also p. 16. The Trapolini woodcut is reproduced in Louise George Clubb, "Pastoral Elasticity on the Italian Stage and Page," in *The Pastoral Landscape*, ed. John Dixon Hunt, Studies in the History of Art 36 (Washington, DC: National Gallery of Art, 1992), 119.

7. Sebastiano Serlio, *Il secondo libro di perspettia di Sebastiano Serlio Bolognese* (Paris, 1545), facsimile reprint in *L'Architettura: I libri I–VII e Extraordinario nelle prime edizioni*, ed. Francesco Paolo Fiore (Milan: Polifilo, 2001), 2:64v–73.

8. Lawrenson and Purkis, "Les éditions illustrées," 17.

9. Reproduced in Louise George Clubb, *Italian Drama in Shakespeare's Time* (New Haven, CT: Yale University Press, 1989), 124, 155.

10. Katritzky, *The Art of Commedia.*

11. Edward Dent proposed in 1911 that Giulio Cesare Croce wrote the poems for *L'Amfiparnaso,* or at least advised Vecchi about them, on the basis of isolated resemblances between Croce's voluminous writings and details of Vecchi's text and of evidence that the two were at some point acquainted. While Croce may have influenced some elements in the text, however, close resemblances between poems in *L'Amfiparnaso* and other works more securely attributable to Vecchi (notably no. 2, "O Pierulin"; see below) argue that Vecchi wrote both the words and music. Edward J. Dent, "Notes on the 'Amfiparnaso' of Orazio Vecchi," *Sammelbände der Internationalen Musikgesellschaft* 12, heft 3 (April–June 1911): 330–347.

12. It has often been claimed that the performance Alessandro heard took place in 1594, but there is no evidence for this; the date appears to have been proposed first by Fétis in his *Biographie universelle* of 1844.

13. On the development and distinguishing characteristics of the new genre of pastoral tragicomedy, see Clubb, *Italian Drama,* chaps. 4–6; and Lisa Sampson, *Pastoral Drama in Early Modern Italy: The Making of a New Genre* (London: Legenda, 2006).

14. Battista Guarini, *Il pastor fido e Il compendio della poesia tragicomica,* ed. Gioachino Brognolio (Bari: Laterza, 1914). The *Compendio* was not published until 1601, but preliminary formulations of Guarini's theory, prompted by attacks on *Il pastor fido* by Giasone Denores and others, were printed as *Il verrato* and *Il verrato secondo* in 1588 and 1593; see Bernard Weinberg, *A History of Literary Criticism in the Italian Renaissance* (Chicago: University of Chicago Press, 1961), 2:656–662, and chap. 21.

15. Orazio Vecchi, *L'Amfiparnaso: Il testo letterario e il testo musicale,* ed. Renzo Bez (Bologna: Forni, 2007), x. Subsequent references to *L'Amfiparnaso* refer to this edition.

16. Guarini, *Il Pastor Fido e il compendio della poesia tragicomica,* ed. Gioachino Brognoligo, 234, trans. in Allan H. Gilbert, *Literary Criticism: Plato to Dryden* (Detroit: Wayne State University Press, 1962), 513. The association of comedy with the *uomo privato* is reconfirmed by the first edition of the *Vocabolario degli Accademici della Crusca* (Florence: G. Alberti 1612), 197, http://www.lessicografia.it/pagina.jsp?ediz=1&vol=0&pag=197&tipo=1 (accessed June 15, 2013), which defines *commedia* simply as "a poem representing private persons."

17. *Poetics* chap. 5, 1449ª32 (from the Bekker edition of Aristotle), trans. Ingram Bywater in *The Rhetoric and Poetics of Aristotle* (New York: Random House, 1954), 229.

18. Lodovico Castelvetro, *Poetica d'Aristotele vulgarizzata et sposta* (Basel: Pietro de Sedabonis, 1576), 189, trans. in Gilbert, *Literary Criticism,* 320.

19. Guarini, *Il Pastor fido e il compendio*, 268, trans. in Gilbert, *Literary Criticism*, 530.

20. Quoted and trans. in Weinberg, *A History of Literary Criticism*, 2:680.

21. It has often been assumed that the *argomenti* are meant to be read aloud before each piece, as Banchieri later suggested for his own books, but Vecchi nowhere makes this suggestion.

22. In the musical setting of line 2, "rimirar" is replaced by "contemplar."

23. Flamino Scala, *Il Teatro delle favole rappresentative* (Venice: Pulciani, 1611), modern ed. by Ferrucio Marotti in *Archivio del teatro italiano* 7, 2 vols. (Milan: Polifilo, 1976). See also *Scenarios of the Commedia dell'Arte: Flaminio Scala's "Il Teatro delle favole rappresentative,"* trans. and ed. Henry F. Salerno (New York: New York University Press, 1967; repr., New York: Limelight Editions, 1996).

24. This scene is discussed in Emily Wilbourne, "*Lo Schiavetto* (1612), Travestied Sound, Ethnic Performance, and the Eloquence of the Body," *Journal of the American Musicological Association* 63 (2010): 17–20.

25. Various names were in use for Spanish captains in sixteenth-century theater, usually associated with particular actors. Capitan Cardon was the role played by Valentino Cortesei, who may have been a direct model for Vecchi; see Schleuse, "A Tale Completed in the Mind," 104–108.

26. "Thus, just as a painter who wishes to include in a small picture a great many figures will show the principal or most famous ones in full length, the less important only from the chest, and others only from the top of the head . . . so in my Harmonic Comedy I represent only what is necessary" (*L'Amfiparnaso*, ed. Bez, x).

27. These are no. 8, "La finta pazza"; no. 9, "Il marito"; no. 13, "Il dottor disperato"; no. 20, "Li duo fidi notari"; and no. 25, "La gelosa Isabella." Scala, *Il teatro delle favole rappresentative*, ed. Marotti.

28. Adriano Banchieri, *La pazzia senile* (Venice: Amadino, 1598), facsimile and score ed. Renzo Bez (Bologna: Forni, 2003).

29. David Allen Nutter, "The Italian Polyphonic Dialogue of the Sixteenth Century" (PhD diss., University of Nottingham, 1977).

30. Louise George Clubb, "Pictures for the Reader: Illustrations to Comedy, 1591–1592," *Renaissance Drama* 9 (1966): 265–277. NB: In the 1966 article, the captions listing the pages on which the illustrations originally appeared are incorrect; see the "Corrigenda" in *Renaissance Drama*, n.s., 1 (1968): 340–341.

31. Many plots turn on characters who are mistaken as dead years before the play's action begins; one that includes a mistaken death during the play itself is no. 22, "Il creduto morto," in which Isabella confesses her love for Oratio only after she commands, and receives (false) news of his death. Scala, *Il teatro delle favole rappresentative*, ed. Marotti, 2:223–230.

32. Isabella Andreini published a serious speech for an *innamorato* who speaks of killing himself as "Della disperazione" in her *Lettere* (1607); see Ferruccio Marotti and Giovana Romei, eds., *La professione del teatro*, vol. 2 of *La commedia dell'arte e la società barocca* (Rome: Bulzoni, 1991), 169.

33. Gerbino, *Music and the Myth of Arcadia*, 247. By contrast, in literary urban comedies such as Oddi's *Prigione d'amore*, characters may seek self-sacrifice to save the life of another but not purely out of heartbreak. See Clubb, *Italian Drama*, esp. chap. 2, "Commedia Grave and The Comedy of Errors."

34. *Aminta*, 3.2, lines 134–143; see Torquato Tasso, *Aminta*, ed. and trans. Charles Jernigan and Irene Marchegiani Jones (New York: Italica Press, 2000), 126–127.

35. Tasso, *Aminta, favola boschereccia del Torquato Tasso, novo coretta, & di vaghe figure adornata* (Venice: Aldo [Mannucci], 1589), 72.

36. Gary Tomlinson, *Monteverdi and the End of the Renaissance* (Berkeley: University of California Press, 1987), chap. 3, "Wert, Tasso, and the Heroic Style," 58–72.

37. In the facsimile edition published by Studio per edizioni scelte, based on the copy in the Museo Internazionale e Biblioteca della Musica di Bologna, the Basso part book shows the best detail of Isabella's face, though the rest of the image is somewhat underinked. In the copy of *L'Amfiparnaso* held by the British Library, the Alto and Quinto part books reflect the best impressions of this woodcut.

38. Pancaldi and Roncaglia, *Orazio Vecchi,* 40–41.

39. Lodovico Antonio Muratori, *Della perfetta poesia italiana,* ed. Ada Ruschioni (Milan: Marzorati, 1971), 570–571.

40. Apostolo Zeno to Muratori, August 1701, in *Lettere di Apostolo Zeno cittadino veneziano istorico e poeta cesareo* (Venice: Valvasense, 1752), 55.

41. "Ma nel decimo sesto secolo con ottimo avviso si cantarono molte volte con regolata musica i Cori, recitandosi il rimanente; e finalmente nel 1597 Orazio Vecchi modanese, con nuovo esempio, nel suo Amfiparnaso fece cantare anche gli attori, non eccettuando Pantalone, Zane, dottor Graziano, Capitano Spagnuolo, che tutti in verso ed in musica fanno la parte loro" (Scipione Maffei, *Discorso intorno al teatro italiano* [Verona, 1723], repr. in *Opuscoli Letterarii di Scipione Maffei* [Venice: Alvisopoli, 1829], 73).

42. Johan C. Hol, "Orazio Vecchi scrittore," in Pancaldi and Roncaglia, 137. Hol reports that the only copy of this print is in the Biblioteca Estense in Modena, but it is not now listed in their catalog.

43. "Nell'anno 1597, nel quale la prime Opera, a bello studio per la Musica fatta da Ottavio Rinuccini, fu recitata in Casa di Jacopo Corsi, uscì veramente in Venezia appresso Angelo Gardano un Opera in Versi di Orazio Vecchi de Modena con Note Musicali, e con questo titolo, *L'Amfiparnaso, Commedia Harmonica in 4.* [sic]; nella cui Dedicatoria si vanta l'Autore, esser questa sua nuova invenzione. Ma sì fatta Opera è un lavoro scipito, e da non farne alcun conto. Esse è però corredata di Note Musicali dal medesimo Vecchi, che in questo fare era assai buono" (Francesco Saverio Quadrio, *Della storia, e della ragione d'ogni poesia,* vol. 3, pt. 2 [Milan: Agnelli, 1744], 462–463). Quadrio had also mentioned Vecchi in book 2 of his enormous work in an entry mostly derived from Picinelli (including his incomplete list of Vecchi's works) but that also mentions *Selva di varia ricreatione* and confirms that Vecchi was Modenese, not Milanese.

44. "Fu il primo di mettere in musica le comedie a molte voci, come si puol vedere dalla sua commedia intitolata *Anfiparnaso* a 5, stampata in Venezia l'anno 1597, a dì 20 maggio, posta da esso in musica con grand'arteficio et industria, dove, nella lettera ai lettori racconta esser stato il primo che vestisse di musica la comedia" (Giuseppe Ottavio Pitoni, *Notitia de' contrapuntisti e compositori di musica,* ed. Cesarino Ruini [Florence: Olschki, 1988], 157).

45. Le voci *armonica* del frontespizio del libro, e *harmoniam* del marmo sepocrale, sono state in que'luoghi adoprate in senso technico. I nostri letterati, che sono inteneramente digiuni di tali materie e poco versati nell'erudizion musicale, han creduto che *armonia,* la quale è termine specifico, e *musica,* che è termine generico, significhino la stessa cosa. Ma *armonia* nel suo tecnico senso indica, come dice il P. Martini all pag. 175 del Tomo I. della sua *Storia della Musica,* un *accordo contemporaneo di cantilene diverse,* dovecchè *musica* secondo il Rousseau nel suo Dizionario, significa l'arte in genere *de combiner les sons d'une maniere agréable à l'oreille.* Ecco dunque spiegato l'enimma: 'l'Amfiparnaso' è un pezzo d'armonia, ossia un com-

posto di diverse cantilene simultanee (Giambatista Dall'Olio, "Sull'Amfiparnaso d'Orazio Vecchi modenese [Creduto prima dramma buffo]," repr. in Angelo Catelani, *Della vita e delle opere di Orazio Vecchi* [Milan: Ricordi, 1864], 44).

46. See Gioseffo Zarlino, *Istitutioni armoniche,* book 3, chap. 26, trans. Guy A. Marco and Claude V. Palisca, *The Art of Counterpoint: Part Three of "Le istitutioni harmoniche"* (New Haven, CT: Yale University Press, 1968), 51–52. The definition of harmony as requiring movement is in pt. 2, chap. 12 (1n1).

47. "Nè la musica nè la poesia meriterebbono, che se ne facesse menzione, se la circostanza d'esser la prima ne suo genere non m'obbligasse a darle qualche luogo in questa Storia" (Stefano Arteaga, *Le rivoluzioni del teatro musicale italiano dalla sua origine al presente* [Bologna: Trenti, 1783], 203).

48. "Dicendo, che la musica non si disconviene a cosi fatta poesia, ho renduto la dovuta giustizia all'una, e all'altra" (Arteaga, *Le rivoluzioni,* 206).

49. For a more detailed consideration of the original performance date of *L'Amfiparnaso,* see Schleuse, "'A Tale Completed in the Mind,'" 104–115.

50. "Questa è l'opera, per qui nell'Iscrizion sepolcrale riferita poc'anzi si dà al Vecchi l'onore di avere il primo congiunta la Musica alla Poesia Teatrale. Ma, a dir vero, si può ben concedergli il vanto di essere stato tra' primi; ma ch'ei fosse il primo, non par che possa affermarsi. Jacopo Peri nella lettera premessa all' *Euridice* di Ottavio Rinuccini stampata in Firenze nel 1600 dice: *Benché dal Sig Emilio del Cavaliere prima che da ogni altro, ch'io sappia, con meravigliosa invenzione si fosse fatta udire la nostra Musica sulle Scene, piacque nondimeno a' Signori Jacopo Corsi ed Ottavo Rinuccini fin l'anno 1594, ch'io adoprandola in altra guisa mettessi sotto le note la* Favola di Dafne *dal Sig. Ottavio composta, per fare una semplice pruova di quello che potesse il canto dell' età nostra.* Fu dunque la *Dafne* del Rinuccini composta e messa in Musica fin dal 1594, benchè molti anni più tardi si publicasse; e perciò pare, che ad esso convenga prima che ad ogni altro il titolo di Dramma per Musica" (Girolamo Tiraboschi, *Biblioteca modenese* [Modena: Società Tipografica, 1784], 5:358–359). On Tiraboschi's quotation from Peri, see Jacopo Peri, *Euridice: An Opera in One Act, Five Scenes,* ed. Howard Mayer Brown, Recent Researches in the Music of the Baroque Era 36–37 (Madison, WI: A-R Editions, 1981), xlii.

51. See James Haar, "Music of the Renaissance as Viewed by the Romantics," in *The Science and Art of Renaissance Music,* ed. Paul Corneilson (Princeton, NJ: Princeton University Press, 1998), 366–382; see pp. 373–375. Originally published in *Music and Context: Essays for John M. Ward,* ed. Anne Dhu Shapiro (Cambridge, MA: Harvard University Press, 1985), 108–125.

52. Romain Rolland, *Les origines du théatre lyrique moderne: Histoire de l'opéra en Europe avant Lully et Scarlatti* (Paris: Thorin, 1895), 36–39.

53. François-Joseph Fétis, *Biographie universelle des musiciens* (Paris: Didot, 1844), 8:435.

54. Fétis, *Biographie universelle des musiciens,* 2nd ed. (Paris: Didot, 1867), 8:312.

55. Catelani, *Della vita,* 3–4.

56. August Wilhelm Ambros, *Geschichte der Musik,* vol. 4, ed. Gustav Nottebohm (Leipzig: F. E. C. Leuckart, 1878), 65.

57. Ambros, *Geschichte der Musik,* 3rd ed., ed. Otto Kade (Leipzig: F. E. C. Leuckart, 1893), 3:562.

58. Ambros, *Geschichte der Musik,* rev. ed., ed. Hugo Leichtentritt (Leipzig: F. E. C. Leuckart, 1909; repr., Hildesheim: Georg Olms, 1968), 4:264.

59. Striggio's *Il cicalamento* had been published in *Rivista musicale italiana* 12–13 (1905–1906).

60. Nicola D'Arienzo, "Origini dell'Opera comica," *Rivista musicale italiana* 2 (1895): 609. The performance practice D'Arienzo suggests may be based on Banchieri's instructions for staging *Prudenza giovenile* (1608); see Martha Farahat, "On the Staging of Madrigal Comedies," *Early Music History* 10 (1991): 123–143.

61. C. Hubert H. Parry, *The Music of the Seventeenth Century,* Oxford History of Music 3 (Oxford: Clarendon, 1902), 26.

62. Parry, *Music of the Seventeenth Century,* 30.

63. Edward J. Dent, "The 'Amfiparnaso' of Orazio Vecchi," *Monthly Musical Record,* March 1, 1906, 50–52, and April 1, 1906, 74–75; and "Notes on the 'Amfiparnaso' of Orazio Vecchi," *Sammelbände der Internationalen Musikgesellschaft* 12 (1911): 330–347.

64. Dent, "The 'Amfiparnaso,'" 52.

65. Henry Prunières, *Monteverdi: His Life and Work,* trans. Marie D. Mackie (London: J. M. Dent and Sons, 1926; repr., Westport, CT: Greenwood Press, 1974), 26.

66. Gino Roncaglia, "Orazio Vecchi e il 'madrigale drammatico,'" in Pancaldi and Rongaclia, *Orazio Vecchi,* 145–159; "Orazio Vecchi, precursore drammatico, ed umorista," *Rivista musicale italiana* 51 (1949): 265–273; "Gli elementi precursori del melodramma nell'opera di Orazio Vecchi: Attuazioni e limiti," *Rivista musicale italiana* 55 (1953): 251–256. Although Vito Pandolfi, in his study of the *commedia dell'arte* from 1957, presents *L'Amfiparnaso* in a chapter titled "Verso l'opera buffa," he describes Vecchi as an experimentalist *sui generis* rather than as an influence on later developments. Vito Pandolfi, *La commedia dell arte: Storia e testo,* 6 vols. (Florence: Sansoni, 1957), 2:261–262.

67. Einstein, *The Italian Madrigal,* 2:743.

68. Einstein, *The Italian Madrigal,* 2:636–637. See Luca Marenzio, *Il secondo libro de madrigali a sei voci* (Venice, 1584), in *Opera Omnia,* vol. 4, ed. Bernhard Meier (American Institute of Musicology, 1978), 206–218.

69. Einstein, *The Italian Madrigal,* 2:796.

70. Einstein, *The Italian Madrigal,* 2:779. Einstein must have had in mind Bonaventura Somma's series Capolavori polifonici, which was issued only sporadically and in the end included only *L'Amfiparnaso, Il Convito musicale,* and *Le Veglie di Siena,* as well as works by Banchieri, Croce, Striggio, and Torelli.

71. Einstein, *The Italian Madrigal,* 2:605.

72. Nino Pirrotta and Elena Povoledo, *Music and Theatre from Poliziano to Monteverdi,* trans. Karen Eales (Cambridge: Cambridge University Press, 1975), 113–119.

73. Alessandro Striggio, *Il cicalamento delle donne al bucato, et la caccia di Alessandro Striggio, con un Lamento di Didone Ad Enea, per la sua partenza* (Venice: Scotto, 1567).

74. DonnaMae Gustafson, "Giovanni Croce's *Mascarate piacevoli et ridicolose per il carnevale:* A Contextual Study and Critical Edition" (PhD diss., University of Minnesota, 1992); Giovanni Croce, *Triaca musicale,* ed. Achille Schianelli (Rome: De Santis, 1942).

75. Gustafson, "Giovanni Croce's *Mascarate,*" chap. 1, and 157–158; the translation is adapted slightly from Gustafson.

76. Modern eds. in Simone Balsamino, *Le Novelette a sei voci di Simone Balsamino: Prime musiche su Aminta di Torquato Tasso (1594),* ed. Andrea Chegai (Florence: Olschki, 1993); Gasparo Torelli, *I fidi amanti,* ed. Bonaventura Somma and Lino Bianchi (Rome: De Santis, 1967).

5. Competition and Conversation

1. Antonfrancesco Doni, *Dialogo della musica,* ed. G. Francesco Malipiero (Venice: Fondazione Giorgio Cini; Vienna: Universal Edition, 1965). See also James Haar, "Notes on

the *Dialogo della Musica* of Antonfrancesco Doni," *Music and Letters* 47 (1966): 198–224, reprinted in Haar, *The Science and Art of Renaissance Music,* ed. Paul Corneilson (Princeton, NJ: Princeton University Press, 1998), 271–299.

2. *Sdegnosi ardori* (Munich: Berg, 1585), ed. in *Settings of "Ardo sì" and Related Texts,* ed. George Schuetze, Recent Researches in the Music of the Renaissance 78–81 (Madison, WI: A-R Editions, 1981); *I lieti amanti: Primo libro de madregali a cinque voci di diversi eccellentissimi musici* (Venice: Vincenzi and Amadino, 1586), ed. in *I lieti amanti: Madrigali di venti musicisti ferraresi e non,* ed. Marco Giuliani (Florence: Olschki, 1990); *L'Amorosa Ero* (Brescia: Sabbio, 1588), ed. in *The Madrigal Collection "L'Amorosa Ero,"* ed. Harry B. Lincoln (Albany: State University of New York Press, 1968).

3. Girolamo Bargagli, *Dialogo de' giuochi che nelle vegghie sanesi si usano di fare* (Siena: Bonetti, 1572), modern ed. by Patrizia D'Icalci Ermini (Siena: Accademia Senese degli Intronati, 1982); Orazio Vecchi, *Le veglie di Siena* (Venice: Gardano, 1604), modern ed. by Donald Beecher (Ottowa: Institute of Mediæval Music, 2004).

4. Bargagli, *Dialogo,* ed. Ermini, 40.

5. Luca Colombini, "Orazio Vecchi a Siena," in *Theatro dell'udito, Theatro del mondo: Atti del convegno internazionale, nel IV centenario della morte di Orazio Vecchi, Modena-Vignola, 29 settember–1 ottobre 2005,* ed. Massimo Privitera (Modena: Mucchi, 2010), 31–35.

6. Laura Riccò, *Giuoco e teatro nelle veglie di Siena* (Rome: Bulzoni, 1993), 15 and chap. 1.

7. Quoted in Riccò, *Giuoco e teatro,* 118.

8. In particular, see James Haar, "On Musical Games in the Sixteenth Century," *Journal of the American Musicological Society* 15 (1962): 22–34; and Massimo Privitera, "Democrito a teatro: Le poetiche di Orazio Vecchi e le allegoriche malinconiche" (PhD diss., Università degli Studi di Bologna, 1990), 205–215.

9. Alessandro Striggio, *Il cicalamento delle donne al bucato et La caccia . . . con il Gioco di primiera* (Venice: Scotto, 1569). The "Gioco di primiera" is transcribed in Einstein, *Italian Madrigal,* 3:285–294.

10. *Il cicalamento delle donne al bucato, et La caccia di Alessandro Striggio, con un Lamento di Didone ad Enea, per la sua partenza, di Cipriano Rore* (Venice: Scotto, 1567).

11. Francesco Berni, *Capitolo del Gioco della Primiera col commento di Messer Pietropaulo da San Chirico* (Rome: Calvo, 1526), modern ed. in *Ludi esegetici,* ed. Danilo Romei (Rome: Vecchiarelli, 2005), 29–96; Gerolamo Cardano, *The Book of Games of Chance: "Liber de ludo aleae,"* trans. Sydney Henry Gould (New York: Holt, Rinehart and Winston, 1961). Cardano is also known to musicologists for two treatises on music; see Hieronymus Cardanus, *Writings on Music,* trans. and ed. Clement A. Miller (n.p.: American Institute of Musicology, 1973).

12. Some variability of the rules clearly existed as well; Cardano declares that draws should come from the deck, and that to draw from the discards is cheating (chap. 18), while a comic poem printed around 1600 describes a game between Caesar, Saint Mark, the pope, and the French king, among others, in which cards are exchanged between players. See Giulio Mantoano, *Opera Nova . . . Nella qual si contiene un Capitolo di Primiera, e molti bellissimi Sonetti, etc.* (n.p., [ca. 1600]), transcription at http://jducoeur.org/game-hist/Giulio.doc (accessed September 25, 2012).

13. Einstein, *Italian Madrigal,* 2:768.

14. Ed. in Einstein, *Italian Madrigal,* 3:li–lii (text and translation), 285–294 (music). I have adjusted Einstein's layout to indicate midline textural shifts, as in line 4. The original clefs are Canto = c1, Alto = c1, Quinto = c3, Tenore = c4, Basso = f3.

15. Berni's commentary explains that *a monte* is colloquially used synonymously with *passa,* though the third edition of the *Vocabolario della Crusca* of 1691 defines it as signifying

withdrawing or folding. See *Ludi esegetici,* ed. Romei, 69–70; *Vocabolario degli Accademici della Crusca,* 3rd ed. (Florence: Accademia della crusca, 1691) 2:87, at http://www.lessicografia.it /cruscle/pagina.jsp?ediz=3&vol=2&tipo=1&pag=87 (accessed October 27, 2012).

16. Baldessar Castiglione, *Il cortegiano,* ed. Bruno Maier (Torino: UTET, 1955; repr., 1964), 239. Trans. in Castiglione, *The Book of the Courtier,* trans. George Bull (New York: Penguin, 1967), 140.

17. Cardano, *The Book of Games of Chance,* 4.

18. Cardano, *The Book of Games of Chance,* 2.

19. Cardano, *The Book of Games of Chance,* 3.

20. Castiglione, *Il cortegiano,* ed. Maier, 313–316.

21. Cardano, *The Book of Games of Chance,* 26.

22. Pericolo's reading brings the painting into narrative alignment with Giambattista Marino's sonnet "Con venti e venti effigiate carte," in which the erotic metaphor of primero is more explicit. See Lorenzo Pericolo, *Caravaggio and Pictorial Narrative: Dislocating the "Istoria" in Early Modern Painting* (London: Harvey Miller, [2011]), chap. 5, "Behind the Comical Trick: Caravaggio's *The Cardsharps* and Giovan Battista Marino's 'Gioco di Primera,'" 157–175.

23. Though partly concealed by the cheat's thumb, the visible suit marks on the cards are enough to confirm these ranks, remembering that the eights, nines, and tens are not used in primero. In La Tour's slightly earlier *The Cheat with the Ace of Clubs* (ca. 1630–1634), the same rank of cards is visible in the cheat's hand, but they are clubs, to match the concealed ace. See Jacques Thuillier, *Georges de La Tour,* trans. Fabia Claris (Paris: Flammarion, 1993), 134–135, 138–141.

24. Giovanni Croce, *Triaca musicale,* ed. Guido Camilucci (Rome: De Santis, 1942), 41–54.

25. David Parlett, *The Oxford History of Board Games* (Oxford: Oxford University Press, 1999), 95–98. For images of a range of historical game boards and related information, see Luigi Ciompi and Adrian Seville, *Giochi dell'Oca e di percorso,* at http://www.giochidelloca.it.

26. Croce, *Triaca musicale,* ed. Camillucci, iv–v. Subsequent textual quotes are from this edition.

27. The Inn and the Well have slightly different penalties in some versions of the rules. According to the 1598 Gargano board, they both require the player to wait for another before departing, but Croce either knew a more lenient rule or deliberately kept the game moving by limiting the number of lost turns.

28. Evelyn Welch, "Lotteries in Early Modern Italy," *Past and Present,* no. 199 (May 2008): 80–81.

29. On Miklós Zrínyi, associated with the sixth motto, see Lórant Czigány, *The Oxford History of Hungarian Literature from the Earliest Times to the Present* (Oxford: Clarendon Press, 1984), 55–60.

30. The lines are from poem no. 325, "Tacer non posso, et temo non adopre," lines 61–62.

31. Bargagli, *Dialogo,* ed. Ermini, 76.

32. Vecchi, *Convito musicale,* ed. Martin, 100–104, translation adapted from Martin's, p. 237.

33. Measure numbers are from the edition by William Martin.

34. Haar cites this as the only game in Bargagli to refer to music, but he does not relate it to the "Bando del asino" ("On Musical Games," 25n15). The text quote is from Bargagli, *Dialogoi,* ed. Ermini, 76.

35. Vecchi, *Convito,* ed. Martin, 110–112, translation adapted from p. 238.

36. Although an Accademia degli spensierati did exist in Rossano, in Calabria, there is no evidence to connect it either to game playing or to Vecchi, so it seems more likely that the term here is intended to sound more generically academic. *Archivio Storico per le Province Napoletane*, Anno Terzo, fasc. 1, ed. Società della storia patria (Naples: F. Giannini, 1878), 298–304.

37. Bargagli, *Dialogo*, ed. Ermini, 68–69.

38. Bargagli, *Dialogo*, ed. Ermini, 69.

39. Bargagli, *Dialogo*, ed. Ermini, 69.

40. Bargagli, *Dialogo*, ed. Ermini, 72.

41. Bargagli, *Dialogo*, ed. Ermini, 72.

42. The distinction between sight-reading and singing embellished music only after rehearsal is attested even within the *concerto*; see Alessandro Striggio's letter of 29 July 1584, quoted in Newcomb, *Madrigal at Ferrara*, 270, translated at 77.

43. The dialogic roles are more clearly presented in "Il giuoco del Conte," a game of *bisticci* from Banchieri's *Festino del giovedì grass avanti cena* that is clearly modeled on Vecchi's, with the two lowest voices representing the leader and the upper three portraying the lady playing the game. Banchieri also introduces a different *bisticcio*: "Sopra il ponte a fronte del fonte vi stava un Conte, / Cadd'il ponte nel fonte e il Conte si rupp'il fronte" (On a bridge by the spring there stood a Count; the bridge fell in the spring, and the Count smashed his face). See Adriano Banchieri, *Festino del giovedì grassa avanti cena*, ed. Bonaventura Somma (Rome: De Santis, 1939), 53–57.

44. Technically, the tempo relationship might be *tripla* or *sesquialtera*, but as contemporary theorists complained, in practice singers often sped up tempos nonproportionally in triple-meter passages such as this one. See Ruth I. DeFord, "Tempo Relationships between Duple and Triple Time in the Sixteenth Century," *Early Music History* 14 (1995): 1–51.

45. Bargagli, *Dialogo*, ed. Ermini, 72.

46. Bargagli, *Dialogo*, ed. Ermini, 74.

47. Of the named humors Lodovico Casali wrote, "In truth, searching in these notes, or the manner of their melodies, few or no one will find them, and fewer still will understand them" (*Generale invito alle grandezze, e maraviglie della musica* [Modena: Gadaldino, 1629], 184, cited in Privitera, "Democrito a teatro," 222).

48. See Haar, "On Musical Games," 32 and passim; and Vecchi, *Le veglie*, ed. Beecher, xviii–xv.

49. Bargagli, *Dialogo*, ed. Ermini, 109.

50. This style of game play is first described in connection with the "Giuoco delle parole e de' cenni." See Bargagli, *Dialogo*, ed. Ermini, 60.

51. Vecchi had done the same for his only other French-texted composition, the bilingual *vinata* in *Selva*, "Je veu le cerf du bois salir / Ecco il buon Bacco," though in that case the Italian *contrafactum* is not a translation, as it is in the example in *Le veglie* (see chapter 6).

52. Note that this table shows only the representations of individual speakers; each *proposta* ends with a *tutti* section, and each *applauso* employs all six voices more or less equally throughout; such passages represent the generalized speech of the entire company.

53. As Massimo Ossi has shown, the use of voices and instruments together is described in the "Avvertimenti" to Claudio Monteverdi's *Scherzi musicali* (1607) and is central to the emergence of formal ritornello-based structures in early opera. Vecchi's short trios in *Le veglie*, like his *Canzonette a tre* (with lute) of 1597, may represent a similar but less explicitly notated

practice. See Massimo Ossi, "Monteverdi's 'Ordine novo, bello, e gustevole': The Canzonetta as Dramatic Module and Formal Archetype," *Journal of the American Musicological Society* 45, no. 2 (Summer 1992): 261–304.

54. The leader asks, "But will you put your heart into it [i.e., the imitation of a Venetian]?" to which Giocoso replies, "Of course, for Cupid is with me" (Ma vi dà egli, il core? / Anzi sì, chè meco è Amore).

55. This translation is from Don Harrán, "Between Acculturation and Exclusion: Jews as Portrayed in Italian Music from the Late Fifteenth to the Early Seventeenth Centuries," in *Acculturation and Its Discontents: The Italian Jewish Experience between Exclusion and Integration*, ed. David N. Myers (Toronto: University of Toronto Press, 2008), 78.

56. Harrán relates this pursuit to the Roman carnival practice of chasing Jews, stripped naked, through the streets ("Between Acculturation and Exclusion," 78).

57. See Harrán, "Between Acculturation and Exclusion," passim; and Wilbourne, "*Lo Schiavetto* (1612)."

58. The "Stella Giulia," besides punning on the player's name, refers to the Great Comet of 44 CE. It was widely taken as a sign of the recently deceased Julius Caesar's deification, as described in Ovid, *Metamorphoses* 15.745–842. Vecchi also refers to a "Giulia stella" in his four-voice canzonetta "Chi vuol veder l'Aurora" (from book 3), which is addressed to "Giulia" throughout.

59. Sonnet LVII in *Rime di Pietro Bembo, corrette, illustrate, ed accresciute*, ed. Anton-Federigo Seghezzi (Bergamo: Lancelotti, 1753), 45.

60. Beecher provides possible English alternatives, but these are somewhat interpretive, as he notes. See Vecchi, *Le veglie di Siena*, ed. Beecher, lvi.

61. Newcomb's categorization is an emendation and elaboration of Privitera's. See Privitera, "Democrito al Teatro," 228–229; Anthony Newcomb, "Gli Humori di Horatio: On a Few Madrigals from the *Veglie di Siena*," in *Theatro dell'udito*, 383–399.

62. Newcomb, "Gli humori di Horatio."

63. Measure numbers refer to the Beecher edition, which numbers measures continuously within each *parte*.

64. Newcomb, "Gli humori di Horatio," 395.

65. The six-voice version in *Le veglie* is an expanded version of Vecchi's five-voice setting, which appeared in *De floridi virtuosi d'Italia* (Venice: Vincenti and Amadino, 1583). On that anthology, see Emma Hilary Wakelin, "*De floridi virtuosi d'Italia*: A Study of Three Italian Madrigal Anthologies of the 1580s" (PhD diss., Royal Holloway, University of London, 1997).

66. See Orazio Vecchi, *"Battaglia d'Amor e Dispetto" and "Mascherata della Malinconia et Allegrezza,"* ed. David Nutter, Recent Researches in Musics of the Renaissance 72 (Madison, WI: A-R Editions, 1987), x–xiii.

67. Newcomb, "Gli humori di Horatio," 383.

68. The significance of the relationship between the *Dichiaratione* and the *scherzi* themselves has been established by Massimo Ossi. See Ossi, "Monteverdi's 'Ordine novo,'" and the same author's *Divining the Oracle: Monteverdi's "Seconda Prattica"* (Chicago: University of Chicago Press, 2003), 111–119.

69. Giovan Battista Spaccini, *Cronaca di Modena,* ed. Albano Biondi, Rolando Busi, and Carlo Giovannini (Modena: Panini, 1993), 2:339, 346.

70. This and subsequent citations of the dedication and preface are from Pancaldi and Roncaglia, *Orazio Vecchi,* 76–77, and adapted from the translation in Vecchi, *Le veglie,* ed. Beecher, lvii–lx.

71. John Bergsagel, "Borchgrevinck, Melchior," in *Grove Music Online, Oxford Music Online,* http://www.oxfordmusiconline.com/subscriber/article/grove/music/03563 (accessed October 6, 2012).

72. This is a reference to Aristotle's discussion of music as a pastime in book 8 of the *Politics;* of particular relevance here is chapter 5, in which Aristotle describes the benefits of music in terms of its imitation of ethoses. See *Source Readings in Music History,* rev. ed. by Leo Treitler (New York: Norton, 1998), 27–30.

73. Scipione Bargagli, *I trattenimenti,* ed. Laura Riccò (Rome: Salerno, 1989).

74. Vecchi's references are traced in *Le vegle di Siena,* ed. Beecher, lviii–lix.

75. Homer is credited with both the *Odyssey* and the mock-epic *Batrachmyomachia* ("The Battle of Frogs and Mice," known in Italian as the *Topeide;* the attribution to Homer was denied by Plutarch), and Virgil is cited as authoring the *Aeneid* as well as the *Bucolics.*

76. Torquato Tasso, *Gerusalemme liberata,* ed. Lanfranco Carretti (Turin: Einaudi, 1971), canto 1, lines 9–20, pp. 13–14, trans. in Tasso, *Jerusalem Delivered,* trans. Anthony M. Esolen (Baltimore, MD: Johns Hopkins University Press, 2000), 17.

77. Quoted in Claude V. Palisca, *Music and Ideas in the Sixteenth and Seventeenth Centuries* (Urbana: University of Illinois Press, 2006), 163.

78. Vecchi's closest personal connection to the debates over the *seconda prattica* was his friendship with Alfonso Fontanelli, a nobleman who had moved with what was left of the Este court from Ferrara to Modena in 1598. Vecchi contributed a preface to the second edition (1603) of Fontanelli's first book of five-voice madrigals in which he defends the "novelty, dignity, delight, and affect" of his friend's music from "superstitious" attacks. See Pancaldi and Roncaglia, *Orazio Vecchi,* 78–79.

79. Tomaso Garzoni, *L'hospidale de' pazzi incurabili* (Ferrara: Cagnacini, 1586); Bargali, *Dialogo,* ed. Ermini, 114–115.

6. Representation and Identity in Musical Performance

1. David O. Frantz, *Festum Voluptatis: A Study of Renaissance Erotica* (Columbus: Ohio State University Press, 1989), 4–5; Roger Thompson, *Unfit for Modest Ears* (London: Macmillan, 1979), ix–x.

2. Giovanni Giacomo Gastoldi, *Balletti a cinque voci* (Venice: Amadino, 1591), modern ed. in Giovanni Giacomo Gastoldi, *Balletti a cinque voci, 1591,* ed. Michel Sanvoisin (Paris: Heugel, 1968).

3. Orazio Vecchi, *Selva di varia ricreatione (1590),* ed. Paul Schleuse (Middleton, WI: A-R Editions, 2012), 79–80.

4. Modena, Biblioteca Estense Ms. C 311, facsimile ed. in Cosimo Bottegari, *Il libro di canto e liuto,* ed. Dinko Fabris and John Griffiths (Bologna: Forni, 2006), fol. 5r. On Bottegari's career and lute book, see Warren Kirkendale, *The Court Musicians in Florence during the Principiate of the Medici* (Florence: Olschki, 1993), 251–255.

5. Vecchi, *Selva,* ed. Schleuse, xvi.

6. Joseph Kerman, *The Elizabethan Madrigal* (New York: American Musicological Society and Galaxy Music, 1962), 140.

7. Cesare Negri, *Le Gratie d'Amore* (Milan: Pontio & Piccaglia, 1602, facsimile ed., New York: Broude Brothers, 1969), 222, trans. and transcribed in Yvonne Kendall, "*Le Gratie d'Amore* by Cesare Negri: Translation and Commentary" (DMA diss., Stanford University, 1985), 377–382.

8. Negri, *Gratie d'Amore*, 21, 28.

9. The metaphorical sense of the word *martello* (hammer) is given in the *Vocabolario della crusca* (1612): "E MARTELLO lo diciamo per una certa passione amorosa, che è quando si dubita, che la cosa amata non ti sia tolta da altri" (And we say *hammer* for a certain amorous passion, that is, when one fears that the beloved will be taken away by others) (Accademia dela Crusca, *Lessicografia della Crusca in rete*, http://www.lessicografia.it/pagina.jsp?ediz=1& vol=0&pag=512&tipo=1).

10. Harry Berger, Jr., *The Absence of Grace: Sprezzatura and Suspicion in Two Renaissance Courtesy Books* (Stanford, CA: Stanford University Press, 2000), 14.

11. Berger, *The Absence of Grace*, chap. 2.

12. On relationships between jesters and comic theater, see Beatrice K. Otto, *Fools Are Everywhere: The Court Jester around the World* (Chicago: University of Chicago Press, 2007), chap. 6, "All the World's a Stage."

13. Vecchi, *Convito musicale*, ed. Martin, 157–158; I have adapted Martin's translation on pp. 241–242.

14. Barbara Correll, *The End of Conduct: "Grobianus" and the Renaissance Text of the Subject* (Ithaca, NY: Cornell University Press, 1996), 45–46.

15. Berger, *The Absence of Grace*, 45.

16. Melanie Marshall, "Cultural Codes and Hierarchies in the Mid-Cinquecento Villotta" (PhD diss., University of Southampton, 2004), chap. 2, "Cinquecento Sexual Representation."

17. Toscan, *Le carnaval du langage: Le lexique érotique des poètes de l'équivoque de Burciello à Marino (XVe–XVIIe siècles)* (Lille: Atelier Reproduction des Thèses, 1981), 1:423–425 (on *sù* and *giù*), 2:1137 (on *impiccarsi*).

18. *Il primo libro del opere burlesche* (Usecht al Reno: Broedelet, 1771) [fictional city and publisher], 143. Cited in Toscan, *Le carnaval du langage*, 1:389.

19. Toscan, *Le carnaval du langage*, 1:531 (on *asciutto* and *molle*).

20. Toscan, *Le carnaval du langage*, 3:1274–1276.

21. Toscan, *Le carnaval du langage*, 1:458–461 (on *bugie* and falsehoods), 3:1493 (on *tinella*).

22. Marshall describes one potentially homosexual relationship between the Reverend Monsignor Girolamo Fenaruolo and Marco Silvio, members of the Venetian circle around Domenico Venier. Marshall, "Cultural Codes," 1:111–115.

23. On the earlier phase, see William F. Prizer, "Games of Venus: Secular Vocal Music in the Late Quattrocento and Early Cinquecento," *Journal of Musicology* 9 (1991): 17 ff. On later developments, see Marshall, "Cultural Codes," 1:26–32.

24. Marshall, "Cultural Codes," 1:11.

25. Prizer, "Games of Venus," 24–25. Mathias Werrecore describes his *villotte* as being written for an all-sung context in the dedication to *La bataglia taliana* (1549), trans. in Marshall, "Cultural Codes," 2:11–12.

26. Claudio Gallico, *Damon pastor gentil: Idilli cortesi e voci popolari nelle "Villotte mantovane" (1583)* (Mantua: Gianluigi Ancari, 1980).

27. Prizer, "Games of Venus," 37. While Prizer's notion of a distancing effect certainly applies to the *villotta*, Vecchi's *arie* discussed above suggest that evocations of popular culture are not always necessary for critiques of courtly manners.

28. Toscan, *Le carnaval de langage*, 3:1462. See also Valter Boggione and Giovanni Casalegno, *Dizionario storico del lessico erotico italiano: Metafore, eufemismi, oscenità, doppi sensi, parole dotte e parole basse in otto secoli di letteratura italiana* (Milan: TEA, 1999), 352 (on *caglio*), 458–459 (on *insalata*).

29. Toscan, *Le carnaval du langage*, 4:1767. See also Boggione and Casalegno, *Dizionario*, 426.

30. Christina Fuhrmann, "Gossip, *Erotica*, and the Male Spy in Striggio's *Il Cicalamento delle donne al bucato* (1567)," in *Gender, Sexuality, and Early Music*, ed. Todd M. Borgerding (New York: Routledge, 2002), 181.

31. As with "O bella ò bianca" the cleffing, though generally high, emphasizes the lower part of the ambitus: Canto = g2, Alto = c1, Sesto = c2, Tenore = c3, Quinto = c3, Basso = c4.

32. Girolamo Bargagli, *Dialogo de' giuochi che nelle vegghie sanesi si usano di fare* (Siena: Bonetti, 1572), modern ed. by Patrizia D'Icalci Ermini (Siena: Accademia Senese degli Intronati, 1982), 93.

33. *Vinate* are described as "the slightest kind of music (if they deserve the name of music)" in Thomas Morley, *A Plaine and Easie Introduction to Practicall Musicke* (London: Short, 1597), 180, modern edition ed. Alex Harman (New York: Norton, 1952), 295.

34. Concetta Assenza, *Giovan Ferretti tra canzonetta e madrigale, con l'edizione critica del quinto libro di canzoni alla napolitana a cinque voci (1585)* (Florence: Olschki, 1989), 210–216.

35. This sense of *montare* is attested in John Florio, *A World of Wordes* (London: Bradwood, 1611), 321.

36. Bargagli, *Dialogo*, ed. Ermini, 57–59.

37. "Del che mi fa fede, il vedere nelle ville e nelle nostre castelle alcuni giuochi usarli, che noi nella Città facciamo. Et non mi par possibile, che in si pochi anni l'havessero quelli huomini appresi da noi, e tanto piu in alcuni salvatichi, e alpestre luoghi, dove faccia di persona nobile non si vede mai, la onde mi stimo piu tosto che noi alcuni presi n'habbiamo da loro, si come molte delle lor canzoni, e de' balli si onde chiaramente che tolti habbiamo. Confermami in cotal credenza il gioco della Cicirlanda, che tanto è usanza, il quale se cosi moderno fosse, non avrebbe mai un nome, che da' moderni inteso non sia. La onde convien che lo tenghiamo per molto antico poiche venga da una molto antica derivatione. Percioche Cicirlanda . . . è parola corrotta da ghirlanda perchioche colui che haveva la potestà del domandare si poneva, come ancor hoggi s'usa, in luogo eminente, e chiamando quei, che stavano in giro, acciò che ascoltassaero, e ubidissera diceva o ghirlanda? et il cerchio rispondeva, come adesso ancor si costuma, che commanda, e quel che intendeva che far si dovesse, comandava" (Bargagli, *Dialogo*, ed. Ermini, 60).

38. Giovanni Della Casa, *Galateo: A Renaissance Treatise on Manners*, trans. Konrad Eisenbichler and Kenneth R. Bartlett (Toronto: Centre for Reformation and Renaissance Studies, 1994), 93–95.

39. Adriano Banchieri, *Festino nella sera del giovedì grasso avanti cena a 5 voci miste (1608)*, ed. Bonaventura Somma (Rome: De Santis, 1939), 61–66.

40. The Bolognese setting of the *Festino* is implied by the encounter described in the preface between the allegorical figures of "Diletto Moderno"—explicitly identified as the author, Banchieri himself—and "Rigore Antico"—a figure identifiable as Giovanni Maria Artusi. It was clearly Banchieri's intent to insert himself into the debates over modern music then raging between Artusi, Monteverdi, and others. Banchieri takes the side of the moderns, of course, though his counterpoint in *Festino* contains little to offend the precepts of Zarlino that Artusi defended. The preface is given and translated in Einstein, *Italian Madrigal*, 2:813–816.

41. Pierre de Manchicourt, *Twenty-Nine Chansons*, ed. Margery Anthea Baird, Recent Researches in the Music of the Renaissance 11 (Madison, WI: A-R Editions, 1972), 72–76.

42. Baird characterizes "J'ay veu le cerf du bois sallir" as Parisian in style despite its scant resemblance to the syllabic, homorhythmic, and sectional form associated with "Parisian" *chansons*, apparently on the basis of the Attaingnant publication. Lawrence Bernstein has

shown that Attaingnant's *chanson* prints in fact transmit songs from a wide variety of overlapping styles and geographical origins. Lawrence F. Bernstein, "The 'Parisian Chanson': Problems of Style and Terminlogy," *Journal of the American Musicological Society* 31 (1978): 193–240.

43. *La grand bible des noelz, tant vieux que nouveaux* (Lyon: Rigaud, [1554]), fols. 86v–88v.

44. *Airs de Cour comprenans le trésor des trésors, le fleur des fleurs, & eslite des Chansons amoureuses* (Poitiers: Brossart, 1607), 544.

45. Vecchi, *Selva*, ed. Schleuse, xxiv.

46. C = Canto (c1), A = Alto (c2), 6 = Sesto (c3), T = Tenore (c4), 5 = Quinto (c4), B = Basso (f4), [Pass.] = Passagiero, [Giard.] = Giardino.

47. "Fare il saggio" may literally be read as "to come to know," that is, to have sexual relations. See Boggione and Casalegno, *Dizionario*, 137.

48. On equivocal uses of *giardino*, see Boggione and Casalegno, *Dizionario*, 427–428.

49. Similar imagery appears, though in a heterosexual sodomitical context, in the "Canzona di donne che vendono agresto" by Guglielmo detto il Giuggiola, first published in *Tutti i Trionfi, Carri, Mascherate, ò canti Carnascialeschi* (Florence: [n.p.], 1559), modern ed. in *Canti carnascialeschi del rinascimento,* ed. Charles S. Singleton (Bari: Laterza, 1936), 272–273.

50. The Secchia River runs around the western and northern sides of Modena; the gardener's pride may therefore indicate the music's Modenese provenance.

51. The *Crusca* confirms this alternate definition "Diciamo anche incarnare, per ferire, e ficcar nella carne" (*Vocabolario della Crusca,* 1st ed., 427, http://www.lessicografia.it/pagina .jsp?ediz=1&vol=0&pag=427&tipo=1).

52. On *vengo meno,* see Toscan, *Le carnaval du langage,* 3:1348–1349, and on *grilli,* see 4:1859n67.

53. Gino Roncaglia, *La cappella musicale del duomo di Modena* (Florence: Olschki, 1957), 57–58.

54. *Trionfo di musica di diversi a 6 voci* (Venice: Scotto, 1579). The book is described, and Vecchi's piece is transcribed, in Federico Ghisi, *Feste musicali della Firenze Medicea (1480–1589)* (Florence: Vallecchi, 1939; repr., Bologna: Forni, 1969), xxxviii–xl, 79–84.

55. *Dialoghi musicali de diversi* (Venice: Gardano, 1590), facsimile ed. in *Corpus of Early Music* 29 (Brussels: Éditions culture et civilisation, 1970).

56. Vecchi, *"Battaglia d'Amor e Dispetto" and "Mascherata della Malinchonia et Allegrezza,"* ed. Nutter.

57. Anthony Cummings, "On the Testimony of Fragments (or, Alessandro Striggio the Elder and the Genesis of the *Genere Concitato*)," *Studi musicali,* n.s., 4 (2013): 52–53.

58. "È uscito una mascherata di pastori con Diana che va a caccia, con assai buona musica di Ercole Sforzini cantore. Non è quelli mascheri in volta che potrìa essere, per il cattivo tempo che è, e nevica del continuo. Dopo desinaro uscì tre carroze discoperte piene di burattini; in una di quelle v'era una buona musica d'Oracio Vecchi che andavano cantando alle finestre, e nevicava molto forte" (Spaccini, *Cronaca di Modena,* 1:325).

59. Roncaglia, *La cappella musicale del duomo di Modena,* 34, 58.

60. "È uscita una mascherata di Pantaloni che in gondola andavano vogando, e cantavano in lingua veneziana le antichità di questa città, et are composizione di Oracio Vecchi, cosa invero delle più belle che ancor se siano fatte. Un'altra n'è uscita della Gran Madre, ch'era in cima a un carro tirato da leoni; lei avèa in capo una corona fatta a torri, la veste è tessuta di verde erbe e circondata da fronzuti rami. Ha lo scetro in mano et una chiave nell'altra, intorno le stanno alcuni seggi vuoti, e vi sono i risuonanti timpani, e l'accompagnano certi sacerdoti

con gli elmi in testa, con gli scudi al braccio, e con le aste in mano, e questi facevano gran concerto, ch'era di Geminiano Capilupi" (Spaccini, *Cronaca di Modena,* 1:327).

61. Spaccini, *Cronaca di Modena,* 1:211.

62. "Gionto in castello, nelle camere, vi vien incontra due principine et una dama vestite da grazie molto adorno, dove cantorno un madrigale, et in ultimo diceva 'Maschere, mascare!' Doppo questo li principi comparsero vestiti da Pantaloni, e cantorono una pantalona molto ridicolosa; questa è stata invenzione d'Oracio Vecchi loro mastro da cantare" (Spaccini, *Cronaca di Modena,* 1:433).

63. Spaccini, *Cronaca di Modena,* 1:443.

64. Roncaglia, *La cappelle musicale del duomo di Modena,* 87 ff.

65. Gismondo Florio, *Tomba d'Atlante avventurosa. Feste, giostre, e tornei bellissimi nell'accoglienze fatte in Modona . . .* (Modena: Gadaldino, 1604). The relevant description is translated in Vecchi, *"Battaglia d'Amor e Dispetto"* and *"Mascherata della Malinchonia et Allegrezza,"* ed. Nutter, x–xi. See also Spaccini, *Cronaca di Modena,* 2:105–106.

66. Spaccini, *Cronaca di Modena,* 2:137.

67. Pancaldi and Roncaglia, *Orazio Vecchi,* 36.

68. Spaccini, *Cronaca di Modena,* 2:136.

69. Pancaldi and Roncaglia, *Orazio Vecchi,* 36 and 54; see also Massimo Privitera, "Orazio Vecchi, musico-poeta all'autunno del Rinascimento," in *Il Theatro dell'udito: Società, musica, storia, e cultura nell'epoca di Orazio Vecchi,* ed. Ferdinando Taddei and Alessandra Chiarelli (Modena: Mucchi, 2007), 125.

70. Spaccini, *Cronaca di Modena,* 2:158–159; Pancaldi and Roncaglia, *Orazio Vecchi,* 37.

Works Cited

Adkins, Cecil. "Vecchi and the Madrigal Comedy." In Orazio Vecchi, *"L'Amfiparnaso": A New Edition of the Music with Historical and Analytical Essays.* Edited by Cecil Adkins, 5–12. Chapel Hill: University of North Carolina Press, 1977.

Agee, Richard. *The Gardano Music Printing Firms, 1569–1611.* Rochester, NY: University of Rochester Press, 1998.

Ambros, August Wilhelm. *Geschichte der Musik.* Vol. 4. Edited by Gustav Nottebohm. Leipzig: F. E. C. Leuckart, 1878.

———. *Geschichte der Musik.* Vol. 3. 3rd edition, edited by Otto Kade. Leipzig: F. E. C. Leuckart, 1893.

———. *Geschichte der Musik.* Vol. 4. Revised edition, edited by Hugo Leichtentritt. Leipzig: F. E. C. Leuckart, 1909. Reprint, Hildesheim: Georg Olms, 1968.

Archivio Storico per le Province Napoletane. Anno Terzo, fasc. I. Edited by Società della storia patria. Naples: F. Giannini, 1878.

Arteaga, Stefano. *Le rivoluzioni del teatro musicale italiano dalla sua origine al presente.* Bologna: Trenti, 1783.

Assenza, Concetta. *Giovan Ferretti tra canzonetta e madrigale, con l'edizione critica del Quinto libro di canzoni alla napolitana a cinque voci (1585).* Florence: Olschki, 1989.

Aulus Gellius. *The Attic Nights, Books I–IV.* Translated by John C. Rolfe. Cambridge, MA: Harvard University Press, 1927.

Bargagli, Girolamo. *Dialogo de' giuochi che nelle vegghie sanesi si usano di fare.* Siena: Bonetti, 1572. Modern edition by Patrizia D'Icalci Ermini. Siena: Accademia Senese degli Intronati, 1982.

Bargagli, Scipione. *I trattenimenti.* Edited by Laura Riccò. Rome: Salerno, 1989.

Bembo, Pietro. *Rime di Pietro Bembo, corrette, illustrate, ed accresciute.* Edited by Anton-Federigo Seghezzi. Bergamo: Lancelotti, 1753.

Berger, Harry, Jr. *The Absence of Grace: Sprezzatura and Suspicion in Two Renaissance Courtesy Books.* Stanford, CA: Stanford University Press, 2000.

Berni, Francesco. *Capitolo del Gioco della Primiera col commento di Messer Pietropaulo da San Chirico.* Rome: Calvo, 1526. Modern edition, *Ludi esegetici,* edited by Danilo Romei. Rome: Vecchiarelli, 2005.

Bernstein, Jane A. *Music Printing in Renaissance Venice: The Scotto Press (1539–1572).* New York: Oxford University Press, 1998.

———. *Print Culture and Music in Sixteenth-Century Venice.* Oxford: Oxford University Press, 2001.

Bernstein, Lawrence F. "The 'Parisian Chanson': Problems of Style and Terminology." *Journal of the American Musicological Society* 31 (1978): 193–240.

Boetticher, Wolfgang. *Aus Orlando di Lassos Wirkungkreis.* Kassel: Bärenreiter, 1963.

Boggione, Valter, and Giovanni Casalegno. *Dizionario storico del lessico erotico italiano.* Milan: TEA, 1996.

Bywater, Ingram, trans. *The Rhetoric and Poetics of Aristotle.* New York: Random House, 1954.

Calcagno, Mauro. *From Madrigal to Opera: Monteverdi's Staging of the Self.* Berkeley: University of California Press, 2012.

Cardamone, Donna G. *The* canzone villanesca alla napolitana *and Related Forms, 1537–1570.* 2 vols. Ann Arbor, MI: UMI Research Press, 1981.

Cardano, Gerolamo. *The Book of Games of Chance: "Liber de ludo aleae."* Translated by Sydney Henry Gould. New York: Holt, Rinehart and Winston, 1961.

Carter, Tim. "Music Publishing in Italy, c. 1580–c. 1625: Some Preliminary Observations." *Royal Musical Association Research Chronicle* 20 (1986–87): 19–37.

Castelvetro, Lodovico. *Poetica d'Aristotele vulgarizzata et sposta.* Basel: Pietro de Sedabonis, 1576.

Castiglione, Baldessar. *Il cortegiano.* Edited by Bruno Maier. Torino: UTET, 1955. Reprint, 1964. Translated by George Bull, *The Book of the Courtier.* New York: Penguin, 1967.

Catelani, Angelo. *Della vita e delle opere di Orazio Vecchi.* Milan: Ricordi, 1864.

Chater, James. "'Such Sweet Sorrow': The *dialogo di partenza* in the Italian Madrigal." *Early Music* 27, no. 4 (1999): 576–590.

Chew, Geoffrey. "A Model Musical Education: Monteverdi's Early Works." In *The Cambridge Companion to Monteverdi,* edited by John Whenham and Richard Wistreich, 31–44. Cambridge: Cambridge University Press, 2007.

Cicero. *De finibus bonorum et malorum.* Edited by M. A. Rackham. Loeb Classical Library. London: Heineman; New York: Macmillan, 1914.

———. *On Moral Ends.* Edited and translated by Julia Annas. Cambridge Texts in the History of Philosophy. Cambridge: Cambridge University Press, 2001.

Ciompi, Luigi, and Adrian Seville. *Giochi dell'Oca e di percorso.* http://www.giochidelloca.it (accessed June 15, 2013).

Clubb, Louise George. *Italian Drama in Shakespeare's Time.* New Haven, CT: Yale University Press, 1989.

———. "Pastoral Elasticity on the Italian Stage and Page." In *The Pastoral Landscape,* edited by John Dixon Hunt. Studies in the History of Art 36. Washington, DC: National Gallery of Art, 1992.

———. "Pictures for the Reader: Illustrations to Comedy, 1591–1592." *Renaissance Drama* 9 (1966): 265–277. See also "Corrigenda." *Renaissance Drama,* n.s., 1 (1968): 340–341.

Colombini, Luca. "Orazio Vecchi a Siena." In Privitera, *Theatro dell'udito,* 31–35.

Conati, Marcello. "Theatro dell'udito: Appunti su Orazio Vecchi e il suo tempo." *Ricerche musicali* 2, no. 2 (1978): 41–69.

Correll, Barbara. *The End of Conduct: "Grobianus" and the Renaissance Text of the Subject.* Ithaca, NY: Cornell University Press, 1996.

Cummings, Anthony. "On the Testimony of Fragments (or, Alessandro Striggio the Elder and the Genesis of the *Genere Concitato*)." *Studi musicali,* n.s., 4 (2013): 39–59.

Czigány, Lórant. *The Oxford History of Hungarian Literature from the Earliest Times to the Present.* Oxford: Clarendon Press, 1984.

D'Accone, Frank. *The Civic Muse: Music and Musicians in Siena during the Middle Ages and the Renaissance.* Chicago: University of Chicago Press, 1997.

Dall'Olio, Giambatista. "Sull'Amfiparnaso d'Orazio Vecchi modenese (Creduto prima dramma buffo)." In Catelani, *Della vita e delle opere di Orazio Vecchi,* 42–51.

Dalmonte, Rossana, and Massimo Privitera. *Gitene, canzonette: Studio e trascrizione delle "Canzonette a sei voci d'Horatio Vecchi" (1587).* Florence: Olschki, 1996.

D'Arienzo, Nicola. "Origini dell'Opera comica." *Rivista musicale italiana* 2 (1895): 597–628.

DeFord, Ruth I. "The Evolution of Rhythmic Style in Italian Secular Music of the Late Sixteenth Century." *Studi musicali* 10 (1981): 43–74.

———. "Marenzio and the *villanella alla romana*." *Early Music* 27 (1999): 535–552.

———. "Musical Relationships between the Italian Madrigal and Light Genres in the Sixteenth Century." *Musica Disciplina* 39 (1985): 107–168.

———. "Orazio Vecchi's Treatise on the Modes and Its Application to His Four-Voice 'Canzonette.'" In Privitera, *Theatro dell'udito*, 335–356.

———. "Tempo Relationships between Duple and Triple Time in the Sixteenth Century." *Early Music History* 14 (1995): 1–51.

Della Casa, Giovanni. *Galateo: A Renaissance Treatise on Manners.* Translated by Konrad Eisenbichler and Kenneth R. Bartlett. Toronto: Centre for Reformation and Renaissance Studies, 1994.

Dent, Edward J. "The 'Amfiparnaso' of Orazio Vecchi." *Monthly Musical Record,* March 1906 and April 1906.

———. "Notes on the 'Amfiparnaso' of Orazio Vecchi." *Sammelbände der Internationalen Musikgesellschaft* 12, no. 3 (1911): 330–347.

Doni, Antonfrancesco. *Dialogo della Musica.* Edited by Gian Francesco Malipiero. Vienna: Universal, 1964.

Durante, Elio, and Anna Martellotti. *Don Angelo Grillo O.S.B. alias Livio Celiano: Poeta per musica del secolo decimosesto.* Florence: Studio per Edizioni Scelti, 1989.

Eco, Umberto. *The Open Work.* Translated by Anna Cancogni. Cambridge, MA: Harvard University Press, 1989.

Einstein, Alfred. *The Italian Madrigal.* 3 vols. Translated by Alexander H. Krappe, Roger H. Sessions, and Oliver Strunk. Princeton, NJ: Princeton University Press, 1949.

Eitner, Robert. *Biographisch-bibliographisches Quellen-Lexikon der Musiker und Musikgelehrten christlicher Zeitrechnung bis zur Mitte des neunzehnten Jahrhunderts.* 10 vols. Leipzig: Breitkopf & Härtel, 1898–1904. Reprint, Graz: Akademische Druck- und Verlagsanstalt, 1959.

Fabbri, Paolo. *Monteverdi.* Translated by Tim Carter. Cambridge: Cambridge University Press, 1994.

Farahat, Martha. "Adriano Banchieri and the Madrigal Comedy." 2 vols. PhD dissertation, University of Chicago, 1991.

———. "On the Staging of Madrigal Comedies." *Early Music History* 10 (1991): 123–143.

———. "Villanescas of the Virtuosi: Lasso and the *Commedia dell'arte.*" *Performance Practice Review* 3, no. 2 (1990): 121–137.

Federhofer, Hellmut. *Musikpflege und Musiker am Grazer Habsburgerhof der Erzherzöge Karl und Ferdinand von Innerösterreich (1564–1619).* Mainz: B. Schott's Söhne, 1967.

Feldman, Martha. *City Culture and the Madrigal at Venice.* Berkeley: University of California Press, 1995.

Fenlon, Ian. *Music and Patronage in Sixteenth-Century Mantua.* Cambridge: Cambridge University Press, 1980.

Fétis, François-Joseph. *Biographie universelle des musiciens.* 8 vols. Paris: Didot, 1844.

———. *Biographie universelle des musiciens.* 2nd edition. 8 vols. Paris: Didot, 1867.

Florio, John. *A World of Wordes.* London: Bradwood, 1611.

Frantz, David O. *Festum Voluptatis: A Study of Renaissance Erotica.* Columbus: Ohio State University Press, 1989.

Fuhrmann, Christina. "Gossip, *Erotica,* and the Male Spy in Striggio's *Il Cicalamento delle donne al bucato* (1567)." In *Gender, Sexuality, and Early Music,* edited by Todd M. Borgerding, 167–197. New York: Routledge, 2002.

Galen. *On the Properties of Foodstuffs (De alimentorum facultatibus).* Translation and commentary by Owen Powell. Cambridge: Cambridge University Press, 2003.

Gallico, Claudio. *Damon pastor gentil: Idilli cortesi e voci popolari nelle "Villotte mantovane"* *(1583)*. Mantua: Gianluigi Ancari, 1980.

Garzoni, Tomaso. *L'hospidale de' pazzi incurabili.* Ferrara: Cagnacini, 1586.

Gerbino, Giuseppe. *Music and the Myth of Arcadia in Renaissance Italy.* Cambridge: Cambridge University Press, 2009.

Ghisi, Federico. *Feste musicali della Firenze medicea (1480–1589).* Bologna: Forni, 1939.

Gilbert, Allan H. *Literary Criticism: Plato to Dryden.* Detroit: Wayne State University Press, 1962.

Giustiniani, Vincenzo. *Discorsi sulle arti e sui mestieri.* Edited by Anna Banti. Florence: Sansoni, 1981.

La grand bible des noelz, tant vieux que nouveaux. Lyon: Rigaud, [1554].

Guarini, Giovanni Battista. *"Il pastor fido" e "Il compendio della poesia tragicomica."* Edited by Gioachino Brognolio. Bari: Laterza, 1914.

———. *Opere.* Edited by Luigi Fassò. [Torino]: U T E T, 1950.

———. *Rime.* Venice: Ciotti, 1598.

Gustafson, Donna Mae Jenon. "Giovanni Croce's *Mascarate piacevoli et ridicolose per il carnevale:* A Contextual Study and Critical Edition." PhD dissertation, University of Minnesota, 1993.

Haar, James. "Music of the Renaissance as Viewed by the Romantics." In *The Science and Art of Renaissance Music,* edited by Paul Corneilson. Princeton, NJ: Princeton University Press, 1998.

———. "Notes on the *Dialogo della Musica* of Antonfrancesco Doni." *Music and Letters* 47 (1966): 198–224. Reprint, Haar, *The Science and Art of Renaissance Music.*

———. "On Musical Games in the Sixteenth Century." *Journal of the American Musicological Society* 15 (1962): 22–34.

———. "Popularity in the Sixteenth-Century Madrigal: A Study of Two Instances." In *Studies in Musical Sources and Style: Essays in Honor of Jan LaRue,* edited by Eugene K. Wolf and Edward H. Roesner, 191–212. Madison, WI: A-R Editions, 1990.

Harrán, Don. "Between Acculturation and Exclusion: Jews as Portrayed in Italian Music from the Late Fifteenth to the Early Seventeenth Centuries." In *Acculturation and Its Discontents: The Italian Jewish Experience between Exclusion and Integration,* edited by David N. Myers, 72–98. Toronto: University of Toronto Press, 2008.

Horace. *The Art of Poetry.* Translated by Burton Raffel and James Hynd. Albany: State University of New York Press, 1974.

Huizinga, Johan. *Homo Ludens: A Study of the Play-Element in Culture.* Boston: Roy, 1950.

Il primo libro del opere burlesche. Usecht al Reno: Broedelet, 1771 [fictional city and publisher].

Katritzky, M. A. *The Art of Commedia: A Study of the Commedia dell'arte 1560–1620 with Special Reference to the Visual Records.* Amsterdam: Rodopi, 2006.

Kerman, Joseph. *The Elizabethan Madrigal.* New York: American Musicological Society and Galaxy Music, 1962.

King, Jennifer L. "The *Proposta e risposta* Madrigal, Dialogue, Cultural Discourse, and the Issue of *Imitatio.*" PhD dissertation, Indiana University, 2007.

Kirkendale, Warren. *The Court Musicians in Florence during the Principiate of the Medici.* Florence: Olschki, 1993.

———. "Franceschina, Girometta, and Their Companions in a Madrigal 'a diversi linguaggi' by Luca Marenzio and Orazio Vecchi." *Acta Musicologica* 44 (1972): 181–235. Reprint, Kirkendale and Kirkendale, *Music and Meaning,* 125–204.

Kirkendale, Warren, and Ursula Kirkendale. *Music and Meaning: Studies in Music History and the Neighbouring Disciplines*. Florence: Olschki, 2007.

Landulphi Senioris. *Mediolanensis historiae*. Edited by Alessandro Cutulo. Rerum Italicarum Scriptores. Bologna: Zanichelli, 1942.

Lawrenson, T. E., and Helen Purkis. "Les éditions illustrées de Térence dans l'histoire du théatre." In *Le lieu theatral à la renaissance,* edited by Jean Jacquot. Paris: Éditions du centre national de la recherche scientifique, 1964.

Lesure, François, and Claudio Sartori. *Il nuovo Vogel: Bibliografia della musica italiana vocale profana pubblicata dal 1500 al 1700*. 3 vols. Pomezia: Staderini, 1977.

Lupo, Bettina. "Scene e persone musicale dell' *Amfiparnaso*." *Rassegna musicale* 11 (1938): 445–459.

MacClintock, Carol, trans. *Hercole Bottrigari: "Il Desiderio" & Vincenzo Giustiniani: "Discorso sopra la musica*." Musicological Studies and Documents 9. [Rome]: American Institute of Musicology, 1962.

Mace, Dean T. "Pietro Bembo and the Literary Origins of the Italian Madrigal." *Musical Quarterly* 55 (1969): 65–86.

Macy, Laura. "Speaking of Sex: Metaphor and Performance in the Italian Madrigal." *Journal of Musicology* 14 (1996): 1–34.

Maffei, Scipione. *Discorso intorno al teatro italiano*. Verona, 1723. Reprint, *Opuscoli Letterarii di Scipione Maffei*. Venice: Alvisopoli, 1829.

Mangani, Marco. "Un'*alta impresa* di Vecchi e Capilupi: Le canzonette a tre voci del 1597." In Privitera, *Teatro dell'udito,* 315–333.

Mantoano, Giulio. *Opera Nova . . . Nella qual si contiene un Capitolo di Primiera, e molti bellissimi Sonetti, etc.* [ca. 1600]. Transcription, http://jducoeur.org/game-hist/Giulio.doc (accessed September 25, 2012).

Marotti, Ferruccio, and Giovana Romei, eds. *La professione del teatro*. La commedia dell'arte e la società barocca, vol. 2. Rome: Bulzoni, 1991.

Marshall, Melanie. "Cultural Codes and Hierarchies in the Mid-Cinquecento Villotta." PhD dissertation, University of Southampton, 2004.

Mason, Kevin. "Accompanying Italian Lute Song." In *Performance on Lute, Guitar, and Vihuela,* edited by Victor Anand Coelho, 72–106. Cambridge: Cambridge University Press, 1997.

Menichetti, Aldo. *Metrica Italiana: Fondamenti metrici, prosodia, rima*. Padua: Antenore, 1993.

Morgan, Jonathan. Review of *"Gitene, canzonette": Studio e trascrizione delle "Canzonette a sei voci" d'Horatio Vecchi* by Rossana Dalmonte and Massimo Privitera. *Music and Letters* 79 (1998): 103.

Morley, Thomas. *A Plaine and Easie Introduction to Practicall Musicke*. Edited by Alex Harman. New York: Norton, 1952.

Muratori, Lodovico Antonio. *Della perfetta poesia italiana*. Edited by Ada Ruschioni. Milan: Marzorati, 1971.

Newcomb, Anthony. "Gli Humori di Horatio: On a Few Madrigals from the *Veglie di Siena*." In Privitera, *Theatro dell'udito,* 385–403.

———. *The Madrigal at Ferrara, 1579–1597*. Princeton, NJ: Princeton University Press, 1980.

The New Grove Dictionary of Music and Musicians. 2nd edition, edited by Stanley Sadie and John Tyrrell. New York: Grove's Dictionaries; London: Macmillan, 2001.

Nutter, David. "The Italian Polyphonic Dialogue of the Sixteenth Century." PhD dissertation, University of Nottingham, 1977.

Ossi, Massimo. *Divining the Oracle: Monteverdi's* Seconda prattica. Chicago: University of Chicago Press, 2003.

———. "Monteverdi's 'Ordine novo, bello, e gustevole': The Canzonetta as Dramatic Module and Formal Archetype." *Journal of the American Musicological Society* 45, no. 2 (1992): 261–304.

Otto, Beatrice K. *Fools Are Everywhere: The Court Jester around the World.* Chicago: University of Chicago Press, 2007.

Palau y Dulcet, Antonio. *Manual de Librero Hispanoamericano.* 10 vols. 2nd edition. Barcelona: Libreria Palau, 1956.

Palisca, Claude V. *Music and Ideas in the Sixteenth and Seventeenth Centuries.* Urbana: University of Illinois Press, 2006.

Pancaldi, Evaristo, and Gino Roncaglia, eds. *Orazio Vecchi: Precursore del melodramma (1550–1605).* Modena: Accademia di scienze lettere e arti di Modena, 1950.

Pandolfi, Vito. *La commedia dell'arte: Storia e testo.* 6 vols. Florence: Sansoni, 1957.

Parlett, David. *The Oxford History of Board Games.* Oxford: Oxford University Press, 1999.

Parry, C. Hubert H. *The Music of the Seventeenth Century.* Oxford History of Music 3. Oxford: Clarendon, 1902.

Pericolo, Lorenzo. *Caravaggio and Pictorial Narrative: Dislocating the* Istoria *in Early Modern Painting.* London: Harvey Miller, [2011].

Petrarch, Francesco. *Petrarch's Lyric Poems: The* Rime sparse *and Other Lyrics.* Translated and edited by Robert M. Durling. Cambridge, MA: Harvard University Press, 1976.

Piccinelli, Filippo. *Ateneo dei letterati milanesi.* Milan: Vigone, 1670.

Pirrotta, Nino, and Elena Povoledo. *Music and Theatre from Poliziano to Monteverdi.* Translated by Karen Eales. Cambridge: Cambridge University Press, 1975.

Pitoni, Giuseppe Ottavio. *Notitia de' contrapuntisti e compositori di musica.* Edited by Cesarino Ruini. Florence: Olschki, 1988.

Poliziano, Angelo. *Stanze, Orfeo, Rime, con il saggio Delle poesie toscane di messer Angelo Poliziano di Giosuè Carducci.* Edited by Sergio Marconi. Milan: Feltrinelli, 1981.

Powers, Harold. "Tonal Types and Modal Categories in Renaissance Polyphony." *Journal of the American Musicological Society* 34 (1981): 428–470.

Praetorius, Michael. *Syntagma musicum III.* Translated and edited by Jeffery T. Kite-Powell. New York: Oxford University Press, 2004.

Privitera, Massimo. "Democrito a teatro: Le poetiche di Orazio Vecchi e le allegoriche malinconiche." PhD dissertation, Università degli Studi di Bologna, 1990.

———. "Orazio Vecchi, musico-poeta all'autunno del Rinascimento." In *Il Theatro dell'udito: Società, musica, storia, e cultura nell'epoca di Orazio Vecchi,* edited by Ferdinando Taddei and Alessandra Chiarelli. Modena: Mucchi, 2007.

———, ed. *Theatro dell'udito, theatro del mondo: Atti del convegno internazionale nel IV centenario della morte di Orazio Vecchi, Modena-Vignola, 29 settembre–1 ottobre 2005.* Modena: Mucchi, 2010.

Prizer, William F. "Games of Venus: Secular Vocal Music in the Late Quattrocento and Early Cinquecento." *Journal of Musicology* 9 (1991): 3–56.

Prunières, Henry. *Monteverdi: His Life and Work.* Translated by Marie D. Mackie. London: J. M. Dent and Sons, 1926. Reprint, Westport, CT: Greenwood Press, 1974.

Quadrio, Francesco Saverio. *Della storia, e della ragione d'ogni poesia.* Vol. 3, pt. 2. Milan: Agnelli, 1744.

Quintilian. *Institutioni Oratoria.* Translated and edited by H. E. Butler. Cambridge, MA: Harvard University Press, 1922.

Raby, F. J. E., ed. *Oxford Book of Medieval Latin Verse.* Oxford: Oxford University Press, 1959.

Riccò, Laura. *Giuoco e teatro nelle veglie di Siena.* Rome: Bulzoni, 1993.

Ringhieri, Innocentio. *Cento giuochi liberali.* Bologna: Giaccarelli, 1551.

Rolland, Romain. *Les origines du théatre lyrique moderne: Histoire de l'opéra en Europe avant Lully et Scarlatti.* Paris: Thorin, 1895.

Roncaglia, Gino. "Gli elementi precursori del melodramma nell'opera di Orazio Vecchi: Attuazioni e limiti." *Rivista musicale italiana* 55 (1953): 251–256.

———. *La cappella musicale del duomo di Modena.* Florence: Olschki, 1957.

———. "Orazio Vecchi, precursore drammatico, ed umorista." *Rivista musicale italiana* 51 (1949): 265–273.

Sampson, Lisa. *Pastoral Drama in Early Modern Italy: The Making of a New Genre.* London: Legenda, 2006.

Sannazaro, Jacopo. *Arcadia & Picatorial Eclogues.* Translated by Ralph Nash. Detroit: Wayne State University Press, 1966.

Sartori, Claudio. "Orazio Vecchi e Tiburzio Massaino a Salò: Nuovi documenti inediti." In *Renaissance-Muzeik 1400–1600: Donum naticalum René Bernard Lenaerts,* edited by Jozef Robijns, 233–240. Leuven: Kothlieke Universiteit Seminarie voor Muzeikwetenscap, 1969.

Scala, Flamino. *Il Teatro delle favole rappresentative.* Venice: Pulciani, 1611. Modern edition edited by Ferrucio Marotti. *Archivio del teatro italiano* 7. 2 vols. Milan: Polifilo, 1976.

———. *Scenarios of the Commedia dell'Arte: Flaminio Scala's "Il Teatro delle favole rappresentative."* Translated and edited by Henry F. Salerno. New York: New York University Press, 1967. Reprint, New York: Limelight Editions, 1996.

Schleuse, Paul. "*Balla la mona e salta il babuino:* Performing Obscenity in a Musical Dialogue." In *Sexualities, Textualities, Art and Music in Early Modern Italy: Playing with Boundaries.* Edited by Melanie L. Marshall, Katherine McIver, and Linda Carroll, 41–72. Farnham: Ashgate, 2014.

———. "Genre and Meaning in Orazio Vecchi's *Selva di varia ricreatione* (1590)." PhD dissertation, City University of New York, 2005.

———. "Italian Genres in Morley's *Introduction.*" In a volume of essays to accompany Thomas Morley, *A Plaine and Easie Introduction to Practicall Musicke,* edited by Jessie Ann Owens and John Milsom. Farnham: Ashgate, forthcoming.

———. "On the Origin of the Work 'A diversi linguaggi' Attributed to Luca Marenzio and Orazio Vecchi." In Privitera, *Theatro dell'udito,* 121–153.

———. "'A Tale Completed in the Mind': Genre and Imitation in *L'Amfiparnaso* (1597)." *Journal of Musicology* 29 (2012): 101–153.

Serlio, Sebastiano. *Il secondo libro di perspettia di Sebastiano Serlio Bolognese.* Paris, 1545. Facsimile reprint, *L'Architettura: I libri I–VII e Extraordinario nelle prime edizioni.* Edited by Francesco Paolo Fiore. 2 vols. Milan: Polifilo, 2001.

Singleton, Charles S., ed. *Canti carnascialeschi del rinascimento.* Bari: Laterza, 1936.

Spaccini, Giovan Battista. *Cronaca di Modena.* 5 vols. Edited by Albano Biondi, Rolando Bussi, and Carlo Giovannini. Modena: Franco Cosimo Panini, 1993.

Statius, Papinius. *Statius.* 2 vols. Translated and edited by J. H. Mozley. Cambridge, MA: Harvard University Press, 1928.

Sternfeld, Frederick W. *The Birth of Opera.* Oxford: Clarendon Press, 1993.

Strozzi, Giovanni Battista. *Madrigali*. Edited by Luigi Sorrento. Strasbourg: Heitz, 1909.

Strunk, Oliver. *Source Readings in Music History*. Revised edition, edited by Leo Treitler. New York: W. W. Norton, 1998.

Talvacchi, Bette. *Taking Positions: On the Erotic in Renaissance Culture*. Princeton, NJ: Princeton University Press, 1999.

Tasso, Torquato. *Aminta*. Edited and translated by Charles Jernigan and Irene Marchegiani Jones. New York: Italica Press, 2000.

———. *Aminta, favola boschereccia del Torquato Tasso, novo coretta, & di vaghe figure adornata*. Venice: Aldo [Mannucci], 1589.

———. *Gerusalemme liberata*. Edited by Lanfranco Carretti. Turin: Einaudi, 1971.

———. *Jerusalem Delivered*. Translated by Anthony M. Esolen. Baltimore, MD: Johns Hopkins University Press, 2000.

Thompson, Roger. *Unfit for Modest Ears*. London: Macmillan, 1979.

Thuillier, Jacques. *Georges de La Tour*. Translated by Fabia Claris. Paris: Flammarion, 1993.

Tiraboschi, Girolamo. *Biblioteca modenese*. 6 vols. Modena: Società tipografica, 1781–1786.

Tomlinson, Gary. *Monteverdi and the End of the Renaissance*. Berkeley: University of California Press, 1987.

Toscan, Jean. *Le carnaval de langage: Le lexique érotique des poètes de l'équivoque de Burchiello à Marino (XVᵉ–XVIIᵉ siècles)*. 4 vols. Lille: Atelier Reproduction des Thèses, 1981.

Vecchi, Orazio. *Mostra delli Tuoni della Musica*. Edited by Mariarosa Pollastri. Modena: Aedes Muratoriana, 1987.

Vocabolario degli Accademici della Crusca. Florence: G. Alberti 1612. http://www.lessicografia.it (accessed June 15, 2013).

Wakelin, Emma Hilary. *"De floridi virtuosi d'Italia:* A Study of Three Italian Madrigal Anthologies of the 1580s." PhD dissertation, Royal Holloway, University of London, 1997.

Weinberg, Bernard. *A History of Literary Criticism in the Italian Renaissance*. 2 vols. Chicago: University of Chicago Press, 1961.

Welch, Evelyn. "Lotteries in Early Modern Italy." *Past and Present*, no. 199 (May 2008): 71–111.

Wilbourne, Emily. "*Lo Schiavetto* (1612), Travestied Sound, Ethnic Performance, and the Eloquence of the Body." *Journal of the American Musicological Association* 63 (2010): 1–44.

Wistreich, Richard. *Warrior, Courtier, Singer: Giulio Cesare Brancaccio and the Performance of Identity in the Late Renaissance*. Aldershot, UK: Ashgate, 2007.

Zarlino, Gioseffo. *The Art of Counterpoint: Part Three of "Le istitutioni harmoniche."* Translated by Guy A. Marco and Claude V. Palisca. New Haven, CT: Yale University Press, 1968.

Zeno, Apostolo. *Lettere di Apostolo Zeno cittadino veneziano istorico e poeta cesareo*. Venice: Valvasense, 1752.

Music Editions

Balsamino, Simone. *Le Novelette a sei voci di Simone Balsamino: prime musiche su Aminta di Torquato Tasso (1594)*. Edited by Andrea Chegai. Florence: Olschki, 1993.

Banchieri, Adriano. *Festino del giovedì grassa avanti cena*. Edited by Bonaventura Somma. Rome: De Santis, 1939.

———. *La pazzia senile*. Venice: Amadino, 1598. Facsimile and score edited by Renzo Bez. Bologna: Forni, 2003.

Bellavere, Vincenzo. *Il primo libro delle Justiniane di diversi*. Venice: Scotto, 1570.

Bottegari, Cosimo. *Il libro di canto e liuto*. Edited by Dinko Fabris and John Griffiths. Bologna: Forni, 2006.

Croce, Giovanni. *Triaca musicale*. Edited by Achille Schinelli. Capolavori polifonici del secolo XVI 3. Rome: De Santis, 1942.

Ferretti, Giovanni. *Canzone alla napolitana a cinque voci*. Venice: Scotto, 1567.

———. *Primo libro delle villotte alla Napolitana a tre voci di diversi*. Venice: Scotto, 1565.

Fiorino, Gasparo. *Libro Secondo Canzonelle a tre e a quattro voci*. Venice: Gardano, 1574.

Gastoldi, Giovanni Giacomo. *Balletti a cinque voci*. Edited by Michel Sanvoisin. Paris: Heugel, 1968.

Giamberti, Giuseppe. *Duo tessuti con diversi solfeggiamenti, scherzi, perfidie, et oblighi*. Edited by Andrea Bornstein. Duo 39. Bologna: Ut Orpheus, 2001.

Giulini, Marco, ed. *I lieti amanti: Madrigali di venti musicisti ferraresi e non*. Florence: Olschki, 1990.

Lasso, Orlando. *Sämtliche Werke*. Edited by F. X. Haberl and A. Sandberger. Leipzig, 1894–1926. Reprint, New York: Broude, 1974.

Lincoln, Harry B., ed. *The Madrigal Collection "L'Amorosa Ero."* Albany: State University of New York Press, 1968.

Macey, Patrick, ed. *Savonarolan Laude, Motets, and Anthems*. Recent Researches in Music of the Renaissance 116. Madison, WI: A-R Editions, 1999.

Manchicourt, Pierre. *Twenty-Nine Chansons*. Edited by Margery Anthea Baird. Recent Researches in the Music of the Renaissance 11. Madison, WI: A-R Editions, 1972.

Marenzio, Luca. *The Complete Five Voice Madrigals*. 6 vols. Edited by John Steele. New York: Gaudia, 1996.

———. *The Complete Four-Voice Madrigals*. Edited by John Steele. New York: Gaudia, 1995.

———. *The Secular Works*. Edited by Patricia Myers. New York: Broude Bros., 1980.

Monteverdi, Claudio. *Opera omnia*. Edited by the Fondazione Claudio Monteverdi. Cremona: Athenaeum Cremonense, 1970.

Negri, Cesare. *Affetti Amorosi a tre voci*. Venice: Gardano, 1608.

———. *Le Gratie d'Amore*. Milan: Pontio & Piccaglia, 1602. Facsimile edition, New York: Broude Brothers, 1969. Edited by Yvonne Kendall, "*Le Gratie d'Amore* by Cesare Negri: Translation and Commentary," DMA dissertation, Stanford University, 1985.

Nola, Giovanni Domenico da. *Corona delle napolitane a tre et a quattro voci, di diversi eccellentissimi musici*. Venice: Scotto, 1570.

Nuvoloni, Massimiliano. *Canzonette di Massimiliano Nuvoloni a tre . . . agiontovi alcuni Capricii, & Balletti di Alessandro suo Padre*. Milan: Tini & Lomazzo, 1608.

Peri, Jacopo. *Euridice: An Opera in One Act, Five Scenes*. Edited by Howard Mayer Brown. Recent Researches in the Music of the Baroque Era 36–37. Madison, WI: A-R Editions, 1981.

Rongoni, Francesco. *Selva de varii passaggi*. Edited by Richard Erig. Zurich: Musik Hug, 1987.

Rore, Cipriano de. *Opera Omnia*. Edited by Bernhard Meier. 8 vols. Corpus mensurabilis musicae 14. [Rome]: American Institute of Musicology, 1969.

Schuetze, George, ed. *Settings of "Ardo sì" and Related Texts*. Recent Researches in the Music of the Renaissance 78–81. Madison, WI: A-R Editions, 1981.

Torelli, Gasparo. *I fidi amanti*. Edited by Bonaventura Somma and Lino Bianchi. Rome: De Santis, 1967.

Tudino, Cesare. *Canzon napolitane a tre voci, di L'Arpa, Cesare Todino, Joan Domenico de Nola, Et di altri musici....* Venice: Scotto, 1566.

Vecchi, Orazio. *"Battaglia d'Amor e Dispetto" and "Mascherata della Malinconia et Allegrezza."* Edited by David Nutter. Recent Researches in Music of the Renaissance 72. Madison, WI: A-R Editions, 1987.

———. *Convito musicale.* Edited by William R. Martin. Rome: Edizioni de Santis, 1966.

———. *The Four-Voice Canzonettas.* Edited by Ruth I. DeFord. 2 vols. Recent Researches in Music of the Renaissance 92–93. Madison, WI: A-R Editions, 1993.

———. *L'Amfiparnaso: Il testo letterario e il testo musicale.* Edited by Renzo Bez. Bologna: Forni, 2007.

———. *Le veglie di Siena.* Edited by Donald Beecher. Ottowa: The Institute of Mediæval Music, 2004.

———. *Madrigali a cinque voci (Venezia, 1589).* Edited by Mariarosa Pollastri. Bologna: Ut Orpheus, 1997.

———. *Madrigali a sei voci.* Edited by Mariarosa Pollastri. I Quaderni di *Musicaaa!* 19–20. Mantua: I Quaderni di *Musicaaa!,* n.d. Available in PDF format by request from http://maren.interfree.it.

———. *Selva di varia ricreatione.* Edited by Paul Schleuse. Recent Researches in Music of the Renaissance 157. Middleton, WI: A-R Editions, 2012.

Vecchi, Orazio, and Geminiano Capilupi. *Canzonette a tre voci.* Edited by Andrea Bornstein. Bologna: Ut Orpheus, 1997.

Index

General Index

References to musical examples, figures, and tables are indicated by *italics*.

Striggio, Alessandro (the elder), 11, 48, 170; "La caccia," 174, 179, 227, 292; "Il cicalamento delle donna al bucato," 167, 171, 174, 179, 256–257; "Gioco di primiera," 171, 178–186, 282

Strozzi, Giovanni Battista (the elder), 47, 48–49

subjectivity, 50, 71; double, 17, 25, 75, 78, 95, 140, 251

suicide, 136, 139, 141, 147–160

Susato, Tylman, 273

tablature, 12, 117, 118

Tansillo, Luigi, 329n2

Tasso, Torquato, 99; *Aminta*, 147, 148–151, 153, *154*, 175; "Ardi e gela a tua voglia," 47, 49–52; *Gerusaleme liberata*, 154, 242; "Se 'l vostro volto è d'un aria gentile," 19

tedesca, 115–116

Thompson, Roger, 245

Tiraboschi, Girolamo, 5, 165

tongue twister. *See* games: *bisticcio*

Torelli, Gasparo, 175

Tosca, Jean, 257

tragicomedy, 136–160

Trapolini, Giovanni Paolo, 135–136, *135*

tronche, rime, 86

Tudino, Cesare, 19

Vagnoli, Virginia, 48

Valderrábano, Enriquez de, 97

variety, of genres, 90, 92, 94–100, 137, 240–241

Vecchi, Giovanni di, 4

Vecchi, Orazio: career, 3, 4–6, 44–46, 91–93, 177, 240, 291–294; contemporary references to, 4, 11; dedication and preface to *Convito musicale*, 120–122; dedication and preface to *Le veglie di Siena*, 240–244; dedication to *Selva di varia ricreatione*, 46, 91, 94–95, 98, 100; dedications and prefaces to *L'Amfiparnaso*, 137, 139, 162; dedications to canzonetta books, 16, 29, 45–46; dedications to madrigal books, 46; dedications to sacred music books, 45–46, 91; early life, 4; personality, 4; poetic style, 19–20; ties to Este family, 12, 291–294; tombstone inscription, 162, 294

Vecchi, Orfeo, 339n2

vecchio, 111, 129, 141. *See also* Pantalone

villanella, 11–12, 13, 111, 117, 223–224, 273

villanesca, 6, 13–14, 108, 254

villotta, 110–111, 123, 252–262, 278–279

vinata, 8, 106, 111–113, 123, 125, 262–277, 278

Virgil, 242, 349n75

Visdomini, Sisto, 46

Werrecore, Matthias, 292, 350n25

Wert, Giaches de, 12, 92, 102, 154; "Tirsi morir volea," 65, 70

Wilhelm V (Duke of Bavaria), 46, 91

Willaert, Adriano, 13

woodcuts, 7, 134–136, 145, 151–153, 156–157

zanni, 111, 141, 248–249, 252

Zarlino, Gioseffo, 98–99

Zeno, Apostolo, 163

Zrínyi, Miklós, 197

www.ingramcontent.com/pod-product-compliance
Lightning Source LLC
Chambersburg PA
CBHW070409100426
42812CB00005B/1685